CONTEMPORARY CHINA INSTITUTE PUBLICATIONS

FOOD GRAIN PROCUREMENT AND CONSUMPTION IN CHINA

Publications in the series are:

Party Leadership and Revolutionary Power in China (1970) *edited by John Wilson Lewis*

Employment and Economic Growth in Urban China, 1949–1957 (1971) *by Christopher Howe*

Authority, Participation and Cultural Change in China (1973) *edited by Stuart R. Schram*

A Bibliography of Chinese Newspapers and Periodicals in European Libraries (1975) *by the Contemporary China Institute*

Democracy and Organisation in the Chinese Industrial Enterprise, 1948–1953 (1975) *by William Brugger*

Mao Tse-tung in the Scales of History (1977) *edited by Dick Wilson*

Shanghai: Revolution and Development in an Asian Metropolis (1980) *edited by Christopher Howe*

Mao Zedong and the Political Economy of the Border Region. A Translation of Mao's *Economic and Financial Problems* (1980) *edited and translated by Andrew Watson*

The Politics of Marriage in Contemporary China (1981) *by Elisabeth Croll*

FOOD GRAIN PROCUREMENT AND CONSUMPTION IN CHINA

KENNETH R. WALKER

School of Oriental and African Studies
University of London

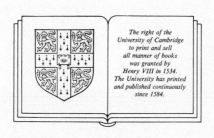

The right of the
University of Cambridge
to print and sell
all manner of books
was granted by
Henry VIII in 1534.
The University has printed
and published continuously
since 1584.

CAMBRIDGE UNIVERSITY PRESS

Cambridge
London   New York   New Rochelle
Melbourne   Sydney

Published by the Press Syndicate of the University of Cambridge
The Pitt Building, Trumpington Street, Cambridge CB2 1RP
32 East 57th Street, New York, NY 10022, USA
296 Beaconsfield Parade, Middle Park, Melbourne 3206, Australia

First published 1984

Printed in Great Britain at the University Press, Cambridge

Library of Congress catalogue card number: 83-7820

British Library cataloguing in publication data

Walker, Kenneth R.
Food grain procurement and consumption in China
—(Contemporary China Institute publications)
1. Grain–China 2. Food supply–China
3. China–Economic conditions–1949–
I. Title II. Series
338.1′731′0951   HD9046.C6

ISBN 0 521 25649 6

SE

CONTENTS

Contents

TABLES

Tables

Tables

FIGURES

To June, Neil and Ruth

PREFACE

The economic development of poor countries is generally accompanied by a marked rise in the demand for food grain, a failure of domestic production and marketed supply to match demand and, consequently, an irresistible pressure to import grain. Demand growth is the combined result of rapid population increase and a high income elasticity of demand for grain at prevailing low levels of income per head. In the developing countries the increase in consumption averaged 3.7 per cent[1] per annum between 1960 and 1976, and the projected growth of demand into the 1990s has been estimated[2] at around 4 per cent per annum.

Empirical studies[3] of food consumption show that the demand for grain passes through two important stages as income per head rises. Initially, at low levels of income, the direct consumption of food grain increases rapidly with rising per capita income but the pattern of grain consumption changes: fine grains (wheat, rice, soya beans, for

[1] W.R. Cline (ed.), *Policy Alternatives for a New Economic Order: An Economic Analysis* (London and New York, 1979).

[2] Kenneth L. Bachman and Leonardo A. Paulino, *Rapid Food Production Growth in Selected Developing Countries: A Comparative Analysis of Underlying Trends 1961–76*, International Food Policy Research Institute Report no.11 (October 1979); also *Food Needs of Developing Countries: Projections of Production and Consumption to 1990*, IFPRI Report no.3 (December 1977).

[3] OECD, *Study of Trends in World Supply and Demand of Major Agricultural Commodities*, Report by the Secretary-General (Paris, 1976); H. Kaneda, 'Long-Term Changes in Food Consumption Patterns in Japan 1878–1964', *Food Research Institute Studies* (vol.8), 1968, pp.3–32; F.H. Sanderson, *Japan's Food Prospects and Policies* (Brookings Institution, Washington DC, 1978); S. Ishikawa, 'China's Food and Agriculture: A Turning Point', *Food Policy*, May 1977, pp.90–102; M.K. Bennett, *The World's Food* (New York, 1954); Ch'en Yueh-eh, 'Food Consumption in Taiwan', in Chinese–American Joint Commission on Rural Reconstruction, Economic Digest Series no.23, *Agricultural Economic Research Papers* (Taipei, Taiwan, October 1978), pp. 187–97; Colin Clark and M.R. Haswell, *The Economics of Subsistence Agriculture* (London, 1967).

example) are substituted for coarse grains (such as millet, maize, barley and sweet potatoes). At higher levels of income, the direct consumption of grain rises more slowly, reaches saturation and then declines. The demand for grain for indirect consumption, however, in the form of livestock products, begins to accelerate. Given the relevant grain–livestock production conversion ratios, this boosts the total demand for grain considerably. The more rapid the growth of the urban population and its income per head, the more pronounced are the shifts in demand towards a diet with more fine grains and more livestock products. If the marketed amount of domestically produced grain of the required kind is insufficient to meet urban demand there is, in the end, little alternative for governments than to import grain.

The history of many less-developed countries during the past fifteen to twenty years shows that increases in the demand for grain of 3–4 per cent per annum have rarely been matched by the growth of production. Between 1961 and 1976 grain production in ninety-four developing market economies[4] increased by 2.6 per cent per year, which was exactly equal to the rate of growth of population. Production rose faster than population in only forty-one out of the ninety-four countries. Declining food grain self-sufficiency and increasing levels of grain imports have thus been a feature of the developing world in recent years.

During the period covered by this study (1952–80) China's experience with grain has, in most respects, been similar to that of a typical underdeveloped country: the population has continually expressed a strong desire to consume more grain, to substitute fine for coarse grain and, especially in the later 1970s, to convert more grain into livestock products. Like those of many less-developed countries, the Government of China has not been able to meet these requirements. People who are not acquainted with trends in the Chinese economy find it almost impossible to believe what the official statistics show – that average grain output per head in 1978–80 was, at best, only 6 per cent above its 1936 level and that, according to one estimate,[5] it may have been 1 per cent *below* that level. The trend of growth of output in 1952–80 was 2.6 per cent per year, while

---

[4] Bachman and Paulino, *Rapid Food Production Growth*, IFPRI Report no.11.
[5] Yang Chien-pai, *Luen Kung-yeh ho Nung-yeh ti Kuan-hsi* (*On the Relations between Industry and Agriculture*) (Peking, 1981).

Table 1. *Long-term changes in grain* production per head*

	Grain output (million tons)	Total population (million)	Average grain output per head (kilograms)
1936	$\begin{cases} 149^a \\ 139^b \\ 144^c \end{cases}$	450	$\begin{cases} 331 \\ 309 \\ 320 \end{cases}$
1952–4	163	588	277
1955–57	186	632	294
1952–57	175	610	287
1978–80	318	971	327

Notes and sources: * In China, 'grain' includes soya beans, potatoes, and pulses.
Production: a and b: Different estimates made by China of 1936 production (including soya beans); see Yang Chien-pai, *On the Relations between Industry and Agriculture.* The origin of a is not given but b is said to be an estimate of the Ministry of Agriculture in 1958. c is the average of a and b. All other production figures are from *Chung-kuo Nung-yeh Nien-chien 1980* (Chinese Agricultural Yearbook 1980) (Peking, 1981), p. 34; with potatoes for 1952–57 reweighted at 5 : 1.
Population: 1936: Yang Chien-pai, *On the Relations between Industry and Agriculture.* 1950s: *TCKT* (no. 11), 1957, p. 24. 1978–80: 1978: *PR* (no. 20), 1980, p. 24 (State Statistical Bureau figures). 1979: *Economic Yearbook* 1981. 1980: State Statistical Bureau figure in *JMJP*, 30 April 1981.

population grew at an annual rate of 2.0 per cent. With per capita output rising at 0.6 per cent per year there was thus little grain available to satisfy the demand associated with rising incomes, including that of an urban population which rose from 80 million during the mid-1950s to at least 150–180 million in 1980. Between 1955–57 and 1978–80 grain production per head declined in eleven out of China's twenty-seven provinces (in existence in 1980), and this group had a total population of 225 million, or 23 per cent of the 1978–80 total. Recent increases in average output per head merely reflect a falling rate of growth of population rather than a rising trend in production. Comparing the five years 1970–74 with the six years 1975–80, we find that the average trend of production growth fell from 3.4 per cent to 3.1 per cent, while population growth declined from 2.4 per cent to 1.3 per cent. Table 1 summarises the long-term changes in average grain production per head.

Since 1953 the Chinese Government has attempted to counter the excess demand for grain by controlling consumption as well as by promoting production. Right from those early years it was determined to manage without foreign grain imports and, indeed, it considered that provided grain distribution within China was efficiently organised, some grain could actually be exported. To achieve these aims the Government created a state system for the procurement, redistribution and rationing of grain covering the entire country and this system has survived, with some modifications, until the present day.

This book traces the progress of that policy between 1953 and 1962 and in the later 1970s. Unfortunately, owing to the lack of statistics, it does not cover the fourteen years from 1962 to 1976. The first period, however, does embody a distinct period in China's recent economic history: the Government's policy for achieving national self-sufficiency in grain was launched in 1953 and finally failed in 1961. Moreover, enough can be said about the problems of the late 1970s to put the entire period from 1953 into historical perspective. Most of the book is concerned with estimating the amounts of grain procured and redistributed, within and between provinces, and between rural and urban areas. It also attempts to measure the effect which redistribution had on grain consumption.

I have taken more than ten years to complete this study. This is mainly because I encountered many difficulties in collecting and analysing the data I required for all the provinces of China. At first I had no intention of covering the whole country but as time passed my search for data developed into a pilgrimage from which there could be no retreat. At times my search was exciting and rewarding, while at other times it was frustrating and endless. Most of the materials I needed were in foreign libraries and I was fortunate to be given several generous research grants which enabled me to visit such libraries and to acquire microfilms of Chinese sources. I gratefully acknowledge grants from the School of Oriental and African Studies (from its Research Committee and from research funds allocated by the former Director, Sir Cyril Philips and by the present Director, Professor C.D. Cowan); from the London–Cornell Project and from the Committee on the Chinese Economy of the US Social Science Research Council.

I am deeply indebted to all the librarians who helped me to locate materials during my visits, and who sent me many items of interest. I extend my warm thanks to the following: John Ma, sometime Curator of the East Asian Collection, the Hoover Library, Stanford; Ramon Myers, the current Curator, and Mark Tam, also of the Hoover

Library; Edwin Beal, formerly of the Orientalia Division, Library of Congress; Eugene Wu, Harvard-Yenching Library; John Lust, Rosemary Stevens and Calliope Caroussis of the SOAS Library; the staff of the British Library, the Lenin Library and Library of the Academy of Science, Moscow, the Institut für Ostasienkunde, Hamburg, the Chinese University of Hong Kong, the Economic Research Institute of the Chinese Academy of Social Sciences, Peking and the City Library of Shanghai.

Many scholars gave me a great deal of advice and encouragement while I was preparing the book. Among the foreign scholars who did so and who I now thank are Shigeru Ishikawa, Robert Michael Field, John S. Aird, J. Philip Emerson, Nicholas Lardy, Charles Liu and Y.Y. Kueh. In China I received insight and information from numerous scholars and officials and although I cannot name them here I am, nevertheless, deeply indebted to them. In England I have encroached on the time of my colleagues and friends over a long period. Dr Werner Klatt, OBE, has always been kind enough to take an interest in my work and he never tired of explaining to me the technical and economic characteristics of various branches of agricultural activity. My close colleagues at SOAS have been an unfailing source of advice and they will be almost as relieved as I am that this study has finally been completed. Christopher Howe provided me with many Chinese sources, economic statistics and ideas. He believed that I would finish the job and he encouraged me to keep right on until I did so. Robert Ash was particularly helpful with data on Kiangsu and Shanghai and with matters relating to presentation. Michael Hodd generously gave his time to put some of the preliminary statistics I collected at the beginning of the project into manageable order and this helped to convince me that it would be possible for me to handle data for all the provinces in a single study. Peter Ayre advised me on the economic analysis of inequality and instability and was willing to discuss any methodological questions I put to him.

On a more general note, over the years I have been conscious of the long-term intellectual debt I owe to two of my former university teachers. Maurice Beresford, Professor of Economic History at the University of Leeds, first introduced me to the study of agrarian history over 25 years ago. I was immediately captivated by his teaching and have never forgotten either his meticulous attention to historical detail or the importance he attached to field studies. Later, when I was a research student at Oxford, I came under the spell of Colin Clark, Director of the Agricultural Economics Research Institute. His breathtaking knowledge of world economic development and his extraordinary ability to use the most fragmentary figures in a meaningful way had a profound effect on my work and subsequently on my approach to Chinese economic studies. I hope that both these great scholars recognise their influence in this book and are not disappointed with the result.

Finally, my wife June, and my children Neil and Ruth, watched the development of the book with interest, and accepted without question the strains on family life imposed by my preoccupation with research. In the winter of 1979–80 they shared with me the rare experience of visiting China – which had absorbed my own interest for twenty years – and I dedicate this book to them.

ABBREVIATIONS

Abbreviations

SHYJP	*Shen-yang jih-pao.* Shenyang Daily.
SIAJP	*Hsi-an jih-pao.* Sian Daily.
SINJP	*Hsin-chiang jih-pao.* Sinkiang Daily.
SNMJP	*Szu-ch'uan Nung-min jih-pao.* Szechuan Peasants' Daily.
SZJP	*Szu-ch'uan jih-pao.* Szechuan Daily.
TCJP	*Ta-chung jih-pao.* Mass Daily (Shantung).
TJP	*T'ien-chin jih-pao.* Tientsin Daily.
TKJJP	*T'ien-chin Kung-jen jih-pao.* Tientsin Workers' Daily.
TKP	*Ta-kung pao.* Impartial Daily.
TSINJP	*Ch'ing-hai jih-pao.* Tsinghai Daily.
TTKP	*T'ien-chin Ta-kung pao.* Tientsin Impartial Daily.
WHP	*Wen-hui pao.* Cultural Exchange News.
YJP	*Yun-nan jih-pao.* Yunnan Daily.

JOURNALS IN CHINESE

CCKH	*Ching-chi K'o-hsüeh.* Economic Science.
CCKL	*Ching-chi Kuan-li.* Economic Management.
CCYC	*Ching-chi Yen-chiu.* Economic Research.
CHCC	*Chi-hua Ching-chi.* Planned Economy.
CHYTC	*Chi-hua yü T'ung-chi.* Planning and Statistics.
CHYYC	*Chiao Hsüeh yü Yen-chiu.* Teaching and Research.
CKCNP	*Chung-kuo Ch'ing-nien pao.* Chinese Youth News.
CKNP	*Chung-kuo Nung-pao.* Chinese Agricultural News.
CKNPTK	*Chung-kuo Nung-pao Tseng K'an.* Chinese Agricultural News Supplement.
CNP	*Ch'ing nien pao.* Youth News.
FCY	*Fu-chien Chiao-yü.* Fukien Education.
HC	*Hung-ch'i.* Red Flag.
HCS	*Hsin Chien-she.* New Construction.
HCTC	*Hsü-chou Ta-chung.* Hsüchow Masses.
HH	*Hsüeh-hsi.* Study.
HHPYK	*Hsin-hua Pan-yueh k'an.* New China Semi-Monthly.
HHYK	*Hsüeh-hsu Yueh-k'an.* Academic Monthly.
HHYP	*Hsin-hua Yueh-pao.* New China Monthly.
HNY	*Hsin Nung-yeh.* New Agriculture (Liaoning).
JKYC	*Jen-k'ou Yen-chiu.* Population Research.
KSUNM	*Chiang-su Nung-min.* Kiangsu Peasants.
KWSINYTH	*Kuang-hsi Nung-yeh T'ung-hsün.* Kwangsi Peasants' Bulletin.
LS	*Liang-shih.* Grain.
LSP	*Liang-shih pao.* Grain News.
NTKTTH	*Nung-ts'un Kung-tso T'ung-hsün.* Rural Work Bulletin.
NYCCTK	*Nung-yeh Ching-chi Ts'ung-kan.* Agricultural Economics Digest.

xviii

NYCCWT	*Nung-yeh Ching-chi Wen-t'i.* Problems of Agricultural Economics.
NYCS	*Nung-yeh Chih-shih.* Agricultural Knowledge (Shantung).
SC	*Shih-chien.* Practice.
SNM	*Hsin-chiang Nung-min.* Sinkiang Peasants.
TC	*Ts'ai-cheng.* Finance.
TCKT	*T'ung-chi Kung-tso.* Statistical Work.
TLCS	*Ti-li Chih-shih.* Geographical Knowledge.

BOOKS IN CHINESE

Collection of Statistical Data (1958)
> *Chung-kuo yü Shih-chieh Chu-yao Kuo-chia Nung-yeh Sheng-ch'an T'ung-chi tzu-liao hui-pien* (Collection of Statistical Data on Agricultural Production in China and other Major Countries of the World). Ministry of Agriculture, Planning Bureau (Peking, 1958).

An Economic Geography of
NE China
> *Tung-pei Ti-ch'ü Ching-chi Ti-li* (An Economic Geography of the North Eastern Region). Edited by Sun Ching-chih (Peking, 1959).

Inner Mongolia
> *Nei-meng-ku tzu-chih-ch'ü Ching-chi Ti-li* (An Economic Geography of the Autonomous Region of Inner Mongolia). Edited by Sun Ching-chih *et al.* (Peking, 1956).

N. China
> *Hua-pei Ching-chi Ti-li* (An Economic Geography of North China). Edited by Sun Ching-chih (Peking 1957).

Central China
> *Hua-chung Ti-ch'ü Ching-chi Ti-li* (An Economic Geography of the Central Region of China). Edited by Sun Ching-chih (Peking, 1958).

East China
> *Hua-tung Ti-ch'ü Ching-chi Ti-li* (An Economic Geography of the East China Region). Edited by Sun Ching-chih (Peking, 1959).

SW China
> *Hsi-nan Ti-ch'ü Ching-chi Ti-li* (An Economic Geography of the South West Region of China). Edited by Sun Ching-chih (Peking, 1960).

South China
> *Hua-nan Ti-ch'ü Ching-chi Ti-li* (An Economic Geography of the South China Region). Edited by Sun Ching-chih (Peking, 1959).

Economic Yearbook (1981)
> *Chung-kuo Ching-chi Nien-chien* (Chinese Economic Yearbook) (Peking, 1981).

Encyclopaedia (1980)
> *Chung-kuo Pai-k'o Nien-chien 1980* (Chinese Encyclopaedia Yearbook 1980) (Peking, 1980).

Encyclopaedia (1981)
> *Chung-kuo Pai-k'o Nien-chien 1981* (Chinese Encyclopaedia Yearbook 1981) (Peking, 1981).

FKHP
> *Chung-hua Jen-min Kung-ho-kuo Fa-kuei Hui-pien* (Collection of Laws and Regulations of the Chinese People's Republic).

HNNY
> *Hu-nan Nung-yeh* (Hunan Agriculture). Compendium of Hunan Province Agricultural Institute (Peking, 1959).

LSWTCC
> *Liang-shih Wen-t'i Chin-chie* (Current and Past Grain Problems). Hupei Province Grain Office (Wuhan, 1957).

Mechanisation Bureau
> *Chung-kuo Nung-yeh Chi-hsie-hua Wen-t'i* (Problems of Agricultural Mechanisation in China). Mechanisation Bureau of the Ministry of Agriculture (Paoting, 1958).

NMKTC
> *Nei-meng-ku tzu-chih-ch'ü Ching-chi ho Wen-hua Chien-she Ch'eng-chiu ti T'ung-chi* (Statistics of the Achievements in Economic and Cultural Construction of the Inner Mongolia Autonomous Region) (Peking, 1960).

NPC (1957)
> *Chung-hua jen-min kung-ho-kuo ti yi ts'eng ch'uan kuo jen-min tai-piao ta-hui ti ssu tz'u hui-yi hui-k'an* (Compendium of the Fourth Session of the First National People's Congress of the Chinese People's Republic) (Peking, 1957).

NYHTH
> *Chung-kuo Nung-yeh ho-tso-hua yün-tung Shih-liao* (Historical Materials on the Agricultural Co-operativisation Movement in China). By Shih Ching-t'ing (2 vols., Peking, 1957).

Rational Transport
> *Liang-shih fen ch'ü ch'an hsiao p'ing-heng ho-li yün-shu* (Rational Transport for Balancing Grain Production and Consumption in Different Areas). Grain Bureau (Peking, 1957).

SNY
> *Hsin-chiang Nung-yeh* (Sinkiang Agriculture). Sinkiang Agricultural Science Institute (Peking, 1965).

TGY
> *Wei-ta ti Shih Nien* (Ten Great Years). State Statistical Bureau (Peking, 1959).

WS (1967) and (1969)
> *Mao Tse-tung Ssu-hsiang Wan-sui* (Long Live Mao Tse-tung's Thought). Chinese Red Guard Publications (Taiwan Reprints, 1967 and 1969).

Abbreviations

MATERIALS IN ENGLISH

CIAAA	Central Intelligence Agency. *Agricultural Acreage in Communist China 1949–68. A Statistical Compilation.* August 1969. Mimeo.
CNS	*China News Service*
CQ	*China Quarterly*
FBIS	*Foreign Broadcast Information Service*
JCRR	Joint Commission on Rural Reconstruction (US–China)
JEC 1967	*An Economic Profile of Mainland China*, Studies Prepared for the Joint Economic Committee, Congress of the United States, February 1967 (Washington, 1967)
JPRS	*US Joint Publications Research Service* (translations of Chinese materials), Washington DC.
NCNA	*New China News Agency*
PAS	*Provincial Agricultural Statistics for Communist China.* Committee on the Economy of China. Social Science Research Council of the USA (Ithaca, New York, 1969).
PR	*Peking Review*
SCMM	*Survey of the China Mainland Magazines* (translations by US Consulate General, Hong Kong)
SCMP	*Survey of the China Mainland Press* (translations by US Consulate General, Hong Kong)
SWB	*Summary of World Broadcasts*
Tuan (1981)	*People's Republic of China Provincial Total Grain Production 1969–79.* Research Notes on Chinese Agriculture, no.2. Francis C. Tuan, International Economics Division, Economics and Statistics Service, USDA (Washington DC, 1981). Mimeo.

1

THE NATURE OF CHINA'S GRAIN PROBLEM IN THE 1950s

The size and diversity of China are great enough to invalidate most generalisations about the economic characteristics of the country. One generalisation which can be made, however, is that during the 1950s, irrespective of region, food consumption consisted overwhelmingly of grain (defined by the Chinese to include pulses, potatoes and soya beans, as well as cereals). In this respect China was a typical low-income, densely populated country in which the struggle to provide enough calories was the main preoccupation of the population. Only small amounts of meat (mainly pork), eggs, fish, edible oil and sugar were consumed, as the figures for several rural and urban areas of China, presented in Table 2, show. According to this evidence, grain accounted for between 81 and 91 per cent of total calories in our urban 'sample', and between 92 and 97 per cent of calories in the rural areas covered. Essentially, therefore, food consumption in China was synonymous with grain consumption.

China's grain 'problem' is not illuminated merely by looking at the statistics of average grain output per head of population during the six years 1952–57. Taking the period as a whole, average output per head was 293 kilograms (unhusked) and it grew from 187 kilograms in 1952 to 300 kilograms in 1957. At this level of generality, therefore, China was not particularly poor. Given the commodity composition of grain output, and after deducting seed, feed, grain for industrial use, and waste, 293 kilograms of grain produced were sufficient to provide approximately 2000 calories per head per day. It could then be claimed that China was 'self-sufficient' in grain.

The heart of China's problem, however, was distribution. National figures obscure considerable regional differences in (1) output per head; (2) the growth of output; and (3) the stability of output. All these elements indicated a need for large-scale grain redistribution – between rural areas of a single province and between provinces. Some

Table 2. *Food consumption per head in selected areas of China, 1950s*

	Urban				Rural		
	North East (Harbin and Heilung-kiang cities)	North (Peking)	East (Shang-hai)	South (Canton and Kwang-tung cities)	North (Shansi)	Central (Chek-iang)	South (Kwang-tung)
Kilograms							
Grain	275	240	263	217	196	271	276
Vegetables	147	107	99	158	33	91	90
Meat	5.3	11.238	11.066	9.915	1.478	2.7	6.722
Edible oil	c.3.6	6.418	6.288	4.500	1.026	1.59	1.582
Eggs	n.a.	2.489	2.677	1.363	0.641	0.864	n.a.
Fish	c.1.64	n.a.	11.422	6.289	0.058	7.65	10.970
Sugar	3.3	4.65	2.047	4.000	0.252	1.00	3.436
Alcohol	4.55	n.a.	2.627	n.a.	n.a.	1.5	1.720
Poultry	n.a.	n.a.	1.198	4.399	n.a.	n.a.	6.063
Calories							
Grain	2539	2194	1873	1546	1726	1973	2041
Other	237	355	336	317	56	124	187
Total	2776	2549	2209	1863	1782	2097	2228
Grain %	91	86	85	83	97	94	92

n.a. not available.
Source: Appendix 1.

grain was needed to meet chronic deficits and some was required to offset short-term fluctuations in production. And, in addition, grain had to be mobilised from the rural to the urban areas. This chapter examines these three elements of China's grain problem in turn. It attempts to measure the scale of the problem and to set out its geographical complexion.

RURAL INEQUALITY OF GRAIN OUTPUT: THE PROBLEM OF INTRA-PROVINCIAL RURAL GRAIN TRANSFERS

The need to mobilise grain surpluses for redistribution among rural areas reflects the great inequalities of production per head of rural population. Approximately 97 million people[1] living in the country-side (18 per cent of China's rural population, 1952–57) permanently produced insufficient grain, in addition to those who suffered temporary deficits as a result of natural disasters. Of the 97 million, 35 million peasants[2] were in deficit because they specialised in the growing of industrial crops ('economic crops' in Chinese terminology) such as cotton, other fibre crops, tea and oil seeds. A further 50 million people[3] were in grain deficit simply because they were poor, living in low yielding areas. The remaining 12 million were fishermen,[4] forestry workers, salt producers or livestock rearers. Although they do not identify the location of rich or poor areas, interesting figures are available for 1951–52 from which a picture of inequality of production per head of rural population in China's 2200 *hsien* (counties) can be drawn. The results are given in Table 3. The national average for 1951–52 was 320 kilograms.

At the lowest end of the distribution were 72 million rural inhabitants in 343 *hsien* with an average output per head below 200 kilograms. This was very poor indeed: 200 kilograms of unhusked grain, after provision for seed and some livestock feed, could provide 1200–1400 calories, depending on the type of grain (different grains have different edible ratios). A good 'self-sufficiency' level would be around 275 kilograms per head providing (net) 1700–1900 calories, and it is interesting that Chen Yün, one of China's leading economic planners of the 1950s, in an important speech on the grain situation,[5] cited 280 kilograms per head of rural population as 'sufficient' for all uses. In this study 'self-sufficiency' is thus assumed to begin at 275 kilograms per head and amounts below that level are classified as 'deficit'. Moreover, 'self-sufficiency' is assumed to include all per capita levels from 275 kilograms to 309 kilograms. At 310 kilograms

[1] Total from figures in Sha Chien-li (Minister of Food), 'Glorious Achievements of the Grain Front', *JMJP*, 25 October 1959; and Pan Ching-yuan, 'Two Years of Planned Purchase and Planned Supply of Grain', *HCS* (no. 9), 1955.

[2] Sha Chien-li, 'Glorious Achievements of the Grain Front'.

[3] Pan Ching-yuan, 'Two Years of Planned Purchase'.

[4] Sha Chien-li, 'Glorious Achievements of the Grain Front'.

[5] Ch'en Yün, 'Questions Concerning the Central Purchase and Supply of Grain' (speech, 21 July 1955), *HHYP*, vol. 70 (no. 8), 1955, pp. 50–4. Note, however, that Chu Hang, 'The Basic Condition of China's Grain This Year', *HHPYK*, vol. 98 (no. 24), 1956, pp. 71–3, claimed that 305 kilograms per head of rural population (which according to Chu would provide 270 kilograms for consumption) was inadequate.

Table 3. *Distribution of grain production* per head of rural population by hsien, 1951–52*

Grain output per head of rural population (kg)	Number of *hsien*	Rural population (million)	Percentage of rural population	Percentage of national grain output
750+	107	15.02	3.00	8.5
500.5–750	145	28.58	5.63	10.8
400.5–500	257	55.92	11.13	14.8
300.5–400	523	122.75	24.43	25.4
200.5–300	834	208.02	41.42	32.6
Under 200	343	72.01	14.34	7.9
	2209	502.30		

* This was said to refer to the 'usual' level of production in each *hsien*.
Source: Li Ch'eng-jui, *Chung-hua Jen-min Kung-ho-kuo Nung-yeh Shui Shih-kao* (*History of Agricultural Taxation in the Chinese People's Republic*) (Peking, 1959), p. 134.

per head (giving 1900–2100 calories per day) peasants might be expected to sell grain on a voluntary basis and this level is adopted as the beginning of the 'surplus' category.

Unfortunately, the figures which form the basis of Table 3 could not be grouped in these categories, but nevertheless they show that *at least* 72 million people were in considerable deficit, with under 200 kilograms per head, and that approximately 280 million people (56 per cent of China's rural population) were *not* in surplus. At the top end of the scale, Table 3 also shows that there were 107 *hsien* in which 15 million peasants produced, on average, more than 750 kilograms per head. Undoubtedly the bulk of surpluses would be expected from the 509 *hsien* where 95.5 million people produced over 400 kilograms per head, although some would also be forthcoming from the 122.7 million people in the 300–400 kilogram band.

It would probably be impossible for even a large team of research workers to discover enough data to map the figures in Table 2 for China's 2200 *hsien*, and an attempt to chart the geographical distribution of grain output has therefore been largely limited to the province and special district levels of administration. Data have, however, been discovered which enable two detailed studies of inequality at the *hsien* level to be presented, and they undoubtedly highlight problems that were widespread throughout China.

4

Table 4. *Inequality of grain output per head of rural population, averages for 1952–57 (kilograms of unhusked grain)*

Province (ranked highest to lowest)	Output per head (kilograms)	Average size of rural population (million)	Average annual grain output (million tons)	Rank in output	Percent of national output
1. Heilungkiang	905	8.640	7.818	10	4.4
2. Kirin	656	8.525	5.592	14	3.1
3. Inner Mongolia	521	6.920	3.602	22	2.0
4. Tientsin	475	0.385	0.183	25	0.1
5. Kiangsi	402	15.440	6.204	13	3.5
6. Sinkiang	396	4.643	1.838	23	1.0
7. Liaoning	389	16.070	6.245	12	3.5
8. Hupei	370	25.270	9.342	8	5.2
9. Chekiang	359	20.633	7.405	11	4.1
10. {Kwangtung	356	30.885	10.993	5	6.2
{Fukien	356	11.300	4.024	20	2.3
12. Anhwei	348	28.943	10.076	7	5.6
13. Kansu	340	12.082	4.105	19	2.3
China average	339	526.535	178.293		
14. Yunnan	338	16.443	5.561	15	3.1
15. Hunan	334	31.390	10.472	6	5.9
16. Shensi	327	14.378	4.698	17	2.6
17. Kwangsi	326	16.850	5.486	16	3.1
18. Szechuan	320	62.748	20.076	1	11.3
19. Kiangsu	314	37.772	11.872	4	6.7
20. Shansi	302	13.183	3.985	21	2.2
21. Tsinghai	301	1.699	0.512	24	0.3
22. Kweichow	300	14.332	4.298	18	2.4
23. Honan	277	43.005	11.892	3	6.7
24. Shantung	272	47.862	13.000	2	7.3
25. Hopei	245	36.103	8.840	9	5.0
26. Peking	200	0.664	0.133	26	0.1
27. Shanghai	111	0.370	0.041	27	negligible

Source: Appendices 2 and 3.

The provincial distribution of production per head of rural population

Figures in Table 4 show the average annual production of grain per head of rural population during the six years 1952–57 and the relative importance of the twenty-seven provinces (and large cities) as grain producers. Three points must be made about the data in Table 4.

5

First, excluding the tiny rural populations and production of Peking and Shanghai, there was more than a threefold difference between the highest provincial output per head (Heilungkiang) and the lowest (Hopei): in other words, production per head in Hopei was only 27 per cent of that in Heilungkiang.

Secondly, even at this early stage in the discussion, without reference either to the size and distribution of urban population or to the extent of annual output fluctuations, these provincial averages indicate that large potential rural surpluses clearly existed in many provinces, for no less than nineteen of them had levels of per capita output above the 'surplus' level of 310 kilograms.

Thirdly, and equally clear, is the evidence suggesting that little or no potential surplus would be available in the rural sectors of Honan, Hopei and Shantung, with average levels of output per head around or below the 'deficit' level of 275 kilograms.

These figures, however, only indicate broadly the extent of the margin above subsistence which existed in each province's rural sector. The need for grain transfers between rural areas of the same province, and the opportunity to make such transfers, depended on the degree of production inequality within each province. Some evidence of this must now be examined.

Sub-provincial distribution of grain production per head of rural population

Special District data

In 1957 China had 180 Special Districts (the exact figure depends on how self-governing cities are counted) each with an average rural population of around 3 million. There was, however, considerable size variation between provinces. Some, for example Szechuan, had Special Districts with 6–8 million rural inhabitants, while some Special Districts in Kansu and Fukien had rural populations of under 2 million. Special District data relating to grain production and population are difficult to find in the Chinese source materials. When compiling Table 5, therefore, the main aim was to provide as good a sample as possible, covering China's major geographical areas. In particular a great effort was made to include most of the provinces in which China's important 'mini-granaries' or 'commercial (i.e. sur-

Table 5. *Inequality of grain output per head of rural population at the Special District level in eleven provinces, 1952–57*

Province	Special district	Average rural population (million)	Average grain output per head of rural population (kg)	Provincial average grain output per head of rural population (kg)
Kansu	Yinch'uan[a]	0.70	465	
	Changyeh[b]	2.08	400	
	P'ingliang[c]	2.05	392	340
	Tinghsi[d]	2.21	384	
	Wutu[e]	0.89	341	
	Kan-nan[f]	0.30	240	
Shensi	Hanchong[g]	2.12	363	
	Yenan[h]	0.79	270	327
	Yülin[i]	1.45	122	
Hopei[j]	T'angshan	4.28	407	
	Ch'engte	1.92	342	
	Ts'anghsien	4.60	269	
	T'unghsien	3.01	266	245
	Tientsin	3.21	265	(1957: 258)
	Changchiak'ou	3.15	256	
	Paoting	5.65	226	
	Hantan	3.32	212	
	Shihchiachuang	5.80	207	
	Hsingt'ai	3.05	175	
Shansi	Ch'angchih[k]	2.61	440	
	Chin-nan[l]	3.46	298	302
	Ying-pei[m]	1.50	273	
	Yütze[n]	3.10	262	
Shantung[o]	Laiyang	7.40	356	
	Changwei	7.81	332	
	Tsining	4.68	331	272
	Taian	4.79	303	(1956: 295)
	Hweimin	6.23	288	
	Liaoch'eng	6.71	279	
	Hotseh	4.83	278	
	Linyi	6.33	267	
Hunan[p]	Ch'angte	6.14	392	
	Hsiangt'an	6.81	379	
	Hsiang-nan	7.82	333	334
	Ch'ienyang	2.34	309	(1952: 341)
	Hsianghsi	1.59	281	
	Shaoyang	5.73	263	
Anhwei	Wuhu[q]	5.00	500	
	Anking[r]	4.58	368	348
	Fouyang[s]	7.60	257	(1956: 372)
Kiangsu	Soochow[t]	5.11	486	
	Sungkiang[u]	2.30	468	

Table 5 (*cont.*)

Province	Special district	Average rural population (million)	Average grain output per head of rural population (kg)	Provincial average grain output per head of rural population (kg)
	Yangchow[v]	6.58	296	314
	Yench'eng[w]	3.99	289	(1956: 308)
	Hsüchow[x]	4.65	254	
	Nant'ung[y]	5.42	206	
	Hwaiyin[z]	5.23	183	
Szechuan	Wenchiang[aa]	4.63	435	
	Chiangchin[bb]	6.02	373	
	Neichiang[cc]	5.32	337	320
	Suining[dd]	6.75	266	
	Yaan[ee]	0.89	242	
	Hsichang[ff]	1.29	203	
	Nanch'ung[gg]	8.10	191	
Fukien[hh]	Nanp'ing	1.63	551	
	Lungch'i	1.50	529	
	Fuan	1.65	338	356
	Minhou	1.76	321	(1957: 374)
	Chinchiang	4.37	300	
	Lungyen	2.04	282	
Kwangtung	Fatshan[ii]	4.18	487	
	Swatow[jj]	6.10	384	356
	Hainan[kk]	2.50	284	
	'N. Kwangtung'[ll] (inc. Chaokuan)	3.50	226	

Notes

a Average for 1952, 1955 and 1956.
b Average for 1952, 1953 and 1957.
c Average for 1952, 1955, 1956 and 1957.
d 1957.
e Average for 1955, 1956 and 1957.
f Average for 1952, 1955 and 1957.
g 1957.
h Average for 1952 and 1957.
i Average for 1954, 1955 and 1957.
j All Hopei figures are for 1957.
k Average for 1956 and 1957.
l Average for 1952, 1955 and 1956.
m Average for 1953–57.
n Average for 1955 and 1956.
o All Shantung figures are for 1956.
p All Hunan figures are for 1952.
q 1956.
r 1956.

plus) grain bases' were located and also those in which China's poorest Districts were to be found.[6]

Having identified these provinces, every effort was made to discover the range of per capita output between the richest and poorest Special District of each province. Some evidence was collected for eleven provinces, including a complete breakdown for all the Special Districts of four provinces. In general, data for rich Districts were more easily discovered than data for the very poor areas.[7]

The figures in Table 5 show (1) that potentially surplus Districts with very high levels of grain output per head existed in provinces where the *average* output per head was not particularly high (for example, Kiangsu and Szechuan); (2) that some Special Districts involving millions of people were, by any standards, very poor in grain,

[6] An excellent discussion of China's grain problem which includes a list of both mini-granaries and very poor areas is given by Wang Kuang-wei (Vice-Chairman of the State Planning Commission), 'Several Views on the Development of Agriculture', *HH* (no. 17), 1957, pp. 25–8.
[7] For example, no data were found for the low output districts of northern Anhwei.

Notes to Table 5 (*cont.*)
s   Average for 1953–56.
t   1956.
u   1956.
v   1956.
w   Average for 1955 and 1957.
x   Average for 1952, 1955 and 1956.
y   1956.
z   1956.
aa Average for 1952, 1956 and 1957.
bb Average for 1952–56.
cc Average for 1952 and 1957.
dd Average for 1952 and 1957.
ee Average for 1952, 1955 and 1957.
ff 1957.
gg 1957.
hh All figures for Fukien are for 1957 except Minhou (average for 1954 and 1955).
ii Average for 1952–57.
jj 1957.
kk Average for 1952, 1954, 1955 and 1956.
ll 1955.
Percentage of provincial rural population covered by sample of Special Districts: Kansu 64%: Shensi 30%; Hopei 100%; Shansi 80%; Shantung 100%; Hunan 100%; Anhwei 59%; Kiangsu 85%; Szechuan 52%; Fukien 100%; Kwantung 53%.
Source: Appendix 4.

9

and (3) that in many provinces studied there was clear evidence of a need for considerable rural redistribution of grain between Special Districts. However, in Shantung, Hunan, Fukien and perhaps Kansu this was not so clear, from the available evidence.

The Special District data reveal great inequality between rural areas in Shensi and Kiangsu. Average output per head of rural population in the richest District of Shensi recorded in Table 4 was almost three times that of the poorest, and in Kiangsu the figure was 2.7 times. In Hopei, Szechuan and Kwangtung the richest District produced more than double the amount per head in the poorest, and in all the provinces listed, except Fukien, the poorest District was in the deficit category (with output below 275 kilograms per head). Rich 'mini-granaries' with per capita output even exceeding 350 kilograms existed in all eleven provinces, including the generally poor province of Hopei. Among the poor Districts, Yülin District of North Shensi (with 1.5 million rural population), stands out as an area of extreme poverty,[8] with average output around 122 kilograms per head. Fairly poor Districts, with average output near to 200 kilograms per head, existed in Hopei, where 12 million people in three such Districts produced an average of exactly 200 kilograms; in Kiangsu, where 10.7 million people produced, on average, 195 kilograms; and in two Szechuan Districts of 9.4 million rural inhabitants, with an average output of 193 kilograms per head. By far the most uniformly poor province among the eleven listed in Table 5 was Hopei. No less than eight out of its ten Special Districts were below the self-sufficiency level of per capita output (275 kilograms) in 1957, and these involved a rural population of 31.8 million.

Hsien (county) data

Although the Special District data provide valuable evidence of the relative levels of poverty and wealth, in grain, within the different provinces, they nevertheless cover populations that are still large enough to obscure wide rural inequalities. Shantung province is a good example of this. Average grain output during the good year of 1956 was 295 kilograms per head of rural population (totalling 49 million): that is, the higher end of the self-sufficiency range (275–309 kilograms). Complete figures for all the province's Special Districts

---

[8] This District produced only 46 kilograms per head in 1951: Wang Ch'eng-ching, *Shen-hsi Tu-ti Li-yung Wen-t'i* (*Problems of Land Use in Shensi*) (Shanghai, 1956), p. 22.

Table 6. *Frequency distribution of average grain output per head of rural population in 113* hsien, *Shantung, 1956, grouped by Special District*

Special District	Number of *hsien* in each class							Total *hsien*
	< 200*	201–274	275–309	310–350	351–400	401–450	451 +	
Taian	–	–	8	2	–	–	–	10
Liaoch'eng	5	3	5	4	1	1	–	19
Hotseh	–	7	1	–	–	1	–	9
Laiyang	1	3	–	3	8	1	1	17
Linyi	–	9	2	1	–	–	–	12
Hweimin	1	5	6	3	2	–	–	17
Tsining	1	1	2	5	3	–	–	12
Changwei	–	2	4	6	4	1	–	17
Total Special Districts	8	30	28	24	18	4	1	113

Special District	Rural population in each class (millions)							Total rural population
	< 200*	201–274	275–309	310–350	351–400	401–450	451 +	
Taian	–	–	3.705	1.081	–	–	–	4.786
Liaoch'eng	1.467	0.891	2.115	1.405	0.527	0.305	–	6.710
Hotseh	–	3.675	0.722	–	–	0.431	–	4.828
Laiyang	0.022	1.314	–	1.380	3.793	0.489	0.407	7.405
Linyi	–	4.455	1.249	0.627	–	–	–	6.331
Hweimin	0.295	1.647	2.289	1.240	0.758	–	–	6.229
Tsining	0.014	0.162	0.970	2.589	0.943	–	–	4.678
Changwei	–	0.985	1.656	2.373	1.937	0.857	–	7.808
Total rural population	1.798	13.129	12.706	10.695	7.958	2.082	0.407	48.775

| | 14.927 (30.6%) 'Deficit' | 12.706 (26.1%) 'Self-sufficient' | 21.142 (43.3%) 'Surplus' |

Note: * Classes are kilograms per head of rural population.
Source: TCJP, 21 January 1958, 26 January 1958 and 7 March 1958; *Jen-min Shou-ts'eh* (*People's Handbook*) 1957 (Peking, 1957).

(Table 4) reveal that the spread around the average was narrow, and that only one District was in the deficit range of per capita output. Data for the major administrative division below the Special District – the *hsien*[9] or county – however, portray a different picture. For example, there was only one deficit Special District, with a rural population of 6.3 million people, but there were thirty-eight deficit *hsien* scattered among seven out of the province's eight Special Districts, and in these thirty-eight *hsien* (34 per cent of the total number) were 14.9 million rural inhabitants. Table 6 and Figures 1

[9] *TCJP*, 21 January, 26 January and 7 March 1958.

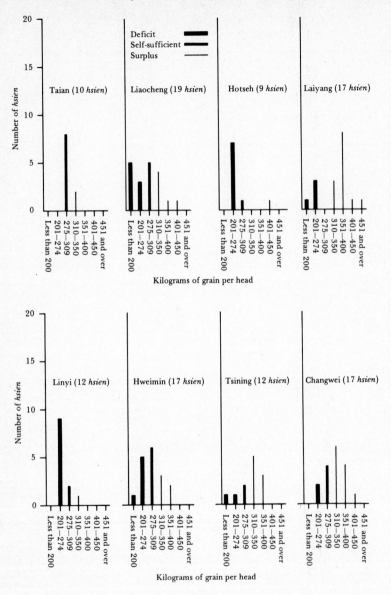

Figure 1. Distribution of grain output per head of rural population in the Special Districts of Shantung, 1956, by number of *hsien*.

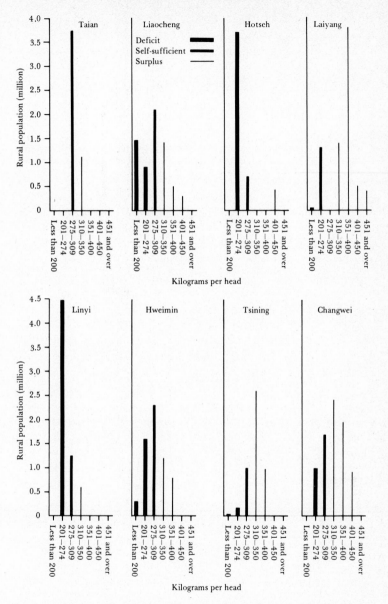

Figure 2. Distribution of grain output per head of rural population in the Special Districts of Shantung, 1956, by the size of rural population.

and 2 summarise the data for the 113 *hsien* in existence during 1956.

From the *hsien* statistics it is immediately apparent that inequality of grain output was considerably greater than that suggested by the Special District averages. The latter reveal a range of per capita production from 267 kilograms (involving 6.3 million people) to 356 kilograms (involving 7.4 million). The range between the richest and poorest *hsien*, however, was from 107 kilograms per head in the small *hsien* of Ch'ang Tao in Laiyang Special District, rural population of 22,000, to 453 kilograms per head in Hwang *hsien*, also part of Laiyang Special District, with 0.4 million people. Excluding the few very small *hsien* in the province (which, however, are included in Table 6), the poorest *hsien* was Linch'ing, Liaoch'eng District, in which 0.5 million people had an average output of 144 kilograms per head. Looking at the inequality between *hsien* more broadly, on the one hand there were 2.5 million rural inhabitants in five *hsien* with an average output of 431 kilograms per head; and on the other hand in eight *hsien* where output per head was below 200 kilograms, the average production of the 1.8 million rural people was only 171 kilograms. Table 7 summarises the range of inequality between *hsien* in all eight Districts.

Thirty out of Shantung's thirty-eight 'deficit' *hsien* were concentrated in four Districts (Liaoch'eng, Hweimin, Linyi and Hotseh) and five of the province's eight *hsien* where average output per head was less than 200 kilograms were in Liaoch'eng. Although it is beyond the scope of this study, it is worthwhile noting that an important reason for the low output in these *hsien* was that they specialised in the growing of either cotton or peanuts.[10] Shantung produced 13.5 per cent of China's cotton in 1956 (third in provincial rank), and it was the largest producer of peanuts. Liaoch'eng grew 34 per cent of Shantung's cotton and Hweimin District grew 30 per cent. Linyi, with nine deficit *hsien*, was an important producer of peanuts. Even so, the *hsien* data also reveal that specialisation in non-grain crops was not the only explanation of low grain output, and that in most deficit *hsien* grain yields per hectare were very low.

Table 6, and the accompanying Figures 1 and 2, indicate the location of Shantung's forty-seven potentially surplus *hsien* (with per capita output above 310 kilograms). The figures show that, although

[10] Distribution of cotton and peanut production by *hsien* is given in *TCJP*, 21 January 1958, p. 3.

Rural inequality of grain output

Table 7. *The range of grain output per head of rural population in the* hsien *of Shantung's eight Special Districts, 1956 (kilograms)*

	Taian	Liao-ch'eng	Hotseh	Laiyang	Linyi	Hwei-min	Tsining	Chang-wei
Special District average	303	279	278	356	267	288	331	332
Richest *hsien*	341	403	431	453	318	367	399	424
Poorest *hsien*	288	130	206	107	229	170	174	226

Source: As Table 6.

they were widely scattered throughout the province, twenty-four of them were concentrated in Laiyang and Changwei Districts, both of which are clearly identified as 'mini-granaries' by the Special District data.

Detailed statistics[11] for production and population in 104 *hsien* of Szechuan province during 1939–43 offer a valuable insight into the historical basis of the unrivalled position held by that province as a supplier of rural grain surpluses during the First Five Year Plan period, 1953–57. These *hsien* have been grouped into their respective Special Districts[12] as of 1957 and, in fact, they make up ten of the sixteen Districts in existence at that time. They mainly exclude *hsien* which belonged to Sikang province, absorbed into Szechuan during 1954, but they include all of the province's 'mini-granaries', and it is primarily because of this that the data are so interesting (Table 8 and Figure 3).

As in the case of Shantung, the *hsien* statistics for Szechuan show a very wide range of per capita output throughout the province. In forty-five *hsien* output per head was at deficit level (below 275 kilograms) and involved 19.6 million rural people, 53 per cent of the provincial total. The rural population in the fifty-one *hsien* where average output was at 'surplus' level totalled 13.61 million, or 37 per cent of the provincial figure. The need for large inter-*hsien* grain movements is further illustrated by figures in Table 9, which shows the

[11] Chou Li-san, Hou Hsüeh-t'ao and Ch'en Ssu-ch'iao, *Ssu-ch'uan Ching-chi Ti-t'u chi shuo-ming (An Annotated Economic Atlas of Szechuan Province)*, Chinese Geographical Research Institute (Peipei, 1946).
[12] Listed in *People's Handbook* 1957.

15

Table 8. *Frequency distribution of average grain output per head of rural population in 104 hsien, Szechuan, 1939–43, grouped by Special Districts of 1957*

Number of *hsien* in each class

Special District	<100*	101–200	201–274	275–309	310–400	401–500	501–600	601–700	701–800	801–900	901–1000	1001–1100	Total *hsien*
Wenchiang	–	1	1	2	5	4	3	–	–	–	–	1	17
Neichiang	–	1	2	1	2	–	1	–	–	–	–	–	7
Suining	–	2	–	1	2	2	–	2	–	–	–	–	9
Mienyang	–	2	1	–	1	2	4	–	1	1	–	1	13
Luchou	1	1	2	–	1	1	1	1	–	–	–	–	8
Chiangchin	–	3	3	1	1	2	–	–	–	–	–	–	10
Loshan	–	5	1	–	2	–	1	–	–	–	1	–	11
Nanch'ung	–	3	4	1	2	–	1	–	2	–	1	–	11
Tahsien	–	3	2	1	2	1	1	–	–	1	–	–	10
Wanhsien	–	3	4	1	–	–	–	–	–	–	–	–	8
Total Special Districts	1	24	20	8	17	12	11	3	3	2	1	2	104

Rural population in each class (million)

Special District	<100*	101–200	201–274	275–309	310–400	401–500	501–600	601–700	701–800	801–900	901–1000	1001–1100	Total rural population
Wenchiang	–	0.37	0.22	0.86	1.05	0.54	0.66	–	–	–	–	0.09	3.79
Neichiang	–	0.88	1.37	0.48	1.19	–	0.32	–	–	–	–	–	4.24
Suining	–	1.44	–	0.60	1.11	0.95	–	0.68	–	–	–	–	4.78
Mienyang	–	0.39	0.19	0.03	0.11	0.32	0.85	–	0.14	0.24	–	–	2.27
Luchou	0.28	0.73	1.25	0.03	–	0.08	0.30	0.37	–	–	–	0.09	3.10
Chiangchin	–	2.22	1.09	0.51	0.29	0.67	–	–	–	–	–	–	4.78

													Total
Loshan	—	1.51	0.08	—	0.23	—	—	—	0.29	—	0.21	—	2.32
Nanch'ung	—	1.45	1.23	0.68	1.18	—	0.33	—	—	—	—	—	4.87
Tahsien	—	1.22	1.13	—	0.70	0.31	0.15	—	—	0.16	—	—	3.67
Wanhsien	—	1.17	1.34	0.57	—	—	—	—	—	—	—	—	3.08
Total rural population	0.28	11.38	7.90	3.73	5.86	2.87	2.61	1.05	0.43	0.40	0.21	0.18	36.90
		19.56 (53.0%) 'Deficit'		3.73 (10.1%) 'Self-sufficient'	13.61 (36.9%) 'Surplus'								

Note: * Classes are kilograms per head of rural population.
Source: Chou Li-san et al., *An Annotated Economic Atlas of Szechuan Province*, and *People's Handbook* 1957.

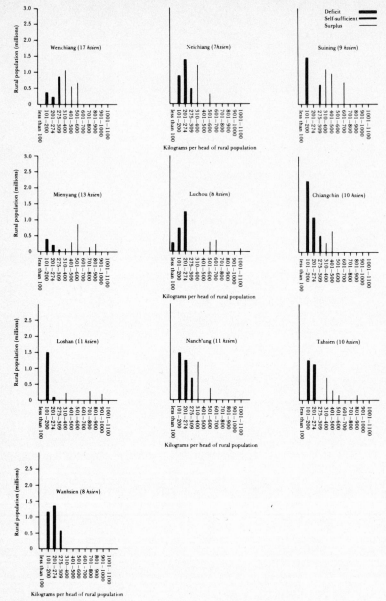

Figure 3. Grain production in 104 *hsien* of Szechuan, 1939–43, grouped by Special Districts of 1957.

Table 9. *The range of grain output per head of rural population in 104 hsien, Szechuan, 1939–43, grouped by Special Districts of 1957 (kilograms)*

	Wen-chiang	Suining	Mieny-ang	Chiang-chin	Luchou	Neichi-ang	Nan-ch'ung	Loshan	Tahsien	Wan-hsien
Average output per head of rural population in Special District	370	352	458	250	312	276	262	308	293	217
Rural population (million)	3.79	4.78	2.27	4.78	3.10	4.24	4.88	2.32	3.67	3.08
Richest *hsien* average output	1041	655	810	463	1066	539	526	901	850	291
Rural population (million)	0.09	0.43	0.24	0.37	0.09	0.32	0.32	0.21	0.16	0.57
Poorest *hsien* average output	123	182	123	154	90	177	116	106	153	124
Rural population (million)	0.37	0.63	0.25	0.66	0.28	0.88	0.63	0.52	0.63	0.75

Note: Comparable figures for average output per head of rural population during the period 1953–57 are: Wenchiang 435 kg, Neichiang 337 kg, and Nanch'ung 191 kg. See Table 8.
Source: As Table 5.

Table 10. *Szechuan's 'granary', 1939–43*

	Special Districts			
	Suining 1	Wenchiang 2	Mienyang 3	Totals 1–3
Number of *hsien*	9	17	13	39
Number of 'surplus' *hsien*	6	13	9	28
Rural population of 'surplus' *hsien* (million)	2.74	2.34	1.66	6.74
Rural population of Special District (million)	4.78	3.79	2.27	10.84
Percentage of population in 'surplus' *hsien*	57.3	61.7	73.1	62.2
Average output per head in 'surplus' *hsien* (kg)	454	451	564	480
Average output per head in Special Districts (kg)	352	370	458	380

Source: As Table 8.

gap between the richest and poorest *hsien* in the ten Special Districts. Although the figures refer to 1939–43, they may undoubtedly be taken as a close approximation to the situation in Szechuan during the early 1950s, before the start of a period of rapid growth which transformed the overall position of the province.

Perhaps the most important revelation of the *hsien* figures, however, is the existence of three adjacent Special Districts, with large potential grain surpluses, concentrated in the Szechuan basin: Suining, Wenchiang and Mienyang Districts. Their combined rural population of 10.8 million produced on average 380 kilograms of grain per head per year. Counting all above 309 kilograms as 'surplus', here then was a single region of Szechuan with a potential surplus of almost 0.8 million tons per year. And if only the twenty-eight surplus *hsien* in the three districts are included, the average output per head was 480 kilograms. The potential surplus from these *hsien* exceeded one million tons per year. The significance of this will become clear when Szechuan's actual contribution to the grain supplies of the rest of China in the 1950s is discussed.

The need for inter-*hsien* rural transfers in many parts of China, to eliminate the extremes of rural poverty and to guarantee adequate supplies for peasants growing industrial crops, cannot therefore be doubted. The actual volume of such transfers varied from province to province, as figures in Chapter 2 for such movements during 1953–57 show. The existence of 'mini-granaries' within provinces provided any government with an opportunity to mobilise the required surpluses. Grain deficit rural areas, however, were but one of the claimants for such surpluses. The urban populations also had to be fed and this task was a daunting one indeed.

THE PROBLEM OF INTRA-PROVINCIAL RURAL–URBAN GRAIN TRANSFERS: A QUESTION OF BOTH QUALITY AND QUANTITY

China had a vast urban population during the 1950s. It was around 69 million in 1952, and it grew at an average rate of 6.3 per cent a year to become 94 million in 1957.[13] On average, during 1952–57, it stood at 82 million. Assuming that average annual grain consumption was 250 kilograms (roughly equal to the rural population's 275 kilograms, gross of seed and feed) some mechanism had to be found to transfer 21 million tons of grain to China's towns each year from the surplus rural areas (foreign imports being ruled out by the Government). With such a large urban population, it only needed a 5 per cent rise in consumption to raise total demand by one million tons.

The problem of supplying the towns was not only one of quantity, but also one of quality, for China's urban populations had a strong preference for fine grain – rice in the southern areas and wheat and soya beans elsewhere. Unlike the southern city dwellers, the urban inhabitants of northern China also consumed considerable amounts of coarse grain – mainly *kaoliang* (sorghum), maize and millet. A common feature of the northern and southern urban populations, however, was

---

[13] These are our estimates from provincial data (see Appendix 3). They differ slightly from several other figures available. Ernest Ni, *Distribution of the Urban and Rural Population of Mainland China: 1953 and 1958* (US Department of Commerce, Bureau of the Census, Foreign Manpower Research Office, International Population Reports, Series P–95, no. 56, October 1960) (see Appendix 3) gives the urban population as 69 million in 1952 and 91.6 million in 1957. The claim that urban population rose by 38.9 per cent in 1953–57 (*KMJP*, 7 October 1963) suggests a rather higher 1957 total than our 94 million, and C.M. Hou cites a figure of 92 million for 1957 (Alexander Eckstein, Walter Galenson and Ta-chung Liu (eds.), *Economic Trends in Communist China* (Chicago, 1968), p. 342).

that none of them regarded potatoes as a 'main grain' at all and in general they did not eat significant amounts. Although the peasants grew and consumed large quantities of potatoes and coarse grains they nevertheless had a high income elasticity of demand for fine grain. The keenest competition between the rural and urban sectors, therefore, was likely to be for *fine* grain as opposed to grain in general, and this section provides evidence of the ability of each province to meet the possible demand for fine grain by the urban population. Table 11 sets out the relevant statistics for 1952 and 1957 (two years for which sufficient data are available). Focusing first on columns 1 and 5 in Table 11, data for 1952 and 1957 show that, quite apart from the question of grain composition, three provinces[14] were not 'self-sufficient' in grain in that their rural sectors could not feed the urban populations without reducing the quantity of grain left per head of rural population to below 275 kilograms. These were Shensi, Shansi and Kiangsu. When, however, the 'cost' to the peasants of supplying the towns is also measured by the small amounts of *fine* grain they would retain (in contrast to the large quantity of potatoes), many more provinces must be provisionally classified as probable grain deficit areas. Thus, Liaoning could not be regarded as potentially self-sufficient in spite of the rural residual of 283 kilograms per head. It is difficult to envisage any means by which the Liaoning peasants could be persuaded to reduce their fine grain availability from 74 kilograms to 6 kilograms per head in order to satisfy the preferences of their 6.22 million urban neighbours. Such considerations also blur, to some extent, the apparently clear status of southern provinces such as Szechuan, Fukien, Kwangsi and even Kwangtung, all of which, on a basis of the figures for total grain left in peasants' hands in column 5, appeared to be quite capable of supplying their towns with grain. Especially interesting are the data for Szechuan. If potatoes were discounted by the rural population,[15] after the required transfers to the

[14] The rural sectors of Honan, Hopei and Shantung were already in a 'deficit' position before any grain had been transferred to the towns.

[15] Further discussion of this topic is found in Chapter 2, but note that the role of potatoes was very important in Szechuan. Yen Hung-yen, addressing the Chinese National People's Congress in 1957, stated that in twenty-seven of Szechuan's *hsien* where there were 15 million people (20 per cent of the provincial population), potatoes were the main grain, supplying around half of the peasants' grain consumption – a problem that called for 'an active plan for its solution', namely the provision of more fine grain: *NPC*, p. 794.

towns had been made, only 255 kilograms per head of rural population would remain. This is important considering the role actually played by Szechuan during the 1950s. In general, however, Table 11 shows how much easier it was likely to be for the provinces of the south, as compared with those of the north, to supply their urban populations with enough grain of preferred quality. In Hunan and Kiangsi it was even possible to feed the towns and still to leave more than 275 kilograms of *fine* grain per head of rural population.

This aspect of the grain imbalance between northern and southern China in the 1950s created much difficulty for the Government. In the north there were several provinces in which low grain output per head of rural population was associated with small quantities of fine grain and large urban populations. In the south, by contrast, many provinces produced 'surplus' levels of grain per head of rural population, composed largely of fine grain, with relatively small urban populations to be fed.

The analysis of the relationship between the rural and urban sectors has of course implications for provincial surpluses and inter-provincial transfers. Data in Table 11 provide some evidence of both the need for such surpluses and their possible sources. In the next section, this is examined in more detail.

INEQUALITY OF GRAIN OUTPUT AND THE PROBLEM OF INTER-PROVINCIAL GRAIN TRANSFERS

Table 12 ranks China's twenty-seven provinces (and autonomous cities) according to their average grain output per head of total population in the six years 1952–57. It illustrates both the wide range between the provinces and also the dispersion around the national average of 293 kilograms per head. Excluding the cities, average per capita output in China's 'poorest' province, Hopei, was only 38 per cent of that in the 'richest', Heilungkiang, and in eleven provinces it was less than 50 per cent of the Heilungkiang level.

For output per head of *total*, as for rural population, defining 'deficit', 'self-sufficient' and 'surplus' as before (0–274 kilograms per head as deficit; 275–309 as self-sufficient; and 310 or above as surplus), during the six year period as a whole, eight provinces and cities were deficit, twelve were self-sufficient and a further seven were surplus. The combined populations of the provinces in the three categories

Table 11. *Provincial production of fine grain per head, 1952–57*

	Output per head of rural population (kg) Average 1952 and 1957			Urban population (million) Average 1952 and 1957	Grain available per head of rural population after meeting basic urban consumption requirements of 250 kg per head including fine grain of assumed percentage[a]			
	Total 1	Fine 2	Fine % 3	4	Total 5	Fine 6	Coarse 7	(of which potatoes)[b] 8
North East								
Heilungkiang	952	338	35.5	4.49	881	248	633	53
Kirin	679	197	29.0	3.34	581	129	452	c.25
Liaoning	381	74	19.4	6.22	283	6	277	19
North West								
IMR	460	78	17.0	1.16	418	48	370	50
Kansu	339	150	44.2	1.54	307	128	170	c.45
Shensi	295	160	54.2	2.51	252	129	123	n.a.
Sinkiang	390	205	52.6	0.56	360	183	177	c.2
Tsinghai	297	129	43.4	0.14	276	115	161	c.48
North								
Honan	262	131	50.0	3.18	244	118	126	39
Hopei	269	65	24.2	3.46	246	48	198	37
Shansi	284	71	25.0	2.00	246	44	202	32
Shantung	267	98	36.7	3.32	250	86	164	62
Centre								
Hunan	343	306	89.2	3.07	319	281	38	26
Hupei	390	303	77.7	3.79	353	266	87	18
Kiangsi	417	392	94.0	2.12	382	358	24	c.22

East							
Anhwei	363	273	75.2	2.71	340	253	87	c.51
Chekiang	360	291	80.8	3.24	321	256	65	c.33
Kiangsu	307	225	73.3	5.30	271	193	78	c.13
South West							
Kweichow	307	214	69.7	1.53	280	190	90	c.21
Szechuan	319	216	67.7	5.71	296	196	100	41
Yunnan	338	215	63.6	1.73	312	191	121	19
South							
Fukien	361	284	78.7	2.40	308	231	77	c.71
Kwangsi	308	256	83.1	1.51	286	233	53	24
Kwangtung	350	295	84.3	4.93	310	256	54	c.49

Notes: a. Percentage of fine grain consumed per head of urban population: 70% in North East, North West and North; 100% in Central and South China; 90% in East and South West China.

b. Assumes no potatoes consumed by urban population.

Table 12. *Average grain output per head of total population, 1952–57, in China's twenty-seven provinces and autonomous cities*

	Average grain output per head 1952–57 (kg)	Average total population 1952–57 (million)	Potential grain surpluses (+) and deficits (−) per annum (million tons)
1. Heilungkiang	593	13.18	+ 3.743
2. Kirin	472	11.85	+ 1.932
3. IMR	448	8.05	+ 1.119
4. Kiangsi	354	17.53	+ 0.789
5. Sinkiang	353	5.21	+ 0.229
6. Hupei	321	29.12	+ 0.349
7. Anhwei	316	31.92	+ 0.223
8. Chekiang	309	23.93	
9. Kwangtung	306	35.88	
9. Yunnan	306	18.20	
11. Hunan	303	34.52	
12. Kansu	301	13.65	
13. Kwangsi	298	18.39	
14. Szechuan	293	68.55	'Self-sufficient'
CHINA	293	608.70	
15. Fukien	292	13.76	
16. Liaoning	283	22.07	
17. Shensi	278	16.88	
17. Tsinghai	278	1.84	
19. Kiangsu	275	43.18	
20. Kweichow	270	15.89	− 0.079
21. Shansi	265	15.04	− 0.150
22. Honan	258	46.17	− 0.785
23. Shantung	254	51.13	− 1.074
24. Hopei	223	39.61	− 2.060
25. Tientsin	63	2.93	− 0.621
26. Peking	37	3.59	− 0.854
27. Shanghai	6	6.63	− 1.783
		Total surpluses	+ 8.384
		Total deficits	− 7.406
		National potential surplus	+ 0.978

Source: Appendices 2 and 3.

were: deficit 180.99 million (29.7 per cent); self-sufficient 310.85 million (51.1 per cent); and surplus 116.86 million (19.2 per cent). The possible implications for inter-provincial transfers, of the distribution of grain output shown in Table 12, are indicated in column 3 of the table, which provides estimates of the potential provincial surplus and deficits according to the self-sufficiency criteria above. The figures reveal that 81 per cent of China's potential surpluses were concentrated in the North East and North West, with Heilungkiang in a dominant position. At the other end of the scale, the largest potential deficits were in Shanghai, Hopei and Shantung. Perhaps surprisingly, the group of provinces falling into the self-sufficient category includes such important rice producers as Hunan, Szechuan and Kwangtung. Finally, it is seen that the total of potential surpluses exceeded the total potential regional deficits by only 0.978 million tons per annum, on average.

THE PROBLEM OF GROWTH AND STABILITY OF GRAIN OUTPUT

So far consideration has been given to the more chronic, long-run grain problems facing China during the 1950s, and it was therefore legitimate and useful to examine them by treating the six years from 1952 to 1957 as a single period. Even in the short-run period of six years, however, significant changes in grain production were taking place, with important implications for grain policy. This section focuses on two facets of change: the trend of growth of output and the degree of stability of output in China's twenty-seven provinces.

Trend of growth of output per head and changes in provincial 'self-sufficiency'

Figures in Table 13 reveal wide regional differences in the six year trend of growth of output per head of total population. On the one hand the trend was downward in no less than nine provinces, of which six were situated in the more northerly part of China. On the other hand, grain output per head in the entire South West Region consisting of Kweichow, Szechuan and Yunnan grew at a rate of more than 4 per cent per annum. Of particular interest for this study is how the provincial trends in Table 13 affected the *absolute* levels of per

27

Table 13. *Growth of grain output per head of total population, 1952–57*

| | Output per head (kg unhusked grain) | | Six-year trend of output per head (% p.a.) |
	1952	1957	
North East			
Heilungkiang	757	529	−5.30
Kirin	549	433	−5.61
Liaoning	269	278	+1.82
North West			
IMR	487	323	−5.91
Kansu	248	347	+9.79
Shensi	254	249	−0.28
Sinkiang	335	361	+1.28
Tsinghai	225	314	+9.41
North			
Honan	235	253	+1.86
Hopei	259	235	−1.81
Peking	43	49	+0.79
Shansi	272	223	−3.85
Shantung	260	240	+0.74
Tientsin	60	78	+7.73
Centre			
Hunan	313	313	+0.01
Hupei	307	368	+4.45
Kiangsi	352	379	+1.81
East			
Anhwei	293	368	+5.43
Chekiang	310	313	+0.30
Kiangsu	267	270	−0.05
Shanghai	7	5	−4.93
South West			
Kweichow	232	317	+6.32
Szechuan	260	322	+4.32
Yunnan	271	338	+4.90
South			
Fukien	292	303	+0.89
Kwangsi	288	279	−1.40
Kwangtung	278	323	+2.89
China	287	300	+1.35

Sources: Appendices 2 and 3.

capita production between 1952 and 1957 and thus the size and distribution of the potential grain surpluses and deficits.

In terms of the three 'self-sufficiency' categories – potentially deficit, self-sufficient and surplus – the change in per capita output between 1952 and 1957 involved no change of 'status' for eighteen provinces. Three provinces (Hupei, Anhwei and Kwangtung) moved from a position of potential self-sufficiency to one of surplus, five provinces (Kansu, Tsinghai, Kweichow, Szechuan and Yunnan) jumped from potential deficit to surplus, while Liaoning improved its status from deficit to self-sufficient. The *extent* to which changes in output per head affected the provincial distribution of potential deficits and surpluses is indicated by Table 14.

The main point to emerge from the figures in Table 14 is that the grain imbalance between north and south China increased between 1952 and 1957: the North Region's potential deficits grew larger, North Eastern and North Western potential surpluses decreased, whereas in the southern regions potential surpluses increased greatly. More specifically, the potential total deficit of the North Region (Honan, Hopei, Shansi, Peking, Tientsin and Shantung) rose from 4.278 million tons to 7.086 million tons. At the same time, the potential surplus of Heilungkiang, Kirin and Inner Mongolia fell by 46 per cent from 9.125 million tons in 1952 to 4.953 million tons in 1957. By contrast, many southern provinces either increased their potential surpluses, or entered the potential surplus category. For example, Kiangsi's potential surplus rose by 84 per cent, while Anhwei and Hupei, which had no potential surplus in 1952, were able to offer 3.797 million tons in 1957.

Even more dramatic were the changing fortunes of the South West Region, where a total potential deficit of 1.682 million tons in 1952 was transformed into a potential surplus of 1.627 million tons in 1957. The overall change in the balance between north and south China, broadly defined, is seen in Table 15.

Stability of grain output 1952–57: the need for reserves

Instability of grain production in China was, of course, a phenomenon which had created famines and malnutrition throughout many centuries. The building up of stocks in order to minimise the hardships imposed by such fluctuations was bound to be a central preoccupation

Table 14. *Potential grain surpluses and deficits in China's provinces, 1952 and 1957 (million tons)*

	1952	1957
Potential deficits		
Liaoning	0.121	
Honan	1.750	1.071
Hopei	0.583	1.721
Shansi	0.042	0.831
Peking	0.610	0.938
Tientsin	0.568	0.634
Shantung	0.725	1.891
Kansu	0.345	
Shensi	0.329	0.471
Tsinghai	0.083	
Kweichow	0.638	
Szechuan	0.975	
Yunnan	0.069	
Kiangsu	0.326	0.226
Shanghai	1.659	1.944
Total	8.823	9.727
Potential surpluses		
Heilungkiang	5.201	3.269
Kirin	2.676	1.556
Inner Mongolia	1.248	0.128
Sinkiang	0.125	0.293
Kiangsi	0.708	1.303
Hunan	0.132	0.145
Chekiang	0.023	0.101
(Total 1952)	10.113	
Anhwei		1.980
Hupei		1.817
Tsinghai		0.010
Kansu		0.554
Kweichow		0.135
Szechuan		0.938
Yunnan		0.554
Kwangtung		0.531
(Total 1957)		13.314
Net potential surplus	1.290	3.587

Table 15. *Regional potential surplus and deficit position, 1952 and 1957 (million tons)*

	'North' China (N, NE, NW)			'South' China (E, Central, SW, S)		
	Potential surplus	Potential deficit	Net ±	Potential surplus	Potential deficit	Net ±
1952	9.250	5.156	+ 4.094	0.863	3.667	− 2.804
1957	5.810	7.557	− 1.747	7.504	2.170	+ 5.334

of the Communist Government. Indeed, one of Mao Tse-tung's most celebrated instructions to the Chinese people was to 'store grain' as a bulwark against war and natural calamities and many vivid statements exhorting the people to save in the good years are to be found in the Chinese literature.[16] Table 16 presents data on the fluctuations in (1) per capita grain output, and (2) the level of total output in the years between 1952 and 1957.

First of all, to put the provincial figures into the national context, in terms of climatic conditions the period 1952–57 witnessed two good years (1952 and 1955), two average years (1953 and 1957), and two bad years (1954 and 1956). In each year, on average, disasters affected 20–30 million rural inhabitants[17] and around 10 million hectares[18] of arable land (9 per cent of the national total). They necessitated the supply of 4–5 million tons of relief grain per annum.[19] In the bad year of 1954 rural disasters hit 12 million hectares of land and 62 million people;[20] in 1956 no less than 15 million hectares of land and 74 million people were devastated.[21]

A glance at the figures in Table 16 for the annual percentage fluctuations in output per head reveals some stark contrasts in

---

[16] For example: 'When drinking water, think of the source; at times of rich harvest, do not forget the State' (*TCJP*, 25 September 1962); 'In the matter of grain consumption we should promote the way of having a river which is small but which, nevertheless, flows continuously' (*HUPJP*, 2 July 1960).

[17] *HKWHP*, 23 September 1957.

[18] *History of Agricultural Taxation*, p. 178.

[19] Sun Wei-tzu, 'Principles for Organising Grain Circulation Planning', *CHCC* (no. 2), 1958, pp. 24–7.

[20] P'eng Hui-fang, 'Refute the Lies of the Capitalist Rightist Class on Questions of the Central Purchase and Supply of Grain', *HHPYK*, vol. 124 (no. 2), 1958, pp. 36–9.

[21] *Ibid.*

Table 16. *Provincial grain output per head of total population, 1952–57*

	Percentage change in output per head on previous year					Output per head of total population (kg)						Change in total grain output on previous year (thousand tons)					Instability index of output per head 1952–57
	1953	1954	1955	1956	1957	1952	1953	1954	1955	1956	1957	1953	1954	1955	1956	1957	
North East																	
Heilungkiang	−33.0	−5.8	+11.1	−8.2	−5.5	757	583	549	610	560	529	−1079	−78	+1173	−295	−51	6.64
Kirin	−6.6	−8.2	+0.8	−15.4	+7.7	549	513	471	475	402	433	−270	−343	+185	−759	+498	5.15
Liaoning	+1.5	+1.5	no ch.	+15.2	−12.9	269	273	277	277	319	278	+275	+300	+155	+1260	−728	3.07
North West																	
IMR	−1.6	+4.0	−20.7	+32.9	−38.5	487	479	498	395	525	323	+127	+340	−630	+1393	−1600	11.70
Kansu	−6.9	+21.6	+6.8	+28.0	−9.6	248	231	281	300	384	347	−140	+750	+375	+1300	−385	6.51
Shensi	+15.7	+2.7	−12.9	+17.1	−19.2	254	294	302	263	308	249	+765	+269	−504	+932	−914	6.71
Sinkiang	+3.9	+2.0	+2.0	−2.2	+2.0	335	348	355	362	354	361	+113	+100	+93	+21	+100	1.37
Tsinghai	−13.8	+52.1	+6.8	−1.3	+1.0	225	194	295	315	311	314	−40	+197	+61	+21	+34	9.13
North																	
Honan	+7.2	+2.4	+7.0	−2.2	−6.3	235	252	258	276	270	253	+955	+560	+1050	+25	−575	3.50
Hopei	−16.6	−5.1	+11.2	−12.7	+18.1	259	216	205	228	199	235	−1315	−135	+1135	−865	+1840	7.90
Peking	−2.3	−42.9	+29.2	+9.7	+44.1	43	42	24	31	34	49	+10	−40	+40	+33	+41	21.61
Shansi	+9.6	−7.0	−11.6	+13.5	−19.8	272	298	277	245	278	223	+477	−207	−390	+610	−770	6.65
Shantung	−13.8	+16.5	no ch.	+6.9	−14.0	260	224	261	261	279	240	−1507	+2110	+322	+1166	−1707	6.15
Tientsin	−18.3	+4.1	+25.5	+9.4	+11.4	60	49	51	64	70	78	−24	+11	+49	+24	+32	8.50
Centre																	
Hunan	−1.6	−11.7	+19.1	−10.2	+7.6	313	308	272	324	291	313	+20	−1056	+1985	−962	+1019	4.90
Hupei	+5.2	−26.3	+37.4	+9.2	+3.1	307	323	238	327	357	368	+642	−2222	+2764	+1152	+584	8.44
Kiangsi	−3.1	−2.6	+6.3	+3.1	+4.1	352	341	332	353	364	379	−40	−8	+525	+350	+443	2.35
East																	
Anhwei	+0.7	−16.6	+44.3	−6.8	+11.2	293	295	246	355	331	368	+275	−1315	+3759	−620	+1441	7.48

Chekiang	− 0.3	− 2.9	+ 5.0	− 1.6	+ 1.0	310	309	300	315	310	313	+ 155	− 70	+ 537	+ 42	+ 240	1.07
Kiangsu	+ 5.6	− 4.6	+ 9.3	− 9.2	+ 1.1	267	282	269	294	267	270	+ 865	− 250	+ 1370	− 870	+ 229	3.16
Shanghai	no ch.	− 14.3 no ch.	+ 16.7	− 28.6		7	7	6	6	7	5	+ 3	− 6	+ 4	+ 6	− 15	7.32
South West																	
Kweichow	+ 6.9	+ 4.8	+ 1.5	+ 11.7	+ 7.5	232	248	260	264	295	317	+ 326	+ 307	+ 184	+ 601	+ 491	1.32
Szechuan	+ 6.2	+ 4.3	+ 1.4	+ 7.9	+ 2.2	260	276	288	292	315	322	+ 1433	+ 1215	+ 705	+ 2025	+ 1003	1.10
Yunnan	+ 3.7	+ 5.3	+ 4.1	+ 8.8	+ 0.9	271	281	296	308	335	338	+ 276	+ 374	+ 320	+ 628	+ 164	1.05
South																	
Fukien	+ 1.4	− 6.8	+ 0.7	+ 10.8	− 1.6	292	296	276	278	308	303	+ 186	− 150	+ 135	+ 545	+ 7	3.48
Kwangsi	+ 6.6	+ 5.5	− 1.9	− 12.9	+ 0.7	288	307	324	318	277	279	+ 445	+ 445	+ 5	− 640	+ 145	5.19
Kwangtung	+ 6.5	+ 4.7	− 2.3	+ 6.9	+ 0.3	278	296	310	303	324	323	+ 810	+ 715	+ 5	+ 1021	+ 260	1.95
China	− 0.7	− 1.4	+ 6.4	+ 1.7	− 1.3	287	285	281	299	304	300	+ 3143	+ 1813	+ 15412	+ 8054	+ 1826	1.60

provincial experience. In Anhwei and Kiangsu, for example, output per head fluctuated in every year from 1952 to 1957, while in the three South West provinces it maintained quite a steady upward trend. Individual years of very wide output fluctuation are to be found in Inner Mongolia, Tsinghai, Hupei and Anhwei. In Hopei and Shantung annual fluctuations resulted in levels of output per head that were well below 'self-sufficiency' standard (275 kilograms) in most years. And as the third set of figures in Table 16 shows, the fluctuations in some provinces involved large amounts of grain, amounting to 1–3 million tons.

The disasters of 1954, mainly in the form of floods, centred on four provinces of central China – Hunan, Hupei, Anhwei and Kiangsu. Grain output here fell by 4.843 million tons. Hunan, Anhwei and Kiangsu suffered a further decline of 2.452 million tons in 1956, when disasters also hit Heilungkiang, Kirin and Hopei, in which production fell by 1.919 million tons. During the summer of 1957, floods in Shantung[22] destroyed 3 million houses and the crops on 2.3 million hectares of land (25 per cent of the province's arable area). The number of people drowned was estimated to be 1500, and 7.4 million people (15 per cent of the rural population) were seriously affected. With production falling by 1.7 million tons, per capita output was reduced to 240 kilograms.

Many more examples of serious local disasters which occurred during the period 1952–57 could be provided, but enough evidence has been given to show that production instability resulting from such disasters was a serious problem. A good measure which shows the relative degree of instability of production per head in each of China's twenty-seven provinces throughout the six years 1952–57 is Coppock's index[23] of instability originally designed to analyse export fluctuations.

---

[22] *TCJP*, 16 August 1957 and *JMJP*, 11 February 1958. In autumn 1957 further disasters affected 5.5 million hectares.

[23] The formula for the index is:

$$\sum_{t=1}^{N} \frac{\left| \dfrac{Y_t - Y'_t}{Y'_t} \right| \cdot 100}{N}$$

where Y_t = the observed value of the variable in t
Y'_t = the logarithmic least squares estimate of the trend value for time period t.
N = the number of time periods

See J.D. Coppock, *International Trade Instability* (New York and Farnborough, 1977), p. 10.

One of the advantages of Coppock's index is that it measures instability in relation to the trend of output. An output with no deviations from the trend would have an instability index of one. The final column of figures in Table 16 gives the provincial indexes for the six years under review. They require little comment at this stage, for it is more interesting to look at instability in the context of growth and level of output. This is done in the next and final section. The small number of stable provinces, however, with indexes close to unity, is striking.

A SUMMARY: THE RELATIONSHIP BETWEEN THE LEVEL OF PER CAPITA OUTPUT, GROWTH AND STABILITY

Earlier sections have examined in turn the 'poverty' (or 'wealth'), growth and degree of stability of grain production per head in each province of China. It is only when the relationship between all three indicators is considered that the 'favourable' and 'problem' areas can be clearly identified. Table 17 and Map 1 bring the relevant figures together.

The three classes of 'poverty' or 'wealth' in Table 17 (poor, adequate and rich) correspond to the per capita output levels designated earlier as deficit, self-sufficient and surplus. Four classes of output growth have been listed: falling per capita output, 'slow' growth (less than 2 per cent per annum), 'medium' growth (2.1–3.5 per cent per annum), and 'fast' growth (over 3.5 per cent). Finally, in Table 16, four degrees of stability have been defined: 'very unstable' (instability index above 6), 'unstable' (index 4–6), 'fairly stable' (index 1.5–4), and 'very stable' (index below 1.5).

From the data in Table 17 it is possible to identify seven major grain-growing provinces in the poor (potentially deficit) or adequate groups which had both growth and stability problems.

1 and 2. In the worst position were Hopei and Shansi, with poor levels of per capita output that was both very unstable and declining, 1952–57.
3. In Shantung, output per head was poor, very unstable and growing only slowly, 1952–57.
4. Marginally better was Shensi, where per capita output was very unstable, declining throughout the six years, but on average just at an adequate level.

35

Table 17. *'Poverty', growth and stability of grain output, 1952–57*

	Average grain output per head, 1952–57 (kg per head)			Trend of per capita grain output, 1952–57				Stability of total grain output, 1952–57			
	Poor (0–274)	Adequate (275–309)	Rich (310+)	Falling	Slow growth (<2% p.a.)	Medium growth (2.1–3.5% p.a.)	Fast growth (>3.5% p.a.)	Very unstable (Index >6)	Unstable (Index 4–6)	Fairly stable (Index 1.5–4)	Very stable (Index <1.5)
North East											
Heilungkiang	—	—	593	−5.30	—	—	—	6.69	—	—	—
Kirin	—	—	472	−5.61	—	—	—	—	—	3.46	—
Liaoning	—	283	—	—	+1.82	—	—	—	—	3.37	—
North West											
IMR	—	—	448	−5.91	—	—	—	11.43	—	—	—
Kansu	—	301	—	—	—	—	+9.79	6.54	—	—	—
Shensi	—	278	—	−0.28	—	—	—	8.31	—	—	—
Sinkiang	—	—	353	—	+1.28	—	—	—	—	—	1.36
Tsinghai	—	278	—	—	—	—	+9.41	9.22	—	—	—
North											
Honan	258	—	—	—	+1.86	—	—	—	—	3.50	—
Hopei	223	—	—	−1.81	—	—	—	7.86	—	—	—
Peking	37	—	—	—	+0.79	—	—	21.61	—	—	—
Shansi	265	—	—	−3.85	—	—	—	6.69	—	—	—
Shantung	254	—	—	—	+0.74	—	—	6.09	—	—	—
Tientsin	63	—	—	—	—	—	+7.73	8.50	—	—	—
Centre											
Hunan	—	303	—	—	+0.01	—	—	—	4.98	—	—
Hupei	—	—	321	—	—	—	+4.45	8.42	—	—	—
Kiangsi	—	—	354	—	+1.81	—	—	—	—	2.29	—

East										
Anhwei	316	—	—	—	—	—	—	—	—	—
Chekiang	—	309	—	+0.30	—	+5.43	—	4.30	—	1.10
Kiangsu	—	275	−0.05	—	—	—	—	—	3.94	—
Shanghai	6	—	−4.93	—	—	—	7.32	—	—	—
South West										
Kweichow	270	—	—	—	—	+6.32	—	—	—	1.31
Szechuan	—	293	—	—	—	+4.32	—	—	—	1.09
Yunnan	—	306	—	—	—	+4.90	—	—	—	1.06
South										
Fukien	—	292	—	+0.89	—	—	—	—	3.25	—
Kwangsi	—	298	−1.40	—	—	—	—	5.20	1.85	—
Kwangtung	—	306	—	+1.35	+2.89	—	—	—	1.62	—
China	—	293	—	—	—	—	—	—	—	—
Hopei, Peking and Tientsin	—	—	−2.08	—	—	—	8.13	—	—	—
Kiangsu and Shanghai	—	—	−0.09	—	—	—	—	—	3.33	—

Map. Level of output per head (kilograms), growth of output per head and
output stability, 1952–57.

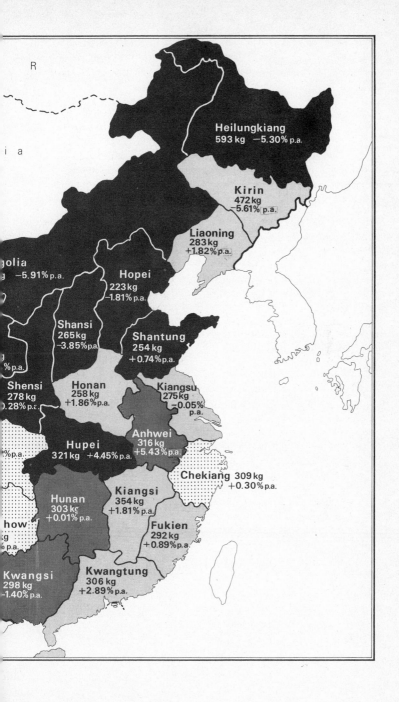

R

i a

Heilungkiang
593 kg −5.30% p.a.

Kirin
472 kg
−5.61% p.a.

Liaoning
283 kg
+1.82% p.a.

golia
g −5.91% p.a.

Hopei
223 kg
−1.81% p.a.

Shansi
265 kg
−3.85% p.a.

Shantung
254 kg
+0.74% p.a.

Shensi
278 kg
0.28% p.a.

Honan
258 kg
+1.86% p.a.

Kiangsu
275 kg
−0.05%
p.a.

Hupei
321 kg +4.45% p.a.

Anhwei
316 kg
+5.43% p.a.

Chekiang 309 kg
+0.30% p.a.

%p.a.

Hunan
303 kg
+0.01% p.a.

Kiangsi
354 kg
+1.81% p.a.

how·

g
p.a.

Fukien
292 kg
+0.89% p.a.

Kwangsi
298 kg
−1.40% p.a.

Kwangtung
306 kg
+2.89% p.a.

These four adjacent provinces occupied a broad 'band' across the northern part of China, from Szechuan to the sea, with a total population of 123 million people (1952–57), equal to 20 per cent of the national population.

5. Kiangsu had an average grain output per head that was on the poverty line of 275 kilograms, a trend of output per head that was slightly downward, and an index of stability (3.94) that was almost in the unstable range.
6. Although the average level of per capita output in Hunan was at the top end of the adequate bracket, growth was stagnant and unstable.
7. Like Hunan, Kwangsi had a very adequate level of per capita production, but the trend was a declining one, and it was also unstable.

In addition to these seven provinces in which all three major problems were combined, there were three *rich* provinces which suffered from serious problems of growth and stability.

1 and 2. In the very rich provinces of Heilungkiang and Inner Mongolia, output per head was both declining and very unstable.
3. In Kirin, too, a high average level of per capita output, far above the beginning of the rich band, was associated with a rapidly declining trend and only moderate stability of production, with an index that was towards the top of the fairly stable limit.

Turning to those provinces where the indicators were relatively favourable, it is interesting that no province of China combined a rich grain output per head with being very stable and growing fast. Seven provinces, however, exhibited some favourable characteristics.

1 and 2. Grain output per head in Sinkiang and Chekiang was rich, very stable but growing only slowly.
3. In Kiangsi it was rich, fairly stable and growing slowly.
4 and 5. Not quite rich, but nearly so, were Szechuan and Yunnan where grain output per head was both very stable and growing quickly.
6. Circumstances in Kwangtung were not dissimilar: per capita output was almost at rich level, it was fairly stable over time and it grew at a medium rate.
7. Kweichow, though poor in output per head, had a very stable production and fast growth rate.

Finally, attention should be drawn to the position of Anhwei and Hupei, where conditions were neither very bad nor very favourable. Both were rich, fast-growing provinces, but at the same time grain output was relatively unstable.

This, then, was the context in which the Chinese Government formulated its policy for grain distribution during the years 1952–57. If inequalities within and between provinces were to be reduced, urban populations supplied from domestic production, and the dire effects of severe fluctuations in output eliminated, the control and mobilisation of large quantities of grain were essential. The Chinese Government decided to take full responsibility for achieving these aims mainly by adopting direct, physical controls. It was an enormous undertaking which presented numerous opportunities for economic and political miscalculation. How much grain was in fact mobilised and transferred, and what effect such redistribution had on consumption in both rich and poor provinces, are the main topics considered by the remaining chapters of this study.

2

GRAIN DISTRIBUTION UNDER
STATE PLANNING, 1953–1957

The Chinese Government did not take complete control of the acquisition and sale of grain until autumn 1953. During the previous three years of post-war recovery, much of the grain marketed passed through the hands of private merchants, although the Government's role had been increasing.[1] In 1952 it purchased 13 million tons of grain, and collected 19 million tons in taxes.[2] Already, therefore, only three years after the Liberation, the state was handling around 32 million tons of grain per year, or 20 per cent of national output. As early as 1950 it had organised the export of approximately 1.7 million tons of surplus grain, mainly from North East and South West China, to deficit areas of the country.[3]

Two important factors led the Government to bring virtually all grain procurement and distribution under its direct control at the end of 1953. In the first place, although it was not published (or even finalised) until July 1955, the broad economic strategy of the First Five Year Plan (1953–57) had been agreed by the leaders of China, with rapid industrial development as its core. The expected rise in employment and incomes – both in town and countryside – implied a rapid growth of demand for grain. The Government, therefore, had to do all in its power to ensure that its economic plans were not frustrated by shortages of grain. The second, and more immediate, factor leading to tighter Government control over grain utilisation in autumn 1953 was the appearance, during the 1952–53 'grain year' (July–June), of serious disequilibrium between the state's grain acquisition and disbursement, amounting to 3.5 million tons.[4] As the summer grain

[1] For a review of this policy see D.H. Perkins, *Market Control and Planning in Communist China* (Cambridge, Mass., 1966).
[2] Sha Chien-li, 'Glorious Achievements of the Grain Front', *JMJP*, 25 October 1959.
[3] Wu Shih, 'A Discussion of the Grain Question in China during the Transition Period', *HHPYK*, vol. 108 (no. 10), 1957, pp. 104–9.
[4] *Ibid.*

harvest of 1953 was gathered, the state buying agencies found it increasingly difficult to fulfil their purchase plans while at the same time the Government's monthly sales of grain greatly exceeded the planned level. One of the reasons for the failure to acquire grain was that the land reform had transferred land to peasants with a high income elasticity of demand for grain; as more and more peasants became members of the 'middle' class, under the impetus to production given by the reform, so their willingness to sell grain declined.[5] The existence of black markets and speculation in grain posed a serious problem for the Government, and the gap between the state's 'list' price for buying grain and the free market price widened to 20–30 per cent.[6] With exports of grain from China running at 1.5 million tons in 1953,[7] the Government had to deplete its inadequate stocks to maintain a balance.

To restore stability, and to ensure that it was maintained in future, the Government decided that it must, as a matter of urgency, bring grain consumption and distribution under state control, and to this end it introduced a scheme for Planned Purchase and Supply of Grain.[8] Under the scheme the state virtually became the sole buyer and seller of grain. Peasant households deemed to have 'surplus' grain (that is, grain in excess of norms set for taxes, 'rations', livestock fodder and seed) were required to sell specified amounts to the state at prices fixed by the state. The grain thus purchased, plus that acquired as taxes, formed the stock out of which the Government hoped to meet all the demands for grain – for rural and urban consumption, for export and for stock accumulation. The Government's directive announcing the scheme also called for the introduction of grain rationing in the towns. Grain coupons were to be issued to households and institutions (factories, schools, etc.) based on 'needs'. It was envisaged that the *hu-k'ou* (population registration) data would serve as the statistical basis

[5] *Ibid.*
[6] Chinese People's University Trade Economic Education Research Bureau, *Kuo Nei Shang-yeh Ching-chi* (*China's Internal Commercial Economy*) (Peking, 1960).
[7] Ch'en Yün, 'Questions Concerning the Central Purchase and Supply of Grain' (speech, 21 July 1955), *HHYP*, vol. 70 (no. 8), 1955, pp. 50–4; also Li Szu-heng, 'On the Export of Grain', *KJJP*, 9 November 1957.
[8] The Government's directive announcing the scheme was issued on 23 November 1953 but it was not published until March 1954, in the *People's Daily* (*JMJP*). The editorial accompanying the directive stated that the scheme had in fact operated throughout the fourth quarter of 1953 and it had, therefore, covered most of the autumn harvest. The scheme was referred to as 'Central' as well as 'Planned' Purchase and Supply.

for this exercise. The entire approach was based on the belief that, although grain production in China was not abundant, provided that its distribution was 'rational'[9] there was enough both to meet internal needs and to provide an export surplus.

For five years, until the virtual disintegration of economic planning in China during the summer and autumn of 1958, the Central Purchase and Supply scheme for grain operated with considerable success. The Government managed to acquire and redistribute enough grain to meet basic requirements, and to export over one million tons per year. It was able, in addition, to transfer grain quickly to areas where major natural disasters had occurred, with the result that only one serious local famine was reported[10] during the period. However, the Government's policy was only implemented with great difficulty. At times there was extreme tension between the cadres and peasants over the level of state acquisition, and the constant struggle between the two groups led to wide fluctuations in procurement and sales. The Government's grain 'account' throughout the period was, in the words of the Chinese State Planning Committee, in a state of 'tense balance'.[11]

Before exploring the nature of the struggle as it developed year by year from 1953 to 1957, evidence of the amounts of grain procured and sold in rural areas must be presented and analysed briefly.

[9] See Ch'en Yün, 'Questions Concerning the Central Purchase and Supply'. Sun Yatsen had held the same opinion: *The International Development of China* (London, 1928). Sun was optimistic about the potential export surpluses which might be obtained from the north eastern and north western provinces. He was a strong advocate of central government control over domestic grain consumption. W.H. Mallory, on the other hand, in his book *China: Land of Famine* (New York, 1926), presented a pessimistic view of the possibility that China could be self-sufficient in grain. He doubted that big enough inter-provincial transfers could be made to prevent famine. Mallory's position was later accepted by R.H. Tawney, *Land and Labour in China* (London, 1932). Ma Yin-ch'u (*JMJP*, 15 June 1957) considered that China's grain output was inadequate for her needs: 'If any maldistribution occurs there will be grain wasted by some people but insufficient grain for others. Right here is the point at issue.' But Ma ruled out grain imports.

[10] This was in Kwangsi province, during the spring of 1956, when 550 peasants were reported to have died of starvation and 14,700 were said to have fled to other areas in search of food: 'How People Died of Famine Last Year and How the Case was Disposed of', *KWSIJP*, 14 June 1957 (*SCMP*, no. 1362).

[11] Sun Wei-tzu, 'Principles for Organising Grain Circulation Planning', *CHCC* (no. 2), 1958, pp. 24–7.

GROSS GRAIN PROCUREMENT

Approximately 50 million tons of grain were acquired on average by the state each year between 1953 and 1957, equal to 28 per cent of average output (Table 18). This procurement level was 57 per cent higher than the 32.2 million tons collected[12] by the Government in the crisis year of 1952–53, when the procurement rate was only 19.7 per cent.[13] The main impact of government intervention was on purchase rather than on tax. The average amount of grain collected as taxes in 1953–57 was 19.1 million tons,[14] compared with 18.9 million tons in 1952–53. State purchases of grain, therefore, rose from 13.4 million tons in 1952–53 to an average of 31.4 million tons per year in 1953–57, an increase of 134 per cent. Table 18 reveals some difference between the official and constructed national totals, the latter indicating wider fluctuations than the former. Both series show very little change in the amount of grain procured between 1953 and 1957. Provincial figures suggest that the total rose by only 1.2 million tons, compared with an increase in output of 27.1 million tons.

Little can profitably be said about the provincial levels of grain procurement at this stage in the discussion, but the generally large amounts acquired in 1954–55 and the small amounts collected in 1956–57 should be noted, for they illustrate two extremes of the competition for grain already mentioned, both of which generated a vigorous response from the opposing sides. By far the biggest procurement *rate* was to be found in the province of Heilungkiang which, as Chapter 1 showed, also had the highest per capita output of grain in China (593 kilograms, 1952–57). The rate of procurement in Heilungkiang, 43.7 per cent throughout the period, was almost double that of the poorer provinces of North and North West China, namely Kansu, Shensi, Honan, Hopei and Shantung. The rate was below 30 per cent in seventeen out of the twenty-four provinces. In general, procurement rates declined between 1953 and 1957, and in contrast to tax policy, this was not what the Government intended.

[12] Cited by Sha Chien-li, 'Glorious Achievements of the Grain Front'.
[13] Total grain production, including soya beans, is from *Collection of Statistical Data* (1958).
[14] Taxes for 1952–56 are given in Li Ch'eng-jui, *Chung-hua Jen-min Kung-ho-kuo Nung-yeh Shui Shih-kao (History of Agricultural Taxation in the Chinese People's Republic)* (Peking, 1959). Grain tax for 1957 is given as 11.3 per cent of output in *SNM*, 5 June 1958.

Table 18. *Gross grain procurement by the state, 1953–57*

	Grain procured (thousand tons)						Grain procured as percentage of grain output					
	1953	1954	1955	1956	1957	Average 1953–57	1953	1954	1955	1956	1957	Average 1953–57
North East												
Heilungkiang	3466	3445	3791	2616	3351	3334	48.7	49.0	46.2	33.1	42.6	43.7
Kirin	2430	2240	2307	1560	1773	2062	41.5	40.7	40.5	31.6	32.6	37.6
Liaoning	1704	1767	1666	1823	1923	1777	29.8	29.4	27.0	24.5	28.7	27.7
North West												
IMR	1276	1656	1496	1756	934	1424	36.0	42.6	46.0	38.5	31.6	39.1
Kansu	629	948	933	893	1105	902	20.8	25.1	22.5	16.4	21.8	21.0
Shensi	944	1294	1054	989	1050	1066	19.9	25.8	23.4	18.2	23.2	22.0
Sinkiang	344	364*	c.225	384	450	353	20.0	20.0	11.8	19.9	22.1	18.7
Tsinghai	77	121	136	120	165	124	23.2	22.9	23.1	19.7	25.6	23.0
North												
Honan	2641	2845	2994	2395	2923	2760	23.5	24.1	23.3	18.6	23.8	22.6
Hopei	1890	2075	1840	1450	2045	1860	23.3	26.0	20.2	17.6	20.2	21.3
Shansi	1150	1254	864	1025	c.975	1054	26.6	30.5	23.2	23.6	c.27.3	26.3
Shantung	2470	2940	2885	2435	2400	2626	22.3	22.3	21.4	16.6	18.5	20.1
Centre												
Hunan	3186	2586	2977	2427	2826	2800	30.8	27.9	26.4	23.6	25.0	26.7
Hupei	2506	1991	2561	2619	2940	2523	27.6	29.1	26.7	24.3	25.9	26.5
Kiangsi	2223	2198	2170	2000	2185	2155	38.7	38.3	34.6	30.2	30.9	34.3
East												
Anhwei	2745	2394	3587	2662	3800	3038	30.2	30.8	31.1	24.4	30.8	29.4
Chekiang	c.2278	2502	2525	2245	c.2361	2382	31.8	35.3	33.1	29.3	29.9	31.8
Kiangsu	4350	4450	4424	3850	4233	4261	37.0	38.7	34.4	32.1	34.6	35.3

South West												
Kweichow	1060	1142	1185	1031	1185	1121	28.1	28.0	27.8	21.2	22.1	25.1
Szechuan	5453	5813	4820	5818	6098	5600	29.8	29.8	23.8	26.1	26.2	27.1
Yunnan	1276	1414	1437	1278	1400*	1361	25.7	26.5	25.4	20.3	21.7	23.7
South												
Fukien	1135	1270	1155	1139	1179	1176	29.1	33.8	29.7	25.7	26.5	28.8
Kwangsi	1563	1750	1428	1170	c.842	1351	28.7	29.7	24.2	22.2	15.6	24.2
Kwangtung	3562	3775	3389	3014	3400	3428	34.7	34.4	30.9	25.1	27.7	30.3
Total (million tons)	50.358	52.234	51.849	46.699	51.543	50.537	30.2	31.0	28.2	24.3	26.6	27.9
Official	48.550	52.700	49.900	48.450	51.150	50.150	29.1	31.2	27.1	25.1	26.2	27.6

* Minimum figure.
Sources and methods: Appendix 5.

Reference has already been made to the division of gross procurement between purchased grain and grain collected as taxes. Incomplete provincial data on grain taxes are collated in Table 19. Three points are noteworthy about the tax figures. First, as would be expected, the annual amount of grain acquired as tax differed greatly between provinces. Seven provinces each contributed over 1 million tons of 'free' grain to the Government each year: Heilungkiang, Shantung, Hunan, Hupei, Kiangsu, Szechuan and Kwangtung. Together, their total accounted for 55 per cent of the national total grain tax.

Secondly, in line with Government policy, grain taxes were stable throughout the period. Bearing in mind the instability of grain procurement (Tables 18 and 22), it follows that grain *purchases* fluctuated very widely indeed. Taxes were, apparently, reduced in provinces affected by severe disasters but not always in proportion to the decline in output. Unfortunately, data for Hunan and Hupei, both of which suffered from serious flooding in 1954, are not available to test this proposition further. Figures are, however, available for Anhwei which was also affected by the 1954 disasters. Output fell by 14 per cent, but grain taxes were reduced by only 4 per cent. However, in Hopei province a production decrease of 9.5 per cent in 1956 was followed by a 26.4 per cent remission of taxes in the grain year 1956–57.

Finally, the tax burden, whether measured by tax as a percentage of output or by the amount of grain handed over per head, was not insignificant. The average rate of tax was 10.5 per cent of output over the five years, and there was only one major deviation from the average – in 1956–57 – when rates fell. The peasants of Heilungkiang gave about 18 per cent of their grain output as tax throughout the five year period,[15] which was 5–6 per cent higher than the rates imposed in most rice-growing provinces. In the relatively poor areas of the North and North West, rates of 8–9 per cent were the norm. Grain tax per head of rural population was around 30 kilograms in the North and North West, up to 50–55 kilograms in the central provinces and 30–40 kilograms in the South and South West. In Heilungkiang the grain tax

[15] The higher percentage of 20.3 per cent for Inner Mongolia, which relates to the bad harvest year of 1957, cannot be taken as representative of the period. The average tax rate in Inner Mongolia was probably around 16 per cent.

took 160 kilograms out of 868 kilograms per head (1953–57). As Table 19 shows, in almost all provinces just under 40 per cent of the grain handed over each year to the state by the peasants brought them no income. And when the fairly low[16] state purchase price received for the remaining 60 per cent of grain delivered is taken into account, the peasants can hardly have regarded the tax burden as light.

RURAL SALES OF GRAIN AND NET GRAIN PROCUREMENT

To reduce rural inequalities in food consumption, cushion the effects of natural disasters and guarantee adequate grain supplies to the non grain-growing rural populations, the Government sold roughly 21 million tons of grain each year in rural areas, or 42 per cent of the 50–51 million tons it acquired through tax and purchase (Table 20). The consistently large amounts of grain sold annually in the rural areas of some provinces reflect (1) the large populations growing industrial crops, and (2) the poverty of many peasants, often associated with hilly and mountainous conditions. Good examples of both (1) and (2) are Honan, where on average 1.5 million tons of grain were sold in rural areas each year, Hopei with 1.9 million tons of rural sales a year and Shantung with 1.5 million tons. Table 20 also shows for each province the average area of land devoted to non-grain crops in each year, and the percentage of total provincial sown area taken up by such crops.

The annual variations in rural grain sales are only partly explained by output fluctuations. They are also closely related to the level of gross procurement and hence to the demand from peasants to buy grain in the following spring. On average, 42.5 per cent of all grain acquired by the Government was redistributed to rural areas. Table 20 shows a great variety of experience, including one province – Hopei – in which the amount sold exceeded the amount procured by 80 per cent (in 1956–57). The greater the amount sold in rural areas, the smaller was the net rural surplus, or net procurement level. The size of such surpluses is revealed by Table 21.

Once again, some discrepancy between the national aggregate

[16] A discussion of procurement prices is found in D.H. Perkins, *Market Control and Planning*.

Table 19. *Grain collected by the state as taxes, 1953–57*

	Tax (thousand tons)					% Output					% Central purchase and tax					1953–57 averages		
	1953	1954	1955	1956	1957	1953	1954	1955	1956	1957	1953	1954	1955	1956	1957	Average tax per annum (thousand tons)	%Output	%CP/T
North East																		
Heilungkiang	c.1400	—	1408	—	—	—	c.18.8	—	17.8	—	—	c.39.2	—	53.8	—	c.1402	18.5 (4 yrs)	c.42.1
Liaoning	749	—	—	—	—	—	12.5	—	—	—	—	42.4	—	—	—	c.749	12.5 (1 yr)	c.42.4
North West																		
IMR	—	—	—	—	c.600	—	—	—	—	c.20.3	—	—	—	—	64.2	c.600	c.20.3 (1 yr)	c.64.2
Kansu	273	352	338	378	441	9.0	9.3	8.1	6.9	8.7	43.4	37.1	36.2	42.3	39.9	356	8.3 (5 yrs)	39.5
Shensi	446	454	417	406	441	9.4	9.1	9.3	7.5	9.8	47.2	35.1	39.6	41.1	42.0	433	8.9 (5 yrs)	40.6
Sinkiang	c.138	c.146	c.153	c.155	c.163	9.4	—	8.0	8.0	9.2[a]	40.1	40.1	68.0	40.4	36.2	151	8.0 (5 yrs)	42.8
Tsinghai	31	48	51	49	59[a]	—	9.1	8.7	—	—	40.3	39.7	37.5	c.40.8	c.35.8	48	c.8.8 (5 yrs)	38.7
North																		
Hopei	776	757	784	577	—	9.6	9.5	8.6	7.0	—	41.1	36.5	42.6	39.8	—	724	8.6 (4 yrs)	39.9
Shansi	432	—	c.400	—	—	10.0	—	—	—	—	37.6	—	c.38.9	—	—	c.406	c.10.8 (5 yrs)	c.38.5
Shantung	—	—	1174	—	—	—	—	—	8.0	—	—	—	—	48.2	—	c.1174	8.0 (1 yr)	c.48.2
Centre																		
Hunan	1241	—	1196	1031	1103	12.0	—	10.6	10.0	9.7	39.0	—	40.2	42.5	39.0	1143	10.6 (4 yrs)	39.5
Hupei	1171[b]	—	—	1310	—	13.9[b]	—	—	12.2	—	c.46.7	—	—	50.0	—	c.1240	12.9 (2 yrs)	c.48.4
Kiangsi	—	—	879	881	829	—	—	14.0	13.3	11.7	—	—	40.0	38.9	44.1	863	13.0 (3 yrs)	40.7
East																		
Anhwei	812	777	962	965	—	8.9	10.0	8.3	8.8	—	29.6	32.5	26.8	36.3	—	879	8.9 (4 yrs)	30.9

Kiangsu	1328	1507	1514	1520	—	11.3	13.1	11.8	12.7	—	30.5	33.9	34.2	39.5	—	1467	12.2 (4 yrs)	34.4
South West																		
Kweichow	446	464	405	432	443	11.8	11.4	9.5	8.9	8.3	42.1	40.6	34.2	41.9	37.4	438	9.8 (5 yrs)	39.1
Szechuan			2553	2681[a]				11.5	c.11.5				43.9	c.44.0		c.2617	c.11.5 (2 yrs)	c.43.9
Yunnan			582	578				10.3	9.2				40.5	45.2		580	9.7 (2 yrs)	42.7
South																		
Fukien		400	400	378	421		10.7	10.3	8.5	9.5		31.5	34.6	33.2	35.7	400	9.7 (4 yrs)	33.7
Kwangtung	1281	1645	1439	1194	—	12.5	15.0	13.1	9.9	—	36.0	43.6	42.5	39.6	—	1390	12.6 (4 yrs)	40.5
Official total (million tons)	18.46	19.46	18.93	16.36	22.04	11.1	11.5	10.3	8.5	11.3	38.0	36.9	37.9	33.8	42.8	19.1	10.5 (5 yrs)	38.0

Notes: Braces indicate that the figure obtained is an average over the years involved.
  a. Planned figure. b. 1952 figure.

Source: Appendix 6.

Table 20. *Rural sales of grain by the state, 1953–57*

	Rural resales (thousand tons)						Rural sales as percent of gross procurement						Non-grain sown area* 1952–57	
	1953	1954	1955	1956	1957	Average 1953–57	1953	1954	1955	1956	1957	Average 1953–57	Average area (thousand hectares)	% Total sown area
North East														
Heilungkiang	519	390	493	464	293	432	15.0	11.3	13.0	17.7	8.7	13.0	586	8.6
Kirin	180	200	190	410	440	284	7.4	8.9	8.2	26.3	24.8	13.8	278	6.0
Liaoning	1140	1129	931	915	605[a]	944	66.9	63.9	55.9	50.2	c.31.5	53.1	658	13.3
North West														
IMR	148	188	134	100	78	130	11.6	11.4	9.0	5.7	8.4	9.1	542	11.1
Kansu	235	307	321	387	200[b]	290	37.4	32.4	34.4	43.3	c.18.1	32.2	852	18.2
Shensi	208	289	324	237	449	301	22.0	22.3	30.7	24.0	42.8	28.3	1480	27.6
Sinkiang	c.137	c.138	c.74	145	138[b]	126	39.8	37.9	32.9	37.8	30.7	35.8	298	19.8
Tsinghai	43	41	56	97	c.86	65	55.8	33.9	41.2	80.8	52.1	52.1	46	10.9
North														
Honan	1220	1490	1438	1682	1601	1486	46.2	52.4	48.0	70.2	54.8	53.8	1689	11.7
Hopei	1479	2029	1815	2615	1521	1892	78.3	97.8	98.6	180.3	74.4	101.7	1491	14.1
Shansi	275	288	318[b]	245	300[b]	285	23.9	23.0	c.36.8	23.9	c.30.8	27.1	657	13.3
Shantung	c.1769	c.1361	1600	1350	c.1501	1516	c.71.6	c.46.3	55.5	55.4	c.62.5	57.7	1754	13.0
Centre														
Hunan	1195	1702	755	2230	723	1321	37.5	65.8	25.4	91.9	25.6	47.2	1112	18.4
Hupei	1081	1923	1269	1189	1386	1370	43.1	96.6	49.6	45.4	47.1	54.3	1196	17.8
Kiangsi	723	999	823	515	172	646	32.5	45.5	37.9	25.8	7.9	30.0	1528	30.9
East														
Anhwei	1146	2129	1141	2126	1350	1578	41.7	88.9	31.8	79.9	35.5	52.0	1126	11.6

Chekiang	c.1056	1237	968	1112	c.590	993	46.4	49.4	38.3	49.5	c.25.0	41.7	1159	27.5
Kiangsu	1650	1800	1800	2250	2241	1948	37.9	40.4	40.7	58.4	52.9	45.7	1217	12.2
South West														
Kweichow	112	200	188	203	295	200	10.6	17.5	15.9	19.7	24.9	17.8	396	14.1
Szechuan	2421	1870	1835	2698	1799	2125	44.4	32.2	38.1	46.4	29.5	37.9	2095	17.5
Yunnan	393	545	522	615	c.575	530	30.8	38.5	36.3	48.1	c.41.1	38.9	466	13.8
South														
Fukien	310	670	550	601	311	488	27.3	52.8	47.6	52.8	26.4	41.5	274	12.2
Kwangsi	562	789	608	756	550[b]	653	36.0	45.1	42.6	64.6	c.65.3	48.3	477	11.9
Kwangtung	1938	2138	1743	1669	1849	1867	54.4	56.6	51.4	55.4	54.4	54.5	621	8.6
Total (million tons)	19.940	23.852	19.896	24.611	19.053	21.470	39.6	45.7	38.4	52.7	36.9	42.5		
Official total (million tons)	20.050	25.900	21.100	26.700	17.750	22.300								

* Total sown area minus grain sown area (see Appendices 2b and 11b).
a. Planned figure.   b. Assumed.
Source: Appendix 5.

Table 21. *Net grain procurement and net procurement ratios, 1953–57*

	Net procurement (thousand tons)						Net procurement ratio (%)					
	1953	1954	1955	1956	1957	Average 1953–57	1953	1954	1955	1956	1957	Average 1953–57
North East												
Heilungkiang	2947	3055	3298	2152	3058	2902	41.4	43.4	40.2	27.2	38.9	38.1
Kirin	2250	2040	2117	1150	1333	1778	38.4	37.0	37.2	23.3	24.5	32.4
Liaoning	564	638	735	908	1318	833	9.9	10.6	11.9	12.2	19.7	13.0
North West												
IMR	1128	1468	1362	1656	856	1294	31.8	37.8	41.9	36.3	28.9	35.6
Kansu	394	641	612	506	c.905	612	13.0	17.0	14.7	9.3	c.17.9	14.2
Shensi	736	1005	730	752	601	765	15.5	20.1	16.2	13.8	13.3	15.8
Sinkiang	207	226	151	239	312	227	12.0	12.4	7.9	12.4	15.3	12.0
Tsinghai	34	80	80	23	c.79	59	10.3	15.2	13.6	3.8	c.12.3	11.0
North												
Honan	1421	1355	1556	713	1322	1273	12.6	11.5	12.1	5.5	10.7	10.4
Hopei	411	46	25	−1165	524	−32	5.1	0.6	0.3	−14.1	5.2	−0.4
Shansi	875	966	546	780	c.675	768	20.2	23.5	14.7	18.0	c.18.9	19.2
Shantung	701	1579	1285	1085	899	1110	6.3	12.0	9.5	7.4	6.9	8.5
Centre												
Hunan	1991	884	2222	197	2103	1479	19.3	9.5	19.7	1.9	18.6	14.1
Hupei	1425	68	1292	1430	1554	1154	15.7	1.0	13.4	13.3	13.7	12.1
Kiangsi	1500	1199	1347	1485	2013	1509	26.1	20.1	21.5	22.4	28.5	24.0
East												
Anhwei	1599	265	2446	536	2450	1459	17.6	3.4	21.2	4.9	19.8	14.1
Chekiang	1222	1265	1557	1133	1771	1390	17.1	17.9	20.4	14.8	22.4	18.6
Kiangsu	2700	2650	2624	1600	1992	2313	23.0	23.0	20.4	13.3	16.3	19.2

South West												
Kweichow	948	942	997	828	890	921	25.1	23.1	23.4	17.0	16.6	20.6
Szechuan	3032	3943	2985	3120	4299	3476	16.6	20.2	14.8	14.0	18.5	16.8
Yunnan	883	869	915	663	c.825	831	17.8	16.3	16.2	10.6	c.12.8	14.5
South												
Fukien	825	600	605	538	868	687	21.1	16.0	15.6	12.1	19.5	16.8
Kwangsi	1001	961	820	414	c.292	698	18.4	16.3	13.9	7.9	c.5.4	12.5
Kwangtung	1624	1637	1646	1345	1551	1561	15.8	14.9	15.0	11.2	12.6	13.8
Total (million tons)	30.418	28.382	31.953	22.088	32.490	29.067	18.2	16.8	17.4	11.5	16.7	16.0
Official total (million tons)	28.5	26.8	28.8	21.8	33.4	27.9	17.1	15.8	15.7	11.3	17.1	15.3

Net procurement = gross procurement minus rural grain resales.
Net procurement ratio = net procurement as a percentage of total grain production.

figures obtained from the provincial data and the official totals must be noted. The former are found to be somewhat higher than the latter, except in 1957–58, for which the official total seems to be inexplicably high.[17] Both sets of figures show, however, that net procurement averaged 28–29 million tons per annum during the five years, departing significantly from this level only in 1956–57, when it fell (according to provincial figures) by 31 per cent, to 22 million tons. All of China's twenty-four provinces provided rural surpluses of varying size in every year between 1953 and 1957, with the single exception of Hopei where there was a net injection of grain into the rural sector.

Perhaps the most important aspect of the net procurement data is the lack of stability they exhibit. This made the Government's task of balancing its provincial grain budgets so much more difficult to achieve. The failure to maintain a stable flow of rural surpluses resulted from the changes in gross procurement and rural sales, which often reinforced each other. The relationships between annual changes in output, gross procurement, rural sales and, hence, net procurement are brought out by figures in Table 22. Above all, they highlight how difficult it was to fix the 'right' level of procurement: high enough to satisfy national requirements but not so high as to provoke the peasants to exert irresistible pressure for compensatory grain sales or even to sabotage the entire procurement system.

With these figures to serve as a background, a more detailed description of the implementation of rural grain procurement policy can now be given.

THE ADMINISTRATION OF RURAL GRAIN CONTROLS, 1953–57

1953–54: stabilisation of the grain balance

The Central Purchase and Supply scheme was launched essentially as a political campaign, and focused on the question of whether capitalism or socialism was to dominate the rural scene. Peasants were exhorted to sell surplus grain to the state to ensure the success of the

---

[17] Figures relating to all aspects of the 1957–58 national grain 'balance-sheet' are both scarce and inconsistent. There is, therefore, no reason to regard the constructed totals as inferior to offical aggregate figures.

Table 22. *Annual changes in gross and net procurement in relation to change in output, 1953–57 (thousand tons)*

	Change 1953-54 to 1954-55				Change 1954-55 to 1955-56				Change 1955-56 to 1956-57				Change 1956-57 to 1957-58				Change 1953-54 to 1957-58			
	O	GP	RCS	NP	O	GP	RCS	NP	O	GP	RCS	NP	O	GP	RCS	NP	O	GP	RCS	NP
North East																				
Heilungkiang	-78	-21	-129	+108	+1173	+346	+103	+243	-295	-1175	-29	-1146	-51	+735	-171	+906	+749	-115	-226	+111
Kirin	-343	-190	+20	-210	+185	+67	-10	+77	-759	-747	+220	-967	+498	+213	+30	+183	-419	-657	+260	-917
Liaoning	+300	+63	-11	+74	+155	-101	-198	+97	+1260	+157	-16	+173	-728	+100	c.-310	+410	+987	+219	-335	+754
North West																				
IMR	+340	+380	+40	+340	-630	-160	-54	-106	+1303	+260	-34	+294	-1600	-822	-22	-800	-587	-342	-70	-272
Kansu	+750	+319	+72	+247	+375	-15	+14	-29	+1300	-40	+66	-106	-385	+212	-187	+399	+2040	+476	c.-35	+511
Shensi	+269	+350	+81	+269	-504	-240	+35	-275	+962	-65	-87	+22	-944	+61	+212	-151	-217	+106	+241	-135
Sinkiang	+100	+20	+1	+19	+93	-139	-64	-75	+21	+159	+71	+88	+100	+66	c.-7	+73	+314	+106	c.+1	+105
Tsinghai	+197	+44	-2	+46	+61	+61	+15	no change	+21	-16	+41	-57	+34	+45	c.-11	+56	+313	+88	+43	+45
North																				
Honan	+550	+204	+270	-66	+1050	+149	+201	-52	+25	-599	-9	-590	-575	+528	-81	+609	+1060	+282	+381	-99
Hopei	-135	+185	+550	-365	+1135	-235	-214	-21	-865	-390	+800	-1190	+1840	+595	-1094	+1689	+1975	+155	+42	+113
Shansi	-207	+104	+13	+91	-390	-390	+30	-420	+610	+161	-73	+234	-770	-50	+55	-105	-757	-175	c.+25	-200
Shantung	+2110	+470	-408	+878	+322	-55	+239	-294	+1166	-450	-250	-200	-1707	-35	+151	-186	+1891	-70	c.-268	+198
Centre																				
Hunan	-1056	-600	+507	-1107	+1085	+391	-947	+1338	-962	-550	+1475	-2025	+1019	+399	-1507	+1906	+86	-360	-472	+112
Hupei	-2222	-515	+842	-1357	+2764	+570	-654	+1224	+1152	+58	-80	+138	+584	+321	+197	+124	+2278	+434	+305	+129
Kiangsi	-8	-25	+276	-301	+525	-28	-176	+148	+350	-170	-308	+138	+443	+185	-343	+528	+1310	-38	-551	+513
East																				
Anhwei	-1315	-351	+983	-1334	+3759	+1193	-988	+2181	-620	-925	+985	-1910	+1441	+1138	-776	+1914	+3265	+1055	+204	+851
Chekiang	-70	+224	+181	+43	+537	+23	-269	+292	+42	-280	+144	-424	+240	+116	-522	+638	+749	+83	c.-466	+549
Kiangsu	-250	+100	+150	-50	+1370	+23	-26	no change	-870	-623	+401	-1024	+229	+383	-9	+392	+479	-117	+591	-708
South West																				
Kweichow	+307	+82	+88	-6	+184	+43	-12	+55	+601	-154	+15	-169	+491	+154	+92	+62	+1583	+125	+183	-58
Szechuan	+1215	+360	-551	+911	+705	-993	-35	-958	+2025	+998	+863	+135	+1003	+280	-899	+1179	+4948	+645	-622	+1267
Yunnan	+374	+138	+152	-14	+320	+23	-23	+46	+628	-159	+93	-252	+164	+122	-40	+162	+1486	+124	c.+182	-58
South																				
Fukien	-150	+135	+360	-225	+135	-115	-120	+5	+545	-16	+51	-67	+7	+40	-290	+330	+537	+44	+1	+43
Kwangsi	+445	+187	+227	-40	+5	-322	-181	-141	-640	-258	+148	-406	+145	-328	-206	-122	-45	-721	c.-12	-709
Kwangtung	+715	+213	+200	+13	+5	-386	-395	+9	+1021	-375	-74	-301	+260	+386	+180	+206	+2001	-162	-89	-73
China total	+1848	+1876	+3912	-2036	+15319	-385	-3956	+3571	+7991	-5150	+4715	-9865	+1768	+4844	-5558	+10402	+26926	+1185	-887	+2072

Notes: O = output of grain; GP = gross procurement; RCS = rural central sales; NP = net procurement.

socialist transformation of China and to strengthen the rural–urban alliance. To allay the peasants' fear that the state would pay what amounted to 'dead' prices,[18] the buying price of grain was raised by 8 per cent.[19] Some provinces, for example Kwangtung[20] and Honan,[21] appealed to the Centre for a postponement of the introduction of the new scheme, pleading special conditions, but these requests were dismissed.

Government cadres involved in the new exercise lacked experience of such affairs,[22] and had to operate it on a weak statistical basis. No clearly defined norms had been established for consumption, seed and feed. The political enthusiasm of the cadres, therefore, was the main driving force behind the launching of the scheme and from the Government's point of view it had a highly successful beginning. Gross grain procurement rose by 16.3 million tons in 1953–54 and, with total sales more tightly controlled than before, an overall procurement – sales deficit of 3.45 million tons (including urban sales) incurred in 1952–53 was turned into a 7.8 million ton surplus.[23] Compared with subsequent years, the gross and net procurement figures (in Tables 18 and 21) look impressive. The gross procurement *rates* of 1953–54 were not subsequently surpassed in eight provinces (Kirin, Liaoning, Shantung, Hunan, Kiangsi, Kweichow, Szechuan and Kwangtung) and the net procurement rate was at its highest during 1953–54 in nine provinces (Kirin, Honan, Hupei, Kiangsu, Kweichow, Yunnan, Fukien, Kwangsi and Kwangtung). Little is known about the peasants' response to the level of procurement during this year, but in Kwangtung the official provincial newspaper[24] argued that (a) cadres were so keen to display their political activism that some of the grain they acquired should have been left as rations, and (b) deliberations between the Government and peasants over the amounts of rural sales

---

[18] I.e. prices which were so low as to 'kill' the incentive to produce. See, for example, *NFJP*, 28 November 1953 and 25 December 1953.

[19] P'eng Hui-fang, 'Refute the Lies of the Capitalist Rightist Class on Questions of the Central Purchase and Supply of Grain', *HHPYK*, vol. 124 (no. 2), 1958, pp. 36–9.

[20] *SCMP*, no. 4085.

[21] *HONJP*, 4 July 1958.

[22] A good account of the procedure is given in Chinese People's University Trade Economic Education Research Bureau, *China's Internal Commercial Economy.*

[23] The deficit for 1952–53 is in *LS* (no. 1), 1957, pp. 20–5, and the defict for 1953–54 is in *TCKT* (no. 19), 1957, pp. 31–2 and p. 28.

[24] *NFJP*, 19 July 1954.

required took so long that the incentive to produce crops in 1954 was adversely affected.

1954–55: a 'bold advance' against the peasants

Encouraged by the success of the Central Purchase and Supply scheme in its first year, the Government badly miscalculated the 'correct' level of gross procurement from the 1954 harvest, with the result that by the spring of 1954 the peasants were in uproar, clamouring for grain to be resold in rural areas. According to provincial figures, national grain output excluding Peking, Tientsin and Shanghai rose by 1.848 million tons, but gross procurement increased by 1.876 million tons, or 1.5 per cent more than the rise in production. As Table 22 shows, gross procurement was actually raised in five provinces which suffered a decline in output: Hopei, Shansi, Chekiang, Kiangsu and Fukien. In Shensi and Inner Mongolia, the increase in procurement exceeded the rise in output.

One of the reasons for this increase in grain procurement was the very serious fall in production in the Yangtze Valley provinces of Hunan, Hupei and Anhwei, all of which were affected by massive floods. By lowering procurement and increasing grain sales in these areas, the Government was able to stabilise grain availability in Hunan and Anhwei; and to reduce net procurement in Hupei by 61 per cent of the decline in output. When the Central Purchase and Supply scheme came under attack for squeezing the peasants the Government could, with some justification, point to this rescue operation as an outstanding indication of its success. Much of the extra rural grain sold in the disaster areas, however, had to come from increased procurement in other provinces and the peasants reacted angrily to what they regarded as excessive levels of grain extraction. During the winter and spring of 1954–55 their discontent reached crisis point. Mao Tse-tung himself described the situation in remarkably colourful language:

Speaking of bold advance, this [the rise in procurement] was some bold advance! It created a storm, with everyone talking about the central acquisition of grain and every family talking about grain. Chang Nai-ch'i was Minister of Food. In approving this plan was it an attempt to turn the peasants against us? Perhaps it was a conspiracy.[25]

[25] *WS*, 1969, pp. 148–54, especially p. 153.

Again:

In the first half of 1955 a great many people didn't welcome us . . . At that time you said there was no grain crisis but I said there was.[26]

As peasants flocked into the towns, where there was virtually no grain rationing at that time, local cadres criticised the Party for the 'hardships' being borne by the peasants.[27] The consequent rise in rural grain sales more than cancelled the rise in grain procurement in Honan, Hopei, Kiangsu, Kweichow, Yunnan, Fukien and Kwangsi. Provincial figures suggest that the national rise in rural sales during 1954–55 was more than double the rise in gross procurement (Table 22), so that net procurement fell by 2 million tons. Mao[28] and Ch'en Yün[29] claimed that grain sales were inflated by the fraudulent claims of many surplus peasant households masquerading as grain deficient. Many provincial reports[30] provided ample evidence of this phenomenon. There can be no doubt, however, that the Government was disturbed by the way the grain controls had operated and it recognised the force of the peasants' grievances.[31] To win their confidence it therefore announced a modification of the procurement policy for 1955–56, with the introduction of the 'three fix' (*san ting*) scheme.[32]

1955–56: a short-lived attempt at reconciliation

The Government's attempt to improve its relations with the peasants was greatly assisted by the good harvests gathered in most provinces, especially in Hunan, Anhwei and Hupei which had been devastated in

[26] *Ibid.*, pp. 226–37, especially p. 229.
[27] *Ibid.*
[28] *Ibid.*
[29] Ch'en Yün, 'Questions Concerning the Central Purchase and Supply'.
[30] For example, Li Ta-chang's speech on Szechuan (*HHYP* (no. 8), 1955, pp. 46–7), which mentions grain 'frauds' in the immensely rich District of Wenchiang; data on Kiangsu in *HCS* (no. 9), 1955, pp. 13–20, and a report on Kwangsi, *KWSIJP*, 21 August 1955.
[31] Acts of 'sabotage' against the Central Purchase and Central Supply are reported in *SASJP*, 21 May 1955, and there was an armed revolt over the scheme in Fatshan Special District in Kwangtung (*SCMP* supplement, no. 1129).
[32] This was introduced gradually from spring to autumn 1955, and involved fixing norms for each household relating to average grain production, amounts of grain to be sold to the state and the amounts to be sold to households by the state. Such norms were not to be changed for three years.

1954. This was bound to reduce the number of rural deficit households and therefore rural sales. The basis of the procurement (and sales) plan for 1955–56 was the new 'three fix' policy, which aimed at stabilising the obligations and demands of the peasants, and also the amount of grain extracted by the state. Every rural household was to be classified as surplus, self-sufficient or deficit, on a basis of its output ('usual output'), its tax obligations and norms laid down for rations, seed and livestock feed requirements. Output, sales obligations to the state from surplus households, and sales obligations by the state to deficit households, would therefore be 'fixed'. Households would know the extent of their obligations or claims, and the state could more accurately plan its grain 'balance'. The success of the scheme depended on the cadres and peasants reaching agreement and on the flexibility of the norms under rapidly changing economic conditions. In practice, cadres found the work of surveying and classifying households to be a long, controversial exercise. And there were other, pressing demands to be met, such as the reorganisation of individual peasant farmers into co-operatives. For many it was an overwhelming task. Some did the 'three fix' work superficially and as quickly as possible, while others found the stress of rural administration so great that they abandoned their positions and sought refuge in the towns.[33]

The Government's cautious approach to the peasants is evident in the 1955–56 figures relating changes in gross procurement to changes in output (Table 22). Procurement was reduced in eleven provinces in which production increased. In some cases, for example, Hopei[34] and Kiangsu, this was obviously designed to rectify the procurement increases of 1954–55 which had been imposed in the face of declining output. Elsewhere, modest increases in procurement accompanied substantial growth of grain production, and large reductions in procurement were made in provinces with bad harvests. In a revealing comment on the autumn of 1955, however, Mao indicated[35] that the tension over procurement did not subside altogether:

[33] Evidence of this phenomenon in Kwangtung province is given in Kenneth R. Walker, 'Collectivization in Retrospect: the "Socialist High Tide" of Autumn 1955–Spring 1956', *CQ* (no. 26), April–June 1966, pp. 1–43.

[34] 'Oppressive commands' of 1954–55 were attacked in *HOPJP*, 2 February 1955.

[35] *WS* (1967), pp. 156–66, especially p. 160. Note also a report in *KSIJP*, 14 October 1955 on crimes committed against the Central Purchase and Supply of grain, and on the sentences given (including death and imprisonment).

At the end of 1955 less than 90 thousand million catties of grain had been acquired [equivalent to 52.3 million tons of *unhusked* grain] and disturbances were very serious, with everyone talking about grain; and households all talking about central purchase. This was still at the stage of acquisition, not supply. In the end we settled on acquiring 80 thousand million catties [46.5 million tons of unhusked grain] and this eased the tension.

Mao's remarks are particularly interesting because they show that the Government had to lower its procurement target, in the face of the peasants' opposition, to a level that was 6 million tons below the 1954–55 amount. This statement is also interesting in the light of actual procurement for 1955–56. The provincial figures add up to a national total of 52 million tons, which was only 0.4 million tons below the 1954–55 total, but which was collected from an output that was 15 million tons higher. The official total for 1955–56, of 50 million tons, though lower than the reconstructed total, was still well above the target of 46.5 million tons referred to by Mao.

The other side of procurement policy was, of course, the question of rural sales. In the winter and spring of 1955–56 the rural cadres were under strong pressure not to allow such sales to get out of control as they had in the previous year. But a genuine need to *increase* rural sales followed from the rural economic policies being implemented. The first six months of 1956 was a period of unprecedented activity associated with the collectivisation campaign, the drive to speed up the technical reform of agriculture (resulting from the publication of Mao's 'Forty Articles'),[36] and the bid[37] to attain the targets of the First Five Year Plan a year early, that is in 1956.

The details of the upsurge of rural employment have been described elsewhere.[38] The immediate result was a steep rise in the rural demand for grain – for consumption, seed and livestock feed. The classification of rural families based on 1955 data was no longer valid: many

---

[36] '1956 Nien Tao 1967 Nien Ch'üan Kuo Nung Yeh Fa-chan Kang Yao (T'sao-an)' (Draft Outline Plan for the Development of Chinese Agriculture, 1956–1967), *JMJP*, 26 January 1956 (also known as the 'Forty Articles').

[37] Chou En-lai, 'Political Report', 14 January 1956, *HHPYK*, vol. 79 (no. 5), 1956, pp. 1–10.

[38] Kenneth R. Walker, *Planning in Chinese Agriculture: Socialisation and the Private Sector 1956–1962* (London, 1965), chapter 4; also Kenneth R. Walker, chapter 6 of A. Eckstein, W. Galenson and Ta-chung Liu (eds.), *Economic Trends in Communist China* (Chicago, 1968).

households then considered to be in surplus were now in deficit.[39] The political atmosphere, however, militated against making concessions. The relatively moderate line of autumn 1955 became a much more coercive, uncompromising approach as cadres carefully avoided adopting any measures that might be considered to be 'rightist'. It was not long before the issue of rural grain sales became a bone of contention once again. For example, in Liaoning, Kiangsi, Fukien and Kwangtung reductions in sales of grain in rural areas exceeded those already made in gross procurement, so that net procurement rose (see Table 22). The *Kiangsi Daily* reported[40] the existence of vagrancy in the countryside as peasants searched for grain. Reference has already been made to the outbreak of famine in Kwangsi province. Subsequently much of the blame for this was attached to those who were responsible for creating a climate in which cadres were too afraid to report the true facts of natural disasters to their higher authorities with the result that relief supplies of grain were not sent in time to save the starving people.[41]

By the summer of 1956 the peasants were demanding a loosening of controls, less work and more food. Conditions for a smooth passage of the Central Purchase and Supply of grain in the year about to commence were dangerously unfavourable. In fact the system was about to crack.

1956–57: the grain controls under attack

During the summer and autumn of 1956 the Government announced a series of measures which involved a decentralisation of agricultural

---

[39] Chang Nai-ch'i (Minister of Food), Speech to the National People's Congress, 26 June 1956, *HHPYK*, vol. 89 (no. 15), 1956, pp. 47–50. Also *JMJP*, 25 April 1956, which stated that there were 0.5 million *new* deficit rural households in Szechuan province, equal to 3.5 per cent of all rural households.

[40] *KSIJP*, 2 April 1956, which also reported that cadres had failed to observe the 'three fix' norms when allocating grain.

[41] Editorial, 'Bureaucracy Disregarding Human Life Must be Resolutely Combated', *JMJP*, 18 June 1957: 'They [the higher authorities of Kwangsi] were fond of hearing favourable news and not unfavourable news; they were fond of hearing good things, not bad. . . Therefore it is our hope that the disposal of this case will genuinely correct the evil working style of reporting. . .' *KWSIJP*, 24 March 1956 ('Overcome the Spring Famine and Prevent a Summer Famine') had actually warned against turning a blind eye to disasters and grain shortages and had referred to the fear of cadres that if they reported such things they would be attacked as rightists.

planning, fewer controls and a greater emphasis on financial incentives in agriculture.[42] In this new context it proved impossible for the Government to maintain, let alone increase, its level of grain acquisition. Production rose in seventeen out of China's twenty-four provinces, but in eleven of these gross procurement fell, often dramatically (Table 22). Moreover, in seven of the seventeen provinces, a fall in gross procurement was accompanied by a rise in rural sales, so that net procurement declined as output rose. Net procurement increased in only eight provinces. The provincial figures indicate that, against the background of a national increase in grain output of 8 million tons, gross procurement fell by 5.2 million tons,[43] rural sales rose by 4.7 million tons, and net procurement therefore fell by 9.9 million tons. This latter figure is considerably higher than the official figure which shows a decline of 6 million tons, but in spite of this the provincial total should not be discounted: the provincial statistics are well documented in the local sources.

Some of the reductions in procurement were the result of direct confrontation between cadres and peasants, as recorded by Mao Tsetung:[44] 'Old women blocked the road and would not allow the grain to be taken away . . .' In other cases, concessions relating to procurement and sales resulted from successful petitions made by peasants with the support of cadres, including some at the provincial level.[45] Sometimes, in order to justify demands for lower tax and procurement quotas, peasants and *hsien* level cadres[46] connived to falsify the relevant data – relating to sown area, grain yields obtained, the scale of disasters, rural population and the number of livestock in need of grain.[47] Deliveries to

---

[42] See D.H. Perkins, *Market Control and Planning*, and K.R. Walker, *Planning in Chinese Agriculture*, chapter 4.

[43] Even grain tax collections, which had been so stable in previous years, fell, as peasants followed the principle 'kung liang fu-ts'ong k'ou liang' (public grain comes after rations), *KAJP*, 8 March 1957.

[44] *WS* (1967), pp. 3–7.

[45] Nine leading officials of Kansu province were later purged for their opposition to the Central Government's grain policies. It was alleged, for example, that they had incited Kansu peasants not to sell grain to the state or to hand over grain as tax: *KAJP*, 16 August 1958. Purges of provincial party officials also occurred in Shantung: *CKNP* (no. 2), 1959, pp. 2–4.

[46] For example, in Heilungkiang (*JMJP*, 24 August 1957) and in Kwangtung (*NFJP*, 22 October 1956).

[47] Among the many interesting reports on these problems are those for Tsinghai (*TSINJP*, 13 August 1957); Shantung (*TCJP*, 22 September 1957); Chekiang (*CHKJP*, 11 November 1956) and Liaoning (*LJP*, 8 December 1956).

the state were kept down by the giving of short weight and by including soil in the grain.[48]

Peasants not only clamoured for higher grain consumption, but also for better consumption. They attacked the Government for acquiring too much fine grain for the urban populations, and for leaving them with too many potatoes and maize, regarded by many as fit only for animals.[49] In the liberal atmosphere of the 'Hundred Flowers' movement, grain was increasingly sold on black markets, at prices far above those paid by the state.[50]

1957–58: the Government's authority restored

The Government restored its control over grain consumption and distribution only as a result of intensive political activity. The antirightist and socialist education campaigns fought throughout the summer and autumn of 1957 made the correct implementation of the Central Purchase and Supply scheme a major issue throughout China.[51] It was a period of fierce political struggle, with purges of

[48] *KJP*, 20 December 1957 lists the 'Ten Evils', i.e., the ten most common 'grain frauds'.
[49] In Shantung the *san ting* (three-fix) grain consumption norm in twenty-seven *hsien* (out of 113) was below 210 kilograms per head of rural population, of which potatoes exceeded 25 per cent: *NTKTTH* (no. 7), 1957, pp. 1–5. Further evidence for Shantung is found in *TCJP*, 26 April 1957. In Shensi, peasants discounted maize as animal feed, and only regarded wheat as 'real grain': *SIAJP*, 16 January 1958.
[50] *NTKTTH* (no. 8), 1957, pp. 11–14; *TCJP*, 24 March 1957. The Chinese leaders did not know what to do about grain prices. They recognised the importance of cheap grain for the economy as a whole, but they also saw the connection between procurement prices and incentives. In January 1957 Mao Tse-tung wrote: 'The commodity price of grain [i.e., purchase price] should be increased by 5 per cent within a certain period . . . [We wish] to increase the amount of marketed grain greatly but if the price is too low who will till the soil? I am not saying that the price should be raised right now, but that price policy should be studied' (*WS* (1969), Speech of 7 January 1957, pp. 81–90, especially p. 90). The *People's Daily*, 14 October 1957, summed up the dilemma: 'owing to the generally low level of grain prices, most peasants are not keen on producing grain as a [marketed] commodity . . . However, as grain prices form an important factor in our economic life, raising them to a higher level would produce undesirable results. For the time being the only thing we can do is to stabilise grain prices through ideological or economic work, but something will have to be done later. Even after agricultural co-operativisation the law of value still plays an important role in agricultural production, so that in order to increase greatly the production of grain as a commodity we shall have to study further our grain price policy.'
[51] The *People's Daily* editorial of 12 August 1957 was critical of cadres who had bowed to the demands of peasants for higher grain consumption: 'When regional and overall

officials at all levels,[52] and with trials[53] of people charged with 'sabotage' and 'wrecking activities' against the grain controls. According to a report from Yunnan,[54] peasants said that the Central Purchase and Supply of grain was creating 'an atmosphere of terror', and that in spite of a bumper harvest, people were starving under the heavy procurement burdens being imposed.

The Government closed the national free grain markets[55] that had been opened mainly in 1954 to encourage above quota sales, and set about collecting grain from what was a good harvest in many provinces. Officials checked the production figures carefully to prevent under-reporting.[56] To control rural consumption more tightly, the movement towards allocating grain on a basis of the degree of self-sufficiency of the *collective*, as opposed to the household, was accelerated.[57] And to relate rations more closely to needs, collectives were urged to replace the current system under which households were given a basic ration per head, irrespective of age, to one in which ration levels varied according to age and work.[58]

As well as restoring consumption, the Government also called for the speedy achievement of grain self-sufficiency in all agricultural areas,

[i.e., national] interests are in conflict, the masses must be persuaded to abide by the interests of the state.' Note also the following statement from the *People's Daily*, 15 August 1957: 'The grain problem is a complete test for every member and cadre of the co-operatives as to who genuinely supports socialism and who genuinely loves his country. This is a practical test with which verbal expressions of attitude bear no comparison.'

[52] Reference has already been made to purges in Kansu and Shantung. One of the most famous purges was that of Pan Fu-sheng, First Party Secretary of Honan province, in spring 1958. See *HONJP*, 4 July 1958. A good analysis of this subject is found in Frederick C. Teiwes, 'The Purge of Provincial Leaders 1957–1958', *CQ* (no. 27), July–September 1966, pp. 14–32.

[53] Reports are given in *SCMP*, nos. 1757 and 1775.

[54] *FBIS*, 6 September 1957.

[55] Details of their operation are in 'Problems of Strengthening and Developing State Grain Markets', *CHYYC* (no. 5), 1956, pp. 31–5. The directive closing the markets, 9 August 1957, is in *HHPYK*, vol. 116 (no. 18), 1957, pp. 207–8.

[56] Kirin authorities, for example, dismissed the current estimate of output for 1957 as 15 per cent below the actual level. *KJP*, 14 December 1957.

[57] The directive announcing this change was actually issued in 1956 (*JMJP*, 7 October 1956), but it seems that little progress had been made in implementing it by autumn 1957.

[58] State Council, *Supplementary Decision on Grain Central Purchase and Supply*, 11 October 1957. *FKHP* 1957, July–December (Peking 1958), pp. 351–4. This change had been advocated by the *People's Daily*, 28 May 1957.

including those specialising in the production of industrial crops.[59] The new production drive, which became the 'Great Leap Forward' of 1958, gave a special emphasis to potatoes, yields of which were very high indeed.[60] To placate the peasants, procurement agencies were instructed to include some potatoes in urban rations.[61]

Figures in Table 22 testify to the Government's success in both raising gross procurement and in cutting down rural sales. In many provinces, it was a case of reversing the situation prevailing in 1956–57: in four out of the eight provinces where production declined, grain procurement was increased and rural sales were reduced (Heilungkiang, Liaoning, Kansu and Honan). The increase in net procurement exceeded the rise in production in no less than eight provinces. In the country as a whole, the provincial data reveal that grain production (in the twenty-four provinces) rose by 1.8 million tons, grain procurement also rose, by 4.8 million tons, rural sales were reduced by 5.6 million tons and net procurement thus reached its highest level for the 1953–57 period, with a rise of 10.4 million tons.

URBAN GRAIN SALES AND THE PROVINCIAL GRAIN BALANCES

The adequacy of the net rural grain surpluses of each province (i.e. net

[59] A notable example of this was Hopei, where local deficits were often associated with the growing of cotton. In January 1958 all such areas were directed to become self-sufficient in grain (see *HOPJP*, 11 January 1958). Considering Hopei's enormous dependence on grain imports, it is quite extraordinary that under the province's First Five Year Plan (*HOPJP*, 6 December 1955) the emphasis was on increasing cotton production and the grain sown area was to *fall* by 0.33 million hectares in 1953–57. Cotton output was planned to increase by 27 per cent and grain output by only 1.7 per cent (inevitably implying a fall in per capita output). This plan was revised in 1957, however, in order to reduce grain imports: the cotton sown area planned for 1957 involved a reduction of 0.3 million hectares compared with 1956. See *HOPJP*, 18 April 1957 and 30 September 1957.

[60] Average energy yield of potatoes per hectare in China (1952–57) was 23 per cent higher than that of rice and 1.5 times higher than that of wheat.

[61] State Council, *Supplementary Decision*, 11 October 1957. The consumption of fine grain by the urban population, while the peasants who grew the grain ate potatoes was, according to a report from Fukien, 'a most irrational phenomenon . . . which stifles the incentives of the peasants'. The towns were requested to 'share this hardship with the peasants': *FCY* (no. 2), 1958, pp. 20–2. In a bid to persuade the population of Shanghai to eat potatoes as part of their grain ration, the rate for converting potatoes into 'grain equivalent' was made 6:1 instead of the 4:1 rate that was generally used: *HWJP*, 8 October 1957.

procurement) listed in Table 21 can only be judged by relating them to the amounts of grain consumed by the urban populations. Which provinces were able to meet their own urban requirements? Did any provinces change their status in this respect during the years 1953–57? In other words, to what extent did provinces acquire more grain than they sold?

Before presenting the annual 'surplus' and 'deficit' figures, the level of urban grain sales must be discussed briefly. Until the summer of 1955 there was no systematic, comprehensive grain rationing in urban China. Some controls were introduced in 1954, but they were not very effective. For example, in Shanghai,[62] ration coupons, issued in August 1954, were bought and sold on the black market. During the spring of 1955, when city populations were swelled by the migration of discontented peasants, the Government tried to tighten urban grain consumption by allocating grain to cities on a basis of the number of households and this achieved some success, for example, in Shenyang.[63] Urban rationing really began in August 1955,[64] with the setting of ration standards according to the age and employment of each person. This brought about an immediate reduction in urban grain sales. Ration norms were then raised[65] during the spring of 1956 to what was considered to be more realistic levels, and in the summer of 1956 the Government carried out a major wage reform in all urban areas, raising urban wages by as much as 30 per cent. The rapid expansion of urban employment under the stimulus of a construction boom, the raising of ration standards and now, the upward shift in wages all combined to increase the urban demand for grain – and particularly the demand for fine grain.[66] As in rural areas, the Government could not keep grain sales to planned levels, and in 1956–57 they rose by perhaps 4 million tons (see Table 23). Black markets in grain and grain coupons, falsification of population data and flagrant disregard for ration standards were common features of

[62] *CFJP*, 26 March 1955.
[63] *LJP*, 13 September 1955.
[64] 'The Method of Fixing Grain Supplies in the Towns', *FKHP* 1955, July–December (Peking 1956), pp. 567–74.
[65] Chang Nai-ch'i, Speech to the National People's Congress, 26 June 1956.
[66] In Heilungkiang, following the wage reform, the demand for flour rose by 34 per cent and the demand for rice by 15.4 per cent: *HJP*, 5 January 1957. A further factor in the urban demand for grain was that, as a direct result of the wage reform, workers' dependants migrated to the towns. See *KWCJP*, 14 November 1957.

Table 23. *Estimated urban grain sales, 1953–57 (thousand tons)*

	1953	1954	1955	1956	1957	Average 1953–57
North East						
Heilungkiang	1334	1516	1256	1591	c.1290	1397
Kirin	980	1106	946	1070	1095	1039
Liaoning	2125	2369	2253	2562	2645	2391
North West						
IMR	242	284	302	630	444	380
Kansu	415	343	347	441	c.429	395
Shensi	623	645	571	708	515	612
Sinkiang	c.139	c.163	c.143	231	232	180
Tsinghai	37	50	54	77	c.79	59
North						
Honan	1016	907	712	975	1037	929
Hopei	810	930	900	1035	1014	938
Peking	654	925	837	1009	c.802	845
Shansi	635	697[a]	647	830	c.785	719
Shantung	c.848	c.967	896	1346	c.1299	1071
Tientsin	592	680	564	633	525	599
Centre						
Hunan	686	898	770	945	845	829
Hupei	975	1059	884	1106	1098	1012
Kiangsi	635	651	510	778	604	636
East						
Anhwei	821	945	1020	1078	1250	1023
Chekiang	c.783	880	827	939	c.874	861
Kiangsu	1640	1926	1542	1703	1527	1668
Shanghai	1875	2153	1621	1952	1792	1879
South West						
Kweichow	388	530	322	418	455	423
Szechuan	1405	1530	1423	1582	c.1535	1495
Yunnan	513	586	647	732	c.693	634
South						
Fukien	625	555	557	638	589	593
Kwangsi	490	513	423	c.511	c.459	479
Kwangtung	1028	1193	1043	1290	1506	1212
Total (million tons)	22.254	25.001	22.017	26.810	25.409	24.298
Official total (million tons)	20.700	22.800	20.800	24.000	26.150	22.890

a. Assumed.
Source: Appendix 5.

urban China during 1956 and 1957.[67] Towards the end of 1957 the Government called for cuts[68] in urban ration levels for 1957–58 and for much tighter controls to be implemented. The scope of rationing was also extended. For example, flour was, apparently for the first time, rationed in Heilungkiang,[69] while in Canton[70] soya beans, coarse grains and certain 'main grain products' were added to the list of rationed grains. This highlights an important problem when attempting to compare urban and rural grain consumption: how to allow for the fact that the official urban grain ration (*k'ouliang*) was not the only source of all grain consumed. The provincial evidence for urban grain sales in 1957–58 is sketchy and incomplete, while official figures for the national total are also unsatisfactory. Careful analysis of the regional data leads to the conclusion that urban sales were possibly stabilised during 1957–58, but what appears to be the 'best' official figure for China points to a 9 per cent rise above the 1956–57 level. In spite of the high level of urban activity which accompanied the Great Leap Forward, this official figure seems to be somewhat high.

The way is now clear for an examination of the provincial grain surpluses and deficits which resulted from the Government's Central Purchase and Supply of grain. Figures for 1953–57 are given in Table 24. Looking first at the national picture, Table 24 shows that, in spite of the difficulties it encountered in carrying out its plans for grain rationing and redistribution, the Government acquired on average 4.8 million tons per annum more than it sold, during the five years 1953–57. It amassed very big surpluses in 1953–54, 1955–56 and 1957–58, a small surplus in 1954–55, but it incurred a deficit in 1956–57. Although the provincial totals differ somewhat from the official totals in all five years, the greatest discrepancy is for 1956–57. It is possible that the provincial data exaggerate the deficits. There is, however, abundant local evidence for that year including alternative provincial figures which would make the deficits even greater than those presented in Table 24. The official deficit of 2.25 million tons can not be reconciled with the mass of provincial evidence.

[67] *KJP*, 20 November 1957; *PKJP*, 1 November 1957; *AJP*, 21 August 1957; *SIAJP*, 14 January 1958; *SASJP*, 28 July 1957.
[68] State Council, *Supplementary Directive*, 11 October 1957.
[69] *HJP*, 15 December 1957. Note however that flour had been rationed in Tsingtao since November 1956: *CTJP*, 18 November 1956.
[70] *KWCJP*, 1 November 1957.

Table 24. *Provincial procurement–sales surpluses and deficits, 1953–57 (thousand tons)*

	1953	1954	1955	1956	1957	Average 1953–57
North East						
Heilungkiang	+ 1613	+ 1539	+ 2042	+ 561	+ 1768	+ 1505
Kirin	+ 1270	+ 934	+ 1171	+ 80	+ 238	+ 739
Liaoning	− 1561	− 1731	− 1518	− 1654	c. − 1327	− 1558
North West						
IMR	+ 886	+ 1184	+ 1060	+ 1026	+ 412	+ 914
Kansu	− 21	+ 298	+ 265	+ 65	+ 476	+ 217
Shensi	+ 113	+ 360	+ 159	+ 44	+ 86	+ 152
Sinkiang	+ 69	+ 64	+ 8	+ 9	+ 90	+ 48
Tsinghai	− 3	+ 30	+ 26	− 54	Even	Even
North						
Honan	+ 405	+ 448	+ 844	− 262	+ 285	+ 344
Hopei	− 399	− 884	− 875	− 2200	− 490	− 970
Shansi	+ 240	+ 269	− 101	− 50	c. − 110	+ 50
Shantung	− 147	c. + 612	+ 389	− 261	− 400	+ 39
Centre						
Hunan	+ 1305	− 14	+ 1452	− 748	+ 1258	+ 651
Hupei	+ 510	− 991	+ 408	+ 324	+ 456	+ 141
Kiangsi	+ 865	+ 548	+ 837	+ 707	+ 1409	+ 873
East						
Anhwei	+ 778	− 680	+ 1426	− 542	+ 1200	+ 436
Chekiang	+ 439	+ 385	+ 730	+ 195	c. + 897	+ 529
Kiangsu	+ 1060	+ 724	+ 1082	− 103	+ 465	+ 646
South West						
Kweichow	+ 560	+ 412	+ 675	+ 410	+ 435	+ 498
Szechuan	+ 1627	+ 2413	+ 1562	+ 1538	+ 2764	+ 1981
Yunnan	+ 370	+ 283	+ 268	− 69	+ 132	+ 197
South						
Fukien	+ 200	+ 45	+ 48	− 100	+ 279	+ 94
Kwangsi	+ 511	+ 448	c. + 397	c. − 97	c. − 167	+ 218
Kwantung	+ 596	+ 444	+ 603	+ 55	+ 45	+ 349
Total (million tons)	+ 11.286	+ 7.140	+ 12.958	− 1.126	+ 10.201	+ 8.093
Total including estimates for Peking, Tientsin and Shanghai (million tons)	+ 8.165	+ 3.382	+ 9.936	− 4.720	+ 7.082	+ 4.769
Official totals (million tons)	+ 7.80	+ 4.00	+ 8.00	− 2.25	+ 7.25	+ 4.96

Note: Figures for total grain sales are given in Appendix 5.

In every year of our period annual provincial surpluses were acquired in ten out of the twenty-four provinces. Five of these were in the North East and North West Regions (Heilungkiang, Kirin, Inner Mongolia, Shensi and Sinkiang), two were in the central south area of China (Kiangsi and Chekiang), two were in the South West (Szechuan and Kweichow) and the tenth was the Southern province of Kwangtung. Apart from the three great cities, only two provinces – Liaoning and Hopei – incurred procurement–sales deficits in each year. The remaining provinces had both surpluses and deficits during the period. There is little evidence of any significant change in the 'status' of provinces in this respect. Kansu province moved into surplus, and there is some suggestion that its surpluses were growing, while the data for Shantung might possibly be interpreted to indicate a movement in the opposite direction.

Of particular interest is the relationship between the size of the surpluses and deficits and the levels of per capita grain output in the different provinces. A closely associated question is how Government 'extraction' affected the amount of grain used per head (for food and non-food purposes) in each province. The effect of redistribution on food consumption, as opposed to gross use, will be examined in Chapter 4 but at this stage it is worth looking briefly at one aspect of the redistribution process. Table 25 compares (1) the actual and 'potential' average surpluses and deficits during 1953–57 and (2) the levels of per capita production and the amounts used within each province. The figures demonstrate that there was no obvious 'cut-off' level of per capita output at which provincial surpluses ceased. The state acquired surpluses in all the 'rich' provinces where per capita output exceeded 309 kilograms, in most of the provinces falling within the hypothetical 'self-sufficiency' range of 275–309 kilograms per head and even in three out of the four provinces with per capita output in the 'deficit' range (below 275 kilograms). Actual surpluses in the 'rich' provinces were larger than the potential surpluses in four out of the nine provinces, while the potential deficits of the four poorest provinces were largely avoided. A bonus for the Government was provided by surpluses it succeeded in acquiring in the provinces within the range of 'self-sufficiency', with the notable exception of Liaoning.

The enormous annual deficit of Liaoning is a remarkable anomaly when viewed in relation to its average output (1953–57) of 285 kilograms per head of total population. Why was the provincial

Table 25. *Potential and actual provincial grain procurement surpluses, 1953–57*

	Grain output per head (kg)	Potential surplus (million tons)	Actual surplus (million tons)	Effect of procurement on grain used in province	
				Extraction/ injection (kg per head)	Grain available for use (kg per head)
'Surplus' (309 +)					
Heilungkiang	566	+ 3.467	+ 1.505	− 112	454
Kirin	459	+ 1.797	+ 0.739	− 62	397
IMR	444	+ 1.114	+ 0.914	− 111	333
Sinkiang	356	+ 0.249	+ 0.048	− 9	347
Kiangsi	354	+ 0.798	+ 0.873	− 49	305
Hupei	323	+ 0.412	+ 0.141	− 5	318
Anhwei	319	+ 0.323	+ 0.436	− 14	305
Yunnan	312	+ 0.055	+ 0.197	− 11	301
Kwangtung	311	+ 0.073	+ 0.349	− 9	302
Total		+ 8.288	+ 5.202		
'Self-sufficient' (275–309)					
Chekiang	309		+ 0.529	− 22	287
Kansu	309		+ 0.217	− 16	293
Hunan	302		+ 0.651	− 19	283
Kwangsi	301		+ 0.218	− 12	c.289
Szechuan	299		+ 1.981	− 29	270
Fukien	292		+ 0.094	− 7	285
Tsinghai	286		even	nil	286
Liaoning	285		− 1.558	+ 69	354
Shensi	283		+ 0.152	− 9	274
Kweichow	277		+ 0.498	− 31	246
Kiangsu	276		+ 0.646	− 15	261
Total			+ 3.428		
'Deficit' (< 275)					
Shansi	264	− 0.167	+ 0.050	− 3	261
Honan	262	− 0.607	+ 0.344	− 7	255
Shantung	253	− 1.137	+ 0.039	− 1	252
Hopei	217	− 2.335	− 0.970	+ 24	241
Total		− 4.246	− 0.537		
Net position ('Surplus' and 'deficit' range provinces)		+ 4.042	+ 4.665		

Government of Liaoning unable to meet its own grain requirements from such an apparently adequate per capita output? Two reasons may explain this phenomenon. First, the generally high level of grain used per head throughout the North East, and especially in the neighbouring, highly urban, industrial province of Heilungkiang, set a standard for the Liaoning authorities which, for political reasons, had to be met. Liaoning had the biggest urban population in China, averaging 6.4 million per year (1953–57) and the Government attached great importance to its welfare.

The second – and more specific – explanation is found by examining the composition of grain production in relation to the tastes and preferences of the Liaoning population, especially those of the large urban population. This question has already been explored briefly in Chapter 1, when the small amount of *fine* grain produced in Liaoning per head of population was emphasised. Although average grain output per head of rural population was 399 kilograms, only 260 kilograms were regarded as what might be termed 'real' grain: potatoes accounted for 20 kilograms per head,[71] while maize production was approximately 119 kilograms per head.[72] Potatoes were largely discounted by the rural as well as the urban population to such an extent that 0.5 million tons were 'given away' to peasants in 1956.[73] Maize was similarly regarded as an inferior food and, having been 'foisted on the people' by the Government,[74] was often wasted. 'Real grain' therefore consisted of 80 kilograms per head of fine grain[75] (soya beans 46 kilograms, wheat 2 kilograms, rice 32 kilograms) and 180 kilograms of coarse grain (excluding maize, but including 118 kilograms of *kaoliang* (sorghum)[76] and 42 kilograms of millet,[77] both

---

[71] Average for four years (1952, 1955, 1956 and 1957). Output figures for 1952 and 1957 are from *An Economic Geography of NE China*, p. 42. Figures for 1952 and 1955 are obtained by subtracting output net of potatoes (*LJP*, 28 December 1956) from gross output.

[72] Average for three years (1952, 1956 and 1957). Output for 1952 and 1957 is given in *An Economic Geography of NE China*, p. 42. Output for 1956 is calculated from sown area (*LJP*, 14 May 1958) and yield (*LJP*, 10 February 1957).

[73] *JMJP*, 26 June 1957.

[74] *CKNP* (no. 8), 1958 and *LJP*, 10 February 1959. In 1957 it was planned to reduce the sown area of maize in favour of *kaoliang* (sorghum) in an attempt to meet consumers' requirements more closely: *LJP*, 21 May 1957.

[75] Sources of data relating to fine grain output are given in Appendix 2a.

[76] Average for three years (1952, 1956 and 1957). Output for 1952 and 1957 is given in *An Economic Geography of NE China*, p. 42. Output for 1956 is estimated from yield (*LJP*, 10 February 1957) and sown area (roughly estimated from *LJP*, 10 February 1957 and *CIAAA*).

highly favoured for food and other uses). Net procurement from the rural sector averaged 52 kilograms per head per year, including virtually all[78] the 46 kilograms of soya beans produced per head. Even if none of the remaining 6 kilograms of grain per head extracted was fine grain, the amount of fine grain left per head of rural population was only 34 kilograms, plus all the inferior grains. The Government clearly saw no possibility of feeding the urban population with large amounts of maize and it must have regarded the net procurement of 0.833 million tons per year as the maximum politically attainable. This amount provided 130 kilograms of grain per head of urban population: hence the procurement–sales deficit.

In contrast, the Government's procurement policy bore heavily on several of China's important rice, wheat and soya bean producing provinces as the figures in Table 25 reveal. As in the case of Liaoning, this reflects the Government's need to meet the great demand for fine grain (for export as well as for the towns). For example, the acquisition of the provincial surpluses in Hunan, Szechuan, Kiangsu and Kweichow reduced per capita grain use in those provinces to surprisingly low levels, making Kweichow one of the poorest provinces in China, with only 246 kilograms used per head. Similarly, the surpluses, however small, created in the provinces of Shansi, Honan and Shantung, are explained by the importance of these areas as producers of wheat and soya beans. Average annual wheat output, 1953–57, was 1.02 million tons in Shansi[79] (4.5 per cent of the national total), 3.89 million tons in Honan[80] (17.2 per cent of the total) and 3.34 million tons in Shantung[81] (14.8 per cent of the total). Honan, in addition, produced 1.22 million tons of soya beans per annum[82] (12.6

---

[77] Two-year average (1952 and 1957). Output from *An Economic Geography of NE China*, p. 42.

[78] *LJP*, 2 January 1958.

[79] Sources are: 1953 and 1954 – *SASJP*, 23 February 1955; 1955 – from 1954 and percentage in *TKP*, 19 June 1955; 1956 – from 1955 and percentage in *SASJP*, 23 April 1957; 1957 – from five-year total (*SASJP*, 12 May 1958) and four-year total.

[80] *JMJP*, 15 June 1958.

[81] 1953–54: from yield and sown area. Yields are in *TLCS* (no. 8), 1957; sown areas are in *CKNP* (no. 15), 1957; 1955 and 1956 – State Statistical Bureau in *TCJP*, 9 August 1957; 1957 – *TCJP*, 17 August 1957.

[82] 1952–54 and 1957 output are all obtained by subtracting net from gross grain output. Net output for 1952–54 – *CKNP* (no. 15), 1957; net output for 1957 – *HONJP*, 31 December 1957 (17.4 per cent above 1952); 1955 and 1956 – State Statistical Bureau in *HONJP*, 18 September 1957.

per cent of the total), while Shantung's 1.47 million tons of soya beans per annum[83] accounted for 15.2 per cent of the national output.

Finally, attention is drawn to the impact of a net injection of almost one million tons of grain per annum for use in Hopei. Table 25 shows that such supplies increased the amount of grain used per head from a possible 217 kilograms to 241 kilograms, still the poorest province in China but now within close range of the levels enjoyed by the neighbouring provinces of Shantung and Honan.

An important reason for building up provincial grain surpluses was to stabilise consumption within each province in the face of production fluctuations. The bulk of such surpluses, however, was needed for exports to grain deficit provinces, Peking, Tientsin and Shanghai, and to foreign countries: in the years under review, quite apart from exports required to meet temporary provincial deficits, 5.8 million tons were needed each year to eliminate the more chronic procurement deficits of Hopei, Liaoning and the three cities. The availability of adequate provincial exports was fundamental to the success of the Government's entire economic strategy of achieving rapid industrialisation without foreign grain imports. For the people of the exporting provinces, grain going out – compared with grain being stored within their own provinces – was a vastly different proposition, as it was lost to consumption for ever. An examination of the level and pattern of such inter-provincial transfers forms the subject matter of Chapter 3.

[83] 1953–54 and 1957 – gross output minus net output (net output 1953–54: *CKNP*, (no. 15), 1957); 1957 from net grain output index in *NTKTTH* (no. 2), 1958, p. 21; 1955 and 1956 – State Statistical Bureau in *TCJP*, 9 August 1957.

3

INTER-PROVINCIAL GRAIN
TRANSFERS, 1953–1957

In practice the level of provincial grain exports was determined by four 'demand' elements, two of which were fairly predictable and unlikely to change in the medium term; one which varied from year to year; and one which was predictable in so far as it was part of the National Plan. These four elements were:

1. The demand from Peking, Tientsin and Shanghai, of well over 3 million tons per annum.
2. The imports required by China's two deficit provinces – Hopei and Liaoning. It is clear from statements[1] made by the Liaoning provincial authorities that 1.0–1.5 million tons of grain imports were regarded as inevitable until 1962 and it is equally clear that the Hopei Government budgeted for at least the same level. This element, therefore, added up to 2–3 million tons of provincial export demand per year.
3. 'Emergency' grain to stabilise supplies in provinces affected by disasters. As Chapter 1 has shown, production in many north and north western provinces was unstable. The magnitude of the problem is well illustrated by severe harvest fluctuations in three out of the five years of the Plan period. In 1954, disasters in Hupei, Hunan and Anhwei reduced output by 4.6 million tons. In 1956 the provinces of Inner Mongolia, Shensi and Shansi were badly affected by the weather, as was Shantung. Losses of grain in these four provinces amounted to 5 million tons. In 1957 – a good year in general – poor harvests were recorded in Kiangsu, Hopei, Hunan, Anhwei

---

[1] For Liaoning see *SHYJP*, 31 October 1957. *LJP*, 10 November 1957 gives 'self-sufficiency' grain output as 9.5 million tons, which was to be attained in 1962. Liaoning's First Five Year Plan target was 6.5 million tons: *JMJP*, 18 January 1957. For Hopei see First Five Year Plan in *HJP*, 22 September 1955. Note that the plan to increase grain output by only 1.7 per cent between 1952 and 1957 implied roughly a 14 per cent *decline* in per capita output. It was argued in *HJP*, 25 April 1957, that imports could never be adequate to cover the kind of grain deficit envisaged. Self-sufficiency grain output for Hopei (planned for 1962) was set at 15 million tons, implying an average of 300 kilograms per head (see *HJP*, 21 August 1957). The province must, therefore, have envisaged grain imports of 1.0–1.5 million tons, or even 2 million tons, per year.

and Kwangsi. Their combined output fell by 4 million tons. Allowing for the fact that not all such losses could be made good out of imports, it is nevertheless the case that the Government would have to plan for at least 2.5 million tons of provincial exports per annum for this purpose.

4. Grain for foreign exports. At a time when the industrial core of the First Five Year Plan was being imported, China had to mobilise all possible agricultural exports to finance her development. Approximately 2 million tons[2] of grain (unhusked) were in fact exported each year between 1953 and 1957 and it must be assumed that this was around the planned level.

The total demand for provincial exports was therefore in the range of 9.5–10.5 million tons per year and this should be viewed in the context of annual procurement surpluses which averaged 10.6 million tons throughout the period 1953–57 (Table 24 above). Two related consequences arise out of this tight budgeting. First, almost all the provincial surpluses had to be exported immediately, leaving little for the accumulation of stocks. Secondly, the planning of inter-provincial transfers was, inevitably, done on a very short-run, month-by-month basis. Both these policies led to considerable dissension between the Central and provincial Governments.

The figures above suggest that 90–94 per cent of provincial surpluses would have to be earmarked by the Central Government for export to other areas or for overseas trade. Firm evidence for sixteen provinces confirms this. In ten[3] of these provinces 85 per cent or more of the surpluses were exported and in seven such provinces the figure exceeded 90 per cent.[4] It would appear that the Central Government took the level of stocks into account when deciding on the export target for any province, but the views of the Central and provincial Governments did not always coincide. For example, Shantung was required[5] to export grain in 1954–55 partly because stocks (0.9 million tons) had been increased excessively with the importation of grain in 1953–54. On the other hand, anxieties were expressed in Honan[6] that

[2] From *TCKT* (no. 19), 1957, pp. 31–2 and p. 28; and R.H. Kirby, *Agricultural Trade of the People's Republic of China, 1935–69*, Foreign Agricultural Economic Report no. 83, US Department of Agriculture, Economic Research Service (Washington DC, 1972). All figures have been converted, where necessary, to unhusked grain equivalent.

[3] Heilungkiang, Kirin, Inner Mongolia, Shensi, Honan, Shansi, Hupei, Chekiang, Szechuan and Kwangtung.

[4] Heilungkiang, Kirin, Shensi, Shansi, Hupei, Chekiang and Szechuan.

[5] *HHYP*, vol. 70 (no. 8), 1955, pp. 64–5.

[6] *HONJP*, 27 August 1957.

her large volume of grain exports had left insufficient stocks to offset the impact of a possible major natural disaster. The province of Shensi also drew attention[7] to its tiny amount of stocks in September 1955, amounting to 0.315 million tons.

The short-run planning of grain transfers may be illustrated from the experience of Kiangsu, Anhwei and Shansi provinces. On a basis of a 12.7 per cent increase in the production of rice in 1953, Kiangsu[8] exported grain during the first six months of 1954 but as a result of a decline in rice production of 8.9 per cent in 1954, grain was imported during the second half of the year. In 1953–45, the unstable province of Anhwei exported most of its procurement surplus of 0.778 million tons, with the result that a procurement deficit of 0.680 million tons incurred during the following year had to be covered by imports equal to the amount exported in 1953–54. Shansi exported 0.508 million tons in the two years 1953–54 and 1954–55 but in doing so it had insufficient stocks to finance procurement deficits in 1955–56 and 1956–57 amounting to only 0.151 million tons, and 0.183 million tons were imported.

Table 26 attempts to reconstruct the inter-provincial grain transfers of the period 1953–57. It includes actual and estimated figures and although it has been very difficult to establish the precise situation in some provinces, the picture is offered with a certain confidence regarding its accuracy, a confidence that is encouraged by the consistency of the overall, national grain 'account' based on the provincial estimates. Moreover, the national totals thus obtained are in line with the few official statements made about the level of provincial grain transfers. For example, one reference records[9] that transfers in 1956–57 were 'one hundred million catties plus several hundred million catties', which may be interpreted as 140–150 hundred million catties, or 8.0–8.5 million tons (unhusked), compared with the 8.156 million tons of grain exports derived in Table 26. A more specific figure of 8.67 million tons is available[10] for the calendar year 1957 and this compares fairly closely with the

[7] *SESJP*, 4 September 1957.
[8] *Rational Transport*, p. 27.
[9] *HHPYK*, vol. 124 (no. 2), 1958, pp. 36–9.
[10] *LSP* (no. 82), 1959.

reconstructed total of provincial exports amounting to 9.142 million tons.

Viewing the period as a whole, the figures in Table 26 show that average provincial exports were 9.967 million tons and average imports were 7.683 million tons, leaving a surplus of 2.284 million tons per annum. Foreign grain exports averaged 2.105 million tons per annum. Comparing total provincial exports with the sum of procurement surpluses (i.e. from the twenty-one surplus provinces listed), it is seen that exports averaged 93.9 per cent of surpluses over the five years and the Government increased its grain stocks by 12.420 million tons.

GROSS PROVINCIAL GRAIN EXPORTS

First of all, as Table 27 shows, seven provinces (Kansu, Hupei, Chekiang, Kweichow, Yunnan, Fukien and Kwangtung) became grain exporters in the 1950s, having been importers in the 1930s; and Szechuan[11] province moved from a position of self-sufficiency to become an exporter. During the period of 1953–57, Szechuan and Heilungkiang were by far the most important exporters. Together they supplied 3.290 million tons per annum, or 33 per cent of the total. The leading[12] six exporters (Szechuan, Heilungkiang, Inner Mongolia, Kiangsi, Kirin and Kiangsu) accounted for 61 per cent of all provincial exports, while the next four in rank (Anhwei, Hunan, Honan and Chekiang) provided a further 21 per cent.

It is the changing provincial origin of grain exports, however, which provides most interest. Five provinces clearly ceased exporting grain during the period: Shansi, Shantung, Fukien, Kwangsi and Kwangtung. The loss of Kwangtung's 0.475 million tons a year (1953–55) was particularly significant. Perhaps even more dramatic was the probable decline in the combined exports of Heilungkiang and Kirin, from

[11] An interesting analysis of the relationship between Szechuan agriculture and the limited transport facilities available is found in Chang Shan-pao, 'The Economic Importance of the Ch'engtu-Chungking Railway', *Central Bank of China Bulletin*, vol. 3 (no. 4), December 1937, pp. 288–94.

[12] Compare Wang Kuang-wei's list of 'leading grain exporting provinces' during 1953–56: Szechuan, Heilungkiang, Kirin, Inner Mongolia, Hunan, Kiangsi and Chekiang. These accounted for 'over three-quarters' of provincial grain exports: Wang Kuang-wei, 'Several Problems in Developing Agriculture', *HH* (no. 17), 1957, pp. 25–8.

2.674 million tons in 1953, to around 1.189 million tons in 1957, a fall
of 56 per cent. In 1957 the exports of these two provinces were 2.4
million tons (or 66 per cent) below the average amount exported in the
1930s and a major factor in this decline was the falling output of soya
beans. On the other hand, Kweichow and Yunnan both began to
export small, but increasing amounts of grain in the 1950s and, most
remarkable of all, Szechuan's exports quadrupled[13] between 1953 and
1957, from 0.704 million tons to 2.884 million tons. In 1957 Szechuan
alone supplied 31.5 per cent of all provincial grain exports and as
Table 27 shows this was no departure from the trend.

GROSS PROVINCIAL GRAIN IMPORTS

The pattern of provincial grain imports outlined at the beginning of
this chapter is confirmed by the details recorded in Table 28. The total
amount imported each year was made up of a fairly constant quantity
plus an amount which varied with the severity of natural disasters.
Thus, in the three relatively good harvest years 1953, 1955 and 1957,
provincial grain imports were quite constant at around 6 million tons
per year, whereas in the bad years of 1954 and 1956 they rose by 3.6
and 4.3 million tons respectively. The three cities (Peking, Tientsin
and Shanghai) are estimated to have imported 3.489 million tons per
year, accounting for 45.4 per cent of total provincial imports, and the
only other significant consistent importers were Liaoning (with 1.66
million tons or 21.6 per cent)[14] and Hopei (1.114 million tons, or 14.5
per cent). Together, therefore, these 'permanent' importing areas
absorbed 6.263 million tons of grain per year, or 81.5 per cent of the
national total of provincial grain imports.

It is interesting that the grain imports of the cities actually declined
between 1953 and 1957 by 3,000 tons. This was partly because the
grain output of Peking and Tientsin rose by 0.176 million tons
(Shanghai's meagre output fell slightly) but it also reflected the success

[13] As well as the rapid growth of grain output in 1952–57 (at a rate of 6.6 per cent per
annum), an important factor in Szechuan's increasing exports was the development of
transport, including the opening of the Szechuan to Shensi railway in 1956. The
Chengtu to Chungking railway, planned since 1908, had opened in 1952.
[14] Liaoning's pre-war imports were around 1.35 million tons per year: see T.H. Shen,
Agricultural Resources of China (Ithaca, New York, 1951), p. 401; also *LJP*, 3 November
1955.

Table 26. *Estimated and actual provincial grain exports* (+) *and imports* (−), *1953–57*

	1953	1954	1955	1956	1957	Total 1953–57 E/I	Total 1953–57 P/S	Stock change 1953–57
North East								
Heilungkiang	+1600	+1500	+1674	+1470 / −80	+1390 / +1000	+7164	+7523	+359
Kirin	+1074	+1368	+800	−233	+189	+3198	+3693	+495
Liaoning	−1600	−1800	−1600	−1800	−1500	−8300	−7791	−509
North West								
IMR	+923	+1111	+758	+833	+264	+3889	+4568	+679
Kansu	−50	+100	+250	+50	+200	+550	+1083	+533
Shensi	+100	+300	+150	+100	+40	+690	+762	+72
Sinkiang		even	even	even	even		+240	+240
Tsinghai	−10					−10	−5	+5
North								
Honan	+167	+973 / −575 } +398	+505	+766 / −575 } +191	even?	+1261	+1720	+459
Hopei	−598	−905	−1205	−2115	−750	−5573	−4848	+725
Peking	−687	−971	−879	−1059	−842	−4438	−4227	+211
Shansi	+260	+250	−160	−23	−120	+207	+248	+41
Shantung	−395	+490	+300	even	−400	−5	+193	+198
Tientsin	−622	−714	−592	−665	−551	−3144	−2994	+150
Centre								
Hunan	+950	−300	+850	+400	+856	+2756	+3253	+497
Hupei	+405	−1264	+325	+390	+350	+266	+707	+441
Kiangsi	+821	+536	+804	+696	+785	+3642	+4366	+724

82

East								
Anhwei	+700	−713	+1200	−600	+1000	+1587	+2182	+595
Chekiang	+400	+300	+650	+225	+505	+2080	+2646	+566
Kiangsu	+954	+702 / −50 }+652	+974	−1265	+419	+1734	+3228	+1494
Shanghai	−1969	−2260	−1702	−2050	−1882	−9863	−9393	+470
South West								
Kweichow	+150	+302	+324	+299	+350	+1425	+2492	+1067
Szechuan	+704	+1267	+1790	+2560	+2884	+9205	+9904	+699
Yunnan	even	even	+150	+367	+300	+817	+984	+167
South								
Fukien	+205 / −33 }+172	even	even	even	−250	+172	+472	+300
Kwangsi	+267	+419	+250	even	even	+686	+1092	+406
Kwangtung	+390	+535	+500	even	even	+1425	+1743	+318
Total exports (millions tons)	+10.130	+10.153	+12.254	+8.156	+9.142	+49.835	+23.841	+12.420
Total imports (million tons)	−5.964	−9.552	−6.138	−10.465	−6.295	−38.414		
Export/import ±	+4.166	+0.601	+6.116	−2.309	+2.847	+11.421		
Net grain exports from China (calendar year)	+1.863	+2.276	+2.268	+2.473	+1.647	+10.527		

Notes: E/I: Exports and imports. P/S: Procurement–sales surplus (+) or deficit (−).
Source: Appendix 7.

Table 27. *Gross grain exports, 1953–57 (thousand tons)*

	1953	1954	1955	1956	1957	Average 1953–57	Pre-communist position p.a.	Percentage of all exports			Rank		
								1953	1957	Average 1953–57	1953	1957	Average 1953–57
North East													
Heilungkiang	1600	1500	1674	1470	1000	1449	} +3540	15.8	10.9	14.5	1	2	2
Kirin	1074	1368	800		189	686		10.6	2.1	6.9	2	13	5
North West													
IMR	923	1111	758	833	264	778	+	9.1	2.9	7.8	5	11	3
Kansu	100	100	250	50	200	120	−		2.2	1.2		12	18
Shensi	100	300	150	100	40	138		1.0	0.4	1.4	17	14	17
North													
Honan	167	973	505	766		482	+	1.6		4.8	15		9
Shansi	260	250				102	+255	2.6		1.0	13		19
Shantung		490	300			158	+75			1.6			16
Centre													
Hunan	950		850	400	856	611	+200	9.4	9.4	6.1	4	4	6
Hupei	465		325	390	350	306	−225	4.6	3.8	3.1	9	8	11
Kiangsi	821	536	804	696	785	728	+150	8.1	8.6	7.3	6	5	4
East													
Anhwei	700		1200		1000	580	{ +500 falling to +100	6.9	10.9	5.8	8	2	8
Chekiang	400	300	650	225	505	416	−400	3.9	5.5	4.2	10	6	10
Kiangsu	954	702	974		419	610	{ −280 to +400	9.4	4.6	6.1	3	7	7
South West													
Kweichow	150	302	324	299	350	285	small −	1.5	3.8	2.9	16	8	12

							s.s.						
Szechuan	704	1267	1790	2560	2884	1841	−1500	6.9	31.5	18.5	7	1	1
Yunnan			150	367	300	163			3.3	1.6		10	15
South													
Fukien	205					41	−300	2.0		0.4	14		20
Kwangsi	267	419	250			187	+50	2.6		1.9	12		14
Kwangtung	390	535	500			285	−700 to −1000	3.8		2.9	11		12
Total (million tons)	10.130	10.153	12.254	8.156	9.142	9.967					17	14	20

Note: s.s. = self sufficient.
Sources: Appendix 7.

of urban grain rationing (from 1955) and the control of city size. Imports into Liaoning fell by 100,000 tons between 1953 and 1957 and Hopei's imports rose by only 152,000 tons, so that together the demand of the leading principal importers was almost constant.

The impact of agricultural instability on provincial imports is well illustrated by 1954 and 1956. In 1954 total provincial grain imports rose by 3.588 million tons, and 63 per cent of this was accounted for by the imports of three provinces suffering from floods – Hunan, Hupei, and Anhwei – all of which had exported grain in 1953–54. In 1956, 2.775 million tons (64 per cent) of the rise in provincial grain imports (amounting to 4.327 million tons) were taken by Hopei, Anhwei and Kiangsu, which had poor harvests.

NET PROVINCIAL GRAIN TRANSFERS

Table 29 classifies China's twenty-seven provinces (including Peking, Tientsin and Shanghai) according to their net trade in grain during the five years 1953–57. Only seven provinces in China consistently provided net export surpluses throughout the period 1953–57. A further three provinces were net exporters in some years without being net importers in others. (In the latter group, as has been pointed out earlier Kwangtung ceased to be an exporter after 1955–56, whereas Yunnan started to export grain in 1955–56 and continued to do so during 1956 and 1957.) Nine provinces were net importers in some years, but net exporters on balance throughout the period. This group includes Kirin and Shansi, the net exports of which declined between 1953 and 1957 (Table 26).

Hupei's low overall net export level is accounted for by the huge imports of a single year, 1954, and the Government could look forward to consistently high annual exports from that area as production stability increased. The most striking feature of the net importers listed in Table 29 is that they were all located in the north of China. It is worth exploring the broad, regional pattern in some detail for it highlights the problem of how to feed the large deficit area of north China with export surpluses from other provinces. More specifically, it raises the issue of the need to transfer grain from south to north China – an issue which Mao Tse-tung regarded as very important. Table 30 presents the net position of China's different 'regions'.

Table 28. *Gross provincial grain imports, 1953–57*

	Gross imports of grain (thousand tons)						Percentage of total grain imports			Rank			Imports as percent of output		
	1953	1954	1955	1956	1957	Average 1953–57	1953	1957	Average 1953–57	1953	1957	Average 1953–57	1953	1957	Average 1953–57
North East															
Heilungkiang				80		16			0.2			15			0.2
Kirin				233		46			0.6			14			0.8
Liaoning	1600	1800	1600	1800	1500	1660	26.8	23.8	21.6	2	2	2	28.0	22.4	25.9
North West															
Kansu	50					10	0.8		0.1	7		17	0.2		0.2
Tsinghai	10					2	0.2		negligible	9		18	2.7		0.4
North															
Honan	598	575	1205	575	750	230	10.0	11.9	3.0	5	4	9		7.4	1.9
Hopei	687	905	879	2115	842	1114	11.5	13.4	14.5	3	3	3	7.4		12.8
Peking		971		1059		887			11.5			4	558.5	427.4	650.2
Shansi			160	23	120	61		1.9	0.8		8	11		3.4	1.5
Shantung	395				400	159	6.6	6.4	2.1	6	6	10	3.6	3.1	1.2
Tientsin	622	714	592	665	551	629	10.4	8.8	8.2	4	5	5	464.2	220.4	334.2
Centre															
Hunan		300				60			0.8			12			0.6
Hupei		1264				253			3.3			8			2.7
East															
Anhwei		713		600		263			3.4			6			2.5
Kiangsu		50		1265		263			3.4			6			2.2
Shanghai	1969	2260	1702	2050	1882	1973	33.0	29.9	25.7	1	1	1	4475.0	5703.0	4812.0
South															
Fukien	33					7	0.6		0.1	8		16	0.8		0.2
Kwangsi					250	50		0.4	0.7		7	13		4.6	0.9
Total (million tons)	5.964	9.552	6.138	10.465	6.295	7.683									

Source: Appendix 7.

Table 29. *A classification of Chinese provinces according to their net trade in grain, averages for 1953–57* (thousand tons unhusked grain per annum)

Net exporters			Self-sufficient	Net importers	
Consistent net exporters in all five years	Consistent net exporters in some years and no net imports in other years	Net exporters on balance over five years	Minimal trade	Consistent net importers in all five years	Net importers on balance over five years
Szechuan 1841	Kwangtung 285	Kirin 640	Sinkiang	Shanghai 1973	Shantung 1
Heilungkiang 1433	Honan 252	Hunan 551	Tsinghai	Liaoning 1660	
IMR 778	Yunnan 163	Kiangsu 347		Hopei 1114	
Kiangsi 728		Anhwei 317		Peking 887	
Chekiang 416		Kwangsi 137		Tientsin 629	
Kweichow 285		Kansu 110			
Shensi 138		Hupei 53			
		Shansi 41			
		Fukien 34			

Table 30. *Regional balance of trade in grain, 1953–57*
(thousand tons)

Region	1953	1954	1955	1956	1957	Average 1953–57	Average population 1953–57 (millions)
North East	+1074	+1068	+874	−643	−311	+412	47.92
North West	+963	+1511	+1158	+983	+504	+1024	46.37
North	−1875	−1452	−2031	−3671	−2663	−2338	160.59
Central	+2236	−1028	+1979	+1486	+1991	+1333	82.02
East	+85	−2021	+1122	−3690	+42	−892	106.87
South West	+854	+1569	+2264	+3226	+3534	+2289	103.73
South	+829	+954	+750	nil	−250	+457	68.82
North excluding Peking and Tientsin	−566	+233	−560	−1947	−1270	−822	153.82
Peking and Tientsin	−1309	−1685	−1471	−1724	−1393	−1516	6.77
North East excluding Liaoning plus North West	+3637	+4379	+3632	+2140	+1693	+3096	71.84
North including Liaoning, Peking and Tientsin	−3475	−3252	−3631	−5471	−4163	−3998	183.04
East excluding Shanghai	+2054	+239	+2824	−1640	+1924	+1080	100.15
Shanghai	−1969	−2260	−1702	−2050	−1882	−1973	6.72

North East: Heilungkiang, Kirin, Liaoning.
North West: IMR, Kansu, Shensi, Sinkiang, Tsinghai.
North: Honan, Hopei, Peking, Shansi, Shantung, Tientsin.
Centre: Hunan, Hupei, Kiangsi.
East: Anhwei, Chekiang, Kiangsu, Shanghai.
South West: Kweichow, Szechuan, Yunnan.
South: Fukien, Kwangsi, Kwangtung.

The five-year averages show that the North and East Regions were in deficit while the remaining five regions were in surplus. The trends in Table 30 are more important than the averages for the period. First, the North East became a deficit region in 1956 and continued to be so in 1957, as the export surpluses of Heilungkiang and Kirin declined. Secondly, annual exports from the North West were maintained at around one million tons until 1957 when they fell by 50 per cent as a result of bad harvests in Inner Mongolia and Shensi. Third, imports by the North Region tended to rise throughout the period and in 1957 they were 42 per cent higher than in 1953. Fourth, the Eastern Region moved between surplus and deficit positions from year to year. Fifth, net exports from the South West Region quadrupled in five years. Sixth, the South Region moved from a position where it exported 0.8 million tons of grain a year for three years to a deficit position in 1956 and 1957.

Consideration of the possible geographical origin of the grain imports needed by north and east China raises three questions:

1. To what extent were the provinces of the North China Region (that is, excluding the two cities) able to supply grain exports to Peking and Tientsin?
2. If we broaden the north China deficit area to include Liaoning, does this mean that the import requirements of this vast area could be met out of the export surpluses of the North East Region (minus Liaoning) and those of the North West Region?
3. Could Shanghai be fed from the export surpluses of its three neighbouring provinces: Anhwei, Kiangsu and Chekiang?

Turning to the first of our questions, the four provinces of the North China Region, taken together, were only in surplus during 1954 when, however, they exported enough grain to meet a mere 14 per cent of the import requirements of Peking and Tientsin. In the remaining four years the region was itself a net importer. And as Table 30 shows, the region's position deteriorated badly between 1953 and 1957, from an annual deficit of 0.566 million tons to one of 1.270 million tons.

Second, the import needs of the large north China deficit region (including Liaoning) with its 183 million people *could* be met entirely from the combined exports of Manchuria and the North West Region during 1953–54, 1954–55 and 1955–56, but not thereafter. In 1956–57 such exports were only equal to 39 per cent of the deficit area's needs and in 1957–58 they were still only 41 per cent of requirements.

Thirdly, the grain exports of the three provinces of the East China Region were adequate for the needs of Shanghai in three out of the five years under discussion.

The main implication of these findings, therefore, is that large amounts of grain had to be transported from the South West Region and from the Central provinces of Hunan, Kiangsi and Hupei (1) to the deficit provinces of north China, and (2) to Shanghai. This operation imposed an enormous strain[15] on China's limited transport facilities and it led the Government to grant great financial subsidies to keep the retail price of grain down to what it considered to be an appropriate level.[16]

Apart from these considerations of transport and of cost, reliance on southern provinces by the north involved problems relating to taste and to the timing of grain availability. For example, in the first half of 1958 the Government was faced with an acute[17] problem of finding grain imports for north China, following a decline in the exports of the North East and North West amounting to 1.9 million tons over two successive years (a drop of 53 per cent). The Government planned to ship more rice from south China but this met with opposition from the north Chinese on grounds of taste: they preferred certain coarse grains and wheat. Rice stocks in the south were very limited and the first rice crop of the year was not ready for harvesting. The southern provinces were therefore directed to send their early wheat in the first instance, followed by rice when it became available. As well as illustrating yet again the hand-to-mouth approach to grain distribution in China, this case also shows the great amount of persuasion and education needed to ensure its success. The *Ta kung-pao*[18] took the northern people to task for complaining about the *type* of grain they were receiving and appealed for mutual understanding:

[cadres] should appreciate the difficulties of the people in the areas transferring grain away and should persuade the masses to obey the requirements of the state . . . if only the areas exporting grain and the areas importing it can understand each other and support each other, the task of transferring southern grain to the north . . . is sure to be fulfilled smoothly.

---

[15] *LS* (no. 4), 1956, pp. 12–13; also, Li Ch'eng-jui, *Chung-hua Jen-min Kung-ho-kuo-Nung-yeh Shui Shih-kao* (*History of Agricultural Taxation in the Chinese People's Republic*) (Peking, 1959), p. 299. *LJP*, 8 October 1957, gives a figure of 65 *yuan* per ton as the cost of transporting grain from south China to Liaoning.

[16] *LJP*, 20 September 1957 (*SCMP*, no. 1658). According to this source, the subsidy on grain imported by Liaoning, which covered the gap between the real cost (including transport, processing and distribution) and the retail price, was 145 *yuan* per ton.

[17] 'Transfer southern grain from South to North. Let the early crop help the late', *TKP*, 14 June 1958.

[18] *Ibid.*

GRAIN TRANSFERS AND POLITICAL STRUGGLE

There is no doubt that the level of provincial grain exports reflected the power of the Central Government rather than the existence of 'true' surpluses which would have been exported in the absence of state controls. In some instances, provincial leaders clashed with the Central Government over the amounts to be exported, while in other instances the provincial authorities resisted pressures from within their region to cut or eliminate exports and even to import grain.

The best example of a province successfully resisting the Central Government during this period is Kwangtung, under the leadership of T'ao Chu who was purged during the Cultural Revolution and subsequently rehabilitated by Hua Kuo-feng. In a remarkably blunt speech to the Kwangtung People's Committee Conference in August 1956, T'ao announced that the Centre had agreed to cancel Kwangtung's exports for 1956–57. In fact Kwangtung did not export grain either in 1956–57 or in 1957–58. T'ao Chu asserted:[19] 'We must insist (*ch'üe ting*) that in future Kwangtung's grain must fully supply [the needs of] this province, and only then can it be exported.' He attacked the 'style' of Central Government Departments which only looked at 'the system, and not at people's welfare' and argued that the elimination of the 'tense grain situation', by increasing consumption, was a very important factor in raising the incentives of the people of Kwangtung. The effect of T'ao Chu's policy of putting Kwangtung first was to raise the potential grain available per head to the province from 290 kilograms during the three exporting years (1953, 1954 and 1955) to 323 kilograms per head in 1956 and 1957 – a considerable improvement in potential consumption from a base that was neither poor nor rich. If the Central Government had kept the amount of grain available for use in the province constant at 290 kilograms per head, it could have extracted exports in 1957–58 amounting to 1.25 million tons. Instead, it obtained none.

Another province which reduced its export burden was Kirin, where per capita grain output fell steadily throughout the period 1953–57. In 1954–55 and 1955–56 the Centre maintained a high level of exports in spite of falling per capita output but concessions were clearly won by the provincial government in 1956–57, when grain was

[19] *NFJP*, 30 August 1956.

actually imported, and in 1957–58 only a very small volume of grain was exported (see Table 26). The *Kirin Daily*[20] claimed that during the First Five Year Plan period grain exports had been sacrificed in the interest of maintaining consumption and this is, indeed, confirmed by the available data: potential grain (output minus exports) was exactly equal in 1953–54 and 1957–58 at 418 kilograms per head. In a sense the cutback in exports is understandable when set against output per head, which had fallen from 513 kilograms in 1953 to 433 kilograms in 1957, but viewed in isolation the 1957 production level was still very high in relation to consumption requirements.

In many provinces, however, local opposition to grain exports had little success. As early as 1955 there were demands in Kiangsi[21] to replace exports by imports, to relieve the 'tense grain situation' within the province. In 1956, the Grain Bureau of Hunan province rejected[22] a call for grain imports following a decline in grain output of 8.5 per cent. It advocated economies in consumption as the appropriate measure. In Chekiang – another major grain exporting province – 'rightists' argued[23] during the Hundred Flowers period that the province should substitute industrial crops (in which they claimed it had a comparative advantage) for grain, and should import grain from other provinces. This view was attacked as localism. Later references (1959)[24] to people in Chekiang who argued that there was 'no alternative but to import grain' show that the issue was not a temporary one. Those who opposed grain exports from Chekiang had history on their side: during the years 1953–57 the Central Government obtained 0.4 million tons of grain exports per annum, from an average per capita output of 309 kilograms, whereas in the 1930s Chekiang had imported 0.4 million tons a year, on a basis of a higher output per head – 334 kilograms, in 1936.[25]

[20] *KJP*, 12 July 1958.
[21] *KSIJP*, 13 September 1955: 'There are some people who do not understand the real cause of the tense grain situation – believe that it is due to an increase in grain exports. This is completely untrue.' *KSIJP*, 23 September 1955, further stated that, for Kiangsi, 'imports are impossible'.
[22] *HHNP*, 6 January 1957.
[23] *CHKJP*, 23 July 1957.
[24] *CHKJP*, 29 September 1959.
[25] *JMJP*, 14 October 1957. One article pointed out that although Chekiang was a grain exporting province, grain supply within the province was below demand: *CHKJP*, 7 March 1957.

The question of provincial grain exports was an important issue in the purges of high-level officials which as has already been pointed out in Chapter 2[26] took place in Kansu, Shantung and Honan during 1957–58. In Kansu it was reported that there had been a 'fundamental struggle'[27] over grain exports during the period of the First Five Year Plan: people had opposed the ending of imports in 1954–55 and had condemned the subsequent exports as excessive, saying that 'If the strength of the old ox becomes exhausted it will die'.[28] The first Party Secretary of Honan province, Pan Fu-sheng, who was dismissed in 1958, had allegedly[29] criticised Mao himself for failing to understand the grain situation in Honan. Pan argued that Honan was *not*, and could not be, a surplus province. On the contrary, imports of 1.15 million tons per annum were needed to rid the province of its perennial grain 'crisis'.

Did the provinces of the South West Region export their grain without a struggle? Direct evidence on the subject for the 1953–57 period is scanty. In Kweichow, the matter appears to have been discussed, for the provincial Government found it necessary to argue[30] the case for exporting grain in order to import cotton, which was said to be so important to the welfare of the Kweichow people. In Szechuan there can be little doubt that the rapid rise in grain exports was opposed and it is no accident that grain 'frauds' in 1954–55 and 1955–56, involving concealment and false reporting of production, occurred in the richest surplus Special Districts.[31] A great deal of evidence on the question of Szechuan's attitude towards its role in the Chinese economy came to light during the Cultural Revolution and this will be examined in Chapter 5. For the moment, it can be assumed that an attitude[32] exposed in Szechuan by the anti-rightist campaign of autumn 1959 – 'grain exports affect production' – was widespread in earlier years.

Finally, just as the Central Government struggled with surplus provinces to extract grain exports, so it also put pressure on deficit provinces to curb consumption, raise output and to become more self-

[26] See p. 64n.
[27] *KAJP*, 26 February 1958.
[28] *KAJP*, 16 August 1958, i.e., do not kill the goose that lays the golden egg.
[29] *HONJP*, 4 July 1958.
[30] *KCJP*, 28 August 1957.
[31] *HHYP*, vol. 70 (no. 8), 1955, pp. 46–7, and *SZJP*, 12 August 1957.
[32] *LSP* (no. 98), 1959.

sufficient. For example, the increase in imports by Liaoning province in 1956–57 was described as a 'serious mistake',[33] and in 1957 the need to achieve grain self-sufficiency was discussed with an increased sense of urgency. The province was reminded that every ton of extra grain output in Liaoning reduced the burden on other provinces. Liaoning was directed to cut its imports in future: 'That Liaoning province has the obligation to do so is beyond question. It is certainly regrettable that the provincial leadership does not appear to have given enough attention to this problem.'[34] Mao, too, criticised[35] the Liaoning authorities for emphasising the growth of industry, compared with that of agriculture, to the point at which grain had to be imported. In response to this pressure to reduce its reliance on grain imports, in April 1958 Liaoning announced[36] a plan for the attainment of self-sufficiency *that year*. Grain output was to reach 8–10 million tons, a rise of 34 per cent, compared with a 23 per cent rise during the First Five Year Plan period; and grain imports were to cease after autumn 1958. This was but one manifestation of the departure from reality which afflicted China during the Great Leap Forward of 1958–59.

[33] *LJP*, 4 September 1957.
[34] *JMJP*, 26 June 1957. See also *LJP*, 8 October 1957: 'the level of Liaoning's grain consumption is not only a problem of this province, but also that of other provinces'.
[35] *WS* (1969), pp. 373–4 ('Notes on Political Economy, 1961–62').
[36] *LJP*, 3 March 1958.

4

GRAIN CONSUMPTION, 1953–1957

In this chapter, grain consumption under government planning is considered in four sections. The first examines five aspects of rural consumption in China's twenty-four provinces: its adequacy, stability, growth, the degree of inter-provincial inequality, and finally the effect which prevailing levels of rural grain consumption had on livestock. The second section examines the level of urban grain consumption, concentrating on the impact of rationing, introduced in 1955, and on the provincial differences in consumption. The third section compares rural and urban consumption and in the final section the effect of inter-provincial transfers on average consumption is analysed with reference to selected provinces.

RURAL GRAIN CONSUMPTION

The adequacy of rural grain consumption

Did the Chinese peasants have enough grain to eat during the years 1953–57? To answer this question it is necessary to compare estimates of actual consumption with some standard of total food requirement and with the contribution made by grain in that total. No precise levels can be established for either of these standards, but the following have been adopted as an approximate guide.[1] For the twelve provinces in North, North East and North West China, it has been assumed that the total food required per head of rural population is 2000 calories per

---

[1] Important discussion of calorie requirements are found in Colin Clark and M.R. Haswell, *The Economics of Subsistence Agriculture*, third edition (London, 1967); Colin Clark, *Starvation or Plenty?* (New York, 1970); Colin Clark, 'Economic Growth in Communist China', *CQ* (no. 21), January–March 1965, pp. 148–67; and *Energy and Protein Requirements*, Report of a Joint FAO/WHO Ad Hoc Expert Commitee, Food and Agriculture Organisation of the United Nations (Rome, 1973).

day and that 90–95 per cent of calories are derived from grain. Grain consumption levels providing 1800–1900 calories per head are therefore regarded as 'marginal' to basic requirements, while levels below 1800 calories are classified as denoting 'poor' or 'inadequate' consumption. A consumption range of 1901–2000 calories from grain has been defined (somewhat arbitrarily) as 'high' while consumption yielding more than 2500 calories per head has been classed as 'very high'. For the twelve remaining Chinese provinces in the central and southern areas of China, total calorific requirements have been assumed to be 1900 per head per day, the slightly lower figure being a recognition of the higher temperatures of the south and the smaller size of the people. It has further been assumed that 85–90 per cent of all food comes from grain in these provinces. Grain is therefore required to supply 1600–1700 calories per head. Levels of grain consumption below 1600 calories are classified as 'poor' while those between 1701 and 1900 are deemed to be 'adequate'. In the south, the 'high' consumption category embraces the range 1901–2400 calories and amounts exceeding 2400 calories are classified as 'very high'.

The provincial estimates of grain consumption for 1953–57 are based on output and procurement figures, with deductions for seed,[2] for livestock feed[3] and for some losses in storage.[4] Calorie values[5] have

---

[2] These have been calculated from available data on the composition of grain sown area in each province and on the seed rates used for each grain crop. The latter are cited in many Chinese books on all the grain crops grown. For the amounts estimated see Appendix 9.

[3] Deductions for livestock are bound to be somewhat arbitrary, for it is impossible to know exactly how much grain was actually fed to pigs and draught animals. Allocations laid down under the *san ting* (three fix) regulations have been a very important guide when making plausible estimates. However, the low levels of per capita grain availability in rural areas, together with the small livestock populations (including the seriously inadequate number of draught animals), lead to the conclusion that the amounts of grain actually fed to livestock were less than those recommended. The amounts of grain deducted in our consumption estimates, together with figures for draught-type animals and pigs, 1952–57, are given in Appendix 10.

[4] It has been assumed that 15 per cent of potato output was lost. This is a very conservative assumption.

[5] *Shih-wu ch'eng-fen piao* (*Tables of Food Composition*) compiled by the Chinese Academy of Medical Sciences (Peking, 1963). Since extraction rates differ, the calorie values per 'average' kilogram of unhusked, unprocessed, grain grown varied considerably between provinces. Official statements explaining why ration levels in coarse grain areas were lower (in kilograms) than in rice areas emphasise this point. See, for example, 'Why Grain Norms are Different', *JMJP*, 23 August 1957; 'To Oppose the Central Purchase and Central Supply of Grain is to Oppose Socialism', *CHKJP*, 11 January 1958.

been calculated with reference to the composition of grain output in each province. As the allowances made for feed and losses are the minimum consistent with the available evidence, it should be emphasised that grain consumption is shown here in the best possible light. Table 31 presents the estimates of grain consumption per head of rural population in twenty-four provinces, for each year from 1953 to 1957 and for the period as a whole. For provinces with consumption below the 'adequate' level, defined above, figures in brackets show the calories which could have been supplied from the province's net output (gross output net of seed, feed and losses) – that is, without any government transfers from the rural sector.

If the period as a whole is first considered, Table 31 shows that grain consumption in twenty out of the twenty-four provinces was above the minimum level adopted in this study as 'adequate', and that in ten provinces it was either 'high' or 'very high'. There was, however, a core of provinces which fall into our 'poor' class: Honan, Hopei and Shansi, with a combined rural population of 93 million, or 18 per cent of China's rural inhabitants. And although, on average, consumption in Kansu was adequate, it is worth pointing out that in three out of the five years it was poor, averaging 1573 calories per head per day in 1953, 1954 and 1955. None of the southern provinces had poor (inadequate) levels of grain consumption on average during the period, but Kweichow belonged to that category in the first three years, and was marginally below adequate level overall. Only three provinces (Heilungkiang, Kirin and Liaoning) enjoyed consistently 'high' or 'very high' consumption levels during the five years, while four southern provinces (Chekiang, Hupei, Kiangsi and Kwangtung) were in the high consumption classes in four out of the five years.

A comparison of the actual and potential consumption (from net output) in the marginal and poor provinces reveals some striking cases where Government redistribution reduced rural consumption from what were potentially very adequate levels to levels that were below basic requirements: for example, Honan (1953, 1954 and 1957), Shansi (1954, 1955 and 1957), Inner Mongolia (1955 and 1957), Kansu (1954 and 1955) and Kweichow (1953, 1954 and 1955). To a great extent this reflects the Central Government's need to secure grain exports from as many provinces as possible (see Table 26 above). The important role of Szechuan in China's grain account has been emphasised many times in this study and it is interesting to see the low average levels of rural consumption in that province during the early years of the First Five Year Plan period. From 1707 calories per head per day (that is, only just above basic requirements) in 1953, average consumption fell in 1954 to 1691 calories (slightly below the level of adequacy), whereas production could have provided nearly 2200 calories per head.

To return, therefore, to the question posed at the beginning of this section, the data show that large rural populations in at least nine of China's provinces did not have enough grain to eat in some of the years between 1953 and 1957; furthermore, the data also show that in most cases this was a direct consequence of the Government's procurement policy. Bearing in mind the wide differences in production per head of rural population *within* the provinces (discussed in Chapter 1) grain consumption in many *hsien* (counties) and Special Districts must have been exceptionally low in some years.

Stabilisation and growth of rural grain consumption

Stabilisation of consumption

One of the main advantages claimed by the Chinese Government for the central control of grain was that it permitted the stabilisation of consumption in areas subject to sharp and frequent fluctuations in output. The available figures (Table 32) suggest that in this respect the Government's success was variable.

To be completely successful, large increases in output per head should have been accompanied by relatively small increases in consumption, while big reductions in output per head should have been associated with reductions in consumption of a smaller extent. The struggle between the peasants and the Government, however, often resulted in production and consumption changing in the opposite direction. This phenomenon has already been discussed in Chapter 2 with reference to production and procurement. Here we may simply draw attention to the contrast between 1956 and 1957. In 1956 increased consumption accompanied falling production in eight provinces, while in 1957 the opposite relationship held in nine provinces, reflecting the Government's successful attempt to win back some of the excessive concessions extracted by the peasants in the previous year.

Table 31. *Estimated grain consumption per head of rural population, 1953–57* (calories)*

Northern China

Level	1953	1954	1955	1956	1957	Average 1953–57
Very high 2500+	Heilungkiang 3749 Kirin 3097 IMR 2513	Heilungkiang 3159 Kirin 2915	Heilungkiang 3997 Kirin 3000 Liaoning 2613	Heilungkiang 4868 Kirin 3265 Liaoning 3208 IMR 2779 Kansu 2683	Heilungkiang 3738 Kirin 3674 Liaoning 2604	Heilungkiang 3902 Kirin 3190 Liaoning 2641
High 2001–2500	Liaoning 2300 Shensi 2098	Liaoning 2478 IMR 2410	Sinkiang 2138 Tsinghai 2079	Tsinghai 2317 Shensi 2284 Shantung 2229	Kansu 2119 Tsinghai 2118	IMR 2224
Adequate 1901–2000	Sinkiang 1952	Shensi 1990 Sinkiang 1937	Shantung 1979	Honan 1968 Sinkiang 1942 Hopei 1924 Shansi 1912		Shensi 1991 Sinkiang 1909 Shantung 1939 Tsinghai 1921 Kansu 1904
Marginal 1801–1900	Shansi 1895 (2492)	Shantung 1898 (2208) Tsinghai 1816 (2218)	Honan 1890 (2212) Hopei 1881 (1885)		Sinkiang 1877 (2328) Shantung 1869 (2039) Hopei 1839 (1959)	
Poor under 1800	Shantung 1720 (1859) Honan 1669 (1977) Hopei 1628 (1733) Kansu 1327 (1628) Tsinghai 1274 (1340)	Honan 1730 (2011) Shansi 1650 (2290) Hopei 1617 (1628) Kansu 1600 (2073)	Kansu 1793 (2235) Shensi 1785 (2220) IMR 1654 (3401) Shansi 1631 (1977)		Shensi 1797 (2138) IMR 1766 (2797) Honan 1704 (2016) Shansi 1456 (1947)	Honan 1792 (2081) Hopei 1776 (1833) Shansi 1709 (2232)

Southern China

Very high 2400+				Hupei 2453 Anhwei 2425	Hupei 2524	
High 1901–2400	Hupei 2153 Chekiang 1982	Kwangsi 1988 Kwangtung 1964 Kiangsi 1935 Chekiang 1903	Hupei 2228 Anhwei 2171 Kiangsi 2012 Chekiang 1947 Kwangsi 1923 Kiangsu 1916 Kwangtung 1915 Yunnan 1897 Szechuan 1877 Fukien 1827 Hunan 1817	Yunnan 2287 Fukien 2232 Kwangtung 2209 Kiangsi 2091 Chekiang 2067 Szechuan 2056 Hunan 2019	Yunnan 2278 Anhwei 2224 Kwangtung 2145 Kweichow 2002 Szechuan 1999 Kiangsi 1993 Fukien 1922	Hupei 2239 Anhwei 2090 Kwangtung 2014 Yunnan 1995 Kiangsi 1974 Chekiang 1952
Adequate 1701–1900	Kiangsu 1865 Kiangsi 1841 Kwangtung 1835 Anhwei 1834 Fukien 1742 Kwangsi 1740 Szechuan 1707 Hunan 1707	Hupei 1835 Yunnan 1818 Anhwei 1797 Fukien 1771 Kiangsu 1721 Hunan 1712		Kiangsu 1891 Kweichow 1890 Kwangsi 1796	Chekiang 1862 Kwangsi 1831 Hunan 1825 Kiangsu 1812	Fukien 1899 Kwangsi 1884 Szechuan 1866 Kiangsu 1841 Hunan 1816
Marginal 1601–1700	Yunnan 1694 (2140)	Szechuan 1691 (2195)				
Poor under 1600	Kweichow 1339 (1898)	Kweichow 1459 (1995)	Kweichow 1474 (2026)			Kweichow 1633 (2158)

Notes: * Estimates for 1953–57 in kilograms are recorded in Appendix 8.
Figures in parentheses show possible calories from net output (before government transfers).

Nevertheless, the Government achieved a striking success in its bid to stabilise consumption when production declined greatly in central China during 1954. In Hunan, where output per head of rural population fell by 48 kilograms (14 per cent), consumption remained stable at its 1953 level. In Anhwei a bigger reduction in production, of 52 kilograms per head (16 per cent), resulted in only a 5 kilogram reduction (2.2 per cent) in consumption. In the third province devastated by floods, Hupei, output per head of rural population fell by 96 kilograms or 26 per cent, but less than half of this decline was offset by government action, so that consumption fell by 39 kilograms per head, or by 14 per cent. However, reference to Table 31 shows that even with such a drop in consumption the rural population of Hupei still enjoyed an average grain consumption that was both adequate and higher than its neighbouring disaster-affected provinces.

Against these successful attempts at stabilisation must be put some cases of failure. For example, the peasants of Inner Mongolia and Shensi can hardly have been impressed by the Government's claim that the Central Purchase and Supply policy cushioned the impact of output fluctuations on consumption. During 1954 consumption declined in both provinces in spite of rising production per head and in 1955, when production per head fell, it continued to decline, although not by as much as output. Taking 1954 and 1955 together, in Shensi production per head fell by 37 kilograms and consumption by 36 kilograms; in Inner Mongolia consumption declined by 95 kilograms even though production fell by only 72 kilograms per head. Other examples of the ineffectiveness of the Government's stabilisation policy are to be found in 1957, in Heilungkiang, Liaoning, Kansu, Honan, Shensi, Shansi and Shantung. But, as has already been pointed out, in some of these cases the changes in consumption must be seen against the experience of the Government's procurement policy in 1956.

Growth of rural grain consumption

The determination of the Government to take firm control of the distribution and consumption of grain in 1957 makes an examination of the growth of consumption between the two years 1953 and 1957 less meaningful than it might have been in the absence of campaigns launched in 1957 to curb consumption with seemingly little regard for output conditions. The year-by-year changes in consumption are of

Table 32. *Change in output and consumption* of grain per head of rural population (kilograms)*

		Change					Percentage changes, 1953–57 (per head)	
		1954–53	1955–54	1956–55	1957–56	1957–53	Output	Con-sumption
North East								
Heilungkiang	O	−41	+90	−52	−54	−57	−6.5	+1.8
	C	−49	+92	+92	−128	+7		
Kirin	O	−47	+18	−92	+54	−67	−9.7	+17.4
	C	−20	+12	+29	+39	+60		
Liaoning	O	+19	+15	+79	−37	+76	+21.7	+13.9
	C	+20	+12	+71	−67	+36		
North West								
IMR	O	+34	−106	+166	−233	−139	−25.9	−29.3
	C	−9	−86	+128	−115	−82		
Kansu	O	+58	+21	+93	−40	+132	+50.6	+57.9
	C	+31	+22	+99	−64	+88		
Shensi	O	+8	−45	+52	−69	−54	−15.6	−14.9
	C	−13	−23	+55	−55	−36		
Sinkiang	O	+10	+7	−6	+6	+17	+4.4	−3.6
	C	−2	+23	−17	−12	−8		
Tsinghai	O	+111	+22	−3	+5	+135	+64.9	+66.5
	C	+66	+31	+29	−23	+103		
North								
Honan	O	+9	+19	−4	−18	+6	+2.2	+7.6
	C	+9	+19	+15	−29	+14		
Hopei	O	−10	+24	−31	+39	+22	+9.3	+12.9
	C	+1	+29	+2	−9	+23		
Shansi	O	−23	−35	+57	−65	−66	−19.9	−22.7
	C	−28	no ch.	+34	−55	−49		
Shantung	O	+39	+1	+23	−42	+21	+8.8	+9.1
	C	+20	+9	+24	−36	+17		
Centre								
Hunan	O	+48	+56	−33	+25	no ch.	no ch.	+4.9
	C	no ch.	+14	+31	−33	+12		
Hupei	O	−96	+102	+39	+12	+57	+15.4	+19.6
	C	−39	+55	+31	+8	+55		
Kiangsi	O	−8	+15	+19	+20	+46	+11.9	+7.7
	C	+13	+11	+10	−14	+20		
East								
Anhwei	O	−52	+122	−21	+31	+80	+24.8	+23.2
	C	−5	+47	+40	−29	+53		
Chekiang	O	−10	+17	−3	+3	+7	+2.0	−6.2
	C	−11	+6	+17	−29	−17		

Table 32. (*contd.*)

		Change					Percentage changes, 1953–57 (per head)	
		1954–53	1955–54	1956–55	1957–56	1957–53	Output	Con-sumption
Kiangsu	O	−13	+28	−28	+3	−10	−3.1	+5.0
	C	−10	+31	−2	−8	+11		
South West								
Kweichow	O	+14	+4	+37	+24	+79	+28.8	+46.3
	C	+15	+2	+48	+17	+82		
Szechuan	O	+14	+4	+26	+8	+52	+17.3	+15.5
	C	−2	+23	+24	−11	+34		
Yunnan	O	+18	+13	+32	+2	+65	+21.0	+35.9
	C	+18	+8	+46	+3	+75		
South								
Fukien	O	−22	−7	+42	−9	+18	+5.1	+7.5
	C	+3	+8		−41	+18		
Kwangsi	O	+20	−8	−42	+1	−29	−8.7	+6.3
	C	+34	−9	−18	+8	+75		
Kwangtung	O	+17	−8	+28	−2	+35	+10.2	+15.7
	C	+16	−7	+37	−6	+40		

Notes: * The annual estimates are given in Appendix 8.
O = output per head of rural population.
C = consumption per head of rural population.

greater interest than those which took place over the five years. Nevertheless, as Table 32 shows, rural grain consumption per head rose (in some cases by a large amount) in nineteen of the twenty-four provinces between 1953 and 1957. In fourteen of these production per head also increased but in Heilungkiang, Kirin, Kiangsu and Kwangsi it fell. The *percentage* rise in consumption, 1953–57, actually exceeded the percentage rise in production in eleven provinces.

Grain consumption per head of rural population fell between 1953 and 1957 in five provinces, of which three suffered from declining output per head (Shansi, Shensi and Inner Mongolia). The absolute fall in consumption in all three was a high proportion of the decline in output per head, and in Shansi and Inner Mongolia the percentage reduction in consumption exceeded that in production. During the five-year period consumption in Sinkiang and Chekiang declined even though output increased.

Provincial inequality of rural grain consumption

In Chapter 1 evidence was given of the wide inequalities of grain output per head which existed, both at the provincial and local levels. To what extent did Government redistribution policy reduce such inequalities? This section attempts to answer this question with reference to inter-provincial differences. To isolate the effect of government policy, *net output* (i.e. net of seed, feed and losses) per head of rural population has been compared with consumption. Figure 4 shows the comparison for the twenty-four provinces for the period taken as a whole and it is immediately clear that the dispersion around the mean for output was greater than it was for consumption. In other words, over the five years, Government policy succeeded in reducing inter-provincial inequality of rural consumption from what it would have been on a basis of output. The five-year averages show that the provincial range of net output per head of rural population, around the national average of 300 kilograms, was considerable, from 756 kilograms in Heilungkiang to 195 kilograms in Hopei, the former being 3.9 times the latter. By contrast the range of average *consumption* found in the twenty-four provinces was less – from 424 kilograms per head in Heilungkiang to 195 kilograms in Hopei, making the gap between top and bottom 2.2 times. The national average rural consumption level was 245 kilograms per head. Net output per head of rural population in the different provinces was closely correlated with the level of consumption, and the provincial rank by both net output and consumption per head was almost identical. Inner Mongolia was a notable exception to this generalisation: it was third in rank for net output per head but twelfth for consumption.

Using the standard deviation of the logarithms as an 'index of inequality',[6] for the period as a whole the Government's action was such as to reduce the 'index' of 0.277 for net output per head of rural population to 0.178 for consumption. If, however, the annual inequality indices are compared, the Government's impact in this

---

[6] A.B. Atkinson, 'On the Measurement of Inequality', in A.B. Atkinson (ed.), *Wealth, Income and Inequality* (Harmondsworth, 1973), pp. 46–71.

Table 33. *Indexes of 'inequality' of grain output and consumption per head of rural population, 1953–57*

	1953	1954	1955	1956	1957	Average for period 1953–57
Inequality of net output per head	0.339	0.293	0.284	0.282	0.281	0.277
Inequality of consumption per head	0.223	0.170	0.185	0.197	0.211	0.178

sphere is less impressive. As the figures in Table 33 show, output inequality between provinces declined in each year from 1953 to 1957 (although the decline was very slow after 1955), but consumption inequality, having been reduced quite sharply in 1954, *increased* in 1955, 1956 and 1957. This is a surprising result.

Rural grain consumption and livestock

Despite the fact that under the regulations governing the Central Purchase and Central Supply of grain, provision was made for livestock, a striking feature of the First Five Year Plan period is the minute (and fluctuating) number of pigs relative to rural population, and the inadequate number of working draught animals in most parts of China. Although several factors[7] were responsible for this, an important element was the lack of feed grain.[8] In many provinces rural grain consumption (at times very low) was only sustained at the expense of livestock and this had serious implications for the growth of agricultural output.

[7] These include price policy, the collectivisation and consequent management of draught animals, and policy towards the private sector of agriculture after collectivisation.

[8] Good general surveys are: CCP directive on pigs, 28 February 1957, *HHPYK*, vol. 105 (no. 7), 1957, pp. 75–7; also 'The National Situation Regarding Domestic Animals in 1956', *HHPYK*, vol. 99 (no. 1), 1957, pp. 88–90. Innumerable provincial reports are available but note especially that in 1957 Wang Kuang-wei called for a reduction in the extraction of grain from the peasants of Szechuan in order to allow for the promotion of livestock (*HH* (no. 17), 1957, pp. 25–8).

population, averages for 1953–57 (kilograms).

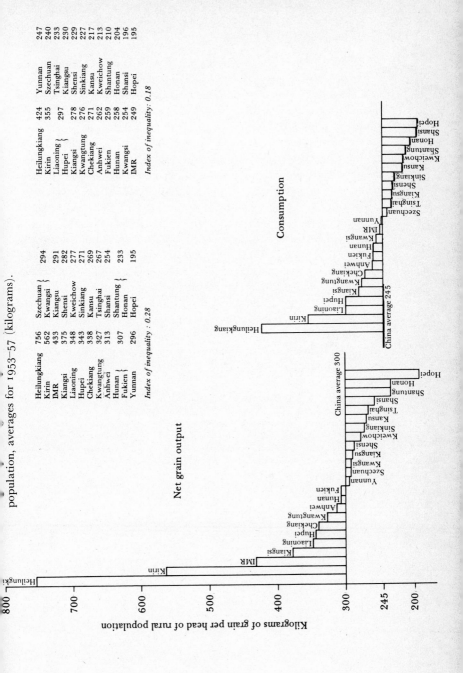

Draught animals

Since 99 per cent of China's arable land relied on draught animals for cultivation and many other kinds of farm work,[9] it might be expected that the preservation of an adequate stock of such animals would be a prime concern of the peasants, and that the necessary grain allocations would be given the same priority as for seed. This was not so. Taking the period 1952–57 as a whole, the number of working animals was below the required level in at least fourteen out of the twenty-four provinces and in many areas the number of draught-type animals declined.[10] Table 34 presents the available data.

The burden of arable land per working animal is ranked in Table 34 from highest to lowest in each of the broad regions of China and in column 4 an approximate figure is given for the maximum area which one strong animal could service in each region. The figures reveal widespread, serious shortages of working draught animals in both 'northern' and 'central' areas. By the end of the First Five Year Plan period this shortage was beginning to impede the growth of grain production,[11] not only because it affected the supply of organic fertiliser, but also because it became increasingly difficult to maintain adequate standards of cultivation on the existing sown area.[12] In

[9] At the end of 1956: Ch'iu Huai, *Yang Niu Hsüeh (Cattle Rearing)*, vol. 1 (Nanking, 1957).

[10] At the end of 1957 the total number of three of China's main working animals – water buffaloes, donkeys and mules – was 4.22 million below the pre-liberation peak: *Duo K'uai Hao Sheng Ti Fa-chan Ch'u-mu (Develop More and Better Livestock Quickly and Economically)* (Peking, 1958).

[11] For a good general analysis see Ch'iao Pei-kuo, 'Research into Problems concerning the Development and Protection of Draught Animals', *NTKTTH* (no. 8), 1957, pp. 22–3.

[12] Note the relationship between changes in the total sown area and in the number of draught-type animals, 1952–57, shown in the table.

	Percentage change in total sown area	Percentage change in draught-type animals
Heilungkiang	+ 18.8	− 18.2
Kirin	no change	− 14.7
Liaoning	no change	− 41.1
Honan	+ 4.8	− 1.6
Hopei	+ 2.3	− 15.5
Shantung	+ 3.3	− 0.2

Source: Appendices 10 and 11.

Table 34. *Provincial distribution of draught animals, 1952–57*

	(1) Net grain available per head of rural population, 1953–57 (kg)	(2) Arable area per working animal, 1952–57 (hectares)	(3) Main change in number of draught-type animals, 1952–57	(4) Maximum burden of land per animal (hectares)
North, NW and NE				
Heilungkiang	514	4.70	−24.2% 1953–57	
Kirin	420	3.98	−26.3% 1954–57	
Liaoning	338	3.85	−41.4% 1952–57	
Hopei	225	2.99	−28.0% 1954–57	
Shansi	230	2.90	+1.1% 1953–57. Constant number	1.0–1.3
Kansu	282	2.38	−11.8% 1954–57. Wide fluctuations	
Shensi	264	2.37	−10.6% 1955–57	
Shantung	234	2.20	Constant number 1952–57	
Honan	233	1.62	−14.2% 1954–57	
IMR	315	1.58	−6.3% in bad year of 1957	
Tsinghai	263	1.50	−11.6% 1952–57	
Sinkiang	342	0.56	Steady increase	
East and Central				
Kiangsu	242	4.30	−7.9% 1956–57	
Anhwei	284	3.48	No increase 1955–57	
Chekiang	284	2.80	−7.6% 1952–57	2.0–2.7
Hupei	314	2.00	−6.1% 1956–57	
Hunan	273	1.73	Upward trend 1952–57	
Kiangsi	294	1.63	Fairly constant 1953–57	
South and SW				
Fukien	285	2.07	−4.9% 1956–57	
Szechuan	262	1.58	Some fluctuations −0.5% 1956–57	
Kwangtung	296	1.12	−5.6% 1956–57	1.6–2.3
Kweichow	236	0.89	Rapid rise 1955–57	
Kwangsi	274	0.85	−10.6% 1955–57	
Yunnan	278	0.73	+39.5% 1952–57	

Sources: Provincial arable areas: Appendix 11a.
Draught animals: Appendix 10b and 10c.

Heilungkiang, where the deficit of working animals was estimated[13] at 3.5 million in 1957 (compared with the existing number of 1.4 million), the decline in average grain yield of 14.7 per cent, 1952–57, was partly attributed to this factor.[14] The deficit in six northern provinces was said[15] to be 8 million, equal to a 40 per cent gap between supply and requirements. Throughout this broad area the substitution of men for animals in ploughing and harrowing was common,[16] while in Hopei[17] there was considerable abandonment of arable land. In East and Central China the main effect of the draught animal shortage was to prevent the extension of double cropping: the increased demand for draught power at the peak seasons, particularly at the turnover period between the harvest of the first crop and the planting of the second, could not be met. This was discovered during 1956 when a bold attempt was made to extend the area of double-crop rice, and the contraction of such activity in 1957 was inevitable.[18] As in the north, the substitution of people for draught animals was reported in provinces such as Chekiang and Kiangsu.

The most authoritative Chinese analysis states categorically[19] that failure to supply adequate feed grain to draught animals was a major factor explaining their shortage and decline during the First Five Year Plan period, and this view is reiterated in many provincial sources. It was pointed out[20] that a large draught animal could eat the grain rations of three people, and some of the recommended grain allocations under the *san ting* (three fix) regulations were indeed very high. For example, the allocation laid down in Liaoning[21] for horses or mules was 500 kilograms per year, while a report in 1957 stipulated[22] that 'large animals' must not be given more than 1278 kilograms per year

[13] *CKNPTK* (no. 5), 1958, p. 14.

[14] See *Mechanisation Bureau*, p. 176 and *HJP*, 25 December 1957.

[15] Hsiao Yü, 'How to Allocate Agricultural Investment', *CHCC* (no. 9), 1957, pp. 5–8.

[16] *Mechanisation Bureau*, p. 4.

[17] *Mechanisation Bureau*, pp. 176–7. In eight special districts of Hopei 1.24 million hectares (equal to 12 per cent of the province's arable land) had not been ploughed 'for several years' in summer 1957, for lack of animal power.

[18] A discussion of this may be found in Kenneth R. Walker, 'Organisation of Agricultural Production' in Alexander Eckstein, Walter Galenson and Ta-chung Liu (eds.), *Economic Trends in Communist China* (Chicago, 1968), chapter 6, pp. 397–458.

[19] *Mechanisation Bureau*, p. 70.

[20] *Ibid.*, p. 4.

[21] *LJP*, 4 September 1957.

[22] *LJP*, 29 September 1957.

(7 catties per day). This must be compared with the peasants' own ration (excluding feed but including seed) of 245 kilograms per head in the province.[23] The livestock feed rates recommended for Liaoning were, it is true, higher than in other provinces, but in Shansi[24] the maximum grain ration per horse and per mule was 400 kilograms, and it was 300 kilograms in Honan.[25] The rate for 'yellow cattle' (*huang niu*) was somewhat lower: 200 kilograms in Honan[26] and 175 kilograms in northern Anhwei.[27] Allowances for water buffaloes were around 30 kilograms per year.[28]

Interestingly Table 34 shows that there was little correlation between net rural grain availability and the adequacy of working animals: Heilungkiang had 514 kilograms of grain per head of rural population (net of seed) and a large deficiency of draught animals while Kweichow, one of the poorest provinces of China, with 236 kilograms of net grain per head, had an export surplus of draught animals.[29] Differences in the type of draught animals used in the two provinces, in the availability of non-grain feed, and in the climate (which affects the death rate) help to explain this paradox. But such contrasts should not obscure the more general point that in eighteen out of China's twenty-four provinces net grain availability was less than 300 kilograms and in thirteen of these there was a deficit of draught animals.

Pigs

The Chinese Government was anxious to increase the number of pigs as they were the country's main source of meat and of fertiliser. Apart from a rapid rise in numbers claimed during 1957, the validity of which must be questioned, China's pig population during the period 1952–57 was small and stationary.[30] On average there was one pig for every 5.2 head of rural population and, excluding Sinkiang with its large Muslim population, the provincial range was from 1:13.0 in

---

[23] *LJP*, 25 October 1956.
[24] *LJP*, 4 September 1957.
[25] *Ibid.*
[26] *HONJP*, 24 October 1956.
[27] *AJP*, 8 October 1957.
[28] See, for example, *ibid.*, and *KSIJP*, 20 September 1955.
[29] *KWCJP*, 31 December 1957.
[30] See Appendix 10a.

Table 35. *The relationship between the number of rural inhabitants per pig and net rural grain availability, 1952–57*

Number of rural inhabitants per pig, 1952–57	Province	Rural population per pig	Net grain available per head of rural population, 1953–57 (kg)
1.00–1.99	nil		
2.00–2.99	nil		
3.00–3.99	Kweichow	3.27	236
	Yunnan	3.27	278
	Szechuan	3.30	262
	Heilungkiang	3.41	514
	Fukien	3.86	285
	Kwangsi	3.90	274
4.00–4.99	Liaoning	4.05	338
	Kirin	4.16	420
	Hunan	4.32	273
	Kwangtung	4.34	296
	Hupei	4.84	314
	Kiangsi	4.88	294
5.00–5.99	Inner Mongolia	5.04	315
	Kiangsu	5.52	242
	Chekiang	5.91	284
6.00–6.99	Hopei	6.68	225
7.00–7.99	Shensi	7.21	264
	Anhwei	7.22	284
8.00–8.99	Kansu	8.48	282
	Shantung	8.50	234
9.00–9.99	Honan	9.70	233
10.00 and over	Tsinghai	11.39	263
	Shansi	13.01	230
	Sinkiang	25.18	342

Sources: Pig numbers: Appendix 10a. Rural population: Appendix 3. Net grain: from output (Appendix 2) and estimates for seed (Appendix 9) and feed (Appendix 10d).

Shansi to 1:3.3 in Yunnan and Kweichow. In Taiwan,[31] where net grain available per head of rural population (1955) was approximately 70 per cent above the average for China, the ratio was 1:1.6. The low consumption of pork in China has already been mentioned in Chapter 1. In the four years 1953–56 average rural consumption was

[31] Data from *Taiwan Statistical Data Book, 1979*, Council for Economic Planning and Development, Executive Yuan (Taipei, Republic of China, 1979) (in English).

4.1 kilograms per head[32] (compared with 11 kilograms in Taiwan)[33] and it fell by 23 per cent[34] during this short period.

As in the case of draught animals, failure to supply enough grain was one of the main reasons for the small and fluctuating number of pigs. Table 36 and Figures 5 and 6 show that the correlation for the period between net grain availability and the rural population–pig ratio was not striking, but it was nevertheless closer than that for draught animals, particularly in the northern provinces. '*San ting*' (three fix) grain allocations laid down for pigs varied from region to region and included 30–70 kilograms per pig per year in north and north east China,[35] 10–50 kilograms in central China[36] and 25 kilograms in the south.[37] Such allowances, however, were not always made by the procurement authorities when transferring grain from the countryside. In 1954–55, for example, peasants slaughtered[38] millions of pigs during the 'storm' which arose over grain procurement.[39] And although, as Chapter 4 has pointed out, some compensation was provided by increased rural resales of grain during the spring of 1955, the imposition of a second round of high grain procurement quotas in autumn 1955, combined with the onset of the collectivisation campaign, led to a further contraction of pig herds. This downward trend continued until summer 1956 when the Government introduced policies designed to reverse the decline. Table 36 shows the extent of the contraction in ten provinces.

The available evidence suggests that a rapid recovery was made throughout China and that by the end of 1957 the number of pigs in many provinces had greatly exceeded their previous peak. Nevertheless, the overall conclusion must be drawn that current levels of grain availability in rural areas were incompatible with the kind of expansion needed to increase pork consumption significantly. The

[32] *Develop More and Better Livestock.*
[33] Ch'en Yueh-eh, 'Food Consumption in Taiwan', in Chinese–American Joint Commission on Rural Reconstruction, Economic Digest Series no. 23, *Agricultural Economic Research Papers* (Taipei, Taiwan, October 1978), pp. 187–97.
[34] *Develop More and Better Livestock.*
[35] See *KJP*, 4 December 1955; *SASJP*, 2 December 1955; *HOPJP*, 10 December 1955; and *HONJP*, 19 June 1956.
[36] *HHJP*, 3 September 1955; *AJP*, 8 October 1957; and *KSIJP*, 20 September 1955.
[37] *FJP*, 24 November 1956.
[38] For example, *NFJP*, 19 January 1955; *SASJP*, 10 February 1955, and *CHKJP*, 5 August 1956.
[39] See Chapter 2.

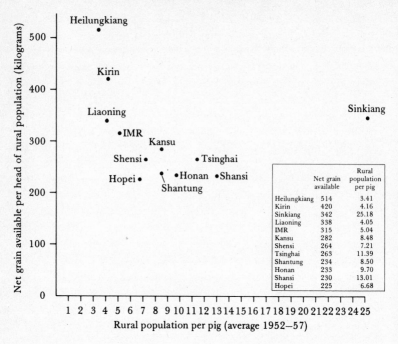

Figure 5. Relationship between net rural grain availability and pig population in twelve north China provinces, 1952–57 (kilograms).

official view expressed[40] in 1958 was that only when grain output per head reached 1000 kilograms would it be possible to carry sufficient livestock to permit the balance of food consumption in China to shift towards animal products and away from grain.

URBAN GRAIN CONSUMPTION

Although many figures relating to urban grain *rations* (theoretical and actual) are available in published Chinese sources they are not by themselves an accurate guide to actual consumption. As has already been pointed out in Chapter 2, some grains were sold off-ration in the towns, both as grain and as processed foods. Fortunately the Grain Bureau published many figures for grain *supplies* to urban and mining

[40] *Develop More and Better Livestock.*

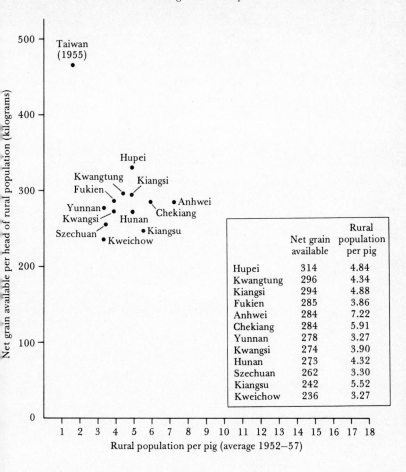

Figure 6. Relationship between net rural grain availability and pig population in twelve south China provinces, 1952–57 (kilograms).

areas during the 1950s and these are a much better basis for consumption estimates. Even so, when using them it is necessary to adopt some assumptions about the percentage of urban supplies consumed by people: some grain was fed to livestock employed in urban transport (especially in north China) and some was used by industry to make non-food products such as starch. Some evidence is

Table 36. *The decline in the number of pigs in ten provinces, 1953–54 to mid-1956*

	Decline in millions	Percentage decline	Time
Honan	−1.317	−31.5	End 1953 (peak) – June 1956
Hopei	−1.214	−22.9	End 1952 (peak) – June 1956
Shansi	−0.242	−28.6	End 1954 – June 1956
Shantung	−2.582	−38.9	End 1953 – June 1956
Hupei	−2.682	−51.8	End 1953 (peak) – Spring 1956
Kiangsi	−0.780	−24.5	End 1953 (peak) – June 1956
Chekiang	−0.965	−25.9	End 1954 (peak) – June 1956
Fukien	−1.460	−41.0	End 1953 – June 1956
Kwangsi	−0.960	−21.1	End 1954 – June 1956
Kwangtung	−2.825	−32.8	End 1954 (peak) – August 1956
China	−17.318	−17.0	June 1954 (peak) – June 1956

Source: Appendix 10a.

available on these allocations.[41] The final consumption estimates, therefore, have been made with reference to both kinds of data. Table 37 presents the results, in calories per head per day, for each of the five years and for the period, classified according to their 'adequacy'.

It will be noticed that the calorie classes in Table 37 differ marginally from those used in Table 31 for rural grain consumption. The same *total* calorie requirements have been assumed for urban as for rural populations, but slightly lower percentage contributions from grain have been adopted for the urban areas: in north China it has been assumed that grain provided 85–90 per cent of total calories, compared with 80–85 per cent in the south.

The most notable feature of the figures in Table 37 is the high average level of urban consumption in most provinces throughout the entire period. In contrast to the situation with regard to rural grain consumption, the urban populations of only four provinces (Shensi, Kwangtung, Fukien and Kweichow) had inadequate levels and only then for part of the five-year period. The exceptionally high consumption in the provinces of the north, north east and north west areas –

[41] See *Nung-ts'un Liang-shih T'ung-kou T'ung-hsiao ho shih-chen Liang-shih Ting liang kung-ying* (*Rural Grain Central Purchase and Central Supply and Urban Grain Supplies*) (Peking, 1955).

with their low winter temperatures and their heavy industrial urban centres[42] – contrasts with the relatively low consumption in the warm, less industrialised provinces of the south, for example, Fukien, Kweichow and Kwangtung. It is interesting that the 'low and stable'[43] grain consumption of the 1.8 million people of Kwangtung's major city, Canton, had to be defended by the authorities, including the Grain Bureau. This was justified in terms of the warm climate, the large supply of non-grain foods available, and the low average age of the population resulting from a high birth rate, so that the number of children under ten years of age accounted for 31–34 per cent of the city's total population. Similarly the high consumption level in urban Shansi (which included the rapidly developing city of Taiyuan) was partly explained[44] by the relatively high average age of the populations in the towns (19 per cent of the province's urban population comprised children under nine years of age compared with 25 per cent in the villages).

Estimates of grain consumption, in kilograms per head of urban population, are recorded in Table 38, together with the average size of urban population in each province during the period. Annual changes in consumption followed a clear pattern. Substantial increases were recorded during 1954 (the year before the introduction of urban rationing) in nineteen of the twenty-six provinces for which estimates can be made. Rationing, implemented in 1955, then reduced average consumption per head by 14.7 per cent: reductions were recorded in twenty-two provinces, in three provinces it remained constant and the only province in which it actually rose was Yunnan. Large increases in urban consumption followed in 1956, however, as a result of the expansion of employment, the urban wage reform, the upward revision of consumption standards allowed and the widespread evasion of rationing. The subsequent general reduction in 1957 reflects the success of the Government's economy drive and a strict enforcement of rationing. If the two pre-rationing years of 1953 and 1954 are compared with the three years when urban rationing was in operation (1955, 1956 and 1957) it is seen from Table 38 that consumption fell

[42] According to *Energy and Protein Requirements*, miners need around 3300 calories per working day, and building labourers need 2880 calories.
[43] *KWCJP*, 11 September 1957; also *LS* (no. 6), 1957, pp. 14–15.
[44] *SASJP*, 11 August 1957 and 15 September 1957.

Table 37. *Estimated grain consumption per head of urban population, 1953–57 (calories)*

Level	1953	1954	1955	1956	1957	Average 1953–57
Northern China						
Very high 2500+	Liaoning 3734 Shansi 3488 Honan 3084 Heilungkiang 2833 Kirin 2758 Shantung 2557 IMR 2542	Shansi 3670 Liaoning 3392 Kirin 2913 Heilungkiang 2879 Tsinghai 2859 Shantung 2773	Shansi 3215 Liaoning 2982 Tsinghai 2859	Tsinghai 3774 IMR 3557 Shantung 2947 Liaoning 2885 Shansi 2664 Heilungkiang 2632	Tsinghai 3558 Shantung 2763 Liaoning 2583	Liaoning 3155 Shansi 3106 Tsinghai 3074 Shantung 2685 Kirin 2560 Heilungkiang 2541 IMR 2530
High 2001–2500	Tsinghai 2319 Peking 2265 Tientsin 2237 Kansu 2222 Hopei 2099 Shensi 2051	Honan 2474 Peking 2446 Tientsin 2400 IMR 2361 Hopei 2237 Shensi 2091	Shantung 2386 Kirin 2315 Heilungkiang 2283 Hopei 2130 Tientsin 2102 IMR 2051 Peking 2021	Kirin 2438 Tientsin 2326 Hopei 2271 Honan 2270 Shensi 2244 Kansu 2210 Peking 2152	Shansi 2494 Kirin 2376 Honan 2271 Hopei 2270 IMR 2244 Peking 2210 Heilungkiang 2152 Kansu 2094 Tientsin 2079 2069 2030	Honan 2360 Tientsin 2219 Peking 2196 Hopei 2179
Adequate 1801–2000			Shensi 1816			Kansu 1992 Shensi 1955
Marginal 1701–1800		Kansu 1730	Honan 1780 Kansu 1728			
Poor under 1700					Shensi 1574	

118

Southern China

	Col 1	Col 2	Col 3	Col 4	Col 5	Col 6
Very high 2300+	Kiangsu 2484 Yunnan 2312	Kiangsu 2677 Yunnan 2498 Kweichow 2448 Anhwei 2424	Yunnan 2726 Anhwei 2424	Yunnan 2890 Kiangsi 2326	Anhwei 3151 Yunnan 2689	Yunnan 2623 Anhwei 2483
High 1801–2300	Kwangsi 2291 Anhwei 2278 Shanghai 2025 Kiangsi 2016 Fukien 1912 Kweichow 1898 Szechuan 1854 Hunan 1839	Kwangsi 2269 Shanghai 2126 Hunan 2008 Kiangsi 1966 Hupei 1948 Szechuan 1921	Kiangsu 2049 Kiangsi 1888 Kwangsi 1849	Anhwei 2136 Kiangsu 2097 Kwangsi 2082 Shanghai 1939 Hunan 1855 Hupei 1838 Szechuan 1815 Kweichow 1804	Kweichow 1927 Kwangtung 1865 Kiangsu 1864 Kwangsi 1830	Kiangsu 2234 Kwangsi 2064 Kiangsi 1981 Kweichow 1907 Shanghai 1892 Szechuan 1826 Hunan 1822
Adequate 1601–1800	Hupei 1782 Chekiang 1682	Chekiang 1791 Kwangtung 1639 Fukien 1602	Hunan 1787 Szechuan 1764 Shanghai 1695 Chekiang 1653	Chekiang 1750 Kwangtung 1636	Hupei 1799 Szechuan 1775 Kiangsi 1710 Shanghai 1673 Chekiang 1626 Hunan 1623	Hupei 1789 Chekiang 1700 Fukien 1607 Kwangtung 1603
Marginal 1501–1600			Hupei 1580	Fukien 1575		
Poor under 1500	Kwangtung 1474		Fukien 1462 Kweichow 1457 Kwangtung 1403		Fukien 1484	

Table 38. *Estimated grain consumption per head of urban population, 1953–57 (kilograms)*

	Consumption in kilograms per head of urban population						Urban population 1953–57 (million)	Pre-rationing consumption 1953 and 1954	Consumption under rationing, 1955, 1956 and 1957	Percentage change (%)
	1953	1954	1955	1956	1957	Average 1953–57				
North East										
Heilungkiang	299	316	250	287	224	275	4.708	308	254	−17.5
Kirin	302	319	255	270	259	281	3.426	311	261	−16.1
Liaoning	419	403	331	325	290	354	6.398	411	315	−23.4
North West										
IMR	282	264	228	399	239	282	1.232	273	289	+5.9
Kansu	253	197	197	250	c.235	c.226	1.666	225	227	+0.9
Shensi	236	240	209	256	180	224	2.518	238	215	−9.7
Tsinghai	279	344	344	454	428	370	0.145	312	409	+31.1
North										
Honan	339	275	199	252	247	262	3.300	307	233	−24.1
Hopei	228	247	234	247	236	238	3.614	238	239	+0.4
Peking	246	270	222	234	229	240	3.782	258	228	−11.6
Shansi	395	417	370	305	278	353	1.946	406	318	−21.7
Shantung	275	298	257	314	298	288	3.398	287	290	+1.0
Tientsin	243	265	231	253	222	243	2.988	254	235	−7.5
Centre										
Hunan	261	285	252	264	226	258	3.220	273	247	−9.5
Hupei	232	256	210	244	239	236	3.944	244	231	−5.3
Kiangsi	283	276	265	325	239	278	2.126	280	276	−1.4
East										
Anhwei	280	298	298	270	394	308	3.074	289	321	+11.1
Chekiang	232	247	228	241	223	234	3.380	240	231	−3.7

Kiangsu	295	329	259	266	239	278	5.550	312	255	−18.3
Shanghai	282	296	236	270	233	263	6.718	289	246	−14.9
South West									
Kweichow	245	316	188	227	245	244	1.596	281	220	−21.7
Szechuan	236	244	224	232	223	232	5.946	240	226	−5.8
Yunnan	284	310	337	354	334	324	1.796	297	342	+15.2
South									
Fukien	259	217	198	208	196	216	2.550	238	201	−15.5
Kwangsi	311	308	251	282	c.251	281	1.576	310	261	−15.8
Kwangtung	201	222	190	219	252	217	5.126	212	220	+3.8
China	270	286	244	268	248	263	85.663	278	253	−9.0
Inequality index	0.160	0.169	0.181	0.177	0.183	0.147		0.157	0.165	

Notes:

a. No figures are available for urban grain supplies in Sinkiang (average urban population 0.580 million, 1953–57). In the national estimate it has been assumed that average urban supplies per head of urban population equalled the *official* national average given in *TCKT* (no. 19), 1957, pp. 31–2 and 28.

b. Figures for Peking, Tientsin and Shanghai are based on *total* population. Rural populations were very small and it was not possible to make separate estimates for rural and urban areas.

considerably in eighteen of the twenty-six provinces listed. And among the eight provinces in which consumption *rose* under rationing, the only areas with sizeable urban populations to record significant increases were Yunnan and Anhwei.

The inequality of urban grain consumption between provinces was less than that of rural areas in all five years, as figures in Tables 33 and 38 show. Urban inequality was greater in the three years of rationing than in the 'free' years of 1953 and 1954. Not surprisingly, therefore, it decreased slightly during the relatively liberal year of 1956 and this suggests that the Government's policy of urban rationing was less geared to improving the consumption of the poorer urban populations than to favouring certain areas which were important in industrial development.

RURAL–URBAN GRAIN CONSUMPTION

Several references have already been made, both in this and in earlier chapters, to differences in grain consumption between rural and urban populations. The higher *quality* of urban consumption – with the fine grains comprising a high proportion of the total and with virtually no potatoes being eaten – was mentioned in Chapter 2. Earlier in the present chapter the relative *needs* of rural and urban populations in Kwangtung and Shansi, as related to their age structure, were touched upon when discussing the level of urban consumption. Thirdly, the relative inequality of grain consumption in rural and urban areas has already been compared.

This section focuses on the ratio of rural to urban grain consumption during 1953–57. In those years there was a great deal of rural–urban migration in China. Peasants moved to the towns (in spite of strict government controls) where there were better employment opportunities, social and educational services, and higher money incomes. It has generally been assumed that such migration was also the result of higher levels of food consumption. Does the evidence for grain consumption support this view? Table 39 gives the provincial ratios of rural to urban grain consumption (by weight).

The first point to be made about Table 39 is that urban grain consumption was *not* universally above rural consumption. Averages for the period reveal that, out of twenty-three provinces for which figures are available, in eight provinces rural consumption exceeded

Table 39. *Rural grain consumption as a percentage of urban consumption,*
1953–57

	1953	1954	1955	1956	1957	Average 1953–57
North East						
Heilungkiang	132.8	110.1	176.0	185.4	180.4	154.2
Kirin	113.9	101.6	131.8	135.2	156.0	126.3
Liaoning	61.8	69.2	87.9	111.4	101.7	83.9
North West						
IMR	99.3	102.7	81.1	78.4	82.8	88.3
Kansu	60.1	92.9	104.1	121.6	c.102.1	96.0
Shensi	102.5	95.4	98.6	102.0	114.4	102.2
Tsinghai	55.6	64.2	73.3	61.9	60.3	63.0
North						
Honan	54.6	70.5	107.0	90.5	80.6	77.9
Hopei	78.1	72.5	88.9	85.0	85.2	81.9
Hopei as % Peking	72.4	66.3	93.7	89.7	87.8	81.3
Hopei as % Tientsin	73.3	67.5	90.0	83.0	90.5	80.2
Shansi	54.7	45.1	50.8	72.8	60.1	55.5
Shantung	67.6	69.1	83.7	76.1	68.1	72.9
Centre						
Hunan	93.5	85.6	102.4	109.5	113.3	100.0
Hupei	121.1	94.5	141.4	134.4	140.6	125.8
Kiangsi	91.9	98.9	107.2	90.5	117.2	100.0
East						
Anhwei	81.4	74.8	90.6	114.8	71.3	85.1
Chekiang	118.5	106.9	118.4	119.1	115.7	115.8
Kiangsu	75.3	64.4	93.8	90.6	97.5	82.7
Kiangsu as %Shanghai	78.7	71.6	103.0	89.3	97.5	87.5
South West						
Kweichow	72.2	60.8	103.2	106.6	105.7	87.3
Szechuan	93.2	89.3	107.6	114.2	113.9	103.4
Yunnan	73.6	73.2	69.7	79.4	85.0	76.2
South						
Fukien	93.1	112.4	127.3	144.2	132.1	119.9
Kwangsi	76.5	88.3	104.8	86.9	100.8	90.4
Kwangtung	126.4	121.6	138.4	137.0	116.7	127.2
China	84.1	79.7	100.4	102.2	101.2	93.2

urban, in thirteen provinces it was less than urban and in two
provinces the levels were equal. In the thirteen provinces where rural
consumption was below the urban level, Shansi had by far the lowest
ratio (55.5 per cent) while the ratio in the other provinces of this group
was not nearly so unfavourable, exceeding 80 per cent in eight of them.
Rural grain consumption failed to reach the urban level in all five

years in six provinces (Tsinghai, Hopei, Shansi, Shantung, Kiangsu and Yunnan) and urban consumption was *below* rural during every year in four provinces (Heilungkiang, Kirin, Chekiang and Kwangtung).

Perhaps the most interesting feature of the figures in Table 39, when used alongside the estimates of calories provided per head from grain (Tables 31 and 34), is that in Shansi, Honan, Hopei and, to some extent, Kweichow, the low average levels of rural, relative to urban, consumption throughout the period meant the difference between inadequate and high consumption levels. In other words, in these four provinces, quite apart from the question of the *quality* of grain consumed, the incentive for peasants to migrate to the towns simply to obtain enough grain to eat was very strong indeed. This was not the case in Tsinghai, Shantung, Yunnan, Kiangsu, Liaoning and Anhwei, even though they all had quite low rural–urban consumption ratios.

GRAIN CONSUMPTION AND INTER-PROVINCIAL TRADE

We have yet to consider the effect of inter-provincial grain transfers on consumption. Table 40 and Figure 7 set out the relevant data for 1953–57. In Figure 7, the grey and white bars indicate what average grain consumption (in calories) might have been without provincial exports or imports respectively, while the black bars show the level of actual consumption, ranked from highest to lowest. The redistributive effect of trade is clearly seen. Without trade, the range of consumption would have been from 4402 calories per head per day (in Heilung-kiang) to 1558 calories (in Hopei), so that Heilungkiang's level would thus have been 2.83 times that of Hopei. Actual consumption, on the other hand, ranged from 3423 calories per head (also in Heilungkiang) to 1681 calories (in Kweichow), making the highest 2.04 times the lowest level.

The main question to be answered is: how deeply did exports cut into potential consumption, and how crucial for the standard of living were provincial grain imports?

The burden of exports

Apart from the issue of the quality or type of grain exported, grain

Table 40. *Grain consumption* per head of total population and provincial trade, average 1953–57*

	Kilograms			Calories		
	Consumption	Consumption + exports – imports	Effect of trade on consumption	Consumption	Consumption + exports – imports	Effect of trade on consumption
North East						
Heilungkiang	372	478	− 106	3423	4402	− 979
Kirin	333	386	− 53	3026	3508	− 482
Liaoning	310	236	+ 74	2761	2100	+ 661
North West						
IMR	255	349	− 94	2274	3117	− 843
Kansu	219	227	− 8	1916	1986	− 70
Shensi	228	236	− 8	1986	2056	− 70
Sinkiang	230	230	nil	1993	1993	nil
Tsinghai	244	243	+ 1	2012	2004	+ 8
North						
Honan	208	213	− 5	1853	1898	− 45
Hopei	200	172	+ 28	1814	1558	+ 256
Peking	240	c.5	+ 235	2196	c.48	+ 2148
Shansi	215	218	− 3	1884	1910	− 26
Shantung	215	215	nil	1991	1991	nil
Tientsin	243	c.33	+ 210	2219	c.300	+ 1919
Centre						
Hunan	258	274	− 16	1815	1927	− 112
Hupei	289	291	− 2	2178	2193	− 15
Kiangsi	278	319	− 41	1973	2266	− 293
East						
Anhwei	266	276	− 10	2122	2202	− 80
Chekiang	266	283	− 17	1918	1982	− 64
Kiangsu	236	244	− 8	1889	1953	− 64
Shanghai	263	negligible	+ 263	1892	negligible	+ 1892
South West						
Kweichow	216	234	− 18	1681	1821	− 140
Szechuan	240	266	− 26	1861	2066	− 205
Yunnan	254	263	− 9	2053	2122	− 69
South						
Fukien	251	253	− 2	1844	1861	− 17
Kwangsi	257	264	− 7	1873	1924	− 51
Kwangtung	268	276	− 8	1956	2015	− 59

Notes:
  * Annual estimates for 1953–57 are recorded in Appendix 8.
a. When comparing kilogram and calorie effects of trade, average calories per kilogram differed between provinces on account of the differences in grain production composition.
b. Imports were for both consumption and stocks. The net output of importing provinces were capable of providing the following calories per head, *without* allowance for stocks: Liaoning 2217; Hopei 1614; Peking 274; Tientsin 475; Shanghai 36.

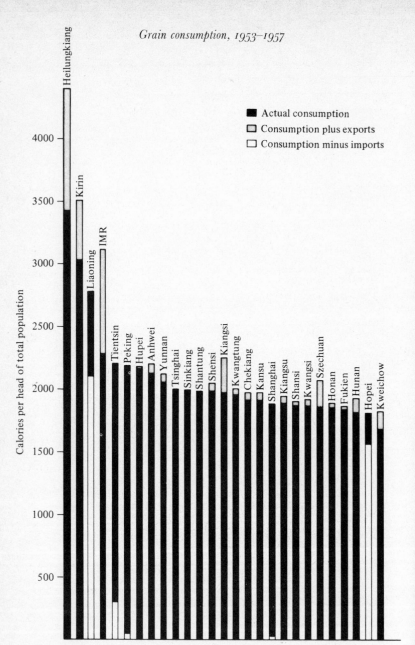

Figure 7. Effect of inter-provincial grain transfers on potential calories from grain per head of total population, 1953–57.

exports from Heilungkiang, Kirin, Inner Mongolia, Anhwei and Yunnan did not seriously reduce consumption to anything approaching insufficiency level: all had consumption levels (from grain) above 2000 calories per head, after exports. Similarly, exports from Shensi, Kiangsi, Chekiang and Kansu did not have a decisive effect on consumption, which remained between 1900 and 2000 calories per head. Although Kwangtung falls into this category of provinces for the five-year period, it must be remembered that T'ao Chu persuaded the Central Government not to demand exports from that province after 1955. The figures for those three exporting years (1953, 1954 and 1955) provide some justification for his stand on this issue: average consumption was 1850 calories per head per day, compared with 1948 calories which would have been possible if all the grain exported had been consumed. This was not a low living standard but it was near enough to the margin for exports to be regarded as an excessive burden. There were nevertheless a number of provinces in which average grain consumption was 1900 per head per day, but which exported enough grain to make a significant difference to the living standard. Among this group it is important to mention Szechuan, Honan, Hunan and Kweichow. Szechuan, as Figure 5 shows, suffered a considerable reduction in consumption as a result of its exports, from a possible 2066 calories per head to 1861 calories. Instead of having quite a high level of consumption the population of Szechuan was among the poorest in China, only slightly better off than Hopei and Honan and considerably poorer than Peking and Tientsin, which consumed Szechuan grain. Allegations made in the 1960s that the leaders of the province refused either to send out grain or even to report production statistics to the Central Government are not, therefore, surprising. In the case of Honan, as we have already pointed out, disagreement between the province and Centre over grain exports became public during the First Five Year Plan period. The basis of Pan Fu-sheng's call for grain *imports* to be substituted for exports is seen in the fact that, in the four years from 1953 to 1956, average grain consumption provided 1807 calories per head, compared with a potential 1870 calories (including the grain exported). Thus, even without exports Honan would not have had a strikingly high level of consumption. Finally, the sacrifices made by Hunan and Kweichow speak for themselves. Perhaps, however, the point should be made that the neighbouring provinces of Kweichow and Szechuan together had a common grievance against the Peking government that should be borne in mind by political analysts of the mid-1960s, when 'independent kingdoms' were set up in various regions of China.

The role of provincial imports

With such small levels of production per head, imports had to provide virtually all the grain required by Peking, Tientsin and Shanghai. That Peking and Tientsin enjoyed such a high level of grain consumption is a reflection of their important status. Hopei, too, was poor in output per head and was therefore dependent on imports. But, unlike Peking, Tientsin and Liaoning, it remained poor, even with the aid of large annual grain imports. Net output in Hopei (with no allowance for stocks) was enough to provide 1614 calories per head, which was approximately 200 calories per head below minimum requirements. Grain imports brought actual consumption up to 1814 calories per head but at this level Hopei was still next to the poorest province in the country. By contrast, among the importing provinces, Liaoning was in a unique position. With grain imports worth 661 calories per head per day, average consumption was 2761 calories, making it third in rank among China's twenty-seven provinces. Without any imports, consumption would have been 2100 calories (after deducting an amount for stock accumulation). Even allowing for the fact that fine grain production per head in the province was low, the high level of imports was, indeed, surprising and must have reflected the demands of the province's heavy industrial cities and the harsh winter climate. However, it is little wonder that in 1957 and 1958 the province was directed to achieve grain self-sufficiency with the utmost urgency.

5

GRAIN PRODUCTION AND DISTRIBUTION, 1958–1962: THE IMPACT OF THE GREAT LEAP FORWARD

During the Great Leap Forward (1958–60) both the production and distribution of grain were seriously disrupted. After an initial increase in production during 1958, national grain output fell as a result of unusually bad weather, bad planning and technical mismanagement. Excessive grain procurement in rural areas reduced the peasants' incentive to grow much more than their subsistence requirements, and this gave the downward spiral a further twist, until output per head fell to the point at which it proved impossible for the Government to mobilise enough grain to meet internal demand, let alone to maintain exports at their previous levels. In 1961, for the first time since the early 1950s, China was forced to become a net importer. And although domestic output recovered fairly quickly after the trough of 1960, grain imports were still required and they continued right through the 1970s. Thus the strategy outlined in 1955 by Ch'en Yün, of achieving national grain self-sufficiency through the 'rational' distribution of domestic production, was no longer tenable in 1961 and the decision to import grain on a large scale marked an historic watershed in economic policy. This chapter argues that the origin of this grain crisis (1959–62) is to be found in the Government's own agricultural policies: even without natural disasters, the agricultural depression was inevitable. Table 41 summarises the chronology of events relevant to this theme.

1958–59: THE COLLAPSE OF ORDERLY PLANNING

Grain production in 1958

Although contemporary provincial statistics relating to grain yields per hectare and to total output in 1958 (and 1959) are useless for

Table 41. *Grain production, distribution and consumption during the Great Leap Forward: a summary*

	Grain production (million tons)	Comments	Grain procurement (million tons)	Distribution and consumption	Foreign trade in grain[t]
1953–57	182[a]	Little change in output structure 1953–57. Output rose by 16.9%; sown area by 5.5%, yield by 10.8%.	GP 50.15 NP 27.85	Central distribution fairly successful. 45 million tons p.a. allocated to rural and urban areas. 10 million tons p.a. inter-provincial transfers.	Net exports of 2.105 million tons p.a.
1958	200[b] 375[c] 365[d] 250[e]	Wild exaggeration of yields led to unrealistic claims of output. Most of increase in output accounted for by potatoes.	GP c.51.00[k] NP 27.5[l]	Rationing relaxed and even abandoned, leading to rapid increase in consumption. Decline in grain circulation. Threat to urban grain supplies.	Net exports of 2.760 million tons.
1959	170[f] (281.55)[g]	Premature contraction of grain sown area following 1958 output claims.	GP 67.49[m] NP 47.60[n]	Some revival of inter-provincial grain transfers in spring associated with implementing Mao's 'chessboard' principle of planning. First sign of local famine, in autumn. Fierce procurement campaign.	Net exports of 3.953 million tons.
1960	144[h]	Technical mismanagement plus declining effort by the peasants. Some severe natural disasters.	GP 51.09[o] NP c.40.18[p]	Distribution system unable to prevent famine and malnutrition in many provinces.	Net exports of 3.241 million tons in spite of internal grain shortage.
1961	147[i]	Search by government for the financial incentives which would restore production.	GP c.54.52[q] NP 25.81[r]	Exhaustion of state grain reserves (30 million tons since 1958) and urgent reduction of urban population implemented to avoid mass hunger in towns. Persistence of famine in some rural areas.	Net imports of 4.460 million tons.
1962	160[j]	New rural policies beginning to show results. Period of 'individual farming'.	GP n.a. NP 25.76[s]	Government discussing how to increase grain circulation. Further reduction in urban population	Net imports of 3.771 million tons.

GP = Gross procurement   NP = Net procurement

Notes and sources:

a. *Collection of Statistical Data* (1958)

b. *HC* (no. 10), 1979, p. 45.

c. SSB Report of 14 April 1959, *HHPYK*, vol. 154 (no. 8), 1959, pp. 51–4.

d. Mao's 'compromise' figure of December 1958 *WS* (1969), p. 268. Mao said that one quarter of the 1958 grain production was sweet potatoes.

e. Chou En-lai, official revision of 1958 estimate of 375 million tons, announced 26 August 1959, *HHPYK*, vol. 163 (no. 17), 1959, pp. 19–24.

f. Calculated from percentages in Yang Chien-pai, *Luen Kung-yeh ho Nung-yeh ti Kuan-hsi* (*On the Relations between Industry and Agriculture*) (Peking, 1981). Confirmed by Hsueh Mu-ch'iao, *Tang ch'ien Wo Kuo Ching-chi roh-kan Wen-t'i* (*Certain Problems at Present in the Economy of our Country*) (Peking, 1980), p. 15.

g. Official figure of the time: *CHYTC* (no. 1), 1960, pp. 1–5.

h. *HC* (no. 5), 1980, p. 28.

i. From percentages in Yang Chien-pai, *On the Relations between Industry and Agriculture.*

j. *HC* (no. 5), 1980, p. 29.

k. 'Over 25 per cent' of output: Yang Chien-pai, *On the Relations between Industry and Agriculture* (25.5 per cent assumed).

l. From gross procurement and rural resales. Rural resales from total sales and urban sales. Total sales: Chinese People's University Trade Economic Education Research Bureau, *Kuo Nei Shang-yeh Ching-chi* (*Chinese Internal Commercial Economy*) (Peking, 1960); Urban sales: *JMJP*, 25 October 1959.

m. Percentage of output given in Yang Chien-pai, *On the Relations between Industry and Agriculture.*

n. *Ibid.*

o. *Ibid.*

p. Assumed to be 28 per cent of output, from evidence in Yang Chien-pai, *ibid.*, p. 149.

q. Can be inferred from data in *Social Sciences in China* (no. 2), 1980, p. 207, if it is assumed that rural grain 'consumption', given as 92.95 million tons, refers to output minus *gross* procurement. Any other assumption is unrealistic.

r. Yang Chien-pai, *On the Relations between Industry and Agriculture*, p. 149.

s. *Ibid.*

t. 1953–56: *TCKT* (no. 19), 1957, pp. 31–2 and p. 28. 1957–62: R. H. Kirby, *Agricultural Trade of the People's Republic of China, 1935–69*, Foreign Agricultural Economic Report no. 83, US Department of Agriculture, Economic Research Service (Washington DC, 1972) (all in raw grain equivalent).

purposes of economic analysis, as they were compiled and published to serve political, rather than economic, ends, the same is not true for grain sown area statistics, which are both plentiful and consistent with those for previous years. They therefore provide an invaluable basis for estimating the level and composition of output in 1958 and because of their importance they are brought together in Table 42. Five main points emerge from these figures:

1. Total grain sown area fell in 1958 by around 2.5 million hectares, or by 2 per cent, compared with 1957.
2. The sown area of rice increased by 1.4 million hectares or by 4 per cent. Particularly noteworthy is the fact that in China's twelve northern provinces the rice sown area expanded by 2 million hectares and was 108 per cent above the 1957 area.
3. The sown area of wheat and soya beans declined.
4. Most dramatic of all, the area under potatoes increased by 7 million hectares, or by 78 per cent. As a percentage of total grain sown area it rose from 7 per cent in 1957 to 13 per cent in 1958.
5. Coarse grains, especially *kaoliang* and millet, contracted by no less than 10 million hectares (21 per cent) and occupied 31 per cent of grain sown area in 1958 compared with 39 per cent in 1957. Within this category, maize sown area (not shown in Table 42) *increased* by around 1.3 million hectares (or 9 per cent).

The 1958 composition of grain sown area was, therefore, reminiscent of 1956 and the logic of the changes was the same: to raise grain output by expanding the sown areas of the three 'high-yielding crops' – rice, maize and potatoes. This policy was to be applied particularly to the poorer, grain deficient areas of north China, as a means of achieving grain self-sufficiency.[1]

In order to estimate grain production from these sown area statistics, the crux of the problem is to apply appropriate yields from the period 1952–57. Three main choices are open: to apply the average annual yields obtained during 1952–57, the worst annual yield of the period or the best yield. On the one hand, it is clear that during the

---

[1] For example, it was planned to increase the rice sown area to the north of the Hwai River from 2 million hectares in 1957 to 5.3 million hectares in 1958 (*CKNP* (no. 10), 1958, pp. 3–8). It was further argued that the extension of the sown area under potatoes in Hopei from 0.5 million hectares in 1957 to 1.8 million hectares in 1958 would 'fundamentally change the grain situation and release Hopei from having to ask other provinces for grain' (*HOPJP*, 6 March 1958). The 'important role' of maize in the attainment of grain self-sufficiency by Liaoning is stressed in *LJP*, 28 July 1958.

Table 42. *Actual and estimated provincial grain sown areas, 1957–58*

	Area (million hectares)		Change in grain sown area 1957–58 (thousand hectares)					
	1957	1958	All grain	Rice	Wheat	Soya	Potato	Coarse grain
North East								
Heilungkiang	6.157	5.839	−318	+83	−270	−356	+225	
Kirin	4.295	4.241	−54	+63	+55	−154	+590	−608
Liaoning	4.330	4.204	−126	+91	−27	+5	+65	−260
North West								
IMR	4.497	4.119	−378	+49	−39	−55	+223	−556
Kansu and Ningsia	3.837	3.903	+66	+304	+153	−96[a]	−295	
Shensi	4.005	3.704	−301	+117	−40	−192[a]	−186	
Sinkiang	1.351	1.517	+166	+37	+43	+13	negligible	+73
Tsinghai	0.388	0.500	+112	+19	n.a.	n.a.	+43	n.a.
North								
Honan	12.800	12.172	−628	+523	+42	−572	+841	−1463
Hopei	9.214	9.295	+81	+600	−70	−155	+1089	−1383
Shansi	4.161	3.648	−513	+27	−153	−132	+262	−517
Shantung	11.676	12.184	+508	+181	+200	+899	+768	−1540
Centre								
Hunan	5.583	5.935	+352	−189	+61	+51	+275	+154
Hupei	5.702	5.700	−2	−29	−45	−74[a]	+110[a]	+36
Kiangsi	3.960	4.011	+51	+117	−67	+29	+70	−98
East								
Anhwei	8.966	8.200	−766	+60	−34	−103	+382	−1071
Chekiang	2.859	2.996	+137	+193	no ch.	−4[a]	+117	−177
Kiangsu	8.854	7.547	−1307	−93	−301	−326	+541	−1128
South West								
Kweichow	2.615	3.061	+446	−95	+39	+14	+333	+155
Szechuan	11.187	11.227	+40	−147	+173	−44	+618	−560
Yunnan	3.443	3.556	+113	+135	+13	+56[a]	+333	−424
South								
Fukien	2.063	1.862	−201	−179	+1	+2	−40	+15
Kwangsi	3.744	3.904	+160	−194	+70[a]	no ch.[a]	+315	−31
Kwangtung	6.804	6.618	−186	−313	+28	+7[a]	+295	−203
Total	132.491	129.943	−2.548	+1.360	−0.168	−1.132	+7.230	−9.388

Notes: a. Assumed figure.
Changes in individual crops do not add up to −2.548 million hectares because of missing figures for Tsinghai.
Braces indicate that figures cannot be separated.
Sources and explanation of estimates: Appendices 2b and 12.

winter of 1957–58 immense efforts were exerted by the rural labour force in applying natural fertilisers to the land and in improving water conservation and irrigation facilities. Such efforts may well have resulted in high grain yields during 1958. On the other hand, it is probable that the *rice* yields achieved, for example on the newly planted areas of north China, were relatively modest, judging from reports, published in the authoritative journal *Chinese Agricultural News*,[2] of the many technical problems encountered in connection with the extension of rice. Secondly, the weather conditions in China were by no means universally favourable in 1958. The wheat-growing area[3] was severely affected by prolonged drought from autumn 1957 to spring 1958 and reports indicate that Liaoning, Shantung, Hopei and Anhwei experienced particularly bad weather.[4] The grain production for these four provinces has therefore been estimated on a basis of the lowest average yield recorded during the period 1952–57. In Honan[5] and Kirin[6] provinces the average yield for the period has been used, while for the remaining eighteen provinces, the best yield has been applied. The national output thus obtained is 201.3 million tons (excluding Peking, Tientsin and Shanghai on a basis of their pre-Great Leap boundaries), an increase of 4 per cent over 1957. This is remarkably close to the official figure, first published in 1979, of 200 million tons. The provincial estimates[7] are given in Table 43.

[2] *CKNP* (no. 4), 1959, pp. 8–12.
[3] *JMJP*, 23 July 1958.
[4] Serious summer drought in Liaoning took a heavy toll of maize production (*LJP*, 28 July 1958). Shantung suffered first from drought and then from floods (*CKNP* (no. 2), 1959, pp. 2–4). Hopei reported its worst drought for fifty years (*SCMP*, no. 1871) while in Anhwei drought hit 49 per cent of the grain sown area: see *HC* (no. 12), 1959, pp. 1–8; also *AJP*, 9 October 1959 and 1 December 1959.
[5] Honan was probably affected by the drought which struck the north China plain.
[6] *KJP*, 23 September 1959.
[7] It is encouraging to find that estimated output is close to the official figure in four provinces for which data are available.

Province	Estimated output (m. tons)	Official output (m. tons)
Heilungkiang	9.3	9.1[a]
Kiangsu	12.6	12.5[b]
Szechuan	25.2	25.3[c]
Kwangtung	12.2	11.7[b]

Attention is drawn to three points arising out of the figures in Table 43. First, the estimates for 1958 reveal that output declined in eight provinces (Liaoning, Kansu and Ningsia, Hopei, Shantung, Anhwei, Fukien, Kwangsi and Kwangtung), and in twelve of the twenty-four provinces grain production failed to reach its previous peak of the 1952–57 period: in addition to the above eight provinces, these included Inner Mongolia, Shensi and Shansi, all of which peaked in 1956, and Kiangsu where output was at its highest in 1955. Secondly, out of a national increase of around 7.8 million tons, the South West accounted for 3.6 million tons, the North West 2.9 million tons, and the Central Region 2.6 million tons. There was only a small rise in output (of 1.3 million tons) in the North East and a decline in the North Region (by 0.8 million tons), in the Eastern Region (by 1.4 million tons) and in the South (by 0.5 million tons). And finally, the changes in the composition of output reflected the changes in sown area: the output of wheat, soya beans and coarse grains declined, but rice production increased by around 3.5 million tons (overwhelmingly due to the expansion in the northern provinces) and potato output rose remarkably, by more than 13 million tons (the increase coming almost equally from the north and south).

More significant, however, are the estimates of grain output per head of total population in 1958 (Table 44). The most important conclusion to be drawn from these figures is that no major change occurred in the provincial pattern of potential grain surpluses and deficits during 1958. The import requirements of the leading deficit provinces actually rose and there were no compensating increases in potential surpluses from traditionally rich provinces. Thus, Liaoning,[8] Hopei and Shantung moved further into deficit and both Fukien and Kwangsi declined into deficit 'range'. However, output per head

a. From a graph in *Chung-kuo Nung-yeh Ti-li Tsung-luen (General Agricultural Geography of China)*, Geography Research Institute, Chinese Academy of Social Sciences (Peking, 1980), p. 343.

b. Supplied to the author in Nanking and Canton, and adjusted to the boundaries of 1957.

c. From 1949 output (*SZJP*, 26 September 1959) and growth rates in *CCYC* (no. 3), 1979, p. 16.

[8] Liaoning was the only deficit province of significance to acknowledge its failure to achieve grain self-sufficiency in 1958 (*JMJP*, 21 October 1958). *JMJP*, 3 October 1958, on the other hand, reported that Hopei had become 'basically self-sufficient'.

Table 43. *Estimated provincial grain production, 1958*

	Total grain (million tons)		Change in production 1957–58 (thousand tons)					
	1957	1958	All grain	Rice	Wheat	Soya	Potato	Coarse grain
North East								
Heilung-kiang	7.859	9.309	+1450	+583	−268	−326	+1461*	
Kirin	5.434	5.797	+363	+227	+25	−122	+937	−704
Liaoning	6.702	6.165	−537	−104	−13	−66	−18	−336
North West								
IMR	2.957	4.523	+1566	+177	+35	+31	+578	+745
Kansu and Ningsia	5.065	4.922	−143	+88	+344	−67	−508*	
Shensi	4.523	5.272	+749	+526	+403	+65	−245*	
Sinkiang	2.034	2.644	+610	+94	+229	+10	nil	+277
Tsinghai	0.644	0.830	+186	n.a.	n.a.	negligible	negligible	n.a.
North								
Honan	12.300	12.960	+660	+872	−276	−279	+1751	−1408
Hopei	10.100	8.984	−1116	+748	−358	−70	+1616	−3052
Shansi	3.565	4.084	+519	+70	+369	−79	+382	−223
Shantung	12.968	12.139	−829	+236	−804	+208	+972	−1441
Centre								
Hunan	11.324	13.277	+1953	+691	+146	+63	+714	+339
Hupei	11.345	11.608	+263	−101	−47	−13	+258	+166
Kiangsi	7.060	7.474	+414	+303	+6	+22	+129	−46
East								
Anhwei	12.350	9.389	−2961	−1267	−989	−551	+817	−971
Chekiang	7.904	9.029	+1125	+708	+27	+60	+545	−215
Kiangsu	12.229	12.623	+394	+414	+144	−152	+1056	−1068
South West								
Kweichow	5.356	6.115	+759	−357	+231	+9	+718	+158
Szechuan	23.258	25.177	+1919	+562	+225	−37	+1680	−511
Yunnan	6.447	7.376	+929	+453	+60	+178	+612	−374
South								
Fukien	4.442	4.048	−394	−399	+17	+87	−118	+19
Kwangsi	5.405	5.367	−38	−373	+63	+16	+279	−23
Kwangtung	12.266	12.813	−83	−642	+20	+13	+511	+15
Total (million tons)	193.537	201.295	+7.758	+3.509	−0.411	−1.000	+13.419	−7.945

Notes: * Included under 'coarse'.

Changes in individual crops do not add up to +7.758 thousand tons because of missing figures for Tsinghai.

For Kirin and Honan, average annual yields for 1952–57 period used.

For Liaoning, Hopei, Shantung and Anhwei, poorest yield for 1952–57 used.

For other provinces, best annual yields for 1952–57 used.

Sources: Yield data, see Appendices 2c and 12.

Table 44. *Estimated grain output per head of total population, 1958 (kilograms)*

	Gross output per head			'Real' output* per head			Changes in gross and real' output per head, 1957–58	
	1957	1958	Change 1957–58	1957	1958	Change 1957–58	Gross	Real
North East								
Heilungkiang	529	596	+67	499	n.a.	n.a.	n.a.	n.a.
Kirin	433	451	+18	419	365	−54	+18	−54
Liaoning	278	247	−31	262	232	−30	−31	−30
North West								
IMR	323	468	+145	292	379	+87	+145	+87
Kansu	347	329	−18	299	n,a.	n.a.	−18	n.a.
Shensi	249	283	+34	n.a.	n.a.	n.a.	+34	n.a.
Sinkiang	361	454	+93	(361)	(454)	+93	+93	+93
Tsinghai	314	386	+72	(314)	(386)	+72	+72	+72
North								
Honan	253	261	+8	217	191	−26	+8	−26
Hopei	235	202	−33	201	132	−69	−33	−69
Shansi	223	249	+26	202	205	+3	+26	+3
Shantung	240	220	−20	175	139	−36	−20	−36
Centre								
Hunan	313	360	+47	285	313	+28	+47	+28
Hupei	368	369	+1	354	347	−7	+1	−7
Kiangsi	379	392	+13	360	366	+6	+13	+6
East								
Anhwei	368	274	−94	320	203	−117	−94	−117
Chekiang	313	349	+36	280	296	+16	+36	+16
Kiangsu	270	274	+4	259	240	−19	+4	−19
South West								
Kweichow	317	353	+36	298	293	−5	+36	−5
Szechuan	322	342	+20	278	276	−2	+20	−2
Yunnan	338	379	+41	320	330	+10	+41	+10
South								
Fukien	303	269	−34	243	218	−25	−34	−25
Kwangsi	279	271	−8	260	238	−22	−8	−22
Kwangtung	323	314	−9	276	254	−22	−9	−22

Notes: * 'Real' output is defined as gross output minus potatoes.

Figures in parentheses indicate no potatoes grown, or amount not known.

Provincial total populations for end of 1958 have been estimated by applying average growth rates for 1953–57.

recovered in some of the provinces that were badly affected by disasters in 1957, such as those of the North West.

Because of the great increase in potato production during 1958, the total output figures obscure a much more delicate situation regarding the availability of 'real' grain and hence the true 'surplus' and 'deficit' position of provinces: increases in 'real' grain availability were much less than those in gross output, and in six provinces increasing gross output per head was actually associated with decreasing 'real' output (Kirin, Honan, Hupei, Kiangsu, Kweichow and Szechuan). It may therefore be concluded that the potential export surpluses of Kirin, Hupei and Szechuan declined in 1958. The figures also show that in five provinces where per capita gross production fell, 'real' or 'net' production declined even more and those provinces would undoubtedly demand more grain imports. This was the position of Hopei, Shantung, Anhwei, Kwangsi and Kwangtung. Attention is drawn to the very low 'net' output per head in the northern provinces of Hopei (34 per cent less than in 1957), Shansi, Honan and Shantung; and to the plight of Liaoning. By contrast, only Anhwei, among the southern provinces of China, suffered a serious fall in per capita 'net' output. The gap between the north and south in grain production per head, therefore, widened somewhat in 1958 and the aim to redress the long-standing grain imbalance between the two regions during the first year of the Great Leap Forward was a spectacular failure.

This was the true position regarding grain production, but it was very different from that claimed by the Central and provincial Governments. As is well known, in the extraordinary political atmosphere of the time, increases of over 100 per cent in output were claimed almost as a ritual and the Central Government accepted[9] the national estimate of 375 million tons for 1958 (excluding soya beans), which represented an increase of 103 per cent over 1957. In December Mao,[10] conceding that much of the increase obtained was accounted for by potatoes, adopted what he clearly considered to be a cautious

---

[9] State Statistical Bureau Report of 14 April 1959 in *HHPYK*, vol. 154 (no. 8), 1959, pp. 51–4.

[10] *WS* (1969), p. 268. By the end of 1958 Mao had begun to hedge his bets: 'Next spring will there be areas which will not be able to eat three meals a day? Kwangtung has sent down an order to eat three meals a day. The masses in Shantung are saying "Now we can eat thin pancakes." Next spring what will they do? At present it is not clear just what the grain production is. Should we eat somewhat less now and more later? All areas should discuss this' (*WS* (1969), pp. 253–4).

estimate of 365 million tons, and in August 1959 Chou En-lai's[11] revised official figure was still 250 million tons, as opposed to the actual level of 200 million tons. It was against this background that the procurement and distribution of grain were carried out for the year from summer 1958 to summer 1959.

Procurement, consumption and distribution 1958–59

Grain procurement in 1958–59 was affected by two contradictory aspects of policy. On the one hand the belief in miracles led senior Government officials to announce that China's 'grain problem' had been solved, so that the people could consume as much as they liked. On the other hand, the formation of the large-scale people's communes in the countryside provided the cadres with the opportunity to mobilise large amounts of grain by depressing the living standards of the relatively rich villages within the communes. As a result there was a violent struggle for grain between the peasants and Government during the autumn and winter of 1958–59.

In summer 1958, there was an unprecedented rise in personal grain consumption in both rural and urban areas. Rationing was relaxed or even abandoned. As P'eng Te-huai later remarked: 'We considered ourselves rich while in fact we were still poor . . . In certain areas where it was believed a bumper grain harvest had been reaped the policy of unified marketing [of grain] was abolished and everyone was encouraged to eat as much as he could.'[12] In urban areas the demand for grain increased with the sudden and large rise in population, associated with the upsurge of employment during the Great Leap Forward in industry and construction. Although accurate figures are not available it is probable that China's urban population[13] rose by at

---

[11] *HHPYK*, vol. 163 (no. 17), 1959, pp. 19–24.

[12] P'eng Te-huai, 'Letter of Opinion', the text of which is published in Union Research Institute, *The Case of P'eng Te-huai 1959–68* (Hong Kong, 1968).

[13] J.P. Emerson considers that the increase in urban population might have been not much below 20 million: John Philip Emerson, 'Employment in Mainland China: Problems and Prospects', in *JEC* 1967, pp. 403–69. C.M. Hou cites a Chinese estimate of 16 million more urban inhabitants in 1958: C.M. Hou, 'Manpower, Employment and Unemployment', in A. Eckstein, W. Galenson and Ta-chung Liu (eds.), *Economic Trends in Communist China* (Chicago, 1968), pp. 329–96. On the other hand, Chinese Peoples' University Trade Economic Education Research Bureau, *China's Internal Commercial Economy* puts the increase in workers and staff at 8 million, and Ernest Ni,

least 13 per cent, or by perhaps 13 million, between the end of 1957 and the end of 1958, and rationing gave way[14] under the strain. In Fukien[15] province, for example, as early as October 1958 it was reported that steel and construction workers would no longer require grain coupons and in November the end of all urban grain rationing in the province was announced.

In rural China the departure from reality was so great that discussions focused on how the embarrassing grain 'surpluses' should be used. The prevailing attitude was one of 'indulge yourself today and tighten up in future' (*hsien k'uan hou chin*)[16] – a view which must have been fostered by Mao Tse-tung himself when he commented on the question of grain supplies in a county of Hopei province during August 1958:[17] 'So your summer harvest will only produce 90 million or so *chin* of grain! And, indeed, your autumn harvest will produce 1100 million *chin*! But since there are only 310,000 or so of you in the whole county, how can you eat your way through so much grain? What are you going to do with the surplus?' Wang Kuo-tsung replied: 'We'll exchange the surplus for machinery.' Chairman Mao said: 'And what will happen if you are not the only ones to have grain surpluses and if every county has them? You may want to exchange your grain for machinery but no

---

Distribution of the Urban and Rural Population of Mainland China: 1953 and 1958 (US Department of Commerce, Bureau of the Census, Foreign Manpower Research Office, International Population Reports, Series P-95, no. 56, October 1960) gives the increase in urban population as 4.5 million (mid-year 1957–58). The Chinese Ministry of Food's figure of 110 million for the urban population at the end of 1959 suggests that the 1958 increase might not have been quite as great as some authors estimate (see *LSP* (no. 79), 1959). In 1981, the new Chinese data which became available added weight to this view – 1958 urban population is estimated 107 million: *JKYC* (no. 1), 1981, p. 20.

[14] See *LSP* (no. 7), 1959 and (no. 9), 1959; also provincial reports for Kwangsi (*KWSIJP*, 19 October 1958), Kweichow (*KCJP*, 9 October 1958) and Inner Mongolia, where the prevailing policy was: 'If they want grain, give it to them' (*LSP* (no. 3), 1959).

[15] *FJP*, 1 October 1958 and 2 November 1958.

[16] *AJP*, 24 November 1958. Many areas did not bother to gather all the autumn harvest and some failed to do so for lack of labour. For example, in Heilungkiang one million tons of grain had not been gathered by mid-October (*HJP*, 13 October 1958). In Kiangsu no effort was made to harvest 2 million hectares of rice (around 2.7 million tons): *HHJP*, 22 October 1958. Livestock were allowed to eat *ad lib* in the maize fields of Inner Mongolia (*LSP* (no. 3), 1959) and in Szechuan a great amount of grain was not harvested (*CKCNP*, 8 November 1958). There were innumerable reports of potatoes rotting in the ground, for example, in Szechuan (*SZJP*, 26 February 1959) and in Shansi (30 per cent of the crop): *SAJP*, 24 October 1958.

[17] *JMJP*, 11 August 1958.

one will want it.' Li Chiang said: 'We are going to make our sweet potatoes into alcohol.' Chairman Mao replied: 'That means that every county will be making alcohol. How can you possibly use so much?' Mao advised the county officials to grow less grain in 1959, to plant more wheat, more oil crops and more vegetables. Wheat should be reserved for people while sweet potatoes and maize should be fed to pigs and cattle.

It is believed[18] that in north China directives were issued at the end of 1958 that maize should be used only for fertiliser and fuel. Many provinces[19] reported the abolition of grain norms for rural rations, seed and feed which, as earlier chapters have shown, had been the foundation of the national plan for grain self-sufficiency. Others raised[20] the norms by as much as 100 per cent. In addition, peasants now consumed higher quality grain at a time when, as we have seen, the production of fine grains in many areas had fallen. For example, in Kweichow,[21] some rural areas in which people had hitherto been accustomed to eating mainly vegetables, potatoes and gourds, now ate only fine grains. In Shantung,[22] peasants criticised cadres who advocated emphasising potatoes in the 1959 plan and they insisted (following Mao's advice) that potatoes should be reserved for livestock.

The formation of the communes brought fundamental changes in the system of food allocation. Grain distribution was carried out on a commune rather than on a household or collective basis, and the principle used for assessing allocations was 'need' rather than work. For a time grain was cooked and consumed in the communal mess-halls. One effect of these changes was that the division of responsibility for grain control between the agencies of the Central Government and the commune was unclear, and there was some duplication of activity. Perhaps the most serious manifestation of this was the phenomenon of 'double grain allocation for the three armies'.[23] This referred to grain

[18] Communication from a former cadre of the Chinese Ministry of Internal Trade.
[19] For example, Fukien (*FJP*, 11 January 1959), Hupei (*CHCJP*, 9 October 1958), Kiangsu (*HHJP*, 8 December 1958), Hunan (*HHNP*, 27 January 1959), and Liaoning (*LSP* (no. 83), 1959).
[20] See *JMJP*, 8 January 1959; also reports from Kweichow (*KCJP*, 19 September 1959), Shensi (*LSP* (no. 3), 1959), Kansu (*KAJP*, 6 October 1959), Inner Mongolia (*NMKJP*, 9 August 1959) and Fukien (*FJP*, 1 October 1958).
[21] *KCJP*, 19 October 1958.
[22] *TCJP*, 28 November 1958.
[23] See *LSP* (no. 7), 1959 and (no. 95), 1959.

allocations made to the large squads of people who were organised by the communes to do water conservation work, road building (and mending) and 'native' steel smelting. Many such groups were given their grain ration by the commune and, in addition, a further grain allocation from the state granaries (under the jurisdiction of the Government, not the communes): overall planning had disintegrated too much to prevent such duplication. It seems clear that the keeping of comprehensive records of grain use in rural areas ceased during the latter part of 1958.

The need for the state to procure and redistribute grain was, however, greater than ever, both in rural and in urban areas. The original target for grain procurement in 1958–59 was set at 51 million tons – the same as had been achieved in 1957–58 – 'in order to remove completely the mental tension which has existed to some extent among the peasants during the past few years over the distribution of grain'.[24] The Ministry of Food later referred to a feasible target of 61 million tons[25] in the light of the enormous national grain output claimed and such a target (9 million tons above 1954–55) must be seen in the context of rising and uncontrolled consumption. The creation of the communes, which for a time established uniform consumption standards covering thousands of households, was, theoretically, conducive to the speedy procurement of a large amount of grain but in fact grain collections were resisted by the peasants probably to a greater extent than in any previous year.

As the 'communist wind' blew throughout rural China during the autumn of 1958, peasants took all manner of action to prevent the state from taking away their grain. They divided it privately among individual households and concealed it in secret underground stores which they guarded with armed sentries. Mao, who actually took the peasants' side over this struggle for grain, later spoke of violence in the countryside in which cadres beat up, arrested and bound peasants in their efforts to lay their hands on grain.[26]

---

[24] Editorial *JMJP*, 27 September 1958.

[25] Twenty per cent above 1957–58: *LSP* (no. 1), 1959.

[26] The most graphic account of these events is given by Mao Tse-tung in speeches at the Chengchow Conference, February–March 1959 (*WS* (1967), pp. 8–49). In February 1959, when addressing provincial and municipal party secretaries, Mao warned that the standard of living of the peasants had declined so much since the summer of 1958 that, unless urgent measures were taken to improve matters, there would be 'tens of thousands of cases of dropsy' (*WS* (1969), p. 278).

How much grain, then, was procured and to what extent did the Government achieve a satisfactory grain balance during 1958–59? The available figures are difficult to interpret and reconcile. According to official figures[27] of the period, gross procurement increased by 8.8 per cent to 55.65 million tons and this national figure is consistent with the provincial data available. However, there can be little doubt that this was a gross exaggeration. The Ministry of Food, for example, reported[28] that by the last week of December 1958, fifteen of China's twenty-four provinces had fulfilled less than half their procurement plans and only three (Honan, Heilungkiang and Kirin) had already attained their targets. Other reports[29] drew attention to slow progress with the collection of the autumn rice crop, to the small amount of coarse grain, soya beans and wheat being procured, and to serious transport and storage bottlenecks, both of which were impeding grain work. As late as February 1959, Mao criticised[30] those provinces which he said had falsely reported the fulfilment of grain procurement targets, with the comment that 'the grain is not yet in our hands', while in March he conceded[31] that the national procurement target for 1958–59 (not specified) had not in fact been attained. More recent evidence[32] suggests that the true level of procurement was 51 million tons and this is the figure adopted here.

As well as the peasants' desire to eat more grain, the Government's difficulty in procuring grain during 1958–59 was partly due to (1) much larger allocations for seed,[33] following directives to introduce close planting; and (2) an increase in the number of grain-deficit households in rural areas, associated with the marked expansion, in some provinces, of the area sown to non-grain crops and the consequent contraction of the grain sown area. Only fragmentary data are available on the scale of the latter phenomenon but as Table 45 shows, in nine northern provinces the grain sown area fell by 1.755

[27] Minister of Food in *JMJP*, 25 October 1959.
[28] *LSP* (no. 1), 1959. Note, too, that according to *LSP* (no. 7), 1959, only 76 per cent of the gross procurement plan had been fulfilled by the end of 1958.
[29] *LSP* (no. 1), 1959.
[30] Speech at the Chengchow Conference, *WS* (1967), p. 13.
[31] *Ibid.*, p. 18.
[32] See Table 41 for source.
[33] A doubling of seed rates was advocated in some areas. See, for example, *SZJP*, 9 October 1958 and *CHCHJP*, 24 March 1959, for reports on Szechuan. The Minister of Food commented on the increased demand for wheat seed: *LSP* (no. 1), 1959.

Table 45. *Changes in sown area in twelve provinces during 1958 (thousand hectares)*

	Grain sown area	Non-grain crop sown area*
North East		
Heilungkiang	−318	+178
Kirin	−54	+120
Liaoning	−126	+86
North West		
IMR	−378	+174
Kansu	+66	+383
Sinkiang	+166	+530
North		
Honan	−628	+479
Hopei	+30	+40
Shansi	−513	+756
East		
Anhwei	−766	+819
Kiangsu	−1307	+966
South West		
Szechuan	+40	+1368
Total for twelve provinces	−3788	+5899

* Sources of provincial total sown area in 1958: Heilung-kiang – *HJP*, 11 November 1958; Kansu – *SCMP*, no. 1924; Sinkiang – *SINJP* 1 October 1958. Remaining provinces: *CIAAA*.

million hectares while the industrial crop area rose by 2.746 million hectares. And in the twelve provinces listed in Table 45 a contraction of the grain sown area, by 3.788 million hectares (worth around 6 million tons of grain), was accompanied by an expansion of the area under other crops of 5.899 million hectares.

Turning to the national grain account during 1958–59, total grain sales were reported[34] to be 50.90 million tons. If this figure is correct, it means that procurement and sales were almost exactly in balance. The official figures show an increase in rural grain sales of 6.1 million tons (34.4 per cent) but only a small rise in urban sales, from 26.15 million

[34] Calculated from percentages in Chinese People's University Trade Economic Education Research Bureau, *China's Internal Commercial Economy*. Urban grain sales are given by the Minister of Food in *JMJP*, 25 October 1959 and rural sales are estimated by deducting urban from total sales.

tons in 1957–58 to 27.05 million tons in 1958–59. The latter seems to be an understatement. However, it was precisely during the winter of 1958–59 that urban grain supplies began to fall short of demand to the point at which China's industrial growth was put in jeopardy. Net procurement per head of urban population[35] was 279 kilograms and if foreign grain exports are deducted, this fell to 253 kilograms. The continuation of the Great Leap Forward in industry thus depended on the Government's ability to increase urban grain supplies during 1959–60.

Provincial figures are almost entirely lacking, but it is clear that until spring 1959, inter-provincial[36] (and intra-provincial) grain transfers declined significantly mainly as a result of the so-called 'base-ist' tendencies of the rural areas. The restoration of a national pattern of grain transfers was one of Mao's main themes in his remarkable speeches to the Chengchow Conference. Describing the nation as 'one chessboard' he advocated a speedy return to the central planning of grain among 'China's 600 million people' including the application of the *san ting* (three fix) norms already abandoned in many areas: upon the 'chessboard' the competing claims between the individual, the collective and the state were to be resolved.[37]

During the spring and summer of 1959 there was an energetic campaign to implement this policy. Many provinces reported that they had both brought grain under tighter control and that they had achieved their plans for grain exports. In Szechuan,[38] for example, a 'great army' of 5 million people was organised to transport grain for export: the guiding slogan for the campaign was 'First the Centre, then the locality; first external [commitments], then internal [commitments].'[39] In spite of the fact that grain output per head, net of potatoes, had fallen in Szechuan during 1958 (Table 44), exports from the province reached their highest point ever, at 2.595 million tons,[40] with obvious implications for the living standards of the local population. National grain exports during the grain year 1958–59 are

[35] Assumed to be 107 million.
[36] Inter-provincial transfers fell in the 1958–59 grain year by 2.1 million tons (unhusked) according to *CCYC* (no. 7), 1959, p. 5.
[37] Speech at Chengchow Conference, *WS* (1967), p. 26.
[38] *SZJP*, 10 September 1959.
[39] *LSP* (no. 111), 1959.
[40] Average of the calendar years 1957 and 1958. (1957 figure from *CHCHJP*, 30 December 1957; 1958 from six-year total (*LSP* (no. 73), 1959 minus five-year total.)

estimated to have risen from 2.37 million tons in 1957–58 to 3.45 million tons, and it appears that by summer 1959 the Government had retrieved some of the control it had lost during the previous eight to ten months.

1959–62: DRAINING THE POND TO CATCH THE FISH

Grain production in 1959–60

In addition to the deleterious effect which a decline in incentives had on grain production in 1959, three factors combined to bring about a 15 per cent reduction in output, to 170 million tons. These were (1) the reduced sown area, (2) widespread natural disasters, and (3) technical mismanagement associated with deep ploughing, close planting and water conservation work. Chinese and Western[41] analyses of the Great Leap Forward have always emphasised the influence of the second and third of these items, but in fact the reduction of the grain sown area played a decisive role and, unlike the other factors, it can be quantified.

The contraction of the grain sown area in 1959 was the result of a directive, initiated by Mao in 1958, to implement the so-called 'three–three system' of arable land utilisation, in which grain would only occupy one-third of the land.[42] The context of this extraordinary proposal, of course, was the claim that the 'grain problem' had been solved by the doubling of output in 1958. Although this revolutionary change in land use was advocated as a long-term measure, the political atmosphere of the time led to an immediate decline in the grain sown area for 1959. The implications of this change were recognised by the Government during the first few months of 1959 but by then it was too late to reverse the process and the spring and summer crops were reduced. Table 46 presents the national figures, and shows that grain sown area contracted by 12.491 million hectares, or by 9.6 per cent. On a basis of average grain yield per sown hectare, 1952–57, this

---

[41] The best study of Chinese agriculture during this period is Kang Chao, *Agricultural Production in Communist China 1949–1965* (Milwaukee and London, 1970).

[42] *JMJP*, 24 October 1958, attributes the system to Mao, but Liu Shao-ch'i was also associated with its inception in Kiangsu during the summer of 1958. See *NCNA*, 29 September 1958. A detailed discussion of the policy is found in *TLCS* (no. 1), 1959, pp. 28–31.

Table 46. *Grain sown area, 1958–59*

	Grain sown area (million hectares)		Change 1959/58 (thousand hectares)	Percentage change 1959/58
	1958	1959		
Rice	33.127	29.667	− 3460	− 10.4
Wheat	26.844	25.330	− 1514	− 5.6
Soya	12.372	9.479	− 2893	− 23.4
Total fine	72.343	64.476	− 7867	− 10.9
Potatoes	c.16.773	11.606	− 5167	− 30.8
Coarse	c.40.827	41.370	+ 543	+ 1.3
Potatoes and coarse	c.57.600	52.976	− 4624	− 8.0
Total (million hectares)	129.943	117.452	− 12.491	− 9.6

Sources:
1958: Author's estimate from provincial figures.
1959: Official figures. Rice: *JMJP*, 8 August 1960. Note that provincial figures suggest a total of 29.9 million hectares. Wheat: *CIAAA*. Provincial figures suggest a total of 25.6 million hectares but *Honan Hsiao-mai Tsai-p'ei Hsüeh* (*A Study of Wheat Cultivation in Honan*), Honan Agricultural Science Academy (Peking, 1960) indicates an area of 23.3 million hectares. Soya, potatoes and coarse: *CIAAA*.
Total area: By addition.

implied a reduction in output of 17 million tons and leaves the remaining reduction of 13 million tons (compared with 1958) to be explained with reference to other factors. The sown area of fine grains declined more than that under coarse grains and among the former the area under soya beans fell the most, by 23 per cent.

Wheat output was badly affected by a prolonged drought[43] during the winter and spring of 1958–59 and many central and southern provinces also reported bad weather.[44] However, relatively high yields may have been obtained in the rice-growing areas in view of their

[43] See, for example, reports on Shansi (where drought affected 30 per cent of total sown area): *SASJP*, 24 May 1960; Shensi: *SESJP*, 25 November 1959; Hopei: *HOPJP*, 31 December 1960; Shantung: *JMJP*, 18 September 1959 (4.7 million hectares drought-stricken, or 40 per cent of the average area sown to grain, 1952–57); Hupei, which had seventy rainless days: *TJP*, 24 November 1959; Anhwei (drought hit 3.6 million hectares, equal to 40 per cent of the average annual sown area, 1952–57): *AJP*, 1 December 1959; Szechuan (3.9 million hectares affected, or 38 per cent of the average annual grain sown area): *TJP*, 24 November 1959.
[44] Hunan: *HHNP*, 6 October 1960; Kiangsu: *HHJP*, 3 November 1959; Fukien: *FJP*, 26 October 1959; Kwangtung: *NFJP*, 3 October 1959; Kweichow: *KCJP*, 12 February 1960; Chekiang: *CHKJP*, 3 October 1960.

Table 47. *Estimated composition of grain output per head in 1959 (kilograms)*

	Actual output per head, 1952–57		Estimated output per head, 1959		Estimated change in output per head, 1952–57 to 1959	
	Per head of total population	Per head of rural population	Per head of total population	Per head of rural population	Per head of total population	Per head of rural population
Rice	125	145	119	145	−6	no change
Wheat	36	42	27	33	−9	−9
Soya	16	18	11	14	−5	−4
Total fine	177	205	157	192	−20	−13
Potatoes	31	36	33	40	+2	+4
Coarse	86	99	63	76	−23	−23
Potatoes and coarse	117	135	96	116	−21	−19
Total	294	340	253	308	−41	−32
Total calculated from official figures	294	340	256	310	−38	−30

Notes:

a. Assumptions for grain yields in 1959 are: poorest average annual yield obtained in 1952–57 for wheat; second highest yield for rice; average yield for other grains.
b. Total population in 1959 assumed to be 664 million and rural population 549 million.

irrigation and drainage facilities and this must be considered when making output estimates for 1959. Such estimates of output per head, based on available sown area figures and assumed grain yields (using those obtained during 1952–57), are given in Table 47.

Average grain output per head of total population in 1959 was only 256 kilograms, compared with 294 kilograms in 1952–57. This was 7 per cent below the self-sufficiency standard of 275 kilograms adopted in this study. The estimates for individual grains in Table 47 indicate that only potato production per head showed any increase over the average for 1952–57. The declining per capita output of wheat, soya beans and coarse grain mainly affected the poor, urbanised area of northern China, and this increased the pressure on the Government to procure more grain in the south for redistribution in the north. Using, once again, the available figures for grain sown area in 1959 and assumed yields based on the years 1952–57, estimates of grain output per head have also been made for fourteen of China's provinces and estimates for a further four provinces have been made from actual output figures. In nine out of the eighteen provinces listed in Table 48, per capita output was below the lowest point of the period 1952–57 and in this respect the provinces of north China were worse than those of central and southern areas. The figures show the erosion and even disappearance of provincial grain surpluses: for example, Szechuan, China's biggest grain exporting province during the period 1953–58, moved into 'deficit' range, with output per head estimated at 214 kilograms. In the four northern provinces of Shensi, Honan, Shansi and Shantung, all of which had provided some grain export surpluses during the previous seven years, output per head fell to below 200 kilograms. And although estimates for 1959 cannot be made, it is likely that the two major importing provinces – Hopei and Liaoning – moved further into deficit, so that the demand for provincial grain imports was probably higher than in any year since 1952.

Grain procurement 1959–60

The low levels of grain output per head of *rural* population meant that the Government was bound to meet strong opposition when it tried to procure enough grain to satisfy requirements right across the national 'chessboard'. It was precisely in this area of activity, however, that it grossly miscalculated. Only months after Mao had warned the Party not to commit 'Stalin's error'[45] when dealing with the peasants, Government cadres were collecting what turned out to be the largest amount of grain ever, during the anti-rightist campaign[46] organised by Mao in answer to P'eng Te-huai's famous attack on the entire Great Leap Forward strategy.

Gross procurement in 1959–60 reached the remarkable level of 67.49 million tons, which was 32 per cent above the 1958–59 amount, from an output of 170 million tons, 15 per cent *below* that of 1958. Even worse, net procurement rose from 15.9 per cent of output in 1958–59 to 28 per cent in 1959–60.[47] As a result the amount of grain left per head

[45] Speech at the Chengchow Conference, *WS* (1967), p. 26.
[46] Described as 'a brutal struggle and a ruthless blow': 'Facts about Liu Chien-hsün's Crimes', *SCMM* supplement no. 32.
[47] The 1953–57 ratio was 15.3 per cent.

Table 48. *Estimated grain output per head in eighteen provinces, 1959*

| | Grain sown area | | | | Estimated and actual grain output (million tons) | Estimated output per head of population | | | |
| | Million hectares | | Thousand hectares ± change | Percentage change | | Per head of rural population (kg) | | Per head of total population (kg) | |
	1958	1959				1959	Lowest 1952–57	1959	1952–57
North East									
Heilungkiang	5.839	5.396	−443	−7.6	8.889[a]	937	822 (1957)	567	529
Kirin	4.241	4.020	−221	−5.2	4.440[b]	517	573 (1956)	344	402
North West									
IMR	4.119	3.825	−294	−7.1	3.179	430	397 (1957)	328	323
Kansu	3.903	3.522	−381	−9.8	3.907	305	261 (1953)	260	231
Shensi	3.704	3.334	−370	−10.0	3.423[b]	222	292 (1957)	183	249
Sinkiang	1.517	1.533	+16	+1.1	2.334	470	372 (1952)	399	335
Tsinghai	0.500	0.403	−97	−19.4	0.500[a]	267	208 (1953)	231	194
North									
Honan	12.172	10.467	−1705	−14.0	9.728	219	249 (1952)	195	235
Shansi	3.648	3.123	−525	−14.4	2.676[b]	202	266 (1957)	163	223
Shantung	12.184	11.066	−1118	−9.2	10.284[b]	207	238 (1953)	186	224
Centre									
Hunan	5.935	5.530	−405	−6.8	11.810	363	297 (1954)	319	272
Hupei	5.700	4.996	−704	−12.4	8.589	325	274 (1954)	272	238
Kiangsi	4.011	3.533	−478	−11.9	6.566	406	380 (1954)	344	332
East									
Anhwei	8.200	7.162	−1038	−12.7	8.943	294	271 (1954)	260	246
Kiangsu	7.547	7.353	−194	−2.6	9.962[a]	274	302 (1952)	231	267
South West									
Szechuan	11.227	10.300	−927	−8.3	15.800[a]	242	282 (1952)	214	260

South									
Fukien	1.862	1.689	−173	−9.3	3.727	316	334 (1954)	247	276
Kwangtung	6.618	5.608	−1010	−15.3	8.875[a]	291	320 (1952)	241	278

Notes:

a. Actual output.

b. Output in these provinces has been estimated by applying *lowest* annual yield in the period 1952–57. Estimates for other provinces are based on the *average* yield for 1952–57 (see Appendix 2c).

Sources: Sources of sown area and yields are given in Appendices 12 and 3. Sources of actual output data: Heilungkiang: *General Agricultural Geography of China*. Tsinghai: *CCYC* (no. 11), 1980, p. 66. Kiangsu, Szechuan and Kwangtung: Figures supplied to author in Nanking, Chengtu and Canton.

Estimates of total population are based on 1958 and a growth rate in 1959 of 0.3 per cent (the national increase). Rural populations have been estimated from 1958 by assuming a decline of 1.1 per cent (following the national estimated change). The latter is based on the assumption that China's urban population was 115 million in 1959.

Table 49. *Grain procurement and estimated consumption in sixteen provinces, 1959–60*

	Maximum annual gross procurement 1953–57 (million tons)	Gross procurement[a] in 1959 (million tons)	Estimated grain consumption per head of rural population (calories per day)	
			Net of seed and feed	Net of seed only
North East				
Heilungkiang	3.791 (1955)	c.4.480	4111	4485
Kirin	2.430 (1953)	2.573	1977	2180
North West				
IMR	1.756 (1956)	1.745	1601	1770
Kansu	1.105 (1957)	1.269	1552	1871
Shensi	1.294 (1954)	1.246	1179	1304
Sinkiang	0.450 (1957)	0.962	1761	2486
Tsinghai	0.165 (1957)	0.250	1192	1287
North				
Honan	2.994 (1955)	c.4.129	1192	1290
Shansi	1.254 (1954)	1.274	936	1035
Shantung	2.940 (1954)	3.000[b]	1458	1523
Centre				
Hunan	3.186 (1953)	3.685	1904	1944
Hupei	2.940 (1957)	2.813	1864	1930
East				
Anhwei	3.800 (1957)	3.749	1574	1635
Kiangsu	4.450 (1954)	c.3.529	1544	1636
South West				
Szechuan	6.098 (1957)	7.187	1380	1457
South				
Kwangtung	3.775 (1954)	c.3.224	1551	1635

Notes and Sources:

a. Heilungkiang: Gross procurement was 12% above 1958–59 (*LSP* (no. 98), 1959). 1958–59 is difficult to assess. Some sources suggest that the plan of 4.4 million tons was fulfilled but *HJP*, 13 October 1958, argued that it had proved difficult to collect 3.2 million tons in 1957–58 and that the creation of the communes had made procurement harder. 1958–59 is therefore put at 4 million tons. Kirin: From figures in *KJP*, 12 July 1958, *LSP* (no. 16), 1959, and *KJP*, 22 November 1958. IMR: *NMKJP*, 10 December 1959. Kansu: From figures in *LSP* (nos 86 and 90), 1959. Shensi: *SESJP*, 21 November 1959. Sinkiang: From figures in *SINJP*, 1 February 1959 and in *LSP* (no. 100), 1960. Tsinghai: *LSP* (no. 88), 1959. Honan: 2.7% above plan (*LSP* (no. 99), 1959). 1959–60 plan not known. 1958–59 plan was 2.814 million tons. Mao revealed that procurement in Honan was particularly high in 1959–60 and we can assume 3.5 million tons. Shansi: *LSP* (no. 89), 1959. Shantung: 'Highest ever' (*LSP* (no. 99), 1959) therefore 3 million tons was minimum in 1959–60. Hunan: From figures in *HHNP*, 20 December 1959 and *LSP* (no. 98), 1959. Hupei: From

of rural population (for seed, livestock feed, stocks and personal consumption) fell from 303 kilograms to 223 kilograms.[48] When commenting on this blunder in 1962, Mao blamed the faulty output statistics: 'When we did not have very much grain we insisted on saying that we had.'[49]

Out of sixteen provinces for which figures are available, gross procurement in 1959–60 was higher than in any previous year. Table 49 presents this evidence, together with estimates of the effect which such procurement levels might have had on rural consumption. In line with the national total of rural grain resales, such provincial sales have been assumed to be 10 per cent below their average for 1953–57. In column (a) an allowance has been deducted for seed and livestock feed, while in column (b) consumption estimates are net of seed only. Table 49 contains some strikingly low estimates of rural grain consumption, even without any deduction for livestock feed. In the northern provinces of Shensi, Tsinghai, Honan and Shansi the peasants clearly did not have enough grain to eat after the state had taken its quotas for the towns and for possible export. And in view of the wide disparities of production *within* provinces, the provincial averages must hide some severe local famines, notably in Shantung and Szechuan.

Although 1960 was worse, hunger and famine began to affect China as early as autumn 1959. According to Hsüeh Mu-ch'iao,[50] 'a great many peasants came close to famine' at that time. An interesting report[51] on Kwangtung published during the Cultural Revolution

[48] Retained grain per head of rural population 1953–57 was 290 kilograms.
[49] Speech of 24 September 1962 at the Tenth Plenum of the Eighth Central Committee held at Peitaiho and Peking, *WS* (1969), p. 432.
[50] Hsüeh Mu-ch'iao, *Certain Problems at Present in the Economy of our Country*, p. 76.
[51] *SCMP*, no. 4018.

Notes and Sources to Table 40 (*cont.*)

figures in *HUPJP*, 15 September 1959 and *LSP* (no. 95), 1959. Anhwei: *AJP*, 1 May 1960, and 1958–59 figure (obtained from six-year total in *LSP* (no. 84), 1959 and five-year total). Kiangsu: Assumed plan fulfilled. *LSP* (no. 98), 1959 and *LSP* (no. 86), 1959. Szechuan: Assumed plan fulfilled. *SZJP*, 1 October 1959 and 26 May 1960. 7 million tons is the figure cited by the Provincial Grain Bureau, Chengtu, in an interview with the author in 1982. Actual rural sales have been used: figures from the Provincial Grain Bureau. Kwangtung: 4% above plan (*LSP* (no. 95), 1959). Plan estimated at 3.4 million tons (from 1957–58 and 1958–59). Cancellation of 0.3 million tons (*SCMP*, no. 2126), hence plan of 3 million tons.

b. Minimum figure.

claimed that in 1959 there was an increase in the number of people suffering from malnutrition – 'characterised by the symptom of swelling'. In Hopu *hsien*, where the situation was particularly bad, 'a large number' of inhabitants were reported[52] to have died of famine.

The slaughter and starvation of livestock[53] affected grain production in two ways. In .the first place it reduced yields via the supply of organic fertiliser. Secondly, as the number of draught animals declined, it restricted the area which the peasants could cultivate: they had neither the strength nor the incentive to pull the ploughs themselves.[54] It is little wonder, therefore, that in Szechuan where a decline in 'activism' was accompanied by 'confusion and disorder'[55] in

[52] *Ibid.*
[53] A process which began in 1958. Only a few figures are available, but they suggest that the decline was considerable.
Livestock during the Great Leap Forward

	Large animals	Pigs
China	−31.0% (1957–61)	−48.3% (1957–61)
IMR	−28.5% (1959–60)	
Tsinghai	−62.1% (1957–60)	−66.0% (1957–60)
Shantung	−41.9% (1957–60)	n.a.
Kwangtung	−23.4% (1957–60)	−37.1% (1957–60)

Sources:
China: *NYCCTK* (no. 4), 1981, pp. 19–23.
    IMR: *Yao Chung-shih Fa-chan Ch'u-mu yeh* (*We Must Emphasise the Development of the Livestock Industry*), Agricultural Economics Research Institute, Chinese Academy of Social Sciences (Peking, 1980); *Nei Meng-ku Tzu-chih-ch'ü Ching-Chi Fa-chan Kai-Luen* (*A Summary of the Economic Development of the Inner Mongolia Autonomous Region*) (Huhehot, 1979), p. 310.
    Tsinghai: Large animals: *Tsinghai She-hui K'o-hsüeh* (*Tsinghai Social Science*) (no. 3), 1980, pp. 13–20 (Peking People's University Reprints F10 (no. 2), 1981, pp. 113–20). Pigs: *Tsinghai Ch'u-mu yeh Ching-chi Fa-chan Shih* (*History of the Economic Development of the Livestock Industry in Tsinghai*), Tsinghai Livestock Office (n.p., 1980).
    Shantung: *NYCCWT* (no. 2), 1981, pp. 13–21 and p. 8.
    Kwangtung: 1960 figures from P. Nolan, 'Rural Incomes in Kwangtung Province 1952–1957' (unpublished PhD thesis, University of London, 1981), quoted with kind permission of the author.
[54] See speech (mimeo) made by Hsüeh Mu-ch'iao at a section meeting of the State Economic Commission, 14 March 1979, entitled 'In Economic Work We Must Grasp the Laws of Economic Development'. In Shantung 0.67 million hectares of wheat (10 per cent of 1957 sown area) were ploughed and harrowed by hand in 1961: *NYCCTK* (no. 4), 1981, pp. 19–23.
[55] *SWB*, 23 December 1967.

production, the provincial newspaper stressed the need to establish the right balance between consumption and procurement 'to prevent the masses from harbouring the misconception that the state has taken away all the grain'.[56]

At the side of the low levels of rural consumption prevailing in 1959–60, the high volume of provincial grain exports is striking: Kansu[57] exported 0.361 million tons, Honan[58] 0.935 million tons, Szechuan[59] 2.244 million tons and Hunan[60] 0.440 million tons (in the third quarter of 1959 alone). As late as March 1960 an 'export high tide'[61] was still running in Honan in the face of a poverty-stricken peasantry. Foreign grain exports reached their highest level, at 3.96 million tons (for the calendar year of 1959), compared with 2.94 million tons in 1958. Moreover, in the short run, by procuring such a large amount of grain, the Government was able to increase urban grain supplies and thus to ensure the continuation of the industrial Great Leap Forward: net procurement in 1959–60 was around 414 kilograms per head of urban population with no allowance for foreign exports, or 380 kilograms per head net of such exports. But it was only a short-run success. In fact it was, as Mao later admitted, a case of 'draining the pond to catch the fish',[62] the full consequences of which were to be faced within the next twelve months.

Production and procurement in 1960–61 to 1962–63: the end of grain self-sufficiency

In 1960 grain production declined by 15.6 per cent, to 143.5 million tons. It then recovered slightly during 1961 and 1962, by 2.8 per cent

---

[56] *SZJP*, 24 May 1960. Reports from Shantung (*TCJP*, 5 June 1960) and Yunnan (*LSP* (no. 129), 1960) also emphasised the need to establish rational *san ting* norms for rations, seed and feed.

[57] *LSP* (no. 94), 1959.

[58] *LSP* (no. 111), 1959.

[59] Plan figure in *LSP* (no. 99), 1959 and report of plan fulfilment in *LSP* (no. 94), 1959.

[60] *LSP* (no. 84), 1959.

[61] *LSP* (no. 126), 1960.

[62] This was Mao's description of the 'erroneous' extractive agricultural policy practised by Stalin. In 1966 Mao commented: 'We have also had several years of experience in draining the pond to catch the fish . . .' *WS* (1969), p. 633. Mao made several other references to the adverse effects of grain procurement policy during the Great Leap Forward period. See *WS* (1969), p. 432 (speech of 24 September 1962); *WS* (1969), p. 456 (speech of 13 February 1964); *WS* (1969), pp. 633 and 639 (speech of 12 March 1966) which specifically mentions excessive (and illegal) grain taxation in Kiangsi.

and 8.5 per cent respectively. Average output per head of total population in 1960 was 217 kilograms, which was 26 per cent below the six-year average for 1952–57 and 7 per cent below the average for 1949–51. Although details have not yet been published in China relating to the severity of the food crisis at this time, it is admitted by leading Chinese officials that 'not a few people'[63] died of starvation. And according to official figures, the shortage of food had a significant effect on the growth of population: the average death rate rose from 11 per thousand in 1957 to 17 per thousand in 1958–61, while the birth rate declined from 34 per thousand in 1957 to 23 per thousand in 1958–61.[64] Total population rose very little in 1959, fell in 1960 by 0.3 per cent and in 1961 by a further 1.7 per cent, but increased by 3.4 per cent in 1962, as food output improved. Total population thus fell by 13 million between the peak of 1959 and the lowest point of 1961.[65]

At the time, matters relating to famine and population were not discussed openly in China. However, some vivid details of conditions in rural areas are to be found in the secret journal of the Chinese People's Liberation Army, *Bulletin of Activities*, copies of which were made available to Western readers in 1963.[66] The journal discusses the incidence of hunger and malnutrition[67] within the army itself, and

---

[63] Hsüeh Mu-ch'iao's speech of 14 March 1979, 'In Economic Work We Must Grasp the Laws of Economic Development'. The decline in incentives is also discussed in several articles published since 1978. See, for example, Wang Keng-chin and others, 'To Speed up the Growth of Agricultural Production we must Fully Pay Attention to the National Interests of the Peasants', *CCYC* (no. 3), 1979, pp. 22–8. (The authors list the 'communist wind', the 'wind of exaggeration', 'high grain procurement' and 'blind targets' as factors which led to a decline in peasants' incentives. A similar analysis is given by Yu Kuo-yao, 'A Few Views on the Question of the Trends in China's Agricultural Production', *HC* (no. 5), 1980, pp. 28–30.)

[64] 1958–61 averages are in *CCKH* (no. 3), 1980, pp. 54–8. 1957 vital rates are in S. Chandrasekar, *China's Population. Census and Vital Statistics* (Hong Kong, 1959).

[65] Total population for 1957 and 1958 are official figures cited by J.S. Aird, 'Reconstruction of an Official Data Model of the Population of China', Foreign Demographic Analysis Division, Bureau of Census, US Department of Commerce, 15 May 1980 (mimeo). Total population for 1959 is from 1961 and information relating to the change in total population, 1959–61, in Yang Chien-pai, *On the Relations Between Industry and Agriculture*, p. 122. Total population for 1960 and 1962: *NYCCWT* (no. 2), 1981, pp. 58–9; and for 1961, from 1962 and natural increase in *JKYC* (no. 1), 1981, p. 20.

[66] For a translation see J. Chester Cheng (ed.), *The Politics of the Chinese Red Army*, Hoover Institution Publications (Stanford, 1966).

[67] A rapid rise in the number of cases of oedema after September 1960 was reported in February 1961: *ibid.*, pp. 295–301. See also pp. 283–95 for a discussion of the reaction of soldiers to deaths in their families from dropsy and oedema.

there are also several references to the condition of the peasants, especially as it affected 'social order' in the countryside. According to the *Bulletin*, people in 1961 were saying:[68]

Chairman Mao lives in Peking. Does he know about the everyday life of the peasant? So much grain was harvested. Where has it gone?

Is it the order of Chairman Mao that people should eat vegetables? The workers repairing the Chung-Nan-hai have a ration of 30 catties [15 kilograms] of grain each month. Still they complain that they have no strength to do the work. The peasants eat only vegetables and sweet potatoes and have no grain. We should not ignore the problems of life and death among the common people.

At present what the peasants eat in the villages is even worse than what dogs ate in the past. At that time, dogs ate chaff and grain. Now the people are too hungry to work and pigs are too hungry to stand up.

Mao Tse-tung described[69] the grain situation in Honan, Shantung and Kansu as 'grave'. In Honan, said to be in 'total darkness'[70] during 1961, output per head may have dropped to 145 kilograms per head, with total output reported at 'pre-liberation'[71] level. In the 'serious famine'[72] which followed in 1962, dropsy, oedema and starvation (of people and draught animals) were widespread and large numbers of peasants migrated from the 'stricken' areas of the province. During the Cultural Revolution, when Liu Chien-hsün (First Party Secretary of Honan) was attacked for implementing 'rightist' agricultural policies, it was claimed[73] that Honan had imported 3 million tons of grain during the five years from 1961 to 1965. Liu's opponents argued that these imports in fact reduced the peasants' incentive to grow grain and that they became too reliant on such aid: Honan, they said, was 'like a beggar carrying a golden bowl'.[74] No firm data, however, were presented in support of such a view. Information collected from the

---

[68] *Ibid.*, p. 13 (December 1960).
[69] *WS* (1967), p. 261 (Speech at the Ninth Plenum of the Eighth Central Committee, 18 January 1961).
[70] 'Honan Paper's Further Denunciation of Wen Min-Sheng', 20 October 1967, *FBIS*. Wen was alleged to have said: 'We will have everything if we have food . . . The less procurement the better.'
[71] 'Facts about Liu Chien-hsün's Crimes'.
[72] A statement attributed to T'ao Chu, first secretary of Kwangtung, who visited Honan in March 1962: *SCMP* supplement, no. 193.
[73] 'Facts about Liu Chien-hsün's Crimes'.
[74] *Ibid.*

hundreds of thousands of refugees who entered Hong Kong in 1961 and 1962 suggests that parts of Kwangsi and Kwangtung also suffered from famine. One Red Guard publication of 1967 reported[75] that 20,000 people had died of starvation in Techeng *hsien*, Kwangtung, in 1960, following the alleged failure of the provincial authorities to send grain to relieve the grain shortage. The few provincial estimates which can be made of per capita grain output in 1960–62, together with the national averages, are given in Table 50.

At a time when provincial grain deficits were increasing to unprecedented heights, Heilungkiang and Szechuan were no longer in a position to act as the nation's granary.[76] Szechuan *imported* grain in 1960, 1961 and 1962, while Heilungkiang imported grain in 1961 and 1962. In 1961 the Szechuan provincial newspaper described the level of agricultural output as 'low'.[77] Shortages of farm labour and draught animals, 'inactivity', 'negative thinking', failure to implement appropriate 'three fix' grain norms, and natural disasters, were all listed[78] as reasons for the 'empty fields' throughout the province. It was further reported in 1961 that the rice sown area had contracted and that potatoes would be of great importance in the food supply during autumn.[79] Living standards showed 'some improvement'[80] during 1962 but by mid-August draught animal shortages were still serious in 'grain bases' such as Wenchiang and Mienyang.[81] This evidence must be borne in mind when considering the allegations[82] made during the Cultural Revolution against Li Ching-ch'uan, Szechuan's First Party Secretary. According to leftist groups, Li made Szechuan an 'independent kingdom' during the early 1960s and to demonstrate the province's independence he suspended grain shipments, thus repudiating Mao's principle of 'the whole nation one chessboard'. Aside

---

[75] *SCMM*, no. 578.

[76] *NYCCTK* (no. 4), 1981, pp. 19–23. Szechuan imported 0.23 million tons of wheat in 1960–62 according to the Provincial Grain Office, Chengtu. (Communication to the author in 1982.)

[77] *SZJP*, 7 September 1961.

[78] See especially *SZJP*, 2 August 1961 on 'Li Ta-chang's Views on Eliminating the Empty Fields'.

[79] *SZJP*, 26 August 1961.

[80] *SZJP*, 20 January 1963.

[81] *SZJP*, 12 August 1962.

[82] Of particular interest are: 'Li Ching-ch'uan's Sabotage of Mao's 1958–59 Agricultural Instruction', *SWB*, 23 December 1967 and other reports in *SWB*, 28 October, 19 November, 12 June and 4 June (all 1967).

Table 50. *Estimated grain output per head of total population in twelve provinces, 1960–62 (kilograms)*

	Average 1952–57	1960	1961	1962
China	293	217	227	238
North East				
Heilungkiang	598	366	335	199
Liaoning	282	—	183	—
North West				
Tsinghai	276	186	—	—
North				
Honan	257	145	—	—
Hopei	244	186	—	—
Shantung	254	151	—	—
Centre				
Hunan	304		220	—
East				
Kiangsu	271	176	214	220
South West				
Kweichow	269	—	—	209
Szechuan	293	181	192	191
South				
Kwangsi	299		*c.*227	
Kwangtung	306	238	247	265

Note: Brace indicates that the figure is an average for 1960–62. Figures for individual years are not known.

Sources: Production

Heilungkiang: From graph in *General Agricultural Geography of China*, p. 343. Liaoning: *Ts'ai-mao Chan-hsien Chi-nien Chou En-lai Tsung-li Wen-chi (Essays Commemorating Premier Chou En-lai on the Finance and Trade Front)* (Peking, 1979), p. 56. Tsinghai: *Tsinghai Social Sciences* (no. 3), 1980, pp. 13–20. Honan: From information in *SCMM* supplement, no. 32, and grain output for 1949 (from figures in *An Economic Geography of N. China*, p. 158). Hopei: Output per head given in *FBIS*: communication from Dr A. L. Erisman. Shantung: *NYCCWT* (no. 2), 1981, pp. 13–21 and p. 8. Hunan: *Hsin Hsiang p'ing-luen (New Human Commentary)* (no. 4), 1979, pp. 2–3. Kiangsu: Figures kindly supplied by Kiangsu Agriculture Office in Nanking. (These relate to the post-1958 boundaries, and the 1952–57 average has therefore been adjusted, for consistency.) Kweichow: From figure for 1957 and information in *JMJP*, 27 December 1979. Szechuan: From production figures given to the author by the Szechuan Provincial Agriculture Office, 1982. Kwangsi: Based on estimated average output for 1949–51 and information in *HC* (no. 9), 1978, p. 41. Kwangtung: Estimates of production department, Ministry of Agriculture, Kwangtung Province, supplied to the author, 1979.

Population

The provincial populations for 1960–62 have been estimated from the 1957 totals, by applying the national rates of increase for each year during the period 1957–62.

from the political issues involved in the attack on Li, the main point here is that there was without doubt an economic basis for the decision to cease exporting grain. And this, of course, is an important reason for the large amount of foreign grain imported by China after 1960, for Szechuan's average annual grain exports during the three years from 1956 to 1958 had amounted to 2.68 million tons, or 50 per cent of China's average foreign imports per year in 1961 and 1962. Such was the importance of Szechuan to the national economy.

In spite of the slump in grain output during 1960, the Government persisted with its procurement policy of 'draining the pond to catch the fish'. Gross procurement was cut to 51 million tons in 1960–61 (equal to the 1958–59 level) but *net* procurement remained at 28 per cent of output. As a result, average per capita grain *availability* in the countryside[83] was only 191 kilograms, compared with 223 kilograms in 1959–60. As in 1959–60, the Government extracted enough grain from the peasants to feed the towns and to continue exporting grain to foreign countries: net procurement was, on average, 308 kilograms per head of urban population after deducting the 3 million tons exported. At the same time, grain stocks[84] accumulated during earlier years were run down. And for the moment, the Great Leap Forward in industry continued, with heavy industrial output growing by no less than 26 per cent in 1960.[85]

At the beginning of 1961, however, the Government was forced[86] to adopt a new economic strategy which involved the provision of more food for the peasants and also the retrenchment of industrial activity. To stimulate agricultural production, the burden on the peasants was, at last, reduced. In 1961–62 net grain procurement fell from 40 million tons in 1960–61 (28 per cent of output) to 26 million tons (17.5 per cent of output) and this left 225 kilograms of grain per head in the peasants' hands.[87] In 1962–63 net procurement was stabilised at around 26

[83] Rural population in 1960 is estimated at 542 million by deducting an assumed urban population of 120 million from the total population of 662 million.
[84] Ch'en Yün, in a secret speech of May 1961, states that stocks, which had totalled 18.2 million tons in June 1957, fell to 7.4 million tons in May 1961, of which 5.1 million tons were old grain (*ch'en liang*). See *Ch'en Yün T'ung-chih Wen-kao Hsüan-pian 1956–1962 (A Selection of Drafts of Comrade Ch'en Yün 1956–62)* (Shanghai, 1982), pp. 122–3.
[85] Yang Chien-pai, *On the Relations Between Industry and Agriculture*, p. 121.
[86] See Mao's speech to the Ninth Plenum of the Eighth Central Committee, 18 January 1961, *WS* (1967), pp. 258–66.
[87] Rural population is estimated at 541 million, from the total population of 651 million and an assumed urban population of 110 million.

million tons, which represents a further reduction in the ratio, to 16 per cent of output, only slightly above the 1953–57 ratio of 15.3 per cent.

The main consequence of the reduction in procurement, however, was that the urban population, which had grown during the Great Leap Forward by 30 per cent, could no longer be fed from domestic supplies: in 1961–62 net procurement per head of urban population was 235 kilograms and in 1962–63 it was still only 258 kilograms. The Government therefore set about organising a massive migration from the towns back to the countryside[88] and this not only reduced the need for marketed grain but it also provided the agricultural labour needed for raising farm production. Secondly, the Government finally accepted the fact that China had no alternative but to import grain from abroad. The changes in production and procurement from 1958–59 to 1962–63, associated with this decision, are summarised in Table 51.

In 1961 (calendar year) China's foreign grain exports fell from 3.281 million tons to 1.168 million tons, while imports rose from 40,000 tons to 5.628 million tons. Having been a net grain exporter of 3.241 million tons in 1960, therefore, China became a net importer, in 1961, of 4.460 million tons. Details of China's grain trade 1958–63 are given in Table 52.

The net imports of 1961 and 1962 were only 2.7 per cent of national grain output but they were nevertheless equal to 55 per cent of the average annual provincial grain exports in the period 1953–57. Here lies their significance. They amounted to approximately 14 per cent of all urban grain requirements and were more than adequate for the combined needs of Peking, Tientsin and Shanghai. As figures in Table 51 show, such imports were sufficient to raise urban grain supplies from 235 kilograms to 274 kilograms per head in 1961 and from 258 kilograms to 296 kilograms in 1962.

The continuation of foreign grain exports throughout 1961–63 (mainly of rice), ranging from 1.2–1.5 million tons a year, indicates that the Government's grain distribution system did not fail altogether: some provincial surpluses were clearly procured and mobilised for foreign trade but no evidence is available to show the origin of these surpluses.

[88] Hsüeh Mu-ch'iao, *Certain Problems at Present in the Economy of our Country*, p. 17. Hsüeh remarks that these people 'changed from being workers who consumed marketed grain to workers who produced grain'.

Table 51. Grain procurement, 1958–59 to 1962–63. A national summary

	Output (million tons)	Procurement Gross (million tons)	Procurement Net (million tons)	Net procurement ratio (%)	Output per head of rural population (kg)	Grain available per head of rural population (kg)	Net procurement per head urban population (kg) Before deducting foreign exports	Net procurement per head urban population (kg) Net of foreign exports
Average 1953–57	181.60	50.15	27.85	15.3	343	290	323	300
1958–59	200.00	51.00	27.15	13.6	360	311	254	228
1959–60	170.00	67.49	47.60	28.0	310	223	414	380
1960–61	143.50	51.09	c.40.18	28.0	265	191	335	308
1961–62	147.47	c.54.52	25.81	17.5	273	225	235	274
1962–63	160.00	n.a.	25.76	16.1	279	234	258	296

Notes: Rural population for the years 1958–62 is estimate from total population and (assumed) urban population.
Total population, 1958: 662 million. 1959: 664 million. 1960: 662 million. 1961: 651 million. 1962: 673 million.
Urban population, 1958: 107 million. 1959: 115 million. 1960: 120 million. 1961: 110 million. 1962: 100 million.

Table 52. *China's foreign trade in grain, 1958–63*

	Exports (thousand tons)			Imports (thousand tons)			Total (million tons)		Net exports (+) and imports (−)
	Rice[a]	Soya[b]	Other[c]	Wheat	Coarse	Rice[a]	Exports	Imports	(million tons)
1958	1807	961	167	127	31	17	2.935	0.175	+2.760
1959	2239	1343	380	9	nil	nil	3.962	0.009	+3.953
1960	1677	1176	428	nil	nil	40	3.281	0.040	+3.241
1961	634	343	191	4093	1446	89	1.168	5.628	−4.460
1962	854	350	149	3957	1160	7	1.353	5.124	−3.771
1963	914	357	181	5455	65	139	1.452	5.659	−4.207

Notes:
a. Whole grain equivalent
b. Including soya bean oil in bean equivalent
c. Coarse grain and wheat
Source: R. H. Kirby, *Agricultural Trade of the People's Republic of China, 1935–69.*

In its 'Resolution on Further Strengthening the Collective Economy of the People's Communes and Expanding Agricultural Production' (December 1962), the Central Committee of the Chinese Communist Party summarised,[89] in the light of many years' experience, its view of the relationship between grain procurement, incentives, and production. The 'Resolution' directed that procurement in different areas should be fixed at 'appropriate levels' and then stabilised for a 'definite period'. Any grain acquired above the quotas laid down was to be bought at prices arrived at by 'discussion':

We should obtain agricultural products by economic rather than by administrative means . . . In this the problem of price is especially important . . . the real interest of the peasants should be given due consideration . . .
. . . The more agricultural products a region sells to the state, the more industrial products it should receive.[90]

[89] A translation of this important, secret document is available in C.S. Chen and Charles Price Ridley, *Rural People's Communes in Lien-chiang. Documents Concerning Communes in Lien-chiang County, Fukien Province, 1962–63*, Hoover Institution Publications (Stanford, 1969), pp. 81–9.
[90] *Ibid.*, p. 84.

Such views had been expressed before, in the 1950s, but had not been heard during the Great Leap Forward. Their expression in 1962 thus marked the beginning of a new attempt to employ a system of grain administration that embodied the right combination of direct controls and market incentives – a combination which had eluded the Chinese Government during the previous nine years. Eighteen years later, in 1979, the Central Government still found it necessary to call for the implementation of the very same policy.

6

CONCLUDING REMARKS: GRAIN PRODUCTION AND DISTRIBUTION IN THE LATE 1970s

1953–62: A SUMMARY

The redistribution of large amounts of grain was needed in China during the 1950s in order to meet the deficits of the many poor rural areas which existed and, secondly, to feed the large and rapidly growing urban population. Average output per head of *rural* population, 1952–57, was 339 kilograms and at the provincial level the range was from 245 kilograms in Hopei to 905 kilograms in Heilungkiang. In the early part of this period, over 72 million peasants lived in 343 *hsien* in which average output per head was below 200 kilograms, while 43.6 million people in 252 *hsien* enjoyed a level of grain output per head above 500 kilograms. Average output per head of *total* population, 1952–57, was 293 kilograms and again, if the three autonomous cities are excluded, Hopei province was the poorest, with 223 kilograms per head, and Heilungkiang the richest, with 593 kilograms. The three autonomous cities – Shanghai, Peking and Tientsin, with a total population (1952–57) of 13.5 million – required 3.5–4.0 million tons of grain a year, but together they only produced 0.4 million tons per annum.

The Chinese Government was determined to meet all the demands for grain from domestic production and to do this it implemented the policy of Central Purchase and Supply. This, as we have seen, involved the central planning of grain distribution throughout the entire country including, of course, rural and urban grain rationing. In relation to the enormity of the task, this policy was effective for several years. During the five years 1953–57, the Government procured 50 million tons of grain per year, of which 22 million tons were sold in rural deficit areas and 23 million tons were sold in urban areas. Provincial grain exports averaged 10 million tons per year while provincial imports were 8 million tons. Two million tons of grain were exported to foreign countries each year and during the period 15 million tons were added to stocks. Redistribution within and between provinces was thus carried out on a considerable scale and this raised consumption where it would otherwise have been below subsistence level. It assisted the chronically poor and in many cases it stabilised consumption in areas affected by severe harvest fluctuations.

Even so, the Government encountered strong opposition from peasants as well as from those provincial authorities which regarded their export burdens as excessive. At prevailing levels of per capita output the maintenance of grain self-sufficiency inevitably involved the forcible acquisition of more grain than the peasants wished to release. In the struggle for grain, procurement fluctuated from year to year, and the Government experienced great difficulty in maintaining a positive balance between grain acquisition and disbursement. The State Planning Committee summed up the problem of implementing the scheme as follows:

> Historical experience shows that when grain acquisition exceeds a certain limit the results are not good. This is because if acquisition is excessive it is easy to create grain deficit households, making grain supplies in rural areas tense. As a result it becomes necessary to sell the extra grain acquired back to the villages or the incentive of the peasants to produce grain will be adversely affected. This therefore impedes the growth of grain production and makes difficulties for increasing grain acquisition in the following year. And this is in the interests of neither the state nor of the peasants.[1]

Some provinces successfully resisted the Centre's demand for grain exports while others, notably Szechuan, supplied amounts which resulted in very significant reductions in 'domestic' consumption. In order to obtain enough grain, the Government used political rather than economic methods. For example, in the anti-rightist campaign of 1957–58, peasants and cadres who allegedly opposed the Central Purchase and Supply of grain found themselves classified as enemies of socialism. There was undoubtedly a great deal of opposition to the policy throughout the Chinese countryside.

Nevertheless, the policy would probably have survived in a less rigorous form if the Great Leap Forward had not occurred. As Chapter 5 showed, the decentralisation of planning which ensued was ac-

[1] Sun Wei-tzu, 'Principles for Organising Grain Circulation Planning', *CHCC* (no. 2), 1958, pp. 24–7.

companied by considerable loss of control over grain consumption and distribution. At the same time the country's statistical services disintegrated so that the Government could no longer calculate the correct level of grain production. In an attempt to restore economic order during 1959–60, the Government imposed the highest rates of grain procurement since 1953 at a time when output per head was at its lowest for many years and this, together with the impact of natural disasters, killed the incentive to produce. In the grain crisis which followed famine appeared in many rural areas and it was no longer possible to mobilise enough grain to feed the greatly enlarged urban population. As domestic stocks became exhausted the Government was forced to import grain from abroad.

Although grain output recovered during the 1960s and continued to grow in the 1970s, China did not regain her former position of self-sufficiency. On the contrary, as the 1970s progressed, her dependence on foreign grain increased. Since the fall of the 'Gang of Four' the Chinese Government has admitted that, for the present, grain imports are needed in view of the tense relationship between production, marketed supply and demand.[2] A review of the grain situation at the end of the 1970s, in the context of the 1950s, forms the subject matter of the remainder of this concluding chapter.

GRAIN PRODUCTION, DISTRIBUTION AND CONSUMPTION IN THE LATE 1970s

Grain production

Figure 8 compares average grain output per head of total population in China's twenty-eight provinces (including the three autonomous cities) during 1955–57 and 1978–80. Data for the 1950s have been adjusted to make the comparison possible. This has involved (1) estimating output on a basis of the provincial boundaries of the late 1970s, and (2) re-calculating the total grain output of each province in which potatoes are weighted at 5:1[3] instead of 4:1 as was the convention until 1962.[4]

[2] See for example *NYCCWT* (no. 2), 1980, pp. 46–9.
[3] Confirmation of the new weighting is found in State Statistical Bureau, 'Communiqué on the Fulfilment of China's 1980 National Economic Plan', *JMJP*, 30 April 1981.
[4] Information from senior Chinese economists who visited London in 1981.

Grain production and distribution in the late 1970s

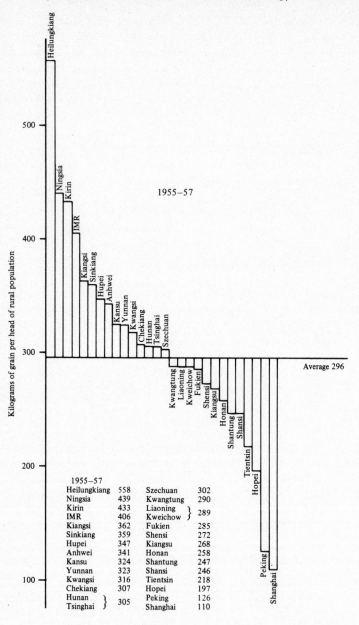

1955–57

1955–57			
Heilungkiang	558	Szechuan	302
Ningsia	439	Kwangtung	290
Kirin	433	Liaoning	289
IMR	406	Kweichow	
Kiangsi	362	Fukien	285
Sinkiang	359	Shensi	272
Hupei	347	Kiangsu	268
Anhwei	341	Honan	258
Kansu	324	Shantung	247
Yunnan	323	Shansi	246
Kwangsi	316	Tientsin	218
Chekiang	307	Hopei	197
Hunan		Peking	126
Tsinghai	305	Shanghai	110

Figure 8. Provincial dispersion of grain output per head around national average, 1955–57 and 1978–80.

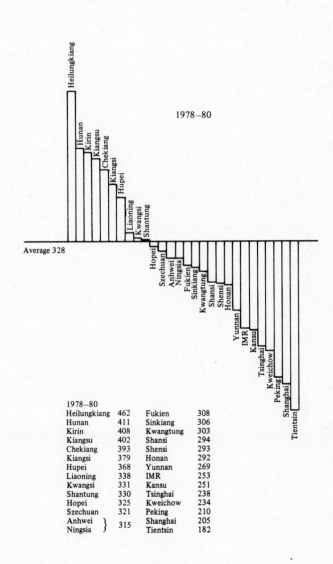

1978–80

Average 328

1978–80			
Heilungkiang	462	Fukien	308
Hunan	411	Sinkiang	306
Kirin	408	Kwangtung	303
Kiangsu	402	Shansi	294
Chekiang	393	Shensi	293
Kiangsi	379	Honan	292
Hupei	368	Yunnan	269
Liaoning	338	IMR	253
Kwangsi	331	Kansu	251
Shantung	330	Tsinghai	238
Hopei	325	Kweichow	234
Szechuan	321	Peking	210
Anhwei }	315	Shanghai	205
Ningsia }		Tientsin	182

It is immediately apparent that in 1978–80 China still had to face one of the major agricultural problems which characterised the 1950s: great provincial inequality of grain output per head. However, there was some improvement between the 1950s and late 1970s. For example the national average rose from 296 kilograms in 1955–57 to 328 kilograms in 1978–80, an increase of 10.8 per cent, and the provincial distribution was narrower around this higher mean. Decreasing provincial inequality of per capita output is also borne out by statistical analysis. Using once again[5] the standard deviation of the logarithms as our measure, the indices for the two periods are:

$$1955\text{–}57\text{: }0.3279$$
$$1978\text{–}80\text{: }0.2228$$

Eight provinces fell into the 'poor' class (compared with nine in 1955–57), but because of the shift in the geographical location of this group its total population in 1978–80 was only 131 million (13 per cent) compared with 234 million (37 per cent) in 1955–57. At the other end of the scale the number of provinces in the 'rich' class rose from eleven to fourteen and the total population in the group increased by 450 million, from 172 million (16 per cent) in 1955–57 to 622 million (64 per cent) in 1978–80. Table 53 summarises the change in status of provinces between the 1950s and late 1970s. As shown, twelve provinces did not change their grain 'wealth' status during the period. Of the remaining sixteen, ten moved to a higher and six to a lower 'wealth' class. Particularly encouraging for the Government was the elevation of Hopei, Shantung and Kiangsu (which had a combined population of 131 million in 1953–57 and 182 million in 1978–80) from the poor to the rich class. On the other hand, five provinces – all located in the North West and South West Regions – moved downwards into the poor class.

It is a startling fact that in 1978–80 average grain output per head in eleven provinces was below what it had been in 1955–57 (Table 54). This group included five out of the six provinces of the North West Region as well as two out of the three provinces in both the North East and the South West Regions. The decline in several of these provinces is not yet easy to explain and in any case such analysis lies outside the scope of this study. The drastic reduction of output in the North West,

[5] See Chapter 4.

Table 53. *Change in status of provinces between 1955–57 and 1978–80 according to categories of grain output per head*

Provinces with no change in status					
Poor		Adequate		Rich	
Peking	126–210	Fukien	285–308	Heilungkiang	558–462
Tientsin	218–182	Kwangtung	290–303	Kirin	433–408
Shanghai	110–205			Ningsia	439–315
				Hupei	347–368
				Kiangsi	362–379
				Anhwei	341–315
				Kwangsi	316–331

Provinces with changed status					
From poor to adequate		From poor to rich		From adequate to rich	
Honan	258–292	Hopei	197–325	Liaoning	289–338
Shansi	246–294	Shantung	247–330	Hunan	305–411
Shensi	272–293	Kiangsu	268–404	Chekiang	307–393
				Szechuan	302–321

From adequate to poor		From rich to adequate		From rich to poor	
Tsinghai	305–238	Sinkiang	359–306	IMR	406–253
Kweichow	289–234			Kansu	324–251
				Yunnan	323–269

Source: Production and population figures for 1974–80 in Appendices 13 and 14.

however, may be attributed primarily to the ploughing up of pasture during and after the Great Leap Forward, when the Government placed the greatest emphasis on grain and on the attainment of regional grain self-sufficiency. This led to a fall in the production of livestock fodder and consequently in the number of livestock, which in turn affected soil fertility. Soil erosion on the newly reclaimed land was widespread, and the yields of grain obtained were small. For example, in Inner Mongolia,[6] where hay production fell by up to 70 per cent, the average yield of grain on reclaimed land ranged from 0.15 to 0.75 tons per hectare, with an average of 0.44 tons per hectare. Average grain

[6] *Chi-shu Ching-chi Ho Kuan-li Hsien-tai-hua Wen chi (Essays on Technical Economics and Management Modernisation)* (Peking, 1979), p. 136.

Table 54. *Percentage change in grain output per head, 1955–57 to 1978–80 by region*

	North East	%	North West	%	North	%
	Heilungkiang	− 17.2	IMR	− 37.7	Honan	+ 13.2
	Kirin	− 5.8	Kansu	− 22.5	Hopei	+ 65.0
	Liaoning	+ 17.0	Ningsia	− 28.2	Peking	+ 66.7
			Shensi	+ 7.7	Shansi	+ 19.5
			Sinkiang	− 14.8	Shantung	+ 33.6
			Tsinghai	− 22.0	Tientsin	− 17.9
	Region	− 0.2	Region	− 15.6	Region	+ 30.9

Central	%	East	%	South West	%	South	%
Hunan	+ 34.8	Anhwei	− 7.6	Kweichow	− 19.0	Fukien	+ 8.1
Hupei	+ 6.1	Chekiang	+ 28.0	Szechuan	+ 6.3	Kwangsi	+ 4.7
Kiangsi	+ 4.7	Kiangsu	+ 50.7	Yunnan	− 16.7	Kwangtung	+ 4.5
		Shanghai	+ 86.4				
Region	+ 16.9	Region	+ 26.3	Region	− 2.6	Region	+ 5.4

output per hectare throughout the province, 1952–57, was 0.83 tons. In Tsinghai,[7] 0.38 million hectares of pastureland – equal to 74 per cent of the entire arable area of the province – were ploughed up in 1958, followed by a further 0.33 million hectares in 1959. The total number of livestock (excluding pigs) fell by 27.4 per cent in 1958, 10.0 per cent in 1959 and 5.2 per cent in 1960. For the three years 1958–60 the decline amounted to 37.9 per cent and involved the loss of 5.7 million head of livestock. Moreover, as the figures for Sinkiang[8] show, the impact of the ploughing-up campaign was not short-lived: total livestock declined by 10 per cent between 1966 and 1975, and grain output fell at a rate of 2.8 per cent per year.

Instability of grain production continued to affect many provinces at the end of the 1970s. Using the same statistical measure as in Chapter 1, the instability of national grain output rose slightly between the 1950s and 1970s, from 1.62 to 2.23. Compared with other large countries this was, however, not a high index. For example, the

[7] See *CCYC* (no. 11), 1980, p. 66; *JMJP*, 30 January 1981; and *Tsinghai ch'u-mu yeh Ching-chi Fa-chan Shih* (*History of the Economic Development of the Livestock Industry in Tsinghai*), Tsinghai Livestock Office (n.p., 1980).

[8] *NYCCWT* (no. 3), 1980, pp. 34–6, and p. 4.

index for the USA (1973–79) was 3.47, for India (1973–79) it was 4.87, and for the USSR (1972–79) it was 13.10. Even so, the implications for China of an unstable agriculture were still as serious in the 1970s as they had been in the 1950s: the undeveloped transport system and the difficulty of building up sufficient stocks meant that local food shortages were a constant threat. In 1980 only 30 per cent[9] of the total arable area could guarantee a stable output in the face of either drought or flood.

A comparison of provincial grain instability for 1952–57 and 1974–80 shows that out of the provinces for which data are available only in Hunan, Fukien and Kwangsi was there a marked increase in grain output stability. Several provinces which were unstable in the 1950s remained so in the 1970s and these included Kansu and Ningsia (taken together), Heilungkiang, Shensi, Tsinghai, Hopei, Shantung, Hupei and Anhwei. Furthermore, Kirin, Chekiang and Kiangsu became significantly more unstable during the period. Chekiang, which was the third most stable province in the 1950s, was one of the most unstable provinces in the 1970s.

Table 55 compares the level, stability and growth of grain output in those provinces for which data are available, in the mid-1950s and the late 1970s. Chapter 1 drew attention to a band of northern provinces embracing Hopei, Shantung, Shansi and Shensi in which all three unfavourable conditions were combined during the 1950s. By the period 1974–80, a considerable improvement had taken place especially in Shantung and Hopei. In the 1950s no province combined all three favourable characteristics of high output per head, rapid and stable growth, but in the 1970s four provinces could be included in such a class: Kiangsi, Szechuan, Hunan and Fukien. The overall improvement in Fukien, Hunan and Kwangsi, all of which had problems in the 1950s, is particularly striking. However, as Table 55 shows, only slow progress was made over our period of twenty-five years toward solving China's 'problem' of grain production.

Grain distribution

At first sight the provincial figures for average grain production per head given in the previous section suggest that it would be easier in the

[9] *NTKTTH* (no. 3), 1981, p. 2.

Table 55. *Changes in grain production per head, output stability and growth between the mid 1950s and late 1970s*

	Output per head		Grain 'sufficiency' status		Index of output stability		Stability category[b]		Trend of growth of output per head	
	1955–57	1978–80	1955–57	1978–80	1952–57[a]	1974–80	1952–57	1974–80	1952–57 % p.a.	1974–80[b] % p.a.
North East										
Heilungkiang	558	462	Rich	Rich	6.69	5.97	Very unstable	Unstable	−5.30	+0.14
Kirin	433	408	Rich	Rich	3.46	4.89	Fairly stable	Unstable	−5.61	−0.83
Liaoning	289	338	Adequate	Rich	3.37	3.89	Fairly stable	Fairly stable	−1.82	+2.54
North West										
IMR	406	253	Rich	Poor	11.43	n.a.	Very unstable	n.a.	−5.91	n.a.
Kansu and Ningsia	344	266	Rich	Poor	6.54	4.64	Very unstable	Unstable	+9.79	+1.17
Shensi	272	293	Poor	Adequate	8.31	8.62	Very unstable	Very unstable	−0.28	+0.33
Sinkiang	359	306	Rich	Adequate	1.36	3.76	Very stable	Fairly stable	+1.28	+4.00
Tsinghai	305	238	Adequate	Poor	9.22	7.37	Very unstable	Very unstable	+9.41	−1.82
North										
Honan	258	292	Poor	Adequate	3.50	2.71	Fairly stable	Stable	+1.86	+0.15
Hopei	197	326	Poor	Rich	7.86	4.86	Very unstable	Unstable	−1.81	+0.58
Shansi	246	294	Poor	Adequate	6.69	n.a.	Very unstable	n.a.	−3.85	n.a.
Shantung	247	330	Poor	Rich	6.09	4.00	Very unstable	Unstable	+0.74	+3.70
Centre										
Hunan	305	411	Adequate	Rich	4.98	1.97	Unstable	Fairly stable	+0.01	+3.04
Hupei	347	368	Rich	Rich	8.42	5.28	Very unstable	Unstable	+4.45	−0.25
Kiangsi	362	379	Rich	Rich	2.29	3.17	Fairly stable	Fairly stable	+1.81	+4.68
East										
Anhwei	341	316	Rich	Rich	4.30	4.67	Unstable	Unstable	+5.43	−2.76
Chekiang	307	393	Adequate	Rich	1.10	10.82	Very stable	Very unstable	+0.30	+3.16

Kiangsu	268	404	Poor	Rich	3.94	5.07	Fairly stable	Unstable	− 0.05	+ 2.68
South West										
Kweichow	289	234	Adequate	Poor	1.31	n.a.	Very stable	n.a.	+ 6.32	n.a.
Szechuan	302	321	Adequate	Rich	1.09	2.50	Very stable	Fairly stable	+ 4.32	+ 4.36
Yunnan	323	269	Rich	Poor	1.06	3.14	Very stable	Fairly stable	+ 4.90	+ 1.93
South										
Fukien	285	308	Adequate	Adequate	3.25	1.36	Fairly stable	Very stable	+ 0.89	+ 5.88
Kwangsi	316	331	Rich	Rich	5.20	1.25	Unstable	Very stable	− 1.40	+ 1.81
Kwangtung	290	303	Adequate	Adequate	1.85	2.98	Fairly stable	Fairly stable	+ 2.89	+ 0.13
China	296	328	Adequate	Rich	1.62	2.23	Fairly stable	Fairly stable	+ 1.35	+ 1.56

Notes:

a. For strict comparability the instability indexes for 1952–57 should be recalculated using grain output in which potatoes are weighted at 5:1, not 4:1. However, the necessary data are only available for nine provinces (including five of China's largest producers of potatoes) and since the revised indexes for these provinces are almost identical to the originals, the latter have been retained.

b. We have defined these categories in Chapter 1 as follows: very unstable, index above 6; unstable 4–6; fairly stable 1.5–4; very stable, less than 1.5. Stability indexes and trends in per capita output are for the seven years 1974–80 except in the cases of Kansu and Ningsia (six years 1976–81), Kiangsi (five years 1975–80), Yunnan (five years 1977–81) and Fukien (five years 1975–80).

late 1970s for the Government to achieve national self-sufficiency via redistribution than in the 1950s: the national average per capita output was higher than in the 1950s and there was less inequality of output per head between provinces. In other words, it might appear that by the end of the 1970s the demand for grain transfers had decreased while the potential supply of 'marketed' grain had increased. There are three reasons, however, why this was not the case. First, a great deal of redistribution was still needed between the rural areas, as the fragmentary data relating to sub-provincial inequality show. Secondly, although when viewed against the provincial levels of output per head in the 1950s the potential provincial surpluses of the 1970s look remarkably high, in reality they were much smaller than they appeared to be, because of the increased use of grain for processing, seed and livestock. Finally, grain procurement by the Government had to be carefully controlled in order to provide the necessary incentive for the peasants to increase grain production. Let us look at these reasons in more detail.

Chapter 1 showed that provincial averages obscured wide local inequalities of grain production per head and the same is true for the late 1970s. Figures for Special Districts and *hsien* comparable with those given in Chapter 1 are not available, but enough is known to conclude that the problem was still acute in the 1970s. For example, in 1979,[10] 338 *hsien* (around 15 per cent of the total number) produced 36 per cent of China's grain. (In 1951–52, we recall from Chapter 1, 252 *hsien* (11.4 per cent) produced 19.3 per cent of output.) It follows that many poor villages and production teams continued to exist during the 1970s. One report,[11] published in 1980, stated that the grain ration of 100 million peasants was below 150 kilograms per year. Income data provide further evidence of local poverty: in 1979[12] average income per head of rural population was less than 50 *yuan* in 377 *hsien* (around 16 per cent). In eleven provinces[13] more than 20 per cent of *hsien* fell into this income class. The group included Kweichow, Yunnan and Fukien in the south, and Kansu, Ningsia, Shensi, Inner Mongolia, Shantung, Honan and Anhwei in the centre and north of China. Average provincial grain output per head (1978–80) in Kansu was only 251

[10] *HC* (no. 5), 1981, pp. 24–6.
[11] *CCYC* (no. 9), 1980, pp. 53–8.
[12] *NYCCWT* (no. 2), 1980, p. 34.
[13] *Ibid.*

kilograms, but figures for 1979 reveal[14] that the rural populations of 44.8 per cent of all *hsien* in the province had a grain ration of under 150 kilograms, and 49.6 per cent of all production teams in the province had less than 40 *yuan* income per head. In eighteen *hsien* of the province, 1100 teams had no draught animals.[15]

Between the 1950s and 1970s the use of grain for processing, seed and above all for livestock, increased considerably.[16] This means that it is incorrect to estimate potential provincial surpluses in the 1970s by using the same criteria as for the 1950s. Our estimates of seed requirements in the 1950s were based on detailed grain sown area statistics and on prevailing seed rates for different grains. From provincial figures the national average amount of seed required per annum, 1953–57, was 8.65 million tons or 67 kilograms per sown hectare. This is close to Ma Yin-ch'u's[17] assumed rate of 75 kilograms per hectare. National use of grain for seed in 1980, however, was stated[18] to be 18.5 million tons, or 154 kilograms per sown hectare. Compared with our estimate for 1953–57, therefore, the average seed rate per hectare rose by 130 per cent. Figures for Heilungkiang[19] and Szechuan[20] provide added evidence of such an increase. In Heilungkiang the rate rose from around 50 kilograms per hectare in the 1950s (our estimate) to 100 kilograms in 1980. In Szechuan it was claimed that 2.6 million tons of grain were used for seed in 1978 compared with our estimate of 0.8 million tons per annum for 1953–57.

But the main difference between the 1950s and the 1970s concerning the use of grain was in the amount consumed by livestock, especially by pigs. The number of pigs in the country rose from 103 million (1952–57) to 309 million (1978–80) and most of the additional 206 million must have been fed on grain. By comparison the number of large animals increased little, from 83.26 million (1952–57) to 94.58 million (1978–80) but, bearing in mind that in the 1950s many such animals were so short of feed that they could not work, it is reasonable

---

[14] *HC* (no. 22), 1980, p. 9.

[15] *NYCCWT* (no. 1), 1980, pp. 26–8 and p. 52.

[16] Increased use of feed for industry and livestock 1955–77 is mentioned by *CCYC* (no. 1), 1980, p. 51.

[17] *JMJP*, 15 June 1957. But note that *LS* (no. 16), 1956, p. 1, assumes an average of 112.5 kilograms of seed per hectare.

[18] *SWB*, 4 February 1981.

[19] *SWB*, 4 March 1981.

[20] *CCYC* (no. 3), 1979, p. 16.

to assume that they all consumed significantly more grain in the 1970s. A report[21] from Heilungkiang, for example, drew attention to the demands of 2 million horses in the province, assessed at 500–650 kilograms of grain per horse, and amounting therefore to over one million tons per year, which was equal to the annual volume of grain exports.

The amount of grain fed to pigs varied from place to place. In south China, for example, where more non-grain feed was available than in the rest of China, there is a tradition of using pond weed, the growth of which is stimulated by pig manure, and of only using grain at the fattening stage.[22] On the other hand, in the suburbs of major cities such as Shanghai, specialist pig farms consumed large amounts of feed grain. Total grain used for livestock feed was 'more than 10 per cent' of national output in the late 1970s, according to an article[23] in the journal *Nung-yeh Ching-chi Wen-t'i* (Problems of Agricultural Economics). For the period 1978–80 this amounts to at least 32 million tons per year. The quantity feed to pigs alone in 1976 is estimated by the Agricultural Economics Research Institute of the Chinese Academy of Social Sciences as 22.5 million tons.[24] By contrast our national estimate for 1953–57, based on provincial livestock figures, was 10.3 million tons or 5.7 per cent of grain output.

Although the precise amounts of extra seed and feed grain used by different provinces are not known, it is possible to make some estimates which illustrate clearly why the provincial grain surpluses were so inadequate toward the end of the 1970s and why, therefore, China was obliged to continue to import large amounts of grain from foreign countries. In Table 56 'adjusted' grain output per head (1978–80) is calculated for each province by deducting estimates of additional grain per head of population used for livestock feed and for seed in the late 1970s compared with the 1950s. Potential surpluses and deficits, based on both actual and adjusted output per head, are given in columns (g) and (h). The difference between the results is con-

[21] *NYCCWT* (no. 1), 1980, pp. 37–9.
[22] *NYCCWT* (no. 2), 1980, p. 40. This is a widespread practice in Taiwan where it has been scientifically developed.
[23] *NYCCWT* (no. 2), 1981, pp. 58–61.
[24] *Yao Chung-shih Fa-chan Ch'u-mu yeh* (*We Must Emphasise the Development of the Livestock Industry*), Agricultural Economics Research Institute, Chinese Academy of Social Sciences (Peking, 1980), p. 302.

siderable. If the effect of higher seed and feed requirements is not taken into account, on a basis of our 'self-sufficiency' criteria, China had potential provincial *net* surpluses of 27.329 million tons per annum in the late 1970s. If such additional grain allocations are deducted, however, the potential surpluses fall by 17.379 million tons to 14.195 million tons, the potential deficits rise from 4.195 million tons to 15.810 million tons, making a net *deficit* of 1.615 million tons. If some of the provincial surpluses were needed for stock accumulation and for export to foreign countries (in reality such exports totalled 1.318 million tons per year, 1977–79), the deficit – foreign import require-ment – becomes considerably higher.

While total grain output increased by 70 per cent between 1953–57 and 1977–80, gross grain procurement only rose by 18 per cent, as Table 57 shows. Procurement declined from 27.6 per cent of grain output to 19.2 per cent. Grain purchases rose by almost 50 per cent, but decreased from 17.1 per cent of output to 14.7 per cent of output, while grain acquired as tax fell from 19.1 million tons (10.5 per cent of output) to around 13.8 million tons (4.5 per cent of output). Rural grain sales declined from 22.3 million tons per annum in the 1950s to 15.48 million tons in 1977–80, and net procurement – the surplus for the towns, for stocks and for exports – therefore rose from 27.85 million tons per annum to 43.69 million tons, which represented a decline in the net procurement ratio from 15.3 per cent to 14.1 per cent. No figure for total urban grain supplies in the late 1970s has been discovered, but the amount must have been around 48 million tons per year. Table 57 includes a tentative figure of 47.93 million tons, based on an assumed per capita consumption of 270 kilograms (unhusked grain) and on the further assumption that personal consumption accounted for 85 per cent of total urban supplies. If this is correct, it is seen that in 1977–80 there was a national procurement–sales *deficit* of 4.24 million tons per year, compared with a *surplus* in 1953–57 of 4.96 million tons. With grain exports running at 1.318 million tons in the late 1970s, the foreign import requirement of grain was therefore at least 5.558 million tons a year, and in fact gross imports were 10.293 million tons.[25]

Here, then, is one of the main contrasts between the national grain

[25] Details are available in *Agricultural Situation. Review of 1979 and Outlook for 1980. People's Republic of China*, USDA, supplement 6 to WAS–21, (Washington DC, June 1980).

Table 56. *Estimated potential grain surpluses and deficits, 1978–80*

	Extra grain required in 1978–80 compared with 1953–57 (thousand tons)			Extra grain required per head of population (kg)	Actual grain output per head (kg)	Adjusted grain output per head (kg) (actual output – extra grain required)	Potential surplus[c] (+) or deficit (−) (thousand tons)	
	Livestock[a]	Seed[b]	Total				From actual output	From adjusted output
North East								
Heilungkiang	1202	427	1629	51	462	411	+4846	+3231
Kirin	767	112	879	40	408	368	+2160	+1287
Liaoning	1259	92	1351	39	338	299	+998	s.s.
North West								
IMR	758	190	948	51	253	202	−407	−1351
Kansu and Ningsia	786	221	1007	45	262	217	−293	−1307
Shensi	832	288	1120	40	293	253	s.s.	−617
Sinkiang	490	223	713	57	306	249	s.s.	−3264
Tsinghai	102	34	136	37	238	201	−137	−274
North								
Honan	1816	388	2204	31	292	261	s.s.	−1005
Hopei	1491	448	1939	38	325	287	+818	s.s.
Peking	397	45	442	51	210	159	−563	−1004
Shansi	678	162	840	34	294	260	s.s.	−367
Shantung	2432	357	2789	39	330	291	+1513	s.s.
Tientsin	163	43	206	28	182	154	−694	−903
Central								
Hunan	1834	512	2346	45	411	366	+5313	+2969
Hupei	1334	420	1754	38	368	330	+2732	+972
Kiangsi	708	287	995	31	379	348	+2257	+1257

East								
Anhwei	1304	292	315	33	1596	282	+289	s.s.
Chekiang	1339	268	393	42	1607	351	+3184	+1592
Kiangsu	2253	334	402	44	2587	358	+5479	+2887
Shanghai	454	44	205	44	498	161	−794	−1293
South West								
Kweichow	594	178	234	28	772	206	−1119	−1884
Szechuan	3590	1802	321	55	5392	266	+1172	−879
Yunnan	939	252	269	38	1191	231	−188	−1378
South								
Fukien	422	201	308	25	623	283	s.s.	s.s.
Kwangsi	890	338	331	35	1228	296	+763	s.s.
Kwangtung	1447	404	303	33	1851	270	s.s.	−284

Total potential surpluses (million tons) +31.524 +14.195
Total potential deficits (million tons) −4.195 −15.810
Balance +27.329 −1.615

Notes:

a. Additional grain requirements of pigs are estimated from provincial meat production for 1979 and from the number of pigs slaughtered (*Encyclopaedia* 1980). An assumption has to be made for each province about the proportion of total meat output accounted for by pork. A check is provided by the figures for number of pigs slaughtered, from which pork output may be estimated, from assuming 55 kilograms of meat per pig. Grain: feed conversion ratios assumed are 3.5:1 in the fourteen northern provinces, and 2.5:1 in the thirteen southern provinces. Extra grain used by draught-type animals is estimated from the number of such animals in 1979 (*Encyclopaedia* 1980) and by assuming that 50 per cent more grain per animal was used in 1979 compared with 1953–57.

b. Except for Szechuan seed is estimated from 1979 provincial grain sown areas (*Chung-kuo Nung-yeh Nien-chien 1980* (*Chinese Agricultural Yearbook 1980*) (Peking, 1981), p. 100), and from the assumption that double the seed rates per sown hectare during 1953–57 were adopted. Seed used in Szechuan is given in *CCYC* (no. 3), 1979, p. 16.

c. 'Potential surplus' is calculated by multiplying total population by the amount of grain output per head above 309 kilograms. 'Potential deficit' is obtained by multiplying population by the amount of grain output per head below 275 kilograms. 's.s.' denotes that production per head fell within our assumed 'self-sufficiency' range of 175–309 kilograms.

Table 57. *China's national grain account, 1953–57 and 1977–80*

| | Annual averages | | | |
| | 1953–57 | | 1977–80 | |
	Million tons	% output	Million tons	% output
Grain output	181.60		309.55	
Grain procurement by government				
Gross procurement of	50.15	27.6	59.17	19.2
which { purchase		31.05	17.1	c.45.36	c.14.7
tax		19.10	10.5	c.13.81	c.4.5
Net procurement (gross procurement minus rural sales)	27.85	15.3	43.69	14.1
Grain disbursement by government				
Sales in rural areas	22.30		15.48	
Sales in urban areas	22.89		47.93[a]	
Total	45.19		63.41[a]	
Grain procurement– disbursement balance: surplus (+) or deficit (−)	+4.96		−4.24	
Foreign grain trade				
Exports	2.037		1.318	
Imports	0.116		10.293	
Net exports (+) or imports (−)	+1.921		−8.975	
Stock accumulation	3.039		4.735	

	Kilograms		Kilograms	
Grain per head of rural population				
Output	343		381	
Net procurement	53		54	
Retained by peasants	290		327	
Grain per head or urban population				
Net procurement	323		290	
Net procurement plus imports minus exports	300		349	

Note: a. Estimated figure.
Sources:
1953–57. Earlier chapters. Note that 1953–57 figures include potatoes weighted at 4:1, compared with 5:1 in 1977–80.

balance of the 1950s and that of the late 1970s. In the 1950s, the procurement–sales surplus allowed for net foreign grain exports of 2 million tons per annum, leaving stock accumulation of 3 million tons each year, while in the years 1977–80, the annual procurement deficit was accompanied by net foreign imports of almost 9 million tons per year, which allowed for annual stock accumulation of around 4.7 million tons.

Perhaps the per capita figures in Table 57 underline these points more clearly than the aggregate statistics. For example, they show that grain output per head of rural population was 11 per cent higher in 1977–80 than in 1953–57 but that gross procurement per head was 23.2 per cent or 22 kilograms less, while net procurement per head was only 1.9 per cent, or one kilogram, more. Retained grain per head of rural population thus increased from 290 kilograms in 1953–57 to 327 kilograms in 1977–80; that is, by 12.7 per cent, compared with the increase in *output* per head of 11 per cent. More important is the fact that *net* procurement per head of *urban* population fell from 323

Sources to Table 57 (*cont.*)

1977–80. Gross procurement: 1977–78 from 1979–80 and *HC* (no. 5), 1981, pp. 24–6. 1978–79 from percentage of output given in *JKYC* (no. 1), 1981, pp. 17–22. 1979–80 from *SWB*, 29 April 1981. 1980–81 from 1979–80 and *SWB*, 29 April 1981; also from 1977–79 increase in *HC* (no. 5), 1981, pp. 24–6. Tax: 1978–79 from *Kuo-chia Shui-shou* (*National Taxation*) (Peking, 1979), p. 118. 1979–80 from 1978–79 and *JMJP*, 31 August 1980. Purchase: by subtraction. Rural resales: From figures in *JMJP*, 9 April 1981, p. 5. A different figure (of around 30 million tons) may be inferred from data in *NYCCWT* (no. 4), 1981, pp. 3–8, which refers to 5 per cent of grain output being exchanged on markets, 20 per cent being procured by the state and 10 per cent returned to villages. In both cases net procurement works out at the same amount. Net procurement: By subtraction. Note that *NYCCWT* (no. 3), 1981, pp. 3–10, gives a figure of 13 per cent of output for net procurement, but this may refer to 1980–81 only. Grain foreign trade: 1953–57: R. H. Kirby, *Agricultural Trade of the People's Republic of China, 1935–69*, Foreign Agricultural Economic Report no. 83, US Department of Agriculture, Economic Research Service (Washington DC, 1972) and *TCKT* (no. 19), 1957. 1977–79: *Agricultural Situation: Review of 1979 and Outlook for 1980*. Rural population: *Encyclopaedia* (1980) gives 1979 rural population for all provinces except Szechuan, Yunnan and Fukien. Szechuan rural population is assumed to be 91 per cent of total, Fukien assumed to be 80 per cent, and Yunnan is from *Ssu-hsiang Chan-hsien* (*Ideological Front*) (no. 1), 1981, pp. 76–8 and p. 37. China's rural population is thus estimated at 818.868 million and, by subtraction, urban population is 152.052 million, in 1979. *Chi-hsu Ching-chi* (*Technical Economics*) (Peking, 1979), p. 177, gives China's city population as 76.04 million, and town population as 114.94 million, making a total 'urban' population of 190.98 million, but this must include rural populations of the cities and towns. The figure of 120 million for the urban population (*HC* (no. 2), 1980, p. 8) must *exclude* all such populations (inner and outer suburbs and rural hinterland). *JMJP*, 9 April 1981, gives 160 million as China's 'non-agricultural' population.

Table 58. *Provincial grain transfers 1953–57, 1965 and 1978: a summary*

	1953–57 average	1965	1978
Number of exporting provinces	19	15	8[a]
Number of importing provinces	7[b]	12	18[c]
Volume of provincial exports (million tons)	10.0	5.7	2.5
Volume of provincial imports (million tons)	7.7	8.0	11.6
Provincial trade surplus (+) or deficit (−)	+ 2.3	− 2.3	− 9.1

Notes:
a. Probably Heilungkiang, Kirin, Hunan, Hupei, Anhwei, Kiangsi, Chekiang and Kiangsu.
b. Counting Tsinghai which had minimal trade.
c. Probably Liaoning, Inner Mongolia, Kansu, Ningsia, Shensi, Sinkiang, Tsinghai, Tibet, Honan, Shansi, Shantung, Kweichow, Yunnan, Fukien, Kwangtung and the three major cities of Peking, Tientsin and Shanghai.
Source: 1953–57: Chapter 3. 1965 and 1978: *JKYC* (no. 1), 1981, pp. 17–22. (Grain statistics converted to unhusked grain.)

kilograms to 290 kilograms, which was said[26] to be insufficient for all non-agricultural requirements. In the 1970s, however, net foreign grain imports worth 59 kilograms per head of urban population increased urban grain availability to 349 kilograms, while in the 1950s net foreign grain exports per head of urban population *reduced* such availability per head to 300 kilograms.

Related to the Government's failure to extract enough grain from the agricultural sector in the late 1970s was the decline in the volume of inter-provincial grain transfers, which were the cornerstone of policy during the 1950s. As Table 58 shows, between 1953–57 and 1978 the number of grain exporting provinces declined from nineteen to eight and the volume of provincial grain exports fell by 75 per cent, from 10 million tons per annum to 2.5 million tons. At the same time the number of importing provinces rose from seven to eighteen, increasing the annual volume of grain imports from 7.7 million tons to 11.6 million tons. The provincial grain trade surplus of 2.3 million tons per annum achieved in the 1950s became a *deficit* of 2.3 million tons in 1965 and further rose to 9.1 million tons in 1978; the net foreign grain

[26] An article in *JMJP*, 9 April 1981, stated that the then current net procurement of around 313 kilograms per head of non-agricultural population was 'not enough'.

imports of 8.975 million tons per annum, 1977–79, recorded in Table 57, reflect this deficit.

The provincial trade deficit of 1978 is much greater than our 'model' presented in Table 56 suggests: the potential exports estimated in Table 56 are 11.7 million tons higher than actual provincial exports but the estimated potential imports are nearer the mark at 15.8 million tons, compared with the actual 11.6 million tons. The model, of course, only took into account the extra grain required for seed and feed, and the fact that actual grain exports fell to only 2.5 million tons in 1978 suggests that there were probably some small increases in personal grain consumption (compared with the 1950s), and that provinces accumulated substantial stocks. Moreover, as the provincial figures for grain exports and imports indicate (Table 59), 1978 was probably a relatively poor year for provincial exports. The greatest impact on the availability of provincial grain exports between 1953–57 and the late 1970s resulted from the loss of Szechuan's massive contribution which, it will be recalled, averaged 1.8 million tons per annum 1953–57, and 2.7 million tons in the three years 1956–58. Judged by average grain output per head, Szechuan was never a rich province, but during the 1960s and 1970s, until 1978, the rate of growth of production was well below that of population. Between 1967 and 1976 grain output grew at only one per cent per annum,[27] compared with a population growth[28] of 3.1 per cent in 1970, 2.9 per cent in 1971 and still 1.2 per cent in 1976, in spite of a vigorous campaign to reduce the birth rate. After 1976, however, population growth fell rapidly to 0.46 per cent in 1980, and with the growth of grain output accelerating, per capita production rose significantly. The slow growth of grain production in Szechuan will require detailed research in future but one factor was the 'arbitrary expansion',[29] under the 'Gang of Four', of double crop rice in areas of the province where this was inappropriate both for technical and economic reasons. The reversal of this policy after 1976 helped to promote the growth of output. Another reason for the decline in Szechuan's grain exports was the increased rural demand for grain for seed and for livestock. The former has already been

[27] *CCYC* (no. 3), 1979, p. 16.
[28] For 1970 see *JMJP*, 11 August 1979; for 1971: *HC* (no. 7), 1979, p. 17; 1976: *PR* (no. 26), 1978, p. 31; 1980: *SJP*, 25 May 1981.
[29] *PR* (no. 48), 1978, pp. 20–3. See also *Technical Economics*, p. 131; and *JMJP*, 23 November 1979.

mentioned. The number of pigs increased from 19.2 million (1952–57) to 50.9 million in 1979.[30] Szechuan's grain exports declined from around 0.321 million tons per year in 1965–70, to 0.146 million tons per year during the period 1970–75.[31] In 1976–77, however, 0.729 million tons of grain were actually imported.[32] Thereafter, annual exports were very small – for example, 0.117 million tons in 1979–80 – and in 1981 the Central Government decided[33] to designate Szechuan as a 'self-sufficient' area: no exports would be required from the province and no imports would be provided. Less significant, but nevertheless important, was the disappearance of regular grain exports from Inner Mongolia, Kweichow and Yunnan, and of irregular exports from Kansu and Shensi, all of which amounted to around 1.61 million tons a year. In addition, the amount of grain exported by Heilungkiang and Kirin declined. By contrast the exports of Hunan, Chekiang, Kiangsu, Hupei and Anhwei increased between the 1950s and 1970s.

Among the big grain-importing provinces of the 1950s, Hopei became an exporter from 1972 until 1979. This was an impressive achievement. However, this was not sustained in 1980–81, as Table 59 shows. Liaoning, China's biggest grain importer in the 1950s (of 1.7 million tons per annum), continued to import grain but on a slightly smaller scale: per capita output rose from 279 kilograms in 1953–57 to 338 kilograms in 1978–80. New deficit provinces included Yunnan, Kweichow and Fukien in the south, as well as all the North Western provinces. And, as before, Peking, Shanghai and Tientsin continued to require large annual imports during the 1970s.[34] Published data on provincial grain transfers in the 1970s are sketchy, but Table 59 summarises the available information and compares the position of provinces in the 1970s with the 1950s.

Grain consumption

The paucity of statistics restricts comment on grain consumption during the late 1970s to a few rather general points.

[30] *Encyclopaedia*, 1980, p. 356.
[31] Information given to the author by the Provincial Grain Office, Chengtu, 1982.
[32] *NYCCTK* (no. 4), 1981, pp. 55–6.
[33] Communication from Provincial Grain Office.
[34] 4.85 million tons (raw grain) in 1979–80: *NYCCTK* (no. 4), 1981, pp. 55–6.

Table 59. *Provincial grain exports and imports, 1953–57 and in the 1970s*

	1953–57	1970s
North East		
Heilungkiang	Consistent exporter, declining volume. Average exports 1.43 million tons p.a.	Consistent but declining exporter. 1960s: average exports 1.349 million tons p.a., reaching 2.6 million tons in 1968. 1970s: 0.919 million tons p.a., but only 0.529 million tons in 1979.
Kirin	Net exporter on balance but exports declining. Average 0.64 million tons p.a.	Still an exporter but amount declining.
Liaoning	China's largest grain importer: 1.66 million tons p.a.	Self-sufficienty claimed in 1975, but annual imports in recent years exceed one million tons: average 1979–81 was 1.3 million tons p.a.
North West		
IMR	Consistent exporter. Average 0.78 million tons p.a.	Regular grain importer: 1980: 1.4 million tons.
Kansu	Net exporter on balance. Average 0.11 million tons p.a.	Importer: average *c.*0.6 million tons p.a.
Ningsia	Probably an exporter.	Importer: 0.145 million tons 1980–81.
Shensi	Consistent exporter. Average 0.14 million tons p.a.	Annual importer of 0.5–0.7 million tons in recent years.
Sinkiang	Self-sufficient.	Was an exporter in 1960s but became a consistent importer during 1967–77. Annual imports 0.5 million tons at end of 1970s and 0.2 million tons 1980–81.
Tsinghai	Self-sufficient.	Importer: 0.203 million tons in 1979.
North		
Honan	Small net exporter. Average 0.25 million tons p.a.	Became self-sufficient and even surplus in early–mid-1970s. Highest exports (1977) were 0.465 million tons. Recent position unclear. Probably self-sufficient.
Hopei	Consistent importer. Average 1.11 million tons p.a.	Exporter in mid-1970s of 0.17–0.23 million tons p.a., but imported 1.28 million tons in 1980.
Shansi	Moved from surplus to deficit, but a net exporter on balance. Average 0.04 million tons p.a.	Exported grain in mid-1970s, but became an importer in late 1970s. 1980–81 imported 0.67 million tons.

Table 59 (*contd*)

	1953–57	1970s
Shantung	Self-sufficient on balance.	Mainly an exporter since mid-1970s: average exports 0.2–0.3 million tons p.a.; highest 0.581 million tons in 1976. Small annual deficits also of around 0.1 million tons p.a. Now self-sufficient.
Centre		
Hunan	Exporter in four years out of the five. Average 0.55 million tons p.a.	One of China's four largest exporters (with Kiangsu, Chekiang, Hupei). 1979: 0.666 million tons.
Hupei	Exporter in four years out of the five. Average 0.05 million tons p.a., but 0.3 million tons p.a. for four years.	One of China's four largest exporters: 0.356 million tons in 1978.
Kiangsi	Consistent exporter. Average 0.73 million tons p.a.	Still an exporter but of a smaller amount than in 1950s: 0.5–0.75 million tons in 1977–79 but only 0.265 million tons in 1978.
East		
Anhwei	Exporter and importer according to harvest fluctuations Net exporter on balance. Average 0.32 million tons p.a.	Exporter: 0.8 million tons in 1979.
Chekiang	Consistent exporter. Average 0.42 million tons p.a.	Was an importer (0.158 million tons p.a.) in 1974–76, but is now one of the leading four exporters.
Kiangsu	Exporter and importer according to harvest fluctuations. Overall a net exporter: average 0.35 million tons p.a.	One of China's leading four exporters. Average $c.$1.0 million tons p.a.
South West		
Kweichow	Consistent exporter. Average 0.29 million tons p.a.	Importer of 0.5–0.7 million tons p.a.
Szechuan	China's biggest exporter. Average 1.84 million tons p.a. (rising from 0.7 million tons in 1953 to 2.9 million tons in 1957).	Annual exports 0.146 million tons 1965–70, and 0.146 million tons 1970–75. Imports of 0.729 million tons in 1976–77. 1977–79 very small amount of grain exported (0.117 million tons in 1979). Since 1980 self-sufficient with neither imports nor exports.
Yunnan	Self-sufficient 1953–54 then a consistent exporter. Average 1955–57: 0.27 million tons p.a.	Importer: 0.26 million tons in 1977, and 0.71 million tons in 1980–81.

Table 59 (*contd*)

	1953–57	1970s
South		
Fukien	Virtually self-sufficient.	Importer since 1976. Average 0.1 million tons p.a.
Kwangsi	Net exporter. Average 0.14 million tons p.a.	Importer since 1976. Average exports 1969–76 were *c*.0.6 million tons p.a.
Kwangtung	Exporter 1953–55 then self-sufficient. Net exporter 1953–57 on average: 0.29 million tons p.a.	Exporter 1963–75. Self-sufficient 1976–78 but an importer 1979 to present: 1980–81 imports 0.7 million tons.

Sources:

1953–57. Chapter 3.

1970s. Heilungkiang: *Encyclopaedia* (1980), p. 76. *HC* (no. 1), 1980, pp. 24–9; *NYCCWT* (no. 1), 1980, pp. 37–9; *SWB*, 18 March 1981; *Luen Ts'ai-cheng Fen-p'ei yü Ching-chi ti Kuan-hsi* (*On the Relationship between Financial Allocation and Economics*), China Financial Committee (Peking, 1981), pp. 185–201; and *NYCCTK* (no. 4), 1981, pp. 55–6. Kirin: *JMJP*, 21 February 1979. Liaoning: *JMJP*, 30 December 1975. *Ching-chi Tung-t'ai* (*Economic Situation*) (no. 4), 1980, p. 7; *NYCCTK* (no. 4), 1981, pp. 5–12 and 55–6. IMR: *Nei-meng-ku She-hui k'o-hsüeh* (*Inner Mongolia Social Science*) (no. 2), 1981, pp. 1–4. *SWB*, 6 December 1980 contains a report that Inner Mongolia plans to achieve grain self-sufficiency in ten years. Kansu and Ningsia: *JKYC* (no. 2), 1981, p. 36. For Kansu see *Economic Yearbook* (1981); also *Kung-yeh Ching-chi Kuan-li Ts'ung-k'an* (*Industrial Economic Management Digest*) (no. 12), 1980. For Ningsia see *NYCCTK* (no. 4), 1981, pp. 5–12. Shensi: *SESJP*, 14 January 1981; *NYCCTK* (no. 4), 1981, pp. 5–12; and statistics from Shensi provincial agriculture office, supplied to the author in 1982. Sinkiang: *NYCCWT* (no. 2), 1981, pp. 28–32; *JMJP*, 4 November 1978; *NYCCTK* (no. 4), 1981, pp. 5–12. Tsinghai: *JKYC* (no. 2), 1981, p. 36; *NYCCTK* (no. 4), 1981, pp. 55–6. Honan: *KMJP*, 18 April 1973; *NYCCWT* (no. 5), 1981, pp. 27–30; *NYCCTK* (no. 4), 1981, pp. 55–6. Hopei: *JMJP*, 18 October 1977; *NYCCWT* (no. 5), 1981, pp. 27–30; *NYCCTK* (no. 4), 1981, pp. 55–6. Shansi: *JMJP*, 8 December 1976; *NYCCWT* (no. 9), 1980, pp. 49–53; *NYCCTK* (no. 4), 1981, pp. 5–12. Shantung: *PR* (no. 34), 1974, p. 14, and (no. 42), 1978, p. 8. Li Hsien-nien in *HC* (no. 9), 1978, p. 6; *NTKTTH* (no. 5), 1981, pp. 27–30, and *ibid.* (no. 8), 1980 (information on the latter kindly supplied by N. Lardy); *NYCCTK* (no. 4), 1981, pp. 55–6. Hunan: *NYCCWT* (no. 3), 1981, pp. 3–10; Ma Hung and Sun Shang-ch'ing (eds), *Chung-kuo Ching-chi Chie-kou Wen-t'i Yen-chiu* (*Research on Questions Relating to China's Economic Structure*), 2 volumes (Peking, 1981), vol. 1, p. 143. Hupei: *NYCCWT* (no. 3), 1981, pp. 3–10; and *Peiching Shih-fan Ta-hsüeh Hsüeh-pao* (*Peking Teachers' College University Journal*), (no. 4), 1981, pp. 17–25. Kiangsi: *Chiang-hsi She-hui K'o-hsüeh* (*Kiangsi Social Science*) (nos. 5–6), 1981, pp. 19–24. Anhwei: *JMJP*, 11 September 1980. Chekiang: *JMJP*, 18 December 1978, and *NYCCWT* (no. 3), 1981, pp. 3–10. Kiangsu: *FBIS*, 14 August 1978 (information kindly supplied by R. F. Ash); also *JMJP*, 29 April 1980 and *NYCCWT* (no. 3), 1981, pp. 3–10. Kweichow: *Kuei-yang Shih-yuan Hsüeh-pao* (*Kweiyang Teachers' College Journal*) (no. 4), 1980, pp. 26–31; *NYCCTK* (no. 4), 1981, pp. 5–12. Szechuan: Export figures for 1965–70 and 1970–75 given to the author by the provincial grain office, 1982. Imports for 1976–77 and exports for 1979: *NYCCTK* (no. 4), 1981, pp. 55–6. Information concerning the designation of

The national average levels of grain consumption per head of total, rural and of urban population at the end of the 1970s were strikingly similar to those of 1953–57. Table 60 compares the figures. These suggest that while average grain consumption in 1978–79 was slightly higher than in 1953–57, it was below the levels attained in the peak years of the 1950s. Rural consumption per head reached its highest level in 1956 but, as earlier chapters have shown, that was a year of planning instability in which grain rationing was only loosely implemented. Urban consumption was highest in 1954 before rationing was introduced in the towns and cities. Compared with many consumption statistics published in China in 1978–80, the figures for the late 1970s in Table 60 may appear to be remarkably high. Official statements have presented figures of around 200 kilograms per head for urban as well as for rural grain 'consumption'. These, however, refer to *ration* levels (*k'ou-liang*) and not to total consumption and their levels are approximately the same as those prevailing in 1955–57. Detailed figures[35] for Shanghai in 1976–79 indicate that average *k'ou-liang* was around 80 per cent of total grain consumed per head in the city. For rural population also, actual consumption may be much higher than the *k'ou-liang* norm suggests. This is partly because, as the evidence of the 1950s shows, rationing is rarely strict enough to adhere to the norms; partly because some of the grain retained by rural households theoretically for seed and feed – under the 'three retained amounts' (*san liou liang*) – may be consumed; and, since 1979 especially, because a significant amount of grain is available from private plots. Peasants were not allowed to grow grain on private plots during the 1950s, but in the late 1970s they were encouraged to do so. A survey of 15,914 rural households in twenty-seven provinces carried

[35] *CCKL* (no. 3), 1981, pp. 27–9.

Sources to Table 59 (*cont.*)
Szechuan as a self-sufficient province was also given to the author by the provincial grain office. Yunnan: *Ssu-hsiang Chan-hsien* (*Ideological Front*) (no. 1), 1981, pp. 26–8 and 37; also *NYCCTK* (no. 4), 1981, pp. 5–12. Fukien: *NYCCWT* (no. 3), 1981, pp. 18–19. Kwangsi: *KMJP*, 28 December 1977; *CCYC* (no. 3), 1978, pp. 26–8, and *Nung-yeh ti Ken-pen chu-lu tsai-yü Chi-hsieh-hua* (*Agriculture's Basic Road is Mechanisation*) (Tientsin, 1979), p. 133. Kwangtung: *NFJP*, 15 February 1981, describes the province as a 'large' grain importer. Other information, including the figure for 1980–81, from Kwangtung Province Agriculture Committee, supplied to the author in 1982; see also *NYCCTK* (no. 4), 1981, pp. 5–12.

Table 60. *Average grain consumption per head, 1953–57 and 1978–79*
(kilograms unhusked grain)

	1953–57		1978	1979	Average 1978–79
	Average	Highest			
Per head of total population	248	273 (1956)			c.257
Per head of rural population	245	274 (1956)	248	257	252
Per head of urban population	263	286 (1954)			c.280

Sources and notes:
1953–57. Chapter 4.
1978–79. Rural consumption: 1978 and 1979 sample survey of 10 282 rural households: *JMJP*, 3 January 1981. Urban consumption: Based on figures for Shanghai which we assume are representative of urban China as it was in the 1950s. Shanghai figures are from *CCKL* (no. 3), 1981, pp. 27–9. Average population: Estimated from urban and rural consumption, and from population figures.

out by the State Statistical Bureau[36] found that the amounts being produced were not inconsiderable: 32.7 kilograms per head in 1979 and 35.7 kilograms in 1980. Data from various provinces confirm this order of magnitude,[37] even in the poor province of Kweichow,[38] where grain from the collective sector amounted to 262 kilograms per head in 1979–80, and the private plots provided 40 kilograms per head. Although this sample was undoubtedly atypically rich, it nevertheless illustrates the dangers of citing *k'ou-liang* figures as an indicator of total grain consumption.

Compared with the 1950s, provincial grain exports of the late 1970s probably had a much smaller impact on the grain consumption of the exporting provinces. Chapter 4 showed how grain consumption in Szechuan, for example, was considerably reduced as a result of the large amount of grain exported. In the 1950s, production per head of rural population was 327 kilograms and consumption has been

[36] *JMJP*, 16 June 1981.
[37] For example, in 1979 the average for the entire province of Kansu was 37 kilograms per head of rural population (*SWB*, 27 May 1981). In Szechuan, the Provincial Statistical Bureau surveyed 2181 households and found that collective grain output per head in 1980 was 285 kilograms and private plot output was 35 kilograms: *SZJP*, 3 June 1981.
[38] *SWB*, 20 May 1981, reporting a survey of 690 households.

estimated at 240 kilograms. Output per head in 1978–80 was 353 kilograms, at 8 per cent higher than in 1953–57, and average consumption was around 267 kilograms,[39] 11 per cent above 1955–56. To take a second example, exports in recent years of one million tons per year from Kiangsu were only worth 17 kilograms per head of population compared with a net output (after allowance for seed and feed) of 334 kilograms per head, and they did not therefore impoverish the local population.

Provincial grain imports of over 11 million tons per year in the late 1970s were still big enough to raise significantly the grain consumption of the poorest provinces, to offset the effects of harvest fluctuations and also to provide some stocks. The total import requirements of Peking, Tientsin and Shanghai were approximately 3.4 million tons per year, which meant that 8 million tons were left for the deficit provinces. In the absence of the necessary statistics it is impossible to measure the effect on consumption of such imports. We note, however, that Kweichow, a province in which consumption was considerably reduced by its grain exports during the 1950s, enjoyed a relatively high level of consumption in the late 1970s with the aid of imports: output per head of rural population was 288 kilograms compared with 308 kilograms in 1953–57, but average consumption was at least 220 kilograms (compared with 213 kilograms in 1953–57) and may have been as high as 300 kilograms.[40] Similarly, in Kwangtung, which was a large grain importer in the late 1970s, rural consumption was 294 kilograms per head[41] compared with 276 kilograms in 1953–57, whereas average *output* per head was almost identical in both periods (363 kilograms in 1953–57 and 362 kilograms in 1978–80). The great contrast between the two periods was, of course, that in the 1970s most of the provincial imports came from foreign countries and not from other Chinese provinces.

Grain consumption figures for the late 1970s must be interpreted against a background of increasing *indirect* consumption of grain in the form of pork, particularly in urban areas of China, as the figures in Table 61 show. More than 90 per cent of meat consumption

---

[39] *SZJP*, 3 June 1981.

[40] Judged from figures in the survey reported by *SWB*, 20 May 1981, and from *JMJP*, 22 April 1981, which gives *k'ou-liang* in 1980 as 75.4 per cent of 1957.

[41] *NFJP*, 21 January 1981. (A Provincial Statistical Bureau survey of 242 households, 1978–79.)

Table 61. *Meat[a] consumption per head in China (kilograms)*

	1953–57	1975	1976	1977	1978	1979	1980
China							
Per head total population	4.74[b]	7.40[b]	8.00	7.50	5.00	11.00	11.20[b]
urban population	8.84[b]				15.50[b]	19.00[b]	18.00
rural population	4.11[b]				3.05[c]	9.51[c]	9.94[c]
Shanghai	11.10[b]					19.00[b]	
Peking	8.65[b]						28.45[b]
Szechuan							
Per head urban population							28.55[b]
rural population					9.25	11.65	13.85
Kwangtung							
Per head rural population	6.72[b]						5.30
Kirin							
Per head urban population						15.25[b]	19.00[b]

Notes:
a. Excludes poultry.
b. Pork only and therefore excludes mutton and beef.
c. Estimated from figures for total and urban populations.
Sources:
1953–57. See Chapter 1.
1970s. China, per head of total population, 1975 and 1980: *SWB*, 8 July 1981. 1976: *NYCCWT* (no. 1), 1980, pp. 23–5. 1977 and 1979: *ibid*. (no. 1), 1981, pp. 24–8. 1978: *CCKH* (no. 4), 1980, p. 3. Per head of urban population, 1978 and 1979: *NYCCWT* (no. 11), 1980, p. 34. 1980: *SWB*, 6 May 1981 (sample of 7962 households). Shanghai, 1979: *CCKL* (no. 3), 1981, pp. 27–9. Peking, 1980: *JMJP*, 22 January 1981. Szechuan, urban, 1980: *ibid*. Rural, 1978–80: *SZJP*, 3 June 1981 (survey of 2181 households). Kwangtung, rural, 1980: *NFJP*, 21 January 1981 (survey of 242 households). Note that poultry consumption was 1.38 kg per head in this sample. Kirin: *SWB*, 1 April 1981.

(excluding poultry) was accounted for by pork.[42] Outside the predominantly livestock areas of the North West, very small amounts of beef and lamb were consumed. Few data on poultry consumption are available but fragmentary evidence[43] suggests that in the late 1970s it amounted to 1.0–1.5 kilograms per head. The increase in meat

[42] *NYCCWT* (no. 11), 1980, pp. 34–9. In Szechuan it was 94 per cent (*SZJP*, 3 June 1981).
[43] Average consumption in Shanghai, 1976–79, was around 1.0 kilograms per head (*CCKL* (no. 3), 1981, pp. 27–9); in rural Kwangtung (1978–9) it was *c*. 1.4 kilograms (*NFJP*, 21 January 1981); and approximately 0.7 kilograms per head of rural population were consumed from the private agricultural sector (*JMJP*, 16 June 1981).

consumption, associated with the Chinese Government's desire to improve the quality of the people's diet,[44] was related to the enlargement of the private agricultural sector as well as to the establishment of specialist livestock farms. At levels of pork production prevailing in the late 1970s the demand for feed grain was already high and further significant increase in the per capita consumption of meat and other livestock products, including poultry, eggs and animal fats, will be limited by the low domestic production of grain per head. The Chinese Government has ruled out importing more grain as a 'solution' to the feed grain deficit.[45]

Eventually, under conditions of rising per capita production, the demand for direct grain consumption will reach saturation point and will then decline in favour of other, including grain-using, foods. In his survey of food consumption patterns, Professor S. Ishikawa[46] drew attention to the economic importance of this turning point but found no clear evidence as to its exact level either in Asian or in socialist countries. The experience of Taiwan may, however, offer an interesting indicator for the large areas of China in which rice dominates food production and consumption. In Taiwan, according to the *Food Balance Sheets* prepared by the Council for Agricultural Planning and Development (formerly the Joint Commission on Rural Reconstruction), direct grain consumption reached its peak in 1969, at 249 kilograms (unhusked grain),[47] and it declined thereafter to reach 211 kilograms in 1979. During that period, rice consumption fell from 198 kilograms to 153 kilograms per head, wheat consumption remained fairly constant at 30 kilograms but sweet potatoes virtually disap-

---

[44] The long-run plan for consumption includes 50–100 kilograms per head per year of meat and 20–30 kilograms of eggs: *NYCCWT* (no. 1), 1980, pp. 23–5. In 1978 the projected improvement in the national diet was given remarkably optimistic publicity by the Chinese leaders, including Hua Kuo-feng who repeated a statement alleged to have been made by Mao: 'A country with the dictatorship of the proletariat can certainly ensure that the people have vegetables, cooking oil, pork, fish, beef, mutton, chickens, ducks, geese, rabbits and eggs to eat.' (Speech at the National Finance and Trade Conference 7 July 1978.) By 1980, however, Government spokesmen had become much more guarded in their predictions concerning such matters. See for example a pessimistic analysis in *CCYC* (no. 3), 1980, p. 8.

[45] *NYCCWT* (no. 2), 1980, p. 44, rejects the example set by Japan in this respect.

[46] S. Ishikawa, 'China's Food and Agriculture: A Turning Point', *Food Policy*, vol. 2 (no. 2), May 1977, pp. 90–102.

[47] Including potatoes, weighted at 5:1, and soya beans (with the bean equivalent of bean curd).

peared from the diet. Soya beans, consumed as beans or as bean-curd, increased slightly from 8 kilograms to 10 kilograms per head. Moreover, in 1969, when grain consumption was 249 kilograms per head, meat consumption (including poultry) was 23.2 kilograms per head, compared with the average in China, 1978–80, of 12 kilograms (including poultry). The consumption of fish, edible oil, milk and eggs also exceeded the Chinese levels of 1980, in most cases by a large margin. Table 62 summarises the data.

The improvement of the Chinese diet along Taiwanese lines involves two important shifts in the demand for grain. First, the consumption of fine grain will grow. This will affect all except the central and southern provinces of China in which rice, wheat and soya beans already account for 90–95 per cent of production. For most other Chinese provinces, however, the production of fine grains presents many problems. The composition of grain output should take account of several factors: the need to save land and to improve soil fertility; the need to produce grains with a high income elasticity of demand; and the need to grow 'multi-purpose' grains which can provide building materials, fuel and other valuable by-products in addition to food.

In practice it is very difficult to fulfil all these criteria. As Chapter 1 pointed out, in order to save land the highest yielding grains should be grown, and these include sweet potatoes, rice and maize, rather than soya beans and pulses. But sweet potatoes and maize are inferior foods, while soya beans and pulses are in high demand. In addition the latter supply valuable protein to a protein-deficient diet and they also improve soil fertility. *Kaoliang* has a relatively low average yield per hectare but in north China it is in great demand both as a food and as a source of fuel and building materials. For over twenty years, from 1958 to 1978, the composition of grain output in China reflected the yield criterion more than any other, as the figures in Table 63 show. Following the fall of the 'Gang of Four' the Government began to adopt a more flexible policy towards grain production, which involved (1) reducing slightly the grain sown area to allow for an increase in the production of industrial crops; and (2) establishing a more balanced composition of grain output, by increasing the production of grains that had been neglected for many years: soya beans, pulses, *kaoliang* and millet.

The declining per capita production of soya beans had particularly

Table 62. *Food consumption in Taiwan, 1969 and 1979, and China, 1978–80 (kilograms per head, unhusked grain)*

	Taiwan		China
	1969	1979	1978–80
Grain	249	211	257^d
Rice	198	153	n.a.
Wheat	31	30	n.a.
Potato^a	8	2	n.a.
Soya beans^b	8	10	n.a.
Other^c	4	16	n.a.
Meat	23.3	40.3	*c.*12.0^e
Pork	17.1	27.2	*c.*10.0
Poultry	5.5	11.7	*c.*1.0
Other	0.7	1.4	*c.*1.0
Eggs	3.9	7.8	2.2
Fish	30.3	38.1	*c.*6.0
Edible oil	6.2	9.9	1.6
Milk	2.1	5.3	*c.*1.0

Notes:
a. Weighted at 5:1.
b. Beans and beancurd converted to bean equivalent.
c. Mainly maize.
d. 1978–79 see Table 9.
e. 1979–80.
Sources: Taiwan data all calculated from *Taiwan Food Balance Sheets* (annual): Joint Commission on Rural Reconstruction until 1977 and Council for Agricultural Planning and Development thereafter.
    Chinese data. Meat: Table 9. Eggs: 1978 only; *NYCCWT* (no. 2), 1980, p. 50. Fish: H.J. Green and J.A. Kilpatrick, 'China's Agricultural Production' in *Chinese Economy Post-Mao*, US Government JEC Washington DC, November 1978, p. 645. Edible oil: 1978: *CCKH* (no. 4), 1980, p. 3. Milk: 1978; *NYCCWT* (no. 2), 1980, p. 50.

serious economic and social implications which have recently been recognised by the Chinese Government.[48] On average in 1977–79 China imported 1.24 million tons of beans per year (including oil in bean equivalent), at an annual cost of around US $150 million.[49] Such imports, however, were only worth 1.3 kilograms per head of total

[48] Good surveys of the contraction of soya bean output are found in *NYCCWT* (no. 7), 1980, pp. 29–32; and *ibid.* (no. 4), 1981, pp. 58–9. The dietary implications are mentioned by T'ung Ta-lin, *PR* (no. 4), 1980, pp. 20–3.
[49] *NYCCWT* (no. 4), 1981, pp. 58–9.

Table 63. *Composition of grain output in China, 1952–57 and 1978–80*

	Output (million tons)		% Output		Output per head (kg)	
	1952–57	1978–80	1952–57	1978–80	1952–57	1978–80
Grain	174.90	318.36	100.0	100.0	287	328
Rice	76.30	139.02	43.6	43.7	125	143
Wheat	21.86	56.54	12.5	17.8	36	58
Soya	9.66	7.65	5.5	2.4	16	8
Total fine	107.82	203.21	61.6	63.9	177	209
Maize	19.25	55.61	11.0	17.5	32	57
Millet	c.9.84	c.6.69	5.6	c.2.1	c.16	7
Kaoliang	c.9.56	c.8.28	5.5	c.2.6	c.16	9
Potatoes	15.02	29.13	8.6	9.2	25	30
Other	13.41	c.15.44	7.7	c.4.7	c.21	16
Total coarse	67.08	115.15	38.4	36.1	110	119

Sources:
Total grain output, 1978 and 1979: *JMJP*, 12 September 1980. 1980: SSB report in *JMJP*, 30 April 1981. Rice, wheat, soya and potatoes, 1978: *Chung-kuo Nung-yeh Ti-li Tsung-luen* (*General Agricultural Geography of China*), Geography Research Institute, Chinese Academy of Social Sciences (Peking, 1980), p. 13 and total output. 1979 and 1980: SSB report in *JMJP*, 30 April 1981. Maize, 1978: *General Agricultural Geography of China*. 1979: SSB report in *JMJP*, 30 April 1981. From figures in *Encyclopaedia* (1981), p. 274. Millet and *Kaoliang*, 1978 only: *General Agricultural Geography of China*. Other: Residual obtained by subtraction.

population, or 8.3 kilograms of urban population. To match Taiwan's soya bean consumption in China – 60.44 kilograms per head in 1979 – would necessitate the provision of an extra 51 million tons per year. Such magnitudes are the reason why the Chinese Government insists that her dependence on foreign grain must be tightly controlled and relatively short-lived.

The second way in which the demand for grain will shift is in the increase of its use for livestock. As this shift accelerates in the rural areas of China it will probably erode the grain surpluses required for the urban population and the pressure on the Government to satisfy urban demand – which will also increase, even more rapidly than in the countryside – by importing grain, will grow. Again, it is worth recording that 59 million tons of grain would be required to raise average pork consumption in China to the 1979 level of Taiwan. Overall, the change in meat consumption throughout China is bound to be slow, with considerable regional variation. In some fairly rich areas, however, it is possible that the direct consumption of grain has already begun to decline. An interesting indication of this is found in the results of a survey[50] in Szechuan to which reference has already been made. It shows that, although the amount of grain available per head of rural population rose from 310 kilograms in 1979 to 320 kilograms in 1980, *consumption* declined from 275 kilograms to 258.5 kilograms. At the same time, meat consumption rose from 11.7 kilograms to 13.9 kilograms, and eggs from 0.8 kilograms to 1.0 kilogram.

The rising demand for grain within China will be difficult to meet unless the rate of growth of production can be increased. Since 1976 the Government has made greater use of financial incentives, to promote both output and marketed supply, than at any time since central planning began in 1952. It has retained the Central Purchase and Supply of grain but has attempted to avoid the harmful effects which excessive procurement in earlier years had on production. Already, however, the dangers of the new policy are apparent. For example, the peasants reduced the grain sown area in 1978–80 to an extent that was unacceptable to the Government, forcing it to restore greater state control over land use.[51] It seems likely that the growth of private sector grain production will create further difficulties for the Government in the realm of consumption and distribution. The Government will doubtless continue to search for the optimum mixture of direct controls and financial inducements but, looking at China's vast population with its regional inequalities of food production and consumption, it seems inevitable that the physical rationing, state procurement and central redistribution of grain will form the basis of food policy in the future.

[50] *SZJP*, 3 June 1981.
[51] The grain sown area decreased by 7.3 million hectares (or by 6 per cent) between 1978 and 1980: see Kenneth R. Walker, 'China's Grain Production 1975–80 and 1952–57: Some Basic Statistics', *CQ* (no. 86), 1981, September, pp. 215–47). A Chinese statement on the problem is found in *JMJP*, 9 February 1981.

APPENDICES

CONTENTS

Appendix 1 Sources of data for Table 2: Food consumption per head in selected areas of China, 1950s

URBAN CONSUMPTION

North East China

Grain. Author's estimate. See Chapter 4. (Average for 1953–57.) *HAJP*, 15 November 1956, gives 256 kilograms per head as the average for the four years 1953–56.

Vegetables. Average for 1956 and 1957: *HHPYK*, vol. 129 (no. 7), 1958.

Meat. Average for 1952 and 1956: *HAJP*, 7 August 1957.

Edible oil. *HJP*, 14 August 1957. (Average per head of total population.)

Fish. Output (not consumption) per head in 1955 is given by *HJP* 22 May 1956.

Sugar. Average for 1952 and 1956: *HAJP*, 7 August 1957.

Alcohol. Ibid.

Peking

Grain. Author's estimate: average for 1953–57.

Vegetables. Average for four years 1951, 1955, 1956 and 1957. 1951 and 1957 are in *Shu-ts'ai Shang-p'in Ching-chi (Vegetable Commodity Economy)* (Peking, 1960), pp. 13–14. 1955 and 1956 are in *HHPYK*, vol. 122 (no. 24), 1957, pp. 62–4.

Meat. 1953–57: Five-year averages for pork, beef and mutton are given in *HHPYK, ibid.*

Edible oil. 1956 only: *PKJP*, 26 July 1957.

Sugar. 1956 only: *ibid.*

Eggs. 1954–57: Four-year average calculated from figures in *HHPYK, ibid.*

Shanghai

Grain. Author's estimate for 1953–57.

Vegetables, pork, beef and mutton. 1952–58, six-year averages. Figures for 1952 are in *HHYK* (no. 16), 1958. 1953–58 are in *HHPYK*, vol. 122 (no. 24), 1957, pp. 62–4.

Edible oil, sugar, fish, poultry and wine. Averages for 1952, 1955 and 1956. Figures are in *HHYK* (no. 16), 1958, and a second figure for 1956 is given in *TCKT* (no. 13), 1957. The average of the two figures for 1956 has been used.

Eggs. Six-year average for 1952–57. Figure for 1952: *HHYK* (no. 16), 1958; 1953–57: *HHPYK*, vol. 122 (no. 24), 1957.

Canton

Grain. Author's estimate for five years 1953–57.

Vegetables. Figure for late 1957: *KWCJP*, 27 November 1957. (1956 consumption was below the level recorded here.)

Meat. Pork only. Averages for 1955, 1956 and 1957. 1955 and 1956 are estimates based on figures in *KWCJP*, 24 December 1956. 1957: *KWCJP*, 26 July 1957 and *NFJP*, 12 October 1957.

Edible oil. NFJP, 12 October 1957.

Eggs. Average for 1955 and 1956: from figures in *KWCJP*, 24 December 1956.

Fish. Figures for 1956 January–October and for summer 1957. See *KWCJP*, 24 December 1956 and *NFJP*, 12 August 1957.

Poultry. Average for 1956 and 1957: from figures in *NFJP*, 12 August 1957 and 25 July 1957.

RURAL CONSUMPTION

North (Shansi province)

Grain. Author's estimate for five years 1953–57.
All other items, except sugar and fish, are for representative households from ninety-nine collectives in Shansi: *Shan-hsi Nung-ts'un Ching-chi Tiao-ch'a (Shansi Rural Economic Surveys)*, vol. 1 (Taiyuan, 1958), pp. 13–14. Figures for sugar and fish are from a survey of forty-one collectives in *ibid.*, pp. 66–84.

Central (Chekiang province)

Grain. Author's estimate for five years 1953–57.
All other items are in *CHKJP*, 6 April 1957: survey of 1000 rural households in the province.

South (Kwangtung province)

Grain. Author's estimate for five years 1953–57.

Vegetables. Average for 1956 and 1957, middle peasants only, in two Special Districts of the province. See *NFJP*, 10 October 1957 and 4 April 1957.

Meat (pork). Average for 1952, 1956 and 1957: *NFJP*, 18 August 1957.

Edible oil. Average for 1955, 1956 and 1957: *KWCJP*, 26 July 1957, *NFJP*, 26 June 1957 and 12 October 1957.

Fish. Average for 1953 and 1957: *NFJP*, 18 August 1957.

Sugar. Average for 1953, 1955, 1956 and 1957: *NFJP*, 18 August 1957 (for 1953 and 1957) and *KWCJP*, 6 July 1957 (for 1955 and 1956).

Alcohol. Average for 1953 and 1957: *NFJP*, 18 August 1957.

Poultry. 1956 only: consumption of middle peasants in one Special District: *NFJP*, 10 October 1957.

Appendix 2 Sources of data for output, sown area and yield per sown hectare of major grain crops and of total grain

a. OUTPUT

Output: grain (million tons)

	1952	1953	1954	1955	1956	1957
North East						
Heilungkiang	8.789	7.110	7.032	8.205	7.910	7.859
Kirin	6.123	5.853	5.510	5.695	4.936	5.434
Liaoning	5.440	5.715	6.015	6.170	7.430	6.702
North West						
IMR	3.417	3.544	3.884	3.254	4.557	2.957
Kansu	3.165	3.025	3.775	4.150	5.450	5.065
Shensi	3.975	4.740	5.009	4.505	5.437	4.523
Sinkiang	1.607	1.720	1.820	1.913	1.934	2.034
Tsinghai	0.371	0.331	0.528	0.589	0.610	0.644
North						
Honan	10.285	11.240	11.800	12.850	12.875	12.300
Hopei	9.440	8.125	7.990	9.125	8.260	10.100
Peking	0.113	0.123	0.083	0.123	0.156	0.197
Shansi	3.845	4.322	4.115	3.725	4.335	3.565
Shantung	12.584	11.077	13.187	13.509	14.675	12.968
Tientsin	0.158	0.134	0.145	0.194	0.218	0.250
Central						
Hunan	10.318	10.338	9.282	11.267	10.305	11.324
Hupei	8.425	9.067	6.845	9.609	10.761	11.345
Kiangsi	5.790	5.750	5.742	6.267	6.617	7.060
East						
Anhwei	8.810	9.085	7.770	11.529	10.909	12.350
Chekiang	7.000	7.155	7.085	7.622	7.664	7.904
Kiangsu	10.885	11.750	11.500	12.870	12.000	12.229
Shanghai	*c*.0.041	*c*.0.044	*c*.0.038	*c*.0.042	*c*.0.048	*c*.0.033
South West						
Kweichow	3.447	3.773	4.080	4.264	4.865	5.356
Szechuan	16.877	18.310	19.525	20.230	22.255	23.258
Yunnan	4.685	4.961	5.335	5.655	6.283	*c*.6.447
South						
Fukien	3.719	*c*.3.905	3.755	3.890	4.435	4.442
Kwangsi	5.005	5.450	5.895	5.900	5.260	5.405
Kwangtung	9.455	10.265	10.980	10.985	12.006	*c*.12.266
Total	163.769	166.912	168.725	184.137	192.191	194.017
Official total	163.900	166.800	169.500	183.900	192.750	195.050

Notes: Official national totals are from Collection of Statistical Data (1958). A discussion of the problems of interpreting the available provincial grain production figures is offered in Kenneth R. Walker, *Provincial Grain output in China 1952–57: A Statistical Compilation*, Research Notes and Studies no. 3, Contemporary China Institute, School of Oriental and African Studies (London, 1977).

Output, sown area and yield per sown hectare

Output: rice (thousand tons)

	1952	1953	1954	1955	1956	1957
North East						
Heilungkiang	329	c.441	459	534	674	491
Kirin	c.278	—	248	454	755	625
Liaoning	300	—	—	420	939	652
North West						
IMR	25	16	21	32	66	42
Kansu	—	—	—	—	—	27
Shensi	467	—	—	541	588	c.440
Sinkiang	c.100	—	—	—	—	188
Tsinghai	—	—	—	—	—	—
North						
Honan	743	758	—	1015	1168	1218
Hopei		c.307		c.336	395	304
Peking	—	—	—	—	—	—
Shansi	—	—	—	—	—	—
Shantung	—	—	—	—	—	—
Tientsin	—	—	—	6	25	c.10
Centre						
Hunan	9151	9188	8221	9900	9203	9667
Hupei	5315	5375	3995	6152	7200	7555
Kiangsi	c.5356	—	5360	5891	6000	6237
East						
Anhwei	4625	—	—	5400	6470	6554
Chekiang	c.5286	5494	—	—	6233	5973
Kiangsu	5634	6350	5785	6700	6161	6711
Shanghai	—	—	—	—	—	—
South West						
Kweichow	2374	2383	2622	—	2829	3360
Szechuan	10504	11000	11560	11893	13299	13687
Yunnan	2566	2673	3006	3111	3341	3562
South						
Fukien	2791	—	—	2854	—	3284
Kwangsi	4040	4356	c.4200	4130	—	4345
Kwangtung	8027	8446	9050	9014	9588	9940

Note: Brace indicates that the figure is an average for the years shown.

Appendix 2

Output: wheat (thousand tons)

	1952	1953	1954	1955	1956	1957
North East						
Heilungkiang	862	c.591	c.746	599	555	901
Kirin	66	—	—	47	13	30
Liaoning	c.62	—	—	—	30	30
North West						
IMR	245	327	516	471	532	495
Kansu	c.1360	—	1350	—	1802	1440
Shensi	1328	2008	2125	1858	2395	1903
Sinkiang	755	793	845	—	992	865
Tsinghai	c.175	c.161	254	c.277	253	n.a.
North						
Honan	3005	2955	4190	4272	4275	3750
Hopei	1300	1123	1908	1773	1935	1950
Peking	—	—	—	—	—	—
Shansi	610	995	1002	1042	1293	748
Shantung	3268	2728	3574	3128	3698	3565
Tientsin	—	—	—	—	—	—
Centre						
Hunan	141	128	118	168	169	151
Hupei	805	950	904	906	952	1220
Kiangsi	—	86	—	—	—	57
East						
Anhwei	1299	—	1239	1390	1044	2005
Chekiang	c.280	—	—	—	—	257
Kiangsu	1652	1458	1900	1962	1732	c.1574
Shanghai	—	—	—	—	—	—
South West						
Kweichow	51	—	94	—	187	203
Szechuan	898	1139	1196	1350	1587	1638
Yunnan	196	219	197	233	305	309
South						
Fukien	117	—	—	—	300	c.169
Kwangsi	30	35	59	—	—	55
Kwangtung	52	57	68	95	163	175

Output, sown area and yield per sown hectare

Output: soya beans (thousand tons)

	1952	1953	1954	1955	1956	1957
North East						
Heilungkiang	1637	1653	1269	1430	1670	1691
Kirin	1200	1115	1117	823	1086	1159
Liaoning	554	665	700	625	900	767
North West						
IMR	122	169	189	157	182	146
Kansu	330	269	338	383	677	492
Shensi	215	190	218	222	340	240
Sinkiang			negligible			
Tsinghai			negligible			
North						
Honan	1070	1285	930	1164	1235	1482
Hopei	356	466	481	526	482	c.453
Shansi	182	277	329	212	320	c.303
Shantung	1620	1410	1653	1531	1855	885
Centre						
Hunan	73	73	62	67	56	90
Hupei	104	287	100	209	319	380
Kiangsi	125	68	65	105	113	228
East						
Anhwei	574	791	281	745	297	824
Chekiang	128	337	335	119	175	111
Kiangsu	c.726	c.748	c.674	c.723	c.655	646
South West						
Kweichow	52	102	144	84	115	102
Szechuan	c.173	c.169	c.180	c.196	c.197	279
Yunnan	252	267	283	291	362	c.197
South						
Fukien	54	55	49	50	65	65
Kwangsi	c.79	c.86	c.93	c.93	c.83	c.86
Kwangtung	67	c.75	65	55	55	c.61

Output: coarse grain (including potatoes)* (thousand tons)

	1952	1953	1954	1955	1956	1957
North East						
Heilungkiang	5961	c.4425	c.4558	5642	5011	4776
Kirin	c.4579	—	—	4371	3082	3620
Liaoning	c.4524	—	—	—	5561	5253
North West						
IMR	3025	3032	3158	2594	3777	2274
Kansu	c.1475	—	2087	—	2971	3106
Shensi	1965	—	—	1884	2114	1940
Sinkiang	752	—	—	—	—	981
Tsinghai	c.196	c.170	274	c.312	357	n.a.
North						
Honan	5467	6242	5884	6399	6197	5850
Hopei	7433	6248	5317	6490	5448	7393
Shansi	3053	3050	2784	2471	2722	2514
Shantung	7696	6939	7960	8844	9097	8508
Centre						
Hunan	953	949	881	1132	877	1416
Hupei	2201	2674	1881	2446	2496	2342
Kiangsi	—	—	—	—	—	538
East						
Anhwei	2312	—	—	3994	3074	2918
Chekiang	c.1306	—	—	—	—	1563
Kiangsu	c.2873	c.3194	c.3141	c.3485	c.3452	3298
South West						
Kweichow	970	—	1220	—	1734	1691
Szechuan	5302	6002	6589	6791	7172	7654
Yunnan	1671	1802	1849	2020	2275	c.2379
South						
Fukien	757	—	—	—	—	c.924
Kwangsi	c.856	c.973	c.1543	—	—	c.919
Kwangtung	1309	c.1687	1797	1821	2200	2090

Note: * Coarse grain output including potatoes equals total output minus fine grain. Fine grains are rice, wheat and soya beans.

Output, sown area and yield per sown hectare

Output: potatoes (4 : 1)* (thousand tons)

	1952	1953	1954	1955	1956	1957
North East						
Heilungkiang	489	340	482	600	307	444
Kirin	—	—	—	265	163	170
Liaoning	210	—	—	354	310	390
North West						
IMR	413	330	282	273	326	278
Kansu	—	—	—	—	—	—
Shensi	—	—	—	—	—	—
Sinkiang	—	—	—	—	—	12
Tsinghai	—	—	—	87	—	—
North						
Honan	1653	1742	2047	1794	2292	1735
Hopei	1237	1185	871	1063	1250	1460
Peking	—	—	—	—	—	—
Shansi	496	380	251	166	211	338
Shantung	2390	2386	2967	2965	3751	3500
Tientsin	—	—	—	—	—	—
Centre						
Hunan	660	602	572	798	572	989
Hupei	460	425	340	457	740	445
Kiangsi	—	—	—	—	—	365
East						
Anhwei	c.1816	—	—	1450	c.1885	1615
Chekiang	—	—	—	—	600	825
Kiangsu	—	—	—	—	—	517
Shanghai	—	—	—	—	—	—
South West						
Kweichow	—	—	—	—	—	317
Szechuan	2030	—	3041	—	2500	3183
Yunnan	274	310	265	294	407	340
South						
Fukien	729	—	—	651	—	c.888
Kwangsi	455	—	—	—	—	370
Kwangtung	c.1266	1451	1640	1656	1712	1798

Note: *During the 1950s potatoes were expressed in grain equivalent by counting 4 units equal to 1 unit of grain. Since 1962 the conversion ratio has been 5 : 1.

Output: coarse grain (net of potatoes) (thousand tons)

	1952	1953	1954	1955	1956	1957
North East						
Heilungkiang	5472	4085	4076	5042	4704	4332
Kirin	—	—	—	4106	2919	3450
Liaoning	4314	—	—	—	5251	4863
North West						
IMR	2612	2702	2876	2321	3451	1996
Kansu			*c.*2010			
Shensi			*c.*1850			
Sinkiang	752	—	—	—	—	969
Tsinghai	—	—	—	*c.*225		
North						
Honan	3814	4500	3837	4605	3905	4115
Hopei	6196	5063	4446	5427	4198	5933
Shansi	2557	2670	2533	2305	2511	2176
Shantung	5306	4553	4993	5879	5346	5008
Centre						
Hunan	293	347	309	334	305	427
Hupei	1741	2249	1541	1989	1756	1897
Kiangsi	—	—	—	—	—	173
East						
Anhwei	*c.*496	—	—	2544	*c.*1189	1303
Chekiang	—	—	—	—	—	738
Kiangsu	—	—	—	—	—	2781
South West						
Kweichow	—	—	—	—	—	1374
Szechuan	3272	—	3548	—	4672	4471
Yunnan	1397	1492	1584	1726	1868	*c.*2039
South						
Fukien	28	—	—	—	—	*c.*36
Kwangsi	401	—	—	—	—	549
Kwangtung	*c.*43	236	157	165	488	292

Note: Braces indicate that the figures are averages over all six years.

Output, sown area and yield per sown hectare

Output: maize (thousand tons)

	1952	1953	1954	1955	1956	1957
North East						
Heilungkiang[a]	2127	—	—	—	—	1867
Kirin	—	c.1345	—	—	—	1389
Liaoning	1258	—	—	—	2694	1729
North West						
IMR			c.498			
Kansu		c.1029				
Shensi	—	—	—	874	1464[b]	
Sinkiang	589	—	—	—	—	721
Tsinghai	—	—	—	—	—	—
North						
Honan	—	—	—	1169	—	—
Hopei	—	—	c.1474	—	2350	—
Shansi	—	—	645	740	—	—
Shantung			c.2015			
Centre						
Hunan	80	92	84	96	95	138
Hupei	—	—	—	597	—	595
Kiangsi	—	—	—	—	—	—
East						
Anhwei	—	—	—	—	—	—
Chekiang	—	—	—	—	—	257
Kiangsu	—	—	—	1001	—	—
South West						
Kweichow	740	—	—	—	—	1116
Szechuan	1475	—	—	—	1956	2100
Yunnan	—	—	—	—	—	1336
South						
Fukien	—	—	—	—	—	—
Kwangsi	—	—	—	—	—	—
Kwangtung	—	—	—	—	—	—

Notes: a. Heilungkiang average for 1953–57 was 1780.
b. Planned figure.
Braces indicate that the figure is an average over the years shown.

Output: millet (thousand tons)

	1952	1953	1954	1955	1956	1957
North East						
Heilungkiang*	1289	—	—	—	—	1356
Kirin	—	—	—	—	—	733
Liaoning	562	—	—	—	—	765
North West						
IMR			c.1436			
Kansu	—	—	—	—	—	—
Shensi	—	—	—	—	—	—
Sinkiang	—	—	—	—	—	—
Tsinghai	—	—	—	—	—	—
North						
Honan	—	—	—	—	—	750
Hopei	—	—	c.1389	—	—	—
Shansi	c.779	—	—	—	—	—
Shantung	—	—	—	—	—	—
Centre						
Hunan	—	—	—	—	—	—
Hupei	—	—	—	—	—	—
Kiangsi	—	—	—	—	—	—
East						
Anhwei	—	—	—	—	—	—
Chekiang	—	—	—	—	—	—
Kiangsu	—	—	—	—	—	—
South West						
Kweichow	—	—	—	—	—	—
Szechuan	—	—	—	—	—	—
Yunnan	—	—	—	—	—	—
South						
Fukien	—	—	—	—	—	—
Kwangsi	—	—	—	—	—	—
Kwangtung	—	—	—	—	—	—

Notes: * Heilungkiang average for 1953–57 was 1156. Brace indicates that the figure is an average over all six years.

Output, sown area and yield per sown hectare

Output: kaoliang (thousand tons)

	1952	1953	1954	1955	1956	1957
North East						
Heilungkiang*	1010	—	—	—	—	682
Kirin	c.1932	—	—	—	—	855
Liaoning	1932	—	—	—	—	1995
North West						
IMR			c.480			
Kansu	—	—	—	—	—	—
Shensi	—	—	—	—	—	—
Sinkiang	—	—	—	—	—	—
Tsinghai	—	—	—	—	—	—
North						
Honan	—	—	—	—	—	—
Hopei	—	—	c.708	—	—	—
Shansi	—	—	—	—	—	—
Shantung	—	—	—	—	—	—
Centre						
Hunan	—	—	—	—	—	—
Hupei	—	—	—	—	—	—
Kiangsi	—	—	—	—	—	—
East						
Anhwei	—	—	—	—	—	—
Chekiang	—	—	—	—	—	—
Kiangsu	—	—	—	—	—	—
South West						
Kweichow	—	—	—	—	—	—
Szechuan	—	—	—	—	—	—
Yunnan	—	—	—	—	—	—
South						
Fukien	—	—	—	—	—	—
Kwangsi	—	—	—	—	—	—
Kwangtung	—	—	—	—	—	—

Notes: * Heilungkiang average for 1953–57 was 867. Brace indicates that the figure is an average over all six years.

SOURCES

Heilungkiang

Total grain. **1952**: *HH* (no. 17), 13 August 1957, pp. 25–8. **1953**: *HJP*, 29 October 1957. **1954**: *HJP*, 10 December 1955. **1955**: *HJP*, 18 October 1957. **1956**: *HJP*, 7 August 1957. **1957**: Calculated from figures *An Economic Geography of NE China*, pp. 173 and 175, relating to the percentage composition of total sown area and to yields of grain crops. Grain production can be calculated by multiplying sown area by yield, once sown areas are known. These are obtained from the figure for kaoliang sown area in 1957 (*An Economic Geography of NE China*, p. 178).

Rice. **1952** and **1957**: *An Economic Geography of NE China*. **1953**: Estimated from yield and approximate sown area. **1954** and **1955**: From yield and sown area. **1956**: From 1955 and percentage in *HJP*, 28 July 1957.

Wheat. **1952** and **1957**: *An Economic Geography of NE China*. **1953** and **1955**: Sown area times yield. **1954**: From sown area and estimated yield. **1956**: SSB in *HJP*, 7 August 1957 and figure for 1955.

Soya. **1952** and **1957**: *An Economic Geography of NE China*. **1953** and **1954**: From gross and net grain output. Net output from index in *NTKTTH* (no. 2) 1958, p. 21. **1955** *JMJP*, 12 October 1956. **1956**: *HJP*, 7 August 1957.

Potatoes. **1952** and **1957**: *An Economic Geography of NE China*. **1953**: Five-year total (*ibid.*) minus four-year total. **1954** and **1955**: *HJP*, 10 December 1955. **1956**: SSB in *HJP*, 7 August 1957.

Maize, millet and kaoliang. **1952** and **1957**: *An Economic Geography of NE China*, which also contains averages for the period 1952–57.

Kirin

Total grain. **1952** and **1956**: *KJP*, 14 August 1957. **1953**: By subtraction. Total output for four years (*KJP*, 21 August 1957) minus total output for the three years 1954–56 (by adding output of individual years). **1954**: *KJP*, 24 April 1955. **1955**: Grain output net of potatoes (*KJP*, 9 July 1957) plus potato output (*KJP*, 20 April 1956), confirmed (rounded) in *KJP*, 18 February 1957. **1957**: Net output (*An Economic Geography of NE China*, p. 109) plus soya beans.

Rice. **1952**: An estimate only, based on sown area and four-year average yields. **1954**: SSB in *KJP*, 20 April 1956 and 1955 figure. **1955**: SSB in *KJP*, 17 April 1954 and 1956 figure. **1956**: SSB in *KJP*, 17 April 1957. **1957**: *An Economic Geography of NE China*.

Wheat. **1952**: *An Economic Geography of NE China*. **1955–57**: Sown area times yield.

Soya. **1952**: *KJP*, 29 April 1956. **1953**: *TKP*, 15 November 1954. **1954**: *KJP* 22 April 1956 and 28 April 1956. **1955**: *KJP*, 22 April 1956. **1956**: *KJP*, 17 April 1956. **1957**: From five-year total (*KJP*, 1 January 1958) and four-year total.

Potatoes. **1955**: SSB in *KJP*, 20 April 1956. **1956**: From gross grain output and gross output net of potatoes (*KJP*, 9 July 1957). **1957**: *An Economic Geography of NE China*.

Maize. **1953**: Estimate based on sown area for 1952 and yield for 1953. **1957**: *An Economic Geography of NE China*.

Millet. **1957**: *An Economic Geography of NE China*.

Kaoliang. **1953**: Using data for Liaoning and Heilungkiang, and information in *TLCS* (no. 9), 1953. **1957**: *An Economic Geography of NE China.*

Liaoning

Total grain. **1952**: *LJP*, 18 September 1957. **1954**: Net output (Chinese figures cited in *PAS*, p. 163), plus soya beans. **1953**: From 1954 – gross grain output in 1954 is reported to have risen by 0.3 million tons (*LJP*, 13 November 1954). **1955**: *LJP*, 18 January 1957. **1956**: *LJP*, 28 January 1958. **1957**: Net output plus soya beans (*An Economic Geography of NE China*, pp. 42 and 41).

Rice. **1952** and **1957**: *An Economic Geography of NE China.* **1955**: *LJP*, 9 October 1956. **1956**: *LJP*, 24 August 1957.

Wheat. **1952**: An estimate from sown area and assumed yield (two-year average for 1956–57). **1956:** From sown area and yield. **1957**: *An Economic Geography of NE China.*

Soya. **1952** and **1957**: *An Economic Geography of NE China.* **1953**: From five-year total (*LJP*, 2 January 1958) and four-year total. **1954** and **1955**: From 1956 and *JMJP*, 5 October 1956. **1956**: *LJP*, 2 January 1958. **1957**: *An Economic Geography of NE China.*

Potatoes. **1952** and **1957**: *ibid.* **1955** and **1956**: From gross grain output and output net of potatoes (*LJP*, 28 December 1956).

Maize. **1952** and **1957**: *An Economic Geography of NE China.* **1956**: From sown area and yield.

Mill(**1952** and **1957**: *An Economic Geography of NE China.*

Kaoliang. **1952** and **1957**: *ibid.*

Inner Mongolia

Total grain. **1953–57**: *NMKTC.*

Rice, wheat, soya and potatoes. All from *ibid.*

Maize, millet and kaoliang. *NMKJP*, 5 February 1958.

Kansu (including the area later called Ningsia)

Total grain. **1952**: *KAJP*, 13 March 1956. **1953–56**: *KAJP*, 1 October 1957. **1957**: *HHPYK*, vol. 130 (no. 8), 1958, pp. 121–5.

Rice. **1957**: From sown area and yield.

Wheat. **1952**: Approximate output estimated from known sown area and assumed yield (that of 1954). **1954**: *TTKP*, 23 August 1956. **1956** and **1957**: From sown area and yield.

Soya. **1952–57**: From gross and net grain output using index in *NTKTTH* (no. 2), 1958. Net output for 1952 is in *KAJP*, 27 February 1954.

Potatoes. A rough estimate for 1952–57 may be obtained from the yields for 1952, 1953 and 1957, and from the planned sown area for 1958.

Shensi

Total grain. **1952–55**: *NPC* (1957), pp. 701–5. **1956–57**: *SESJP*, 4 February 1958.

Rice. **1952**: *SCMP*, no. 1208. **1954** and **1955**: Estimates for consumption figures in *SESJP*, 18 July 1957. **1956**: From 1956 and *SESJP*, 4 May 1957. **1957**: Minimum estimate from known sown area and assumed yield (using yields of 1952, 1954, 1955 and 1956).

Wheat. **1952**: *SCMP*, no. 1208. **1953**: From percentage in *SESJP*, 1 July 1958. **1954**: *CFJP*, 20 June 1957. **1955**: From 1956 and *SESJP*, 4 May 1957. **1957**: *SESJP*, 5 August 1958.

Soya. **1952–57**: From gross and net grain output. 1957 net output: *SESJP*, 31 October 1957. 1952–56 net output: From index in *NTKTTH* (no. 2), 1958.

Potatoes. No data for 1952–57 discovered. 1931–37 figures from T.H. Shen, *Agricultural Resources of China* (Ithaca, New York, 1951), p. 375: 0.126 million tons per annum.

Maize. **1952–55**: *SESJP*, 3 April 1956. **1955**: From sown area and yield. **1956**: Planned output in *SESJP*, 4 April 1956.

Sinkiang

Total grain. **1952**: From figures in *SINJP*, 1 October 1957 and *SNY*, p. 2. **1953** and **1954**: *PAS*, p. 203. **1955**: Yen Kuan-yi, *Hsin-chiang-wei-wu-erh tzu-chih ch'ü (Sinkiang-Uighur Autonomous Region)* (Peking, 1957). **1956**: *SINJP*, 11 August 1957. **1957**: *SINJP*, 1 October 1957.

Rice. **1952**: Minimum estimate, from sown area and from assumed yields. **1957**: *SNM*, 12 March 1958.

Wheat. **1952–54** and **1956**: From sown area and yield. **1957**: *SNY*.

Potatoes. **1957**: *SINJP*, 17 April 1958.

Maize. **1952** and **1957**: *SNY*.

Tsinghai

Total grain. **1952–56**: *TSINJP*, 18 August 1957. **1957**: *TSINJP*, 8 September 1957.

Wheat. **1952, 1953** and **1955**: Estimated from sown area and approximate yields, based on percentage fluctuations in *average* grain yields, and actual *wheat* yields for 1954 and 1956. **1954** and **1956**: From sown area and yield.

Potatoes. **1955**: Estimate based on sown area and planned yield for 1955.

Honan

Total grain. **1952–55**: *HONJP*, 24 August 1957. **1956**: *HONJP*, 30 December 1957. **1957**: *HHPYK*, vol. 129 (no. 7), 1958, pp. 68–9.

Rice. **1952–53**: From sown area and yield. **1955** and **1956**: By subtraction of other main grain crops from total output. **1957**: From 1952 and percentage in *HONJP*, 8 January 1958.

Wheat. **1952–57**: *JMJP*, 15 June 1958.

Soya. **1952–54** and **1957**: By subtracting net from gross grain output. Net output 1952–54 is in *CKNP* (no. 15), 1957, pp. 12–15 and 27. Net output for 1957: *HONJP*, 31 December 1957 and 1952 figure. **1955** and **1956**: SSB in *HONJP*, 18 September 1957.

Potatoes. **1952, 1953, 1954** and **1957**: By subtracting other main grain crops from total grain output. **1955** and **1956**: *HONJP*, 7 June 1957.

Maize. **1955**: *CKNP* (no. 17), 1955, p. 24. **1957**: An estimate, from known sown area and assumed yield.

Millet. **1957**: *JMJP*, 28 September 1958.

Hopei

Total grain. **1952** and **1957**: *HHPYK*, vol. 128, no. 6 (1958), pp. 103–4. **1953–56**: *HOPJP*, 14 August 1957.

Rice. Average for 1952–54: Estimates from known yield and 1955 sown area (known to be quite constant). **1955**: Estimate based on sown area and approximate yield. **1957**: From sown area and yield.

Wheat. **1952–57**: *CKNP* (no. 15), 1957, pp. 12–15 and 27.

Soya. **1952–56**: By subtraction of net from gross grain output. Net output: *CKNP* (no. 15), 1957, pp. 12–15 and p. 27. **1957**: A rough estimate based on assumed sown area and yields. For details see Kenneth R. Walker, *Provincial Grain Output*, pp. 14–15.

Potatoes. **1952–55**: Estimate as a residual. Coarse grains as a group are given in *CKNP* (no. 15), 1957, pp. 12–15 and 27. **1956**: *HOPJP*, 25 October 1956. **1957**: From sown area and yield.

Maize. **1954**: Estimated from known sown area and average yield for 1952–54. **1956**: *HOPJP*, 25 October 1956.

Millet and kaoliang. **1954**: Estimates based on sown area and average yield for 1952–54.

Peking

Total grain. **1956**: *PKJP*, 24 July 1957. **1952–55** and **1957**: From 1956 and the grain output index in *NTKTTH* (no. 2), 1958, p. 21. The index is for net grain output but soya bean production in the Peking suburbs is assumed to have been negligible.

Shansi

Total grain. **1952**: *SASJP*, 5 October 1955. **1953** and **1956**: *SASJP*, 8 December 1956. **1954**: *SASJP*, 21 December 1957. **1955**: *SASJP*, 29 May 1960. **1957**: *SASJP*, 10 October 1959.

Wheat. **1952**: *PAS*. **1953** and **1954**: *SASJP*, 23 February 1955. **1955**: From 1954 and percentage in *TKP*, 19 June 1955. **1956**: From 1955 and percentage in *SASJP*, 23 April 1957 (SSB figure). **1957**: From five-year total (*SASJP*, 12 May 1958) and four-year total.

Soya. **1952** and **1953**: *PAS*. **1954–56**: By subtraction of net from gross grain output. Net output from the index in *NTKTTH* (no. 2), 1958. **1957**: An estimate, from known sown area and approximate yield. For details of estimate see Kenneth R. Walker, *Provincial Grain Output*.

Potatoes. **1952–57**: All obtained as a residual from total grain output and main grains other than potatoes. Coarse grain output: **1952–56**: *CKNP* (no. 15), 1957, pp. 12–15 and 27. **1957**: From five-year total (*SASJP*, 12 May 1958) and four-year total.

Maize. **1954** and **1955**: From sown area and yield.

Millet. **1952**: From percentage of national output given in *TLCS* (no. 9), 1953.

Shantung

Total grain. **1952–55**: *TCJP*, 19 January 1957. **1956**: *TCJP*, 9 August 1957. **1957**: *TCJP*, 6 January 1958.

Rice. **1955** and **1956**: SSB figures in *TCJP*, 9 August 1957. **1957**: From sown area and assumed yield.

Wheat. **1952–54**: Sown area times yield. **1955–56**: SSB figures in *TCJP*, 9 August 1957. **1957**: *CTJP*, 17 August 1957.

Soya. **1952–54** and **1957**: By subtraction, gross output minus net output. Net output **1952–54**: *CKNP* (no. 15), 1957, pp. 12–15 and 27. Net output 1957: From index in *NTKTTH* (no. 2), 1958. **1955** and **1956**: SSB figures in *TCJP*, 9 August 1957.

Potatoes. **1952–54**: Obtained as a residual. Coarse grains: *CKNP* (no. 15), 1957, pp. 12–15 and 27. **1955** and **1956**: SSB figures in *TCJP*, 9 August 1957. **1957**: *TCJP*, 11 October 1957.

Maize. An average output for 1952–57 may be estimated from sown areas (available for all years) and average yield for 1952–57.

Tientsin

Total grain. **1953**: *TJP*, 26 December 1956. **1955–56**: *TJP*, 30 April 1957. **1952, 1954** and **1957**: From the index in *NTKTTH* (no. 2), 1958 (soya bean production was negligible).

Hunan

Total grain. **1952–55** and **1957**: By addition, net output plus soya beans. Net output is in *HNNY*, p. 243. **1956**: *HHNP*, 15 February 1957.

Other grains. HNNY.

Hupei

Total grain. **1952**: *JMJP*, 14 December 1957. **1953–56**: *LSWTCC*. **1957**: By addition, net output plus soya beans. Net output is in *An Economic Geography of Central China*, p. 76.

Rice, wheat and potatoes. **1952–56**: *LSWTCC*. **1957**: *An Economic Geography of Central China*.

Soya. **1952–56**: Gross output minus net output. Net output: *LSWTCC*. **1957**: *An Economic Geography of Central China*.

Maize. **1955**: *LSWTCC*. **1957**: *An Economic Geography of Central China*.

Kiangsi

Total grain. **1952**: *KSIJP*, 1 January 1958. **1953**: *KSIJP*, 12 January 1955. **1954**: *KSIJP*, 27 August 1955. **1955**: *KSIJP*, 25 May 1956. **1956**: *KSIJP*, 9 September 1957. **1957**: By addition, net output plus soya beans. Net output is in *An Economic Geography of Central China*.

Rice. **1952, 1954** and **1955**: From sown area and yield. **1956**: *KSIJP*, 23 February 1957. **1957**: *An Economic Geography of Central China.*

Wheat. **1953**: From sown area and yield. **1957**: *An Economic Geography of Central China.*

Soya. **1952–54**: By subtraction of net from gross output. Net output: from index in *NTKTTH* (no. 2), 1958. **1955** and **1956**: *KSIJP*, 31 March 1956. **1957**: *An Economic Geography of Central China.*

Potatoes. **1957**: *ibid.*

Anhwei

Total grain. **1952**: *AJP*, 1 January 1958. **1953–54**: *AJP*, 6 October 1957. **1955**: *AJP*, 23 September 1957. **1956–57**: *AJP*, 30 April 1958.

Rice. **1952**: *AJP*, 1 January 1958. **1955** and **1956**: *AJP*, 19 January 1957. **1957**: From 1956 output and *AJP*, 30 April 1958.

Wheat. **1952**: *AJP*, 1 January 1958. **1954**: From 1955 and *TKP*, 19 June 1955. **1955**: From potato output and figures in *CKNP* (no. 4), 1956, pp. 13–17. **1956**: From 1957 and figures in *AJP*, 30 April 1958. **1957**: *An Economic Geography of Central China.*

Soya. **1952** and **1957**: *AJP*, 1 January 1958. **1953–56**: By subtraction of net from gross output (net output from index in *NTKTTH* (no. 2), 1958).

Potatoes. **1952**: An estimate, from known sown area and average yield for 1955–57. **1955**: From 1956 and *AJP*, 19 January 1957. **1956**: By subtraction – coarse grains: *An Economic Geography of Central China.* **1957**: *ibid.*

Chekiang

Total grain. **1952**: *CHKJP*, 11 July 1957. **1953**: *CHKJP*, 11 January 1955. **1954**: *CHKJP*, 5 August 1956. **1955–56**: *CHKJP*, 13 August 1957. **1957**: *CHKJP*, 23 January 1958.

Rice. **1952**: A very rough estimate based on rice as a percentage of output in years for which production is known, using sown area (given) and implied yield as a check. **1953**: From yield and sown area. **1956**: An estimate from figures in Mechanisation Bureau of the Ministry of Agriculture, *Chung-kuo nung-yeh chi-hsieh-hua wen-t'i* (*Problems of Agricultural Mechanisation in China*) (Paoting, 1958), p. 290. **1957**: *An Economic Geography of East China.*

Wheat. **1952**: Only a rough estimate possible, using assumed sown area and yields. **1957**: *An Economic Geography of East China.*

Soya. **1952–57**: All obtained by subtracting net output from gross output. Net output from 1952, 1954 and 1956: from index in *NTKTTH* (no. 2), 1958. 1953, 1955 and 1957: *CHKJP*, 29 September 1959.

Potatoes. **1956**: *CHKJP*, 22 October 1957. **1957**: *An Economic Geography of East China.*

Maize. **1957**: *ibid.*

Kiangsu

Total grain. **1952**: *HHJP*, 10 March 1956. **1953**: *HHJP*, 8 May 1957. **1954** and **1956**: *HHJP*, 28 January 1957. **1955**: *KSUNM*, 15 December 1955. **1957**: *HHJP*, 1 October 1959.

Appendix 2

Rice. **1952**: From 1953 and percentage in *Rational Transport*, p. 27. **1953**: From 1955, see *HHJP*, 12 November 1955. **1954**: From 1953 and figures in *Rational Transport*. **1955**: From sown area and yield. **1956**: *JMJP*, 1 December 1957. **1957**: *An Economic Geography of East China*, with a deduction for Shanghai.

Wheat. **1952** and **1954**: *JMJP*, 12 July 1954. **1953**: *PAS*. **1955**: From sown area and yield. **1956**: Using SSB figures in *HHJP*, 4 October 1956. **1957**: *An Economic Geography of East China*.

Soya. **1952–56**: All are estimates, based on 1951 figure (*TLCS* (no. 6), 1959, pp. 244–7) and the index of net output in *NTKTTH* (no. 2), 1958. **1957**: *An Economic Geography of East China*.

Potatoes. **1957**: *ibid.*

Maize. **1955**: From sown area and yield. **1957**: *HHJP*, 4 September 1958.

Shanghai

In spite of the availability of almost complete runs of three Shanghai newspapers from 1949 to the mid-1960s, not a single firm figure for grain production in the six years 1952–57 has been discovered. An estimate for 1956 can be made from the grain arable area (obtained from the total arable area of Shanghai minus the vegetable and cotton areas) and the grain yield per unit of arable land (*HWP*, 28 August 1957). 1956 grain output is reported as 0.124 *yi-chin* (hundred million catties) higher than 1955 (*CNP*, February 1957) and 1955 output is therefore estimated by subtraction. Estimates for 1952–54 and for 1957 are obtained from index in *NTKTTH* (no. 2), 1958.

Kweichow

Total grain. **1952** and **1955–56**: *KCJP*, 8 August 1957. **1953–54**: From index in *LSP* (no. 81), 1959, p. 2. **1957**: By addition: net output is in *An Economic Geography of SW China*, p. 110.

Rice. **1952** and **1957**: *An Economic Geography of SW China*. **1953**: From figures in *Wei ta tzu-kuo ti hsi-nan* (*The Great South West of China*) (Shanghai, 1955), p. 68. **1954** and **1956**: From sown area and yield.

Wheat. **1952** and **1957**: *An Economic Geography of SW China*. **1954** and **1956**: From sown area and yield.

Soya. **1952–56**: By subtracting net from gross output. Net output: **1952**, **1955** and **1956**: *KCJP*, 30 September 1959. **1953–54**: From index in *NTKTTH* (no. 2), 1958. **1957**: From 1952 and *KCJP*, 15 November 1959.

Potatoes and Maize. **1957**: *An Economic Geography of SW China*.

Szechuan

Total grain. **1952** and **1954–56**: *HH* (no. 17), 1957, 13 August 1957, pp. 25–8. **1953**: *CFJP*, 26 September 1959. **1957**: *SZJP*, 26 September 1959.

Rice. **1952** and **1957**: *An Economic Geography of SW China*. **1953**: *SZJP*, 5 October 1954. **1954** and **1956**: From sown area and yield. **1955**: From 1952 and *SZJP*, 2 April 1956.

Wheat. **1952** and **1957**: *An Economic Geography of SW China*. **1953**: From 1954 and *TKP*, 8 August 1954. **1954**: From 1955 and *TKP*, 17 June 1955. **1955** and **1956**: *JMJP*, 11 June 1956.

Soya. **1952**: Estimate, using known sown area and assumed yield. **1953–56**: From 1952 and index in *NTKTTH* (no. 2), 1958. **1957**: *An Economic Geography of SW China.*

Potatoes. **1952** and **1957**: *ibid.* **1954**: *HHYP*, vol. 70 (no. 8), 1955. **1956**: *SZJP*, 3 August 1958.

Maize. **1952** and **1957**: *An Economic Geography of SW China.* **1956**: From sown area and yield.

Yunnan

Total grain. **1952–53**: From an index of grain output (applied to 1951 production) in *YJP*, 31 December 1956. **1954**: From percentage figures in *CHCC* no. 3, 1957, pp. 2–3. **1955–57**: By addition, net output plus soya beans. Net output, 1955: *YJP*, 1 May 1957; 1956: *YJP*, 4 September 1957; 1957: *An Economic Geography of SW China*, p. 157.

Rice. **1952** and **1957**: *An Economic Geography of SW China.* **1953, 1954** and **1955**: From 1952 and index in *YJP*, 31 December 1956. **1956**: From percentage given by SSB in *YJP*, 1 May 1957.

Wheat. **1952** and **1957**: *An Economic Geography of SW China.* **1953–56**: From 1952 and index in *YJP*, 31 December 1956.

Soya. **1952–54**: Gross output minus net output. Net output: 1952: *YJP*, 4 November 1958. 1953: *YJP*, 4 September 1957. 1954: An estimate using figures in *YJP*, 30 July 1955. **1955**: *PAS*. **1956**: From percentages in *YJP*, 1 May 1957. **1957**: Estimated from sown area and assumed yield.

Potatoes. **1952, 1953, 1954** and **1956**: Calculated as a residual. Coarse grains are obtained from index in *YJP*, 31 December 1956. **1955**: From 1954 and SSB figures in *YJP*, 11 June 1956. **1957**: *An Economic Geography of SW China.*

Maize. **1957**: *ibid.*

Fukien

Total grain. **1952**: By addition, net output plus soya beans. Net output is found in *FJP*, 1 January 1958. **1953**: No firm figure is available. An estimate was obtained by assuming that gross grain output rose in 1953 by the same percentage as net output (available from index in *NTKTTH* (no. 2), 1958). **1954**: *FJP*, 6 June 1955. **1955–56**: *FJP*, 26 June 1957. **1957**: By addition, net output plus soya beans. Net output is in *FJP*, 7 October 1959.

Rice. **1952** and **1955**: From sown area and yield. **1957**: *An Economic Geography of South China.*

Wheat. **1952**: From sown area and yield. **1956**: *FJP*, 12 November 1959. **1957**: An estimate, from known sown area and assumed yield.

Soya. **1952**: From 1957 and *FJP*, 1 January 1958. **1953–56**: Gross output minus net output. Net output: 1953: *FJP*, 13 January 1954. 1954: using index in *NTKTTH* (no. 2), 1958. 1955–56: *FJP*, 1 January 1958. **1957**: *FJP*, 7 October 1959.

Potatoes. **1952** and **1955**: From sown area and yield. **1957**: From percentage in *FCY* (no. 2), 1958, pp. 20–2.

Kwangsi

Total grain. **1952**: *KWSIJP*, 25 February 1958. **1953–56**: *KWSIJP*, 3 September 1957. **1957**: *HHPYK*, vol. 167 (no. 21), 1959, pp. 88–92.

Rice. **1952** and **1957**: *KWSIJP*, 25 February 1958. **1953**: From figures in *An Economic Geography of S. China*, p. 75. **1954**: Approximate output, set by the limits of 1953 and 1955 (1955 was below 1954 according to *Shui-tao Sheng ch'an Chi-shu Ts'an-k'ao Tzu-liao (Reference Materials on Rice Production Technology)*, compiled by Ministry of Agriculture Grain Production Bureau (Peking, 1956), p. 7). **1955:** From sown area and yield. **1957:** *KWSIJP*, 25 February 1958.

Wheat. **1952–54** and **1957**: *KWSIJP*, 25 February 1958.

Soya. **1952–57**: No firm figures available but estimates of the small amounts grown are possible from some sown area data and from annual yields. For details see Kenneth R. Walker, *Provincial Grain Output*.

Potatoes. **1952** and **1957**: *KWSIJP*, 25 February 1958.

Kwangtung

Total grain. **1952** and **1956**: *NFJP*, 17 November 1957. **1953**: *NFJP*, 22 January 1956. **1954**: *NFJP*, 12 December 1955. **1955**: *NFJP*, 7 April 1956. **1957**: By addition, net output plus soya beans. Net output is in *NFJP*, 3 September 1959.

Rice. **1952, 1955** and **1956**: *NFJP*, 17 November 1957. **1953**: From sown area and yield. **1954**: SSB figure in *NFJP*, 12 December 1955. **1957**: *NFJP*, 8 December 1957.

Wheat. **1952**: From 1953, percentage given in *NFJP*, 5 December 1953. **1953**: From sown area and yield. **1954** and **1955**: SSB in *NFJP*, 12 December 1955. **1956**: *NFJP*, 27 July 1957. **1957**: *NFJP*, 1 October 1959.

Soya. **1952**: *NFJP*, 7 April 1956. **1953**: From sown area and yield. **1954** and **1955**: SSB in *NFJP*, 12 December 1955. **1956**: *NFJP*, 27 July 1957. **1957**: An estimate only, see Kenneth R. Walker, *Provincial Grain Output*.

Potatoes. **1952**: *NFJP*, 24 September 1955. **1953**: SSB figures in *NFJP*, 5 October 1955, and output for 1954. **1954**: SSB figures in *NFJP*, 12 December 1955. **1955**: *ibid*. **1956** and **1957**: *Liang-shih Sheng-ch'an Su-tu k'o-yi Chia-k'uai (Grain Production Can be Speeded Up)* (Canton, 1958), pp. 11–25.

b. SOWN AREA

Total grain sown area (million hectares)

	1952	1953	1954	1955	1956	1957
North East						
Heilungkiang	6.184	5.714	6.368	6.035	6.342	6.481
Kirin	4.312	4.290	4.258	4.393	4.469	4.295
Liaoning	4.242	—	—	4.276	4.345	4.330
North West						
IMR	4.247	4.143	4.247	4.255	4.603	4.497
Kansu	3.590	—	3.784	3.987	4.166	3.837*
Shensi	—	4.573	4.599	c.4.388	—	—
Sinkiang	1.143	1.201	1.147	1.151	1.267	1.335
Tsinghai	0.331	0.346	0.349	0.356	0.384	0.388
North						
Honan	12.384	12.876	12.984	12.711	12.974	12.800
Hopei	8.883	9.157	9.188	8.827	8.903	9.214
Peking	—	—	—	—	—	—
Shansi	4.363	4.287	4.350	4.238	4.385	4.161
Shantung	11.783	11.920	12.117	11.673	11.496	11.932
Tientsin	—	—	—	—	—	—
Centre						
Hunan	4.221	4.401	4.735	5.161	5.573	5.583
Hupei	—	5.335	—	5.556	5.703	5.702
Kiangsi	—	—	—	3.330	3.463	3.960
East						
Anhwei	8.017	—	—	8.805	9.024	8.966
Chekiang	—	—	3.067	3.127	3.267	2.859
Kiangsu	—	—	8.809	8.686	—	8.854
Shanghai	—	—	—	—	—	—
South West						
Kweichow	1.988	2.051	2.131	2.229	2.541	2.615
Szechuan	9.627	—	—	—	10.533	11.187
Yunnan	—	—	2.764	2.877	3.053	3.443
South						
Fukien	1.860	—	1.948	1.987	2.010	2.063
Kwangsi	—	—	3.620	3.877	3.735	3.746
Kwangtung	6.011	6.475	6.535	6.676	6.979	6.804

* New (1958) boundary grain sown area was 3.177 (SSB in *KAJP*, 12 June 1958).

Appendix 2

Grain sown area: rice (thousand hectares)

	1952	1953	1954	1955	1956	1957
North East						
Heilungkiang	125	—	153	169	293	257
Kirin	113	—	131	149	280	283
Liaoning	128	—	145	215	305	280
North West						
IMR	15	8	10	13	29	40
Kansu	—	—	—	—	—	93
Shensi	139	—	140	—	c.142	133
Sinkiang	—	56	—	—	—	73
Tsinghai			nil			
North						
Honan	411	433	—	458	554	515
Hopei	c.117	—	—	129	276	135
Shansi	—	—	—	6	—	—
Shantung	—	—	—	—	19	9
Centre						
Hunan	3259	3284	3311	3434	3921	3782
Hupei	c.1900	1926	1685	1968	2140	2169
Kiangsi	2747	—	2745	2804	2853	2943
East						
Anhwei	1913	—	2000	—	2816	2241
Chekiang	—	1684	1759	—	2040	1629
Kiangsu	c.2060	—	—	2159	2442	2385
South West						
Kweichow	815	—	800	—	c.820	895
Szechuan	3493	3334	3400	3385	3633	4147
Yunnan	—	—	—	986	1048	1062
South						
Fukien	1431	—	1370	1359	1481	1474
Kwangsi	2299	2319	2342	2426	2774	2261
Kwangtung	4678	4827	4847	4777	4969	4847

Output, sown area and yield per sown hectare

Grain sown area: wheat (thousand hectares)

	1952	1953	1954	1955	1956	1957
North East						
Heilungkiang	1099	998	957	666	605	907
Kirin	117	96	117	65	49	43
Liaoning	142	141	181	115	70	67
North West						
IMR	410	445	542	560	554	591
Kansu	1296	1262	1303	1283	1400	1233
Shensi	1581	1532	1572	1630	1620	1625
Sinkiang	609	609	615	665	685	713
Tsinghai	109	117	117	117	117	143
North						
Honan	4632	4883	5105	4952	4855	4425
Hopei	1845	1876	2445	2325	2125	2730
Shansi	1193	1291	1307	1329	1308	1267
Shantung	3975	4036	4281	4091	4012	4133
Centre						
Hunan	187	199	213	319	290	333
Hupei	769	981	1072	1067	1094	1156
Kiangsi	—	114	127	135	163	151
East						
Anhwei	2600	—	2600	2826	2600	2681
Chekiang	—	—	—	—	415	312
Kiangsu	*c.*1919	2167	2000	2400	2323	2109
South West						
Kweichow	79	93	126	—	133	270
Szechuan	1046	1053	1205	1180	1306	1360
Yunnan	209	216	216	258	287	334
South						
Fukien	104	—	—	—	320	164
Kwangsi	67	84	222	335	304	194
Kwangtung	124	129	190	315	315	239

Grain sown area: soya beans (thousand hectares)

	1952	1953	1954	1955	1956	1957
North East						
Heilungkiang	1390	1409		1467	1530	1515
Kirin	900	828	902	810	954	1017
Liaoning	581	—	500	610	736	730
North West						
IMR	158	218	227	267	242	267
Kansu	516	—	—	—	—	708
Shensi	502	—	—	458	682	c.803
Sinkiang				negligible		
Tsinghai				negligible		
North						
Honan	1564	1643	1619	1543	1933	2346
Hopei	910	—	—	960	916	—
Shansi	250	362	473	460	337	368
Shantung	2300	2236	2308	1911	1903	2687
Centre						
Hunan	105	133	155	157	143	169
Hupei	—	214	—	236	297	348
Kiangsi	—	—	—	231	—	304
East						
Anhwei	1015	—	—	1011	1015	1036
Chekiang	—	—	—	—	140	133
Kiangsu	c.937	—	—	800	767	871
South West						
Kweichow	—	—	—	—	—	153
Szechuan	246	—	—	—	—	335
Yunnan	—	—	—	259	189	140
South						
Fukien	—	35	53	50	43	95
Kwangsi	c.102	—	—	—	—	c.132
Kwangtung	107	117	133	124	—	111

Note: Brace indicates that the figure is an average over the years shown.

Output, sown area and yield per sown hectare

Grain sown area: coarse grains (including potatoes) (thousand hectares)

	1952	1953	1954	1955	1956	1957
North East						
Heilungkiang	3570	—	c.3849	3733	3914	3802
Kirin	3182	—	3108	3369	3186	2952
Liaoning	3391	—	—	3336	3234	3253
North West						
IMR	3664	3472	3468	3415	3778	3599
Kansu	—	—	—	—	—	1803
Shensi	1543	—	—	—	—	1444
Sinkiang	c.478	536	—	—	—	549
Tsinghai	222	229	232	239	267	245
North						
Honan	5777	5917	5827	5758	5632	5514
Hopei	c.6011	—	—	5413	5586	—
Shansi	c.2920	c.2634	c.2570	2443	c.2740	c.2526
Shantung	5508	5648	5528	5671	5573	4847
Centre						
Hunan	670	785	1056	1251	1219	1299
Hupei	—	2214	—	2285	2172	2029
Kiangsi	—	—	—	160	—	562
East						
Anhwei	2489	—	—	—	2593	3008
Chekiang	—	—	—	—	672	785
Kiangsu	—	—	—	3327	—	3489
South West						
Kweichow	—	—	—	—	—	1297
Szechuan	4842	—	—	—	—	5345
Yunnan	—	—	—	1375	1528	1907
South						
Fukien	c.290	—	—	—	166	330
Kwangsi	—	—	—	—	—	c.1159
Kwangtung	1102	1402	1365	1460	—	1607

Grain sown area: coarse grains (net of potatoes) (thousand hectares)

	1952	1953	1954	1955	1956	1957
North East						
Heilungkiang	3366	—	—	3494	3681	3573
Kirin	3071	—	—	—	—	2845
Liaoning	3292	—	—	3176	3034	3078
North West						
IMR	3455	3274	3273	3229	3573	3389
Kansu	—	—	—	—	—	c.1503
Shensi	—	—	—	—	—	—
Sinkiang	c.478	c.536	—	—	—	545
Tsinghai	—	—	—	208	—	—
North						
Honan	4836	4980	4809	4804	4550	4514
Hopei	c.5553	—	—	4952	4981	—
Shansi	—	—	c.2361	2258	c.2491	c.2294
Shantung	4467	4581	4374	4480	4194	3615
Centre						
Hunan	386	493	636	742	768	841
Hupei	—	1991	—	2043	—	1839
Kiangsi	—	—	—	—	—	—
East						
Anhwei	1756	—	—	—	1860	2253
Chekiang	—	—	—	—	420	608
Kiangsu	—	—	—	—	—	2950
South West						
Kweichow	—	—	—	—	—	1150
Szechuan	3504	—	—	—	—	4044
Yunnan	—	—	—	—	—	1722
South						
Fukien	c.20	—	—	—	—	29
Kwangsi	—	—	—	—	—	c.741
Kwangtung	102	489	369	295	—	569

Output, sown area and yield per sown hectare

Grain sown area: potatoes (thousand hectares)

	1952	1953	1954	1955	1956	1957
North East						
Heilungkiang	204	146	—	239	233	229
Kirin	111	—	—	—	—	107
Liaoning	99	—	—	160	200	175
North West						
IMR	209	198	195	186	205	210
Kansu	—	—	—	—	*c.*333	—
Shensi	—	—	—	—	—	—
Sinkiang	—	—	—	—	—	4
Tsinghai	—	—	—	31	—	37
North						
Honan	941	937	1018	954	1082	1000
Hopei	*c.*458	*c.*434	*c.*453	461	605	511
Shansi	—	—	209	185	249	232
Shantung	1041	1067	1154	1191	1379	1232
Centre						
Hunan	284	292	420	509	451	458
Hupei	229	223	169	242	—	190
Kiangsi	—	—	—	—	—	197
East						
Anhwei	733	—	448	533	733	755
Chekiang	—	—	—	—	252	177
Kiangsu	—	—	—	—	—	539
South West						
Kweichow	—	—	—	—	*c.*186	147
Szechuan	1338	1133	1200	—	1533	1301
Yunnan	—	—	—	—	—	185
South						
Fukien	270	—	—	267	—	301
Kwangsi	—	—	—	—	—	418
Kwangtung	1000	913	996	1165	1092	1038

Grain sown area: maize (thousand hectares)

	1952	1953	1954	1955	1956	1957
North East						
Heilungkiang[a]	1243	—	—	—	1698	1271
Kirin	830	—	—	—	—	907
Liaoning	587	—	592	693	1077	697
North West						
IMR	—	321	—	—	—	—
Kansu	—	—	—	—	—	—
Shensi[b]	—	—	—	733	780[c]	—
Sinkiang	305	326	200	233	—	366
Tsinghai	—	—	—	—	—	—
North						
Honan	—	c.937	—	998	1319	800
Hopei	—	—	1365	1548	2075	1560
Shansi	—	375	326	426	614	435
Shantung	979	979	950	1270	1669	1507
Centre						
Hunan	81	93	110	121	145	166
Hupei	—	—	—	496	—	461
Kiangsi	—	—	—	—	—	—
East						
Anhwei	—	—	—	—	—	288
Chekiang	—	—	—	—	—	159
Kiangsu	—	—	—	667	—	603
South West						
Kweichow	676	—	—	—	729	667
Szechuan	1360	—	1333	1200	1600	1645
Yunnan	—	—	—	—	—	925
South						
Fukien	—	—	—	—	—	—
Kwangsi	—	—	—	—	—	555
Kwangtung	—	—	—	—	—	—

Notes: a. Heilungkiang average for 1953–57 was 1313.
　　　b. Shensi average for 1952–55 was 755.
　　　c. Planned figure.

Output, sown area and yield per sown hectare

Grain sown area: millet (thousand hectares)

	1952	1953	1954	1955	1956	1957
North East						
Heilungkiang[a]	1020	—	—	—	1098	1143
Kirin	874	—	—	—	—	713
Liaoning	692	—	—	440	340	633
North West						
IMR	—	1432	—	—	—	—
Kansu	—	—	—	—	—	—
Shensi	—	—	—	—	—	—
Sinkiang	—	—	—	—	—	—
Tsinghai	—	—	—	—	—	—
North						
Honan	—	c.937	—	—	—	—
Hopei	—	—	c.1425	—	—	—
Shansi	—	882	—	868[b]	—	—
Shantung	—	1207	c.1760	—	—	—
Centre						
Hunan	—	—	—	—	—	—
Hupei	—	—	—	—	—	—
Kiangsi	—	—	—	—	—	—
East						
Anhwei	—	—	—	—	—	—
Chekiang	—	—	—	—	—	—
Kiangsu	—	—	—	—	—	—
South West						
Kweichow	—	—	—	—	—	—
Szechuan	—	—	—	—	—	—
Yunnan	—	—	—	—	—	—
South						—
Fukien	—	—	—	—	—	—
Kwangsi	—	—	—	—	—	—
Kwangtung	—	—	—	—	—	—

Notes: a. Heilungkiang average for 1953–57 was 1043.
      b. Planned figure.

Appendix 2

Grain sown area: kaoliang (thousand hectares)

	1952	1953	1954	1955	1956	1957
North East						
Heilungkiang*	684	—	—	—	691	593
Kirin	902	—	—	—	—	713
Liaoning	1538	—	—	—	—	1260
North West						
IMR	—	405	—	—	—	—
Kansu	—	—	—	—	—	—
Shensi	—	—	—	—	—	—
Sinkiang	—	—	—	—	—	—
Tsinghai	—	—	—	—	—	—
North						
Honan	—	—	—	—	—	—
Hopei	—	—	c.916	1245	—	—
Shansi	—	—	—	—	—	—
Shantung	—	1476	c.2150	1670	—	—
Centre						
Hunan	—	—	—	—	—	—
Hupei	—	—	—	—	—	—
Kiangsi	—	—	—	—	—	—
East						
Anhwei	—	—	—	—	—	—
Chekiang	—	—	—	—	—	—
Kiangsu	—	—	—	304	—	219
South West						
Kweichow	—	—	—	—	—	—
Szechuan	—	—	—	—	—	—
Yunnan	—	—	—	—	—	—
South						
Fukien	—	—	—	—	—	—
Kwangsi	—	—	—	—	—	—
Kwangtung	—	—	—	—	—	—

Note: * Heilungkiang average for 1953–57 was 666.

SOURCES

Heilungkiang

Total grain. **1952** and **1957**: *An Economic Geography of NE China.* **1953**: By subtracting four-year total from five-year total (latter is in *ibid.*). **1954**: From 1955 and *JMJP*, 16 December 1955. **1955**: From figures in Twelve-Year Plan, *HJP*, 22 May 1956. **1956**: *HJP*, 1 October 1957.

Rice. **1952** and **1957**: *An Economic Geography of NE China.* **1954**: *CKNP* (no. 23), 1954. **1955**: From 1954 and *JMJP*, 12 December 1955. **1956**: *HJP*, 5 January 1957.

Wheat. **1952** and **1957**: *An Economic Geography of NE China.* **1953–55**: Index in *TLCS* (no. 8), 1957. **1956**: *TLCS* (no. 11), 1957.

Soya. **1952** and **1957**: *An Economic Geography of NE China.* **1953–54** average: From five-year data in *ibid.* **1955** and **1956**: *HJP*, 11 October 1956.

Potatoes. **1952** and **1957**: *An Economic Geography of NE China.* **1953** and **1954**: From output and yield. **1955**: *TLCS* (no. 11), 1957.

Maize, millet and kaoliang. **1952** and **1957** and **1953–57** average: *An Economic Geography of NE China.* **1956**: *TLCS* (no. 11), 1957.

Kirin

Total grain. **1952**: *An Economic Geography of NE China*, and figure for soya (*CIAAA*). **1953** and **1954**: *KJP*, 24 April 1955. **1955** and **1956**: *KJP*, 17 April 1957. **1957**: *An Economic Geography of NE China.*

Rice. **1952** and **1957**: *Ibid.* **1954**: From 1955 and *SCMP*, no. 1206. **1955**: From 1956 and *HJP*, 17 April 1957. **1956**: *HJP*, 11 October 1957.

Wheat. **1952** and **1957**: *An Economic Geography of NE China.* **1953–56**: From index in *TLCS* (no. 8), 1957.

Soya. **1952**: *CIAAA.* **1953**: From output and yield. **1954**: *KJP*, 24 April 1956. **1955** and **1956**: SSB figure in *KJP*, 17 April 1957. **1957**: From five-year average (*An Economic Geography of NE China*) and four-year figures.

Potatoes, maize, millet and kaoliang. **1952** and **1957**: *An Economic Geography of NE China.*

Liaoning

Total grain. **1952** and **1957**: *An Economic Geography of NE China.* **1953** and **1954**: *LJP*, 30 December 1957 and soya bean sown area. **1955** and **1956:** From output and yield.

Rice. **1952** and **1957**: *An Economic Geography of NE China.* **1954**: *PAS.* **1955**: *NCNA*, 10 October 1955. **1956**: *LJP*, 24 August 1957.

Wheat. **1952**: *An Economic Geography of NE China.* **1953–57**: From index in *TLCS* (no. 8), 1957, p. 344.

Soya. **1952**: *An Economic Geography of NE China.* **1954**: *CIAAA.* **1955**: *JMJP*, 5 October 1956. **1956**: From output and yield. **1957**: *LJP*, 2 January 1958.

Potatoes. **1952** and **1957**: *An Economic Geography of NE China.* **1955** and **1956**: *LJP*, 9 May 1957.

Maize. **1952** and **1957**: *An Economic Geography of NE China.* **1954**: *LJP,* 7 June 1955. **1955** and **1956**: *LJP,* 9 May 1957.

Millet. **1952** and **1957**: *An Economic Geography of NE China.* **1955**: From 1956 and *LJP,* 14 January 1957. **1956**: *LJP,* 14 May 1958.

Kaoliang. **1952**: *An Economic Geography of NE China.* **1957**: *LJP,* 14 May 1958.

Inner Mongolia

Total grain. **1952–57**: *NMKTC.*

Rice, wheat, soya and potatoes. Ibid.

Maize, millet and kaoliang. **1953**: *An Economic Geography of Inner Mongolia.*

Kansu

Total grain. **1952**: *KAJP,* 26 September 1957. **1954**: From output and yield. **1955**: From 1956 and information in *CIAAA.* **1956**: *JMJP,* 4 March 1958. **1957**: *SCMP,* no. 1649.

Rice. **1957**: *JMJP,* 30 May 1958.

Wheat. **1952–55**: From index in *CKNP* (no. 12), 1957, p. 19. **1956**: *TTKP,* 23 August 1956. **1957**: *JMJP,* 23 August 1958.

Soya. **1952** and **1957**: *CIAAA.*

Potatoes. No figures found but the plan for 1958 (*KAJP,* 3 April 1958) was probably equal to the actual sown area of 1956.

Shensi

Total grain. **1952**: From figures in *SESJP,* 4 February 1958 and 14 August 1958. **1953**: *PAS.* **1954**: *CIAAA.* **1955**: Approximate estimate from percentage in *SESJP,* 3 April 1956. **1957**: *SESJP,* 4 February 1958.

Rice. **1952** and **1956**: From output and yield. **1954**: *JMJP,* 14 July 1954. **1957**: *JMJP,* 29 September 1957.

Wheat. **1952, 1953** and **1955**: From output and yield. **1954**: *TKP,* 1 July 1954. **1956**: *SESJP,* 9 May 1956. **1957**: *SESJP,* 5 September 1957.

Soya. **1952**: *CIAAA.* **1955**: From output and yield. **1956** and **1957**: From gross and net sown areas. 1956 net sown area: *CIAAA.* 1957 net sown area: *SESJP,* 31 October 1957.

Maize. **1955** and plan for **1956**: *SESJP,* 4 April 1956.

Sinkiang

Total grain. **1952** and **1953**: *SNY.* **1954**: *SINJP,* 7 September 1955. **1955**: *SINJP,* 18 January 1957. **1956**: *SINJP,* 22 February 1957. **1957**: *SINJP,* 1 October 1957.

Rice. **1953**: *SNY.* **1957**: *SNM,* 12 March 1958.

Wheat. **1952, 1953, 1955** and **1956**: From index in *CKNP* (no. 12), 1957, p. 19. **1954**: *TKP,* 27 July 1954. **1957**: *SNY.*

Potatoes. **1957**: *SINJP*, 17 April 1958.

Maize. **1952**, **1953** and **1957**: *SNY*. **1954** and **1955**: *CIAAA*.

Tsinghai

Total grain. **1952–56**: From output and yield. **1957**: SSB figure in *TSINJP*, 30 September 1958.

Wheat. **1952–55**: From index in *CKNP* (no. 12), 1957, p. 19. **1956**: Figure derived from information in *ibid.*

Potatoes. **1955**: *TSINJP*, 19 October 1955. **1957**: *CIAAA*.

Honan

Total grain. **1952–56**: Net grain sown area (*CKNP* (no. 15), 1957), plus soya area. **1957**: *TLCS* (no. 1), 1959.

Rice. **1952** and **1957**: *HONJP*, 6 April 1958. **1953**: *An Economic Geography of N. China*. **1955**: *HONJP*, 30 December 1957. **1956**: *HONJP*, 12 August 1956.

Wheat. **1952–57**: *JMJP*, 15 June 1958.

Soya. **1952** and **1957**: Gross minus net sown area. Net sown area: *Ho-nan Hsiao-mai ts'ai-p'ei hsüeh* (*A Study of Rice Cultivation in Honan*) (Peking, 1959). **1953–55**: From output and yield. **1956**: SSB figure in *HONJP*, 18 September 1957.

Potatoes. **1952**, **1954** and **1956**: Estimated as a residual from total grain sown area and sown area of other main grains. **1953**: *An Economic Geography of N. China*. **1955**: *HONJP*, 30 December 1957. **1957**: *TLCS* (no. 1), 1959.

Maize. **1953**: *An Economic Geography of N. China*. **1955**: From output and yield. **1956**: *HONJP*, 30 December 1957. **1957**: *TLCS* (no. 1), 1959.

Millet. **1953**: *An Economic Geography of N. China*.

Hopei

Total grain. **1952**: From output and yield. **1953–55**: Net grain sown area (*CKNP* (no. 17), 1956), plus soya area. **1956**: *HOPJP*, 25 October 1956. **1957**: *CIAAA*.

Rice. **1952**: A rough estimate from total grain sown area and sown area of major grains, using figure for coarse grains in *CKNP* (no. 15), 1957. **1955** and **1956**: *HOPJP*, 25 October 1956. **1957**: *CIAAA*.

Wheat. **1952–57**: *CKNP* (no. 15), 1957.

Soya. **1952**: Gross area minus net. Net sown area: *CKNP* (no. 15), 1957. **1955**: *CIAAA*. **1956**: Gross area minus net. Net: *HONJP*, 25 October 1956.

Potatoes. **1952–54**: Rough estimates obtained as a residual. **1955** and **1956**: *HOPJP*, 25 October 1956. **1957**: *JMJP*, 17 October 1958.

Maize. **1954**: From 1955 and information in *HOPJP*, 22 September 1955. **1955** and **1956**: *HOPJP*, 25 October 1956. **1957**: *CIAAA*.

Millet. **1954**: Estimate from figures in *An Economic Geography of N. China*.

Kaoliang. **1954**: *ibid.* **1955**: *Kaoliang* (Peking, 1957), p. 3.

Shansi

Total grain. **1952** and **1954**: *SASJP*, 24 February 1955. **1953**: *An Economic Geography of N. China*. **1955**: From output and yield. **1956**: From figures in *SASJP*, 1 August 1956 and 13 February 1957. **1957**: *TLCS* (no. 1), 1959.

Rice. **1955**: *SASJP*, 29 May 1960.

Wheat. **1952** and **1954**: *PAS*. **1953**: *An Economic Geography of N China*. **1955** and **1956**: From output and yield. **1957**: *SASJP*, 13 June 1957.

Soya. **1952** and **1953**: From output and yield. **1954–57**: Gross sown area minus net. Net sown area: **1954–56**: *CKNP* (no. 15), 1957. **1957**: *NCNA*, 17 December 1958.

Potatoes. **1954**: From output and yield. **1955**: *SASJP*, 19 December 1957. **1956**: *SASJP*, 13 February 1957. **1957**: *SASJP*, 18 August 1958.

Maize. **1953** and **1954**: *CIAAA*. **1955**: *SASJP*, 29 May 1960. **1956**: *SASJP*, 13 February 1957. **1957**: *JMJP*, 9 February 1958.

Millet. **1953**: *CIAAA*. **1955**: Plan figure, *SASJP*, 24 February 1955.

Shantung

Total grain. **1952** and **1955**: *TCJP*, 19 January 1957. **1956** and **1957**: from output and yield.

Rice. **1956**: From figures in *TCJP*, 19 January 1957. **1957**: *SCMP*, no. 1707.

Wheat. **1952–56**: *CKNP* (no. 15), 1957. **1957**: *TCJP*, 17 June 1957.

Soya. **1952–55**: From gross grain sown area and net sown area. Net sown areas are in *CKNP* (no. 15), 1957. **1956**: From output and yield. **1957**: Estimated from figures in *NTKTTH* (no. 7), 1957.

Potatoes. **1952–56**: By subtracting sown areas of main grains from total grain sown areas. **1957**: *TCJP*, 11 October 1957.

Maize. **1952** and **1956**: *NYCS* (no. 8), 1957, pp. 234–9. **1953**: *An Economic Geography of N. China*. **1954** and **1955**: Estimated as a residual, using figures in *TKP*, 9 September 1954 and *TCJP* 19 January 1957. **1957**: *TCJP*, 17 June 1957.

Millet. **1953**: *An Economic Geography of N. China*. **1954**: Very rough estimate from figures in *TKP*, 9 September 1954.

Kaoliang. **1953**: *An Economic Geography of N. China*. **1954**: Rough estimate from figures in *TKP*, 9 September 1954. **1955**: *Kaoliang*, p. 3.

Hunan

All grain. **1952–57**: *HNNY*.

Hupei

Total grain. **1952, 1954** and **1955**: Net grain sown area (*LSWTCC*) plus soya area. **1953** and **1956**: *LSWTCC*. **1957**: *An Economic Geography of Central China*.

Rice. **1952**: Approximate figure from information in *LSWTCC*. **1956**: *HUPJP*, 4 November 1957. **1957**: *An Economic Geography of Central China.*

Wheat. **1952**: *PAS.* **1953–56**: *LSWTCC.* **1957**: *An Economic Geography of Central China.*

Soya. **1953**: *LSWTCC.* **1955**: *CIAAA.* **1956**: *HUPJP*, 28 October 1956. **1957**: *An Economic Geography of Central China.*

Potatoes. **1952** and **1954**: Obtained as a residual. **1953** and **1955**: *LSWTCC.* **1957**: *An Economic Geography of Central China.*

Maize. **1955**: *LSWTCC.* **1957**: *An Economic Geography of Central China.*

Kiangsi

Total grain. **1955**: *KSIJP*, 1 September 1955. **1956**: From 1955 and *KSIJP*, 2 November 1956. **1957**: *An Economic Geography of Central China.*

Rice. **1952**: *KSIJP*, 30 September 1952. **1954**: *KSIJP*, 6 February 1955. **1955**: *KSIJP*, 31 March 1956. **1956**: From figures in *Mechanisation Bureau*, pp. 126–7. **1957**: *An Economic Geography of Central China.*

Wheat. **1953–57**: *CIAAA.*

Soya. **1955**: *KSIJP*, 31 May 1956. **1957**: *An Economic Geography of Central China.*

Potatoes. **1957**: *ibid.*

Anhwei

Total grain. **1952** and **1957**: *AJP*, 1 January 1958. **1955** and **1956**: *CIAAA.*

Rice. **1952**: From figures in *AJP*, 30 April 1958. **1954**: *PAS.* **1956**: From figures in *Mechanisation Bureau*, pp. 126–7. **1957**: *AJP*, 12 December 1957.

Wheat. **1952**: From figures in *AJP*, 30 April 1958. **1954**: *PAS.* **1955**: *AJP*, 7 June 1955. **1956**: *CIAAA.* **1957**: *An Economic Geography of East China.*

Soya. **1952**: From figures in *AJP*, 30 April 1958. **1955** and **1956**: *PAS.* **1957**: *An Economic Geography of East China.*

Potatoes. **1952**: From figures in *AJP*, 30 April 1958. **1954**: From 1955 and figures in *CKNP* (no. 4), 1956, pp. 13–17. **1955** and **1956**: *CIAAA.* **1957**: *An Economic Geography of East China.*

Maize. **1957**: *AJP*, 12 December 1957.

Chekiang

Total grain. **1954** and **1955**: *CHKJP*, 5 August 1956. **1956**: *CHKJP*, 29 May 1957. **1957**: *An Economic Geography of East China.*

Rice. **1953**: *CHKJP*, 24 January 1953, also *CHKJP*, 23 February 1957. **1954**: *ibid.* **1956**: From figures in *Mechanisation Bureau*, pp. 126–7, and SSB figures in *CHKJP*, 29 September 1957. **1957**: Figures in *An Economic Geography of East China* and *CHKJP*, 30 September 1957.

Wheat. **1956**: *Mechanisation Bureau*, p. 284. **1957**: *An Economic Geography of East China.*

Soya and potatoes. **1956**: *Mechanisation Bureau*, p. 284. **1957**: *An Economic Geography of East China.*

Maize. **1957**: *ibid.*

Kiangsu

Total grain. **1954** and **1955:** From output and yield. **1957:** *TLCS* (no. 6), 1959.

Rice. **1951:** *TLCS* (no. 6), 1959, p. 245. **1955:** *HHJP*, 29 December 1955. **1956:** From figures in *Mechanisation Bureau*, p. 127, and *HHJP*, 13 May 1956. **1957:** *An Economic Geography of East China.*

Wheat. **1951:** *TLCS* (no. 6), 1959, p. 245. **1953:** *PAS.* **1954:** *HHJP*, 12 July 1954. **1955:** *HHJP*, 6 February 1956. **1956:** *HHJP*, 31 August 1957. **1957:** *An Economic Geography of East China.*

Soya. **1951** and **1957:** *TLCS* (no. 6), 1959, p. 245. **1955** and **1956:** *CIAAA.*

Potatoes. **1957:** *An Economic Geography of East China.*

Maize. **1955:** *Chiang-su Sheng Nung-yeh Sheng-ch'an Ho-tsuo-she Ching-chi Chie-shao (Introduction to Kiangsu Province Agricultural Producers' Co-operative Economy)*, Compilation of Kiangsu Province Rural Work Department (3 volumes, Nanking, 1956), vol 3, pp. 276–80. **1957:** *HHJP*, 4 September 1958.

Kaoliang. **1955:** *Introduction to Kiangsu Province*, vol. 3, pp. 206–13. **1957:** *CIAAA.*

Kweichow

Total grain. **1952–56:** From output and yield, using net output and yield data in *KCJP*, 28 October 1958 and estimates for soya. **1957:** *An Economic Geography of SW China.*

Rice. **1952:** *CIAAA.* **1954:** *TKP*, 30 August 1954. **1956:** Estimate based on rice arable of 1954 (*TKP*, 30 August 1954) and double-cropped area (*HCJP*, 30 June 1956). **1957:** *An Economic Geography of SW China.*

Wheat. **1952:** *CIAAA.* **1953, 1954** and **1956:** *PAS.* **1957:** *An Economic Geography of SW China.*

Soya. **1957:** *ibid.*

Potatoes. **1956:** An estimate using figures in *CIAAA* and *An Economic Geography of SW China.* **1957:** *ibid.*

Maize. **1952:** *CIAAA.* **1956:** From 1952 and *KCJP*, 30 June 1956. **1957:** *An Economic Geography of SW China.*

Szechuan

Total grain. **1952:** *SZJP*, 26 September 1959. **1956:** *PAS.* **1957:** *An Economic Geography of SW China.*

Rice. **1952** and **1957:** *An Economic Geography of SW China.* **1953:** *CIAAA.* **1954:** *TKP*, 30 August 1954. **1955:** From rice arable area (obtained from output and yield: yield in Wang Yung-tse, *Ssu-ch'uan Sheng (Szechuan Province)* (Shanghai, 1956), p. 50, and double-cropped area (*SZJP*, 8 January 1958). **1956:** Same method: rice arable given in *SZJP*, 13 February 1957; double-cropped area is in *SZJP*, 8 January 1958. **1957:** *An Economic Geography of SW China.*

Wheat. **1952, 1953** and **1955:** *PAS.* **1954:** From 1955 and information in *TKP*, 17 June 1955. **1956:** *HHPYK*, vol. 89, (no. 15), 1956. **1957:** *An Economic Geography of SW China.*

Soya. **1952**: *PAS.* **1957**: *An Economic Geography of SW China.*

Potatoes. **1952**: *CIAAA.* **1953**: *PAS.* **1954**: *TKP*, 10 October 1954. **1956**: *JMJP*, 10 September 1956. **1957**: *An Economic Geography of SW China.*

Maize. **1952** and **1955**: *CIAAA.* **1954**: *TKP*, 10 October 1954. **1956**: *JMJP*, 10 September 1956. **1957**: *An Economic Geography of SW China.*

Yunnan

Total grain. **1954**: From 1955 and *YJP*, 11 June 1956. **1955**: From 1956 and *YJP*, 1 May 1957. **1956**: *YJP*, 28 December 1956. **1957**: *An Economic Geography of SW China.*

Rice. **1955**: From figures in *YJP*, 1 May 1957. **1956**: *YJP*, 16 August 1957. **1957**: *An Economic Geography of SW China.*

Wheat. **1952–57**: *YJP*, 21 May 1958.

Soya. **1955** and **1956**: From figures in *YJP*, 1 May 1957. **1957**: *An Economic Geography of SW China.*

Potatoes. **1957**: *ibid.*

Maize. **1957**: *ibid.*

Fukien

Total grain. **1952** and **1957**: *An Economic Geography of S. China.* **1954**: From 1955 and *FJP*, 1 April 1956. **1955** and **1956**: *FJP*, 26 June 1957.

Rice. **1952, 1955** and **1957**: *An Economic Geography of S. China.* **1954**: *PAS.* **1956**: From figures in *FJP*, 25 June 1956 and 26 December 1956.

Wheat. **1952** and **1957**: *An Economic Geography of S. China.* **1956**: From output and yield.

Soya. **1953–55**: *PAS.* **1956**: *FJP*, 16 December 1956. **1957**: *An Economic Geography of S. China.*

Potatoes. **1952** and **1957**: *An Economic Geography of S. China.* **1955**: *PAS.*

Kwangsi

Total grain. **1954** and **1956**: *CIAAA.* **1955**: *PAS.* **1957**: *An Economic Geography of S. China.*

Rice. **1952–56**: From rice arable and double-cropped area. Rice arable for 1955 is in *Reference Materials on Rice Production Technology*, pp. 290–300, and the area for 1952–54 is assumed to be the same. Double-cropped area: 1952: Hsü Chün-ming (ed.), *Liang Kuang Ti li (A Geography of the two 'Kwangs', Kwangsi and Kwangtung)* (Shanghai, 1956), p. 89. 1953: From 1952 and information in *Reference Materials on Rice Production Technology*. 1954: From 1953 and *ibid.* 1955: *ibid.* 1956: Rice arable is in *Mechanisation Bureau*: rice double-cropped area is from 1955 and information in *NTKTTH* (no. 2), 1959. **1957**: *An Economic Geography of S. China.*

Wheat. **1952–56**: *KWSINYTH*, (no. 20), 1957. **1957**: *An Economic Geography of S. China.*

Soya. **1950**: *CIAAA* (assumed the same as 1952 area). **1958**: *CIAAA* (assumed the same as 1957 area).

Potatoes and maize. **1957**: *An Economic Geography of S. China.*

Kwangtung

Total grain. **1952** and **1957**: *An Economic Geography of S. China.* **1953**: Liang Jen-ts'ai, *Kuang-tung Ching-chi Ti-li (An Economic Geography of Kwangtung)* (Peking, 1956). **1954** and **1955**: *NFJP*, 7 April 1956. **1956**: From figures in *NFJP*, 14 June 1956, and *Mechanisation Bureau.*

Rice. **1952**: From rice arable (assumed = 1953) and double-cropped area in *NFJP*, 8 December 1957 (cited by Chao Tzu-yang). **1953**: *Economic Geography of Kwangtung*, p. 28. **1954**: From output and yield. **1955**: SSB figure in *NFJP*, 7 April 1956. **1956**: From rice arable (*NFJP*, 15 January 1957) and double-cropped area (*Mechanisation Bureau*). **1957**: *An Economic Geography of S. China.*

Wheat. **1952** and **1955**: *NFJP*, 9 September 1956. **1953**: *Economic Geography of Kwangtung.* **1954**: From 1955 and SSB figures in *NFJP*, 7 April 1956. **1956**: *PAS.* **1957**: *An Economic Geography of S. China.*

Soya. **1952**: *NFJP*, 8 April 1956. **1953**: *PAS.* **1954**: From 1953 and SSB figures in *NFJP*, 5 October 1955. **1955**: From 1954 and SSB figures in *NFJP*, 7 April 1956. **1957**: *An Economic Geography of S. China.*

Potatoes. **1952**: From output and yield. **1953**: *Economic Geography of Kwangtung.* **1954**: From 1955 and SSB figures in *NFJP*, 7 April 1956. **1955**: SSB figures in *NFJP*, 7 April 1956. **1956** and **1957**: *Grain Production Can be Speeded Up.*

c. YIELD PER SOWN HECTARE

Average grain yield per sown hectare (100 kilograms per hectare)

	1952	1953	1954	1955	1956	1957
North East						
Heilungkiang	14.212	12.443	11.043	13.596	12.472	12.126
Kirin	14.200	13.643	12.940	12.964	11.045	12.652
Liaoning	12.824	13.378	14.554	14.429	17.100	15.478
North West						
IMR	8.046	8.554	9.145	7.647	9.900	6.575
Kansu	8.816	—	9.976	10.409	13.082	13.177*
Shensi	—	10.365	10.891	10.267	—	—
Sinkiang	14.059	14.321	15.867	16.620	15.264	15.236
Tsinghai	11.208	9.566	15.129	16.545	15.885	16.598
North						
Honan	8.305	8.729	9.088	10.109	9.924	9.609
Hopei	10.627	8.873	8.696	10.338	14.461	10.962
Peking	—	—	—	—	—	—
Shansi	8.813	10.082	9.460	8.790	9.886	8.568
Shantung	10.680	9.293	10.883	11.573	12.765	10.868
Tientsin	—	—	—	—	—	—
Centre						
Hunan	24.444	23.490	19.603	21.831	18.491	20.283
Hupei	16.347	16.995	13.748	17.295	18.869	19.897
Kiangsi	—	—	—	18.820	19.108	17.828
East						
Anhwei	10.989	—	—	13.094	12.089	13.774
Chekiang	—	—	23.104	24.375	23.459	27.646
Kiangsu	—	—	13.055	14.817	—	13.812
Shanghai	—	—	—	—	—	—
South West						
Kweichow	17.339	18.396	19.146	19.130	19.146	20.482
Szechuan	17.469	—	—	—	21.129	20.790
Yunnan	—	—	19.302	19.656	20.580	18.725
South						
Fukien	19.995	—	19.276	19.577	20.065	21.532
Kwangsi	—	—	16.285	15.218	14.083	14.429
Kwangtung	15.729	15.853	16.802	16.454	17.203	18.028

Note: All average grain yields are derived from output and sown area unless stated in the provincial notes.

* Grain yield for new (1958) boundary was 13.376 (SSB in *KAJP*, 12 June 1958).

Appendix 2

Grain yields per sown hectare: rice (100 kilograms per hectare)

	1952	1953	1954	1955	1956	1957
North East						
Heilungkiang	26.320	31.500	30.000	31.598	23.003	19.105
Kirin	—	—	18.931	30.470	26.964	22.085
Liaoning	23.398	—	14.759	19.535	30.787	23.286
North West						
IMR	16.667	20.000	21.000	24.615	22.759	10.500
Kansu	—	—	—	—	—	29.025
Shensi	33.600	—	36.857	38.643	41.503	—
Sinkiang	—	—	—	—	—	25.650
Tsinghai	—	—	—	—	—	—
North						
Honan	18.065	17.494	—	22.151	21.074	23.651
Hopei		23.775		—	14.251	22.519
Peking	—	—	—	—	—	—
Shansi	—	—	—	—	—	—
Shantung	—	—	—	—	12.947	—
Tientsin	—	—	—	—	—	—
Centre						
Hunan	28.078	27.977	24.829	28.828	23.471	25.559
Hupei	27.974	27.908	23.709	31.260	33.645	34.832
Kiangsi	21.374	—	19.526	21.009	21.030	21.193
East						
Anhwei	24.177	—	—	27.000	22.976	29.246
Chekiang	—	32.625	—	—	30.464	36.667
Kiangsu	c.27.350	30.166	27.482	31.033	25.229	28.088
Shanghai	—	—	—	—	—	—
South West						
Kweichow	29.129	c.29.788	32.775	—	34.500	37.542
Szechuan	30.072	32.993	34.000	35.175	36.606	33.005
Yunnan	c.27.011	c.28.137	31.642	31.559	31.875	33.540
South						
Fukien	19.500	—	—	21.000	—	22.280
Kwangsi	17.573	18.784	—	17.025	—	19.217
Kwangtung	17.159	17.498	18.671	18.870	19.296	20.508

Note: Brace indicates that figure is an average over years shown.

Output, sown area and yield per sown hectare

Grain yields per sown hectare: wheat (100 kilograms per hectare)

	1952	1953	1954	1955	1956	1957
North East						
Heilungkiang	7.843	—	—	9.000	9.203	9.934
Kirin	5.641	—	—	7.253	2.730	7.020
Liaoning	—	—	—	—	4.253	4.478
North West						
IMR	5.963	7.348	9.520	8.411	9.594	8.376
Kansu	—	—	—	10.522	12.870	11.678
Shensi	8.400	13.104	13.518	11.378	14.783	11.711
Sinkiang	12.397	13.017	13.725	—	14.475	12.127
Tsinghai	—	—	21.690	—	17.715	—
North						
Honan	6.487	6.050	8.210	8.627	8.805	8.475
Hopei	7.046	5.986	7.804	7.626	9.106	7.143
Peking	—	—	—	—	—	—
Shansi	5.113	7.707	7.650	7.950	10.028	5.904
Shantung	8.221	6.759	8.349	6.371	9.217	8.626
Tientsin	—	—	—	—	—	—
Centre						
Hunan	7.540	6.432	5.540	5.266	5.828	4.535
Hupei	10.468	9.684	8.433	8.491	8.702	10.554
Kiangsi	—	7.500	—	—	—	3.775
East						
Anhwei	4.996	—	4.765	4.919	4.015	7.479
Chekiang	—	—	8.204	9.104	—	8.237
Kiangsu	c.8.609	6.728	9.500	8.175	7.456	7.463
Shanghai	—	—	—	—	—	—
South West						
Kweichow	6.456	—	7.425	—	14.060	7.500
Szechuan	8.580	10.817	9.925	11.441	12.152	12.044
Yunnan	9.378	10.139	9.120	9.031	10.627	9.252
South						
Fukien	11.250	—	—	—	9.375	—
Kwangsi	4.478	4.167	2.658	—	—	2.835
Kwangtung	4.194	4.419	3.579	6.375	5.175	7.322

Appendix 2

Grain yields per sown hectare: soya beans (100 kilograms per hectare)

	1952	1953	1954	1955	1956	1957
North East						
Heilungkiang	11.777	10.863	‿	9.748	10.915	11.162
Kirin	13.333	13.460	12.384	10.160	11.384	11.396
Liaoning	9.535	—	14.000	10.246	13.480	10.507
North West						
IMR	7.722	7.752	8.326	5.880	7.521	5.468
Kansu	6.395	—	—	—	—	6.949
Shensi	4.283	—	—	4.847	4.985	2.989
Sinkiang			negligible			
Tsinghai			negligible			
North						
Honan	6.841	7.821	5.744	7.545	6.389	6.317
Hopei	3.912	—	—	5.479	5.262	—
Shansi	7.275	7.650	6.956	4.609	9.496	—
Shantung	7.043	6.306	7.162	8.012	9.750	3.294
Centre						
Hunan	6.952	5.489	4.000	4.268	3.916	5.325
Hupei	—	13.411	—	8.856	10.741	10.920
Kiangsi	—	—	—	4.545	—	7.500
East						
Anhwei	5.655	—	—	7.369	2.926	7.954
Chekiang	—	—	—	—	12.500	8.346
Kiangsu	c.7.748	—	—	c.9.038	c.8.540	7.405
South West						
Kweichow	—	—	—	—	—	6.667
Szechuan	—	—	—	—	—	8.328
Yunnan	—	—	—	11.236	19.153	—
South						
Fukien	—	15.714	9.245	10.000	15.116	6.842
Kwangsi	c.7.745	—	—	—	—	c.6.515
Kwangtung	6.262	—	4.887	4.435	—	—

Note: Brace indicates that figure is an average over years shown.

Output, sown area and yield per sown hectare

Grain yields per sown hectare: coarse grain (including potatoes) (100 kilograms per hectare)

	1952	1953	1954	1955	1956	1957
North East						
Heilungkiang	16.697	—	11.842	15.114	12.803	12.562
Kirin	14.390	—	—	12.974	9.674	12.263
Liaoning	13.341	—	—	—	17.195	16.148
North West						
IMR	8.256	8.733	9.106	7.596	9.997	6.318
Kansu	—	—	—	—	—	17.227
Shensi	12.735	—	—	—	—	13.434
Sinkiang	15.732	—	—	—	—	17.869
Tsinghai	8.829	7.424	11.810	13.054	13.371	—
North						
Honan	9.463	10.549	10.098	11.113	11.003	10.609
Hopei	12.366	—	—	11.990	9.753	—
Shansi	10.455	11.579	10.833	10.115	9.934	9.952
Shantung	13.972	12.286	14.399	15.595	16.323	17.553
Centre						
Hunan	14.224	12.089	8.343	9.049	7.194	10.901
Hupei	—	12.078	—	10.705	11.492	11.543
Kiangsi	—	—	—	—	—	9.573
East						
Anhwei	9.289	—	—	—	11.855	9.701
Chekiang	—	—	—	—	—	19.911
Kiangsu	—	—	—	10.475	—	9.452
South West						
Kweichow	—	—	—	—	—	13.038
Szechuan	10.950	—	—	—	—	14.320
Yunnan	—	—	—	14.691	14.889	12.475
South						
Fukien	26.103	—	—	—	—	28.000
Kwangsi	—	—	—	—	—	7.929
Kwangtung	11.878	12.033	13.165	12.473	—	13.006

Appendix 2

Grain yields per sown hectare: potatoes (100 kilograms per hectare)

	1952	1953	1954	1955	1956	1957
North East						
Heilungkiang	23.971	—	—	20.167	13.176	19.389
Kirin	—	—	—	—	—	15.888
Liaoning	21.212	—	—	21.563	15.500	22.286
North West						
IMR	19.761	16.667	14.462	14.677	15.902	13.238
Kansu	16.485	18.503	—	—	—	25.643
Shensi	—	—	—	—	—	—
Sinkiang	—	—	—	—	—	27.075
Tsinghai	—	—	—	28.125[a]	—	—
North						
Honan	17.567	18.585	20.108	18.805	21.183	17.350
Hopei	27.009	27.304	19.227	23.070	20.670	28.571
Peking	—	—	—	—	—	—
Shansi	—	—	12.000	8.973	8.474	14.569
Shantung	22.959	22.362	25.711	24.895	27.201	28.409
Tientsin	—	—	—	—	—	—
Centre						
Hunan	23.239	20.616	13.619	15.678	12.683	21.594
Hupei	20.087	19.058	20.118	18.884	—	23.421
Kiangsi	—	—	—	—	—	18.503
East						
Anhwei	—	—	—	27.205	25.716	21.391
Chekiang[b]	—	35.550	—	—	23.810	46.610
Kiangsu	—	—	—	—	—	9.590
Shanghai	—	—	—	—	—	—
South West						
Kweichow	—	—	—	—	—	27.450
Szechuan	15.172	—	25.340	—	16.308	24.466
Yunnan	—	—	—	—	—	18.378
South						
Fukien	27.000	—	—	24.375	—	29.502
Kwangsi	—	—	—	—	—	8.852
Kwangtung	15.000	15.893	16.466	14.206	15.675	17.325

Notes: a. Planned figure.
     b. Chekiang average for 1952–54 was 30.000.

Output, sown area and yield per sown hectare

Grain yields per sown hectare: coarse grains (excluding potatoes) (100 kilograms per hectare)

	1952	1953	1954	1955	1956	1957
North East						
Heilungkiang	16.272	—	—	14.430	12.779	12.124
Kirin	—	—	—	—	—	12.127
Liaoning	13.104	—	—	—	17.307	15.799
North West						
IMR	7.560	8.253	8.787	7.188	9.659	5.890
Kansu	—	—	—	—	—	—
Shensi	—	—	—	—	—	—
Sinkiang	—	—	—	—	—	17.780
Tsinghai	—	—	—	10.817	—	—
North						
Honan	7.887	9.036	7.979	9.586	8.582	9.116
Hopei	11.158	—	—	10.959	8.428	—
Shansi	—	—	10.729	10.208	10.080	9.486
Shantung	11.878	9.939	11.415	13.123	12.747	13.853
Centre						
Hunan	7.591	7.039	4.858	4.501	3.971	5.077
Hupei	—	11.296	—	9.736	—	10.315
Kiangsi	—	—	—	—	—	4.740
East						
Anhwei	2.825	—	—	—	6.392	5.783
Chekiang	—	—	—	—	—	12.138
Kiangsu	—	—	—	—	—	9.427
South West						
Kweichow	—	—	—	—	—	11.948
Szechuan	9.338	—	—	—	—	11.056
Yunnan	—	—	—	—	—	11.841
South						
Fukien	14.000	—	—	—	—	12.414
Kwangsi	—	—	—	—	—	7.409
Kwangtung	4.220	4.826	4.255	5.590	—	5.132

Appendix 2

Grain yields per sown hectare: maize (100 kilograms per hectare)

	1952	1953	1954	1955	1956	1957
North East						
Heilungkiang[a]	17.112	—	—	—	—	14.689
Kirin	—	16.200	15.790	—	—	15.315
Liaoning	21.431	—	—	—	25.013	24.806
North West						
IMR			15.525			
Kansu	—	—	—	—	—	—
Shensi[b]	—	—	—	11.925	18.769[c]	—
Sinkiang	19.286	—	—	—	—	19.710
Tsinghai	—	—	—	—	—	—
North						
Honan	—	—	—	11.723	—	—
Hopei		10.800		—	11.324	
Shansi	—	—	19.800	17.363	21.825[c]	—
Shantung			16.436			
Centre						
Hunan	9.877	9.892	7.636	7.934	6.552	8.313
Hupei	—	—	—	12.036	—	12.907
Kiangsi	—	—	—	—	—	—
East						
Anhwei	—	—	—	—	—	—
Chekiang[d]	—	16.050	—	—	—	16.164
Kiangsu	—	—	—	15.000	—	14.428
South West						
Kweichow	10.947	—	—	—	—	16.732
Szechuan	10.846	—	—	—	12.225	12.979
Yunnan	—	—	—	—	—	14.443
South						
Fukien	—	—	—	—	—	—
Kwangsi	—	—	—	—	—	—
Kwangtung	—	—	—	—	—	—

Notes: a. Heilungkiang average for 1953–57 was 13.560.
   : b. Shensi average for 1952–55 was 13.629.
    c. Planned figure.
    d. Chekiang average for 1952–54 was 12.750.
Braces indicate that the figure is an average over the years shown.

Grain yields per sown hectare: millet (100 kilograms per hectare)

	1952	1953	1954	1955	1956	1957
North East						
Heilungkiang*	12.637	—	—	—	—	11.864
Kirin	—	—	—	—	—	10.275
Liaoning	8.121	—	—	—	—	12.085
North West						
IMR			10.028			
Kansu	—	—	—	—	—	—
Shensi	—	—	—	—	—	—
Sinkiang	—	—	—	—	—	—
Tsinghai	—	—	—	—	—	—
North						
Honan	—	—	—	—	—	—
Hopei	9.750		—	—	—	—
Shansi	c.8.832	—	—	—	—	—
Shantung	—	—	—	—	—	—
Centre						
Hunan	—	—	—	—	—	—
Hupei	—	—	—	—	—	—
Kiangsi	—	—	—	—	—	—
East						
Anhwei	—	—	—	—	—	—
Chekiang	—	—	—	—	—	—
Kiangsu	—	—	—	—	—	—
South West						
Kweichow	—	—	—	—	—	—
Szechuan	—	—	—	—	—	—
Yunnan	—	—	—	—	—	—
South						
Fukien	—	—	—	—	—	—
Kwangsi	—	—	—	—	—	—
Kwangtung	—	—	—	—	—	—

Notes: * Heilungkiang average for 1953–57 was 11.078.
Braces indicate that the figure is an average over the years shown.

Grain yields per sown hectare: kaoliang (100 kilograms per hectare)

	1952	1953	1954	1955	1956	1957
North East						
Heilungkiang*	14.766	—	—	—	—	11.501
Kirin	21.419	—	—	—	—	11.992
Liaoning	12.562	—	—	—	—	15.833
North West						
IMR	—	—	—	—	—	—
Kansu	—	—	—	—	—	—
Shensi	—	—	—	—	—	—
Sinkiang	—	—	—	—	—	—
Tsinghai	—	—	—	—	—	—
North						
Honan	—	—	—	—	—	—
Hopei		7.725		—	—	—
Shansi	—		—	—	—	—
Shantung	—	—	—	—	—	—
Centre						
Hunan	—	—	—	—	—	—
Hupei	—	—	—	—	—	—
Kiangsi	—	—	—	—	—	—
East						
Anhwei	—	—	—	—	—	—
Chekiang	—	—	—	—	—	—
Kiangsu	—	—	—	—	—	—
South West						
Kweichow	—	—	—	—	—	—
Szechuan	—	—	—	—	—	—
Yunnan	—	—	—	—	—	—
South						
Fukien	—	—	—	—	—	—
Kwangsi	—	—	—	—	—	—
Kwangtung	—	—	—	—	—	—

Notes: * Heilungkiang average for 1953–57 was 13.020.
Brace indicates that the figure is an average for the years shown.

SOURCES

Heilungkiang

Rice. **1952** and **1956**: From output and sown area. **1953**: *CKNP* (no. 23), 1954. **1954**: *PAS.* **1955** and **1957**: *An Economic Geography of NE China.*

Wheat. **1952**: Output divided by sown area. **1955**: *CKNP* (no. 15), 1956. **1956**: *CKNP* (no. 12), 1957. **1957**: *An Economic Geography of NE China.*

Soya. **1952**, average for **1953–54** and **1957**: *ibid.* **1955** and **1956**: From output and sown area.

Potatoes. **1952, 1955** and **1957**: *An Economic Geography of NE China.* **1956**: From output and sown area.

Maize, millet and kaoliang. **1952** and **1957**: *An Economic Geography of NE China.* Average for 1953–57 given *ibid.*

Kirin

Rice. **1954–56**: From output and sown area. **1957**: *An Economic Geography of NE China.*

Wheat. **1952** and **1957**: *ibid.* **1955**: *PAS.* **1956**: *CKNP* (no. 12), 1957.

Soya. **1952** and **1954–57**: From output and sown area. **1953**: *KJP*, 27 April 1956.

Potatoes. **1957**: *An Economic Geography of NE China.*

Maize. **1953** and **1954**: *KJP*, 24 April 1955. **1957**: *An Economic Geography of NE China.*

Millet. **1957**: *ibid.*

Kaoliang. **1952** and **1957**: *ibid.*

Liaoning

Rice. **1952** and **1957**: *An Economic Geography of NE China.* **1954–56**: From output and sown area.

Wheat. **1956**: *CKNP* (no. 12), 1957. **1957**: From output and sown area.

Soya. **1952, 1954, 1955** and **1957**: From output and sown area. **1956**: *LJP*, 2 January 1958.

Potatoes. **1952** and **1957**: *An Economic Geography of NE China.* **1955–56**: From output and sown area.

Maize. **1952** and **1957**: *An Economic Geography of NE China.* **1956**: *LJP*, 10 February 1957.

Millet. **1952** and **1957**: *An Economic Geography of NE China.*

Kaoliang. **1952**: *ibid.* **1957**: From output and sown area.

Inner Mongolia

Rice, wheat, soya and potatoes: *NMKTC.*

Maize, millet and kaoliang: *NMKJP*, 5 February 1958.

Kansu

Rice. **1957**: *JMJP*, 30 May 1958.

Wheat. **1955**: From output and sown area. **1956**: *CKNP* (no. 12), 1957. **1957**: *JMJP*, 23 August 1958.

Soya. **1952** and **1957**: From output and sown area.

Potatoes. **1952, 1953** and **1957**: *KAJP*, 3 April 1958.

Shensi

Rice. **1952**: *SCMP*, no. 1208. **1954–56**: From output and sown area.

Wheat. **1952**: *SCMP*, no. 1208. **1953**: From 1952 and *SESJP*, 1 July 1958. **1954** and **1957**: From output and sown area. **1955** and **1956**: *TLCS* (no. 8), 1957, p. 341.

Soya. **1952, 1955, 1956** and **1957**: From output and sown area.

Potatoes. No data available.

Maize. **1955**: *SESJP*, 4 April 1956. **1956**: (planned figure) From output and sown area.

Sinkiang

Rice. **1957**: *SINJP*, 17 April 1958.

Wheat. **1952**: *SNY.* **1953**: From 1952 and information in *TKP*, 27 July 1954. **1954**: *JMJP*, 8 July 1958. **1956**: *CKNP* (no. 12), 1957. **1957**: From output and sown area.

Potatoes. *SINJP*, 17 April 1958.

Tsinghai

Wheat. **1954**: *TSINJP*, 1 December 1955. **1956**: *CKNP* (no. 12), 1957, pp. 16–19.

Potatoes. **1955**: (planned yield) *TSINJP*, 19 October 1955.

Honan

Rice. **1952**: *HONJP*, 6 April 1958. **1953**: *HONJP*, 31 December 1957. **1955, 1956** and **1957**: From output and sown area.

Wheat. **1952–57**: *JMJP*, 15 June 1958.

Soya. **1952, 1956** and **1957**: From output and sown area. **1953**: *An Economic Geography of N. China.* **1954**: *PAS.* **1955**: *HONJP*, 14 March 1956.

Potatoes. **1952–57**: From output and sown area.

Maize. **1955**: *CKNP* (no. 17), 1955, p. 24.

Hopei

Total grain. **1952**: *HOPJP*, 1 January 1953.

Rice. **1952–54** average: *CKNP* (no. 17), 1955. **1956**: *HOPJP*, 1 April 1957. **1957**: *HOPJP*, 17 October 1957.

Output, sown area and yield per sown hectare

Wheat. **1952–57**: *CKNP* (no. 15), 1957.

Soya. **1952, 1955** and **1956**: From output and sown area.

Potatoes. **1952–56**: From output and sown area. **1957**: *HOPJP*, 17 October 1958.

Maize. **1952–54** average: *CKNP* (no. 17), 1955. **1956**: From output and sown area.

Millet and kaoliang. **1952–54** averages: *CKNP* (no. 17), 1955.

Shansi

Total grain. **1955**: *JMJP*, 10 September 1956.

Wheat. **1952, 1953** and **1957**: From output and sown area. **1954–56**: *SASJP*, 9 August 1956.

Soya. **1952** and **1953**: *PAS*. **1954–56**: From output and sown area.

Potatoes. **1954**: *SASJP*, 20 February 1955. **1955–57**: From output and sown area.

Maize. **1954, 1955** and plan for **1956**: *CKNP* (no. 23), 1956.

Millet. **1952**: From output and sown area.

Shantung

Total grain. **1956** and **1957**: *TCJP*, 31 December 1957.

Rice. **1956**: From output and sown area.

Wheat. **1952–54**: *TLCS* (no. 8), 1957. **1955–57**: From output and sown area.

Soya. **1952–55** and **1957**: From output and sown area. **1956**: *NYCS* (no. 7), 1957.

Potatoes. **1952–57**: From output and sown area.

Maize. 'Average' for period: *NYCS* (no. 8), 1957.

Hunan

Rice, wheat, soya, potatoes and maize. **1952–57**: *HNNY*.

Hupei

Rice. **1952–57**: From output and sown area.

Wheat. **1952–57**: From output and sown area.

Soya. **1953, 1955–57**: From output and sown area.

Potatoes. **1952–55** and **1957**: From output and sown area.

Maize. **1955** and **1957**: From output and sown area.

Kiangsi

Rice. **1952**: *KSIJP*, 27 April 1957. **1954**: *KSIJP*, 6 February 1955. **1955**: *KSIJP*, 4 January 1956. **1956–57**: From output and sown area.

Wheat. **1953**: *PAS*. **1957**: From output and sown area.

251

Soya. **1955**: From output and sown area. **1957**: *An Economic Geography of Central China.*

Potatoes. **1957**: *ibid.*

Anhwei

Rice. **1952, 1955–57**: From output and sown area.

Wheat. **1952, 1954, 1955** and **1956**: From output and sown area. **1957**: *An Economic Geography of East China.*

Soya. **1952, 1955–57**: From output and sown area.

Potatoes. **1955–57**: From output and sown area.

Chekiang

Rice. **1953**: *CHKJP*, 24 March 1954. **1956–57**: From output and sown area.

Wheat. **1954** and **1955**: *CHKJP*, 2 June 1955. **1957**: *An Economic Geography of East China.*

Soya. **1956** and **1957**: From output and sown area.

Potatoes. **1952–54** average: *CHKJP*, 24 May 1955. **1953**: *CHKJP*, 24 March 1954. **1956**: From output and sown area. **1957**: *An Economic Geography of East China.*

Maize. **1952–54** average: *CHKJP*, 24 May 1955. **1953**: *CHKJP*, 24 March 1954. **1957**: *An Economic Geography of East China.*

Kiangsu

Total grain. **1954** and **1955**: *HHJP*, 28 April 1956.

Rice. **1952, 1953, 1954** and **1956**: From output and sown area. **1955**: *HHJP*, 29 December 1955. **1957**: *An Economic Geography of East China.*

Wheat. **1952, 1953, 1954** and **1956**: From output and sown area. **1955**: *HHJP*, 6 February 1956. **1957**: *An Economic Geography of East China.*

Soya. **1952, 1955, 1956** and **1957**: From output and sown area.

Potatoes. **1957**: *An Economic Geography of East China.*

Maize. **1955**: *Introduction to Kiangsu Province Agricultural Producers' Co-operative Economy*, pp. 276–80. **1957**: *HHJP*, 4 September 1958.

Kweichow

Total grain. **1952–56**: *Net* yield in *KCJP*, 28 October 1958.

Rice. **1952** and **1953**: From output and sown area. **1954**: *PAS*. **1956**: *KCJP*, 12 March 1957. **1957**: *An Economic Geography of SW China.*

Wheat. **1952**: From output and sown area. **1954** and **1956**: *PAS*. **1957**: *An Economic Geography of SW China.*

Soya. **1957**: From output and sown area.

Potatoes. **1957**: *An Economic Geography of SW China.*

Maize. **1952**: From output and sown area. **1957**: *An Economic Geography of SW China.*

Szechuan

Rice. **1952** and **1957**: *An Economic Geography of SW China.* **1953** and **1956**: From output and sown area. **1954**: *NCNA*, 6 December 1955. **1955**: *Szechuan Province.* **1956**: From figures in *SZJP*, 26 December 1957, *JMJP*, 10 September 1956 and *CKNPTK* (no. 2), 1958.

Wheat. **1952–56**: From output and sown area. **1957**: *An Economic Geography of SW China.*

Soya. **1957**: *ibid.*

Potatoes. **1952, 1954** and **1956**: From output and sown area. **1957**: *An Economic Geography of SW China.*

Maize. **1952**: From output and sown area. **1956**: *TKP*, 29 August 1957. **1957**: *An Economic Geography of SW China.*

Yunnan

Rice. **1952–55**: From output and sown area. **1956**: *YJP*, 13 May 1957. **1957**: *An Economic Geography of SW China.*

Wheat. **1952–57**: From output and sown area.

Soya. **1956–57**: From output and sown area.

Potatoes and Maize. **1957**: *An Economic Geography of SW China.*

Fukien

Rice. **1952**: *FJP*, 9 April 1955. **1955**: *FJP*, 23 December 1955. **1957**: *An Economic Geography of South China.*

Wheat. **1952**: *FJP*, 9 April 1955. **1956**: *FJP*, 16 January 1957.

Soya. **1953–57**: From output and sown area.

Potatoes. **1952**: *FJP*, 9 April 1955. **1955**: *FJP*, 23 December 1955. **1957**: From output and sown area.

Kwangsi

Rice. **1952, 1953** and **1957**: From output and sown area. **1955**: *PAS.*

Wheat. **1952, 1953, 1954** and **1957**: From output and sown area.

Soya. **1952** and **1957**: From output and sown area.

Potatoes. **1957**: From output and sown area.

Kwangtung

Rice. **1952, 1955, 1956** and **1957**: From output and sown area. **1953** and **1954**: *Economic Geography of Kwangtung.*

Wheat. **1952, 1954, 1956** and **1957**: From output and sown area. **1953**: *Economic Geography of Kwangtung.* **1955**: *NFJP*, 9 September 1956.

Soya. **1952, 1954** and **1955**: From output and sown area.

Potatoes. **1952**: *NFJP*, 19 February 1955. **1953–55**: From output and sown area. **1956–57**: *Grain Production Can be Speeded Up.*

Appendix 3 Provincial population data, 1952–57 and sources

Estimated total population (end year) (million)

	1952	1953	1954	1955	1956	1957
North East						
Heilungkiang	11.61	12.19	12.81	13.46	14.13	14.86
Kirin	11.15	11.42	11.70	11.98	12.27	12.55
Liaoning	20.20	20.93	21.68	22.27	23.27	24.09
North West						
IMR	7.01	7.40	7.80	8.23	8.68	9.16
Kansu	12.76	13.10	13.45	13.82	14.20	14.58
Shensi	15.65	16.12	16.61	17.11	17.63	18.13
Sinkiang	4.80	4.94	5.12	5.28	5.46	5.64
Tsinghai	1.65	1.71	1.79	1.87	1.96	2.05
North						
Honan	43.74	44.69	45.66	46.63	47.63	48.67
Hopei	36.42	37.65	38.89	40.06	41.61	43.03
Peking	2.63	2.91	3.44	3.97	4.58	4.01
Shansi	14.13	14.48	14.84	15.21	15.59	15.98
Shantung	48.32	49.43	50.58	51.74	52.68	54.03
Tientsin	2.64	2.75	2.86	3.02	3.09	3.22
Centre						
Hunan	32.96	33.59	34.18	34.73	35.46	36.22
Hupei	27.48	28.11	28.76	29.43	30.12	30.79
Kiangsi	16.46	16.87	17.29	17.74	18.20	18.61
East						
Anhwei	30.11	30.79	31.62	32.45	33.00	33.56
Chekiang	22.59	23.12	23.65	24.19	24.74	25.28
Kiangsu	40.76	41.74	42.75	43.74	44.87	45.23
Shanghai	6.19	6.28	6.80	6.50	6.81	7.20
South West						
Kweichow	14.84	15.24	15.69	16.16	16.49	16.89
Szechuan	65.00	66.36	67.77	69.25	70.76	72.16
Yunnan	17.30	17.65	18.01	18.37	18.75	19.10
South						
Fukien	12.75	13.18	13.60	14.00	14.40	14.65
Kwangsi	17.40	17.78	18.18	18.58	18.99	19.39
Kwangtung	33.95	34.68	35.45	36.23	37.03	37.96
Total	570.50	585.11	600.98	616.02	632.40	647.04

Provincial population data, 1952–57

Estimated rural population (end year) (million)

	1952	1953	1954	1955	1956	1957
North East						
Heilungkiang	7.93	8.09	8.39	8.84	9.03	9.56
Kirin	8.36	8.43	8.51	8.57	8.62	8.66
Liaoning	16.17	16.26	16.27	16.01	16.02	15.69
North West						
IMR	6.41	6.61	6.81	7.01	7.23	7.45
Kansu	11.37	11.59	11.85	12.20	12.58	12.90
Shensi	13.26	13.69	14.14	14.60	15.08	15.50
Sinkiang	4.32	4.42	4.56	4.71	4.84	5.01
Tsinghai	1.540	1.588	1.657	1.726	1.804	1.880
North						
Honan	41.25	41.93	42.63	43.34	44.07	44.81
Hopei	33.45	34.39	35.43	36.52	37.75	39.08
Peking	0.544	0.546	0.550	0.554	0.897	0.895
Shansi	12.73	13.00	13.30	13.60	13.09	13.38
Shantung	45.70	46.59	47.60	48.53	48.73	50.02
Tientsin	0.337	0.374	0.389	0.385	0.410	0.419
Centre						
Hunan	30.26	29.93	31.28	31.92	32.17	32.78
Hupei	24.13	24.48	24.95	25.55	25.94	26.57
Kiangsi	14.56	14.81	15.12	15.87	16.00	16.28
East						
Anhwei	27.61	28.09	28.70	29.30	29.32	30.64
Chekiang	19.72	20.01	20.38	20.86	21.16	21.67
Kiangsu	36.05	36.63	37.37	38.26	38.97	39.35
Shanghai	0.357	0.358	0.356	0.361	0.393	0.397
South West						
Kweichow	13.50	13.78	14.15	14.58	14.80	15.18
Szechuan	59.92	60.87	62.01	63.40	64.47	65.82
Yunnan	15.76	15.99	16.27	16.60	16.85	17.19
South						
Fukien	10.72	10.96	11.25	11.41	11.58	11.88
Kwangsi	16.06	16.33	16.65	17.03	17.32	17.71
Kwangtung	29.59	29.96	30.49	31.19	31.61	32.47
Total	501.608	509.706	521.062	532.926	540.734	553.191

Estimated urban population (end year) (million)

	1952	1953	1954	1955	1956	1957
North East						
Heilungkiang	3.68	4.10	4.42	4.62	5.10	5.30
Kirin	2.79	2.99	3.19	3.41	3.65	3.89
Liaoning	4.03	4.67	5.41	6.26	7.25	8.40
North West						
IMR	0.60	0.79	0.99	1.22	1.45	1.71
Kansu	1.39	1.51	1.60	1.62	1.62	1.68
Shensi	2.39	2.43	2.47	2.51	2.55	2.63
Sinkiang	0.48	0.52	0.56	0.57	0.62	0.63
Tsinghai	0.112	0.122	0.133	0.144	0.156	0.170
North						
Honan	2.49	2.76	3.03	3.29	3.56	3.86
Hopei	2.97	3.26	3.46	3.54	3.86	3.95
Peking	2.086	2.364	2.890	3.416	3.683	3.115
Shansi	1.40	1.48	1.54	1.61	2.50	2.60
Shantung	2.62	2.84	2.98	3.21	3.95	4.01
Tientsin	2.303	2.376	2.471	2.635	2.680	2.801
Centre						
Hunan	2.70	3.66	2.90	2.81	3.29	3.44
Hupei	3.35	3.63	3.81	3.88	4.18	4.22
Kiangsi	1.90	2.06	2.17	1.87	2.20	2.33
East						
Anhwei	2.50	2.70	2.92	3.15	3.68	2.92
Chekiang	2.87	3.11	3.27	3.33	3.58	3.61
Kiangsu	4.71	5.11	5.38	5.48	5.90	5.88
Shanghai	5.833	5.922	6.444	6.139	6.417	6.803
South West						
Kweichow	1.34	1.46	1.54	1.58	1.69	1.71
Szechuan	5.08	5.49	5.76	5.85	6.29	6.34
Yunnan	1.54	1.66	1.74	1.77	1.90	1.91
South						
Fukien	2.03	2.22	2.35	2.59	2.82	2.77
Kwangsi	1.34	1.45	1.53	1.55	1.67	1.68
Kwangtung	4.36	4.72	4.96	5.04	5.42	5.49
Total	68.894	75.404	79.918	83.094	91.666	93.849

SOURCES

A general note on sources and methods of estimation. The most important source for all the provincial population estimates is Ernest Ni, *Distribution of the Urban and Rural Population of Mainland China: 1953 and 1958*, (US Department of Commerce, Bureau of the Census, Foreign Manpower Research Office, International Population Reports, Series P–95, no. 56, October 1960). Some missing figures have had to be interpolated in every province, and in very many instances either rural or urban population for a given year has been obtained as a residual.

Heilungkiang

Total population for 1953 (Census) and for 1958 (Ni) provided the basis for interpolating the intermediate years. Evidence of rural and urban population is available in *HJP*, 10 December 1955, 29 October 1956, 5 January 1957, 6 June 1957, 18 October 1957 and 29 October 1957. Evidence is also found in *An Economic Geography of NE China*, and in *TLCS* (no. 11), 1957; and in *JMJP*, 24 August 1957.

Kirin

Total population for 1954–57 was estimated in the same way as for Heilungkiang, using the 1953 Census figure and Ni's 1958 population. A check on the results is found in *KJP*, 21 August 1957 (total populations of 1952 and 1956) and in *KJP*, 13 September 1957 (rural population in 1956). Data on rural and urban populations are also published in *An Economic Geography of NE China*.

Liaoning

Total population for 1954–57 was estimated as for Heilungkiang. Evidence relating to total, rural and urban populations was also used from *An Economic Geography of NE China*, and in *LJP*, 5 May 1957 (natural increase in urban population), 22 May 1957 (growth of population of Fushun), 23 May 1957 (urban population), 8 October 1957 (urban population). Further data on urban population are in *JMJP*, 26 May 1958 and *SHYJP*, 26 March 1957.

Inner Mongolia

The main basis of all the population estimates (total, rural and urban) is the information for 1953 and 1958 in Ni and in *NMKTC*. Further data which assist in the interpolation of estimates for the intervening years have been used from *NMKJP*, 12 April 1957 and 5 August 1957 (for agricultural population), and 10 April 1957 (for urban population).

Kansu

Total population figures are based on Ni, with supporting figures in *KAJP*, 10 July 1957 (figures of the State Statistical Bureau); *KAJP*, 9 October 1957 (total population for 1953 and 1957), and *TCKT* (no. 14), 1957 for 1956. The State Statistical Bureau (*KAJP*, 10 July 1957) also lists useful information on rural population in 1949 and 1956.

Appendix 3

Shensi

Total population figures are estimated from data in Ni, and from figures in *SESJP*, 4 September 1957 (for 1955 and 1956). Indications of rural population are also found in Ministry of Food data in this article. *SESJP*, 6 September 1957 contains the fact that the average number of persons per rural household was 4.7 and this may be applied to data for the number of rural households in Shensi contained in *NYHTH*.

Sinkiang and Tsinghai

All figures are based on Ni.

Honan

Ni again provides the basis of the total population estimates, but many statistics are available for filling in the intervening years. Useful figures, cited by the Ministry of Food, are in *HONJP*, 27 August 1957 and some data on urban population are given in *HONJP*, 15 August 1957 and in 14 December 1957. Other data are in *An Economic Geography of N. China*.

Hopei

Ni's figures for total population in 1953 and 1958 have been supplemented with Ministry of Food figures for 1953–56 inclusive, in *HOPJP*, 9 September 1957. An estimated population for 1957 has been interpolated. Apart from Ni's figures for rural and urban population, other evidence is given in *An Economic Geography of N. China*, and in *HOPJP*, 7 and 14 August 1957.

Peking

For total population, figures are available in Ni for 1953 and 1958, and for 1955–57 in *PKJP*, 6 August 1957, 25 August 1957 and 1 November 1957; and in *TGY*. A figure for 1954 has been interpolated. Rural population has been estimated from the number of farm households (*NYHTH*) and an average size of household assumed to be the same as Hopei (which is known).

Shansi

Apart from information in Ni, total population figures are available in *SASJP*, 24 February 1955 (for 1954) and in 11 August 1957 (for 1953 and 1956). Rural population data have been published for 1953 (*An Economic Geography of N. China*, and in *SASJP*, 4 September 1957), for 1955 (*SASJP*, 4 September 1957 and 12 September 1955) and for 1957 (*SASJP*, 20 November 1957). Urban population in 1952, 1956 and 1957 is recorded in *SASJP*, 28 July 1957, while *SASJP*, 11 August 1957 gives the ratio of agricultural to non-agricultural population in 1952 and 1956.

Shantung

Ni's estimates for total population in 1953 and 1958 have been supplemented by data in *TCJP*, 15 August 1957 (for 1952 and 1956) and in *JMJP*, 29 September 1955 (for 1955). Rural population for 1954, 1955 and 1956 can be estimated from figures used by the Ministry of Food in an article in *TCJP*, 16 August 1957. Missing figures have been interpolated.

Tientsin

Annual total population has been roughly estimated from the figures for 1953 and 1958 in Ni. Rural population estimates are based, as in the case of Peking, on the number of peasant households (*NYHTH*) and the average size of households in Hopei.

Hunan

Good additional data, both for total and for rural population, are available to be used alongside those of Ni. Total population figures 1950–56 are in *HHNP*, 7 August 1957, while rural population for 1953–56 is given in *HHNP*, 19 July 1957. Rural and urban populations for 1957 are found in *An Economic Geography of Central China*. This contains information leading to an estimate of rural population for 1956 and also the rate of growth of urban population in Hunan. 1957 urban population is from *HHNP*, 22 January 1958.

Hupei

Estimates are based primarily on Ni, along with data relating to total population in 1955 (*HUPJP*, 28 October 1956) and in 1956 (*HUPJP*, 21 June 1957). *An Economic Geography of Central China* contains 1957 figures for total, rural and urban population.

Kiangsi

Figures in Ni and in *An Economic Geography of Central China* provide the starting point of the estimates. Other data are found in *KSIJP*, 31 August 1955 (total population for 1954), 13 September 1955 (rural population, 1954), 18 August 1957 (rural population, 1956), and 11 October 1955 (urban population, 1955).

Anhwei

Figures for total population in the years 1953–56 are those published by the Ministry of Food in *AJP*, 20 September 1957 and the 1957 figure is from *TGY*. Rural populations for 1955 and 1956 are in *AJP*, 23 September 1957; rural population for 1957 is given in *An Economic Geography of East China*, which also contains the percentage of total population in urban areas.

Chekiang

Very little evidence is available to fill out the picture provided for 1953 and for 1957 by Ni and by *An Economic Geography of East China*. Estimates for the intervening years are, therefore, mainly based on assumptions concerning rural and urban percentages, with a rough check on rural population provided by some figures for *agricultural* population in *CHKJP*, 25 December 1957, and in *Mechanisation Bureau*.

Kiangsu

Mainly based on Ni and percentages for urban and rural population in *WHP*, 21 March 1957. Many assumptions have had to be made in order to arrive at estimates for the years 1954–56. *HHJP*, 8 May 1957, gives a growth rate of total population for 1953–56 and *HHJP*, 10 July 1957 provides a figure for the rise in rural population in 1955–57.

Appendix 3

Shanghai

Available figures for total population are as follows: 1953, Ni; 1955 (April), *HWP*, 10 August 1955; 1956, *WHP*, 11 February 1957 and *CFJP*, 10 March 1957; 1957, *HWP*, 7 January 1958 and an estimated increase in population from October 1957 (kindly supplied by Professor C.B. Howe, who also supplied most of the other figures for Shanghai). The estimates of rural population 1953–55 and 1957 are based on the number of rural households and the average size of households in Kiangsu. For 1956 we have a figure in *WHP*, 11 February 1957. See also *HHPYK*, vol. 75 (no. 1), 1956, pp. 62–4 for an estimate of rural population.

Kweichow

Little published information is available upon which to build a series. Starting with figures for 1953 and 1957 in Ni and in *An Economic Geography of SW China*, further information includes an estimate of total population in 1956 (*KCJP*, 8 August 1957) and of rural population in 1954 and 1956 (*KCJP*, 28 August 1957, figures of the Ministry of Food).

Szechuan

The only sources of all estimates are Ni and *An Economic Geography of SW China*. Missing figures have been interpolated.

Yunnan

The main basis is Ni and *An Economic Geography of SW China*, with guidance for intervening interpolations from *YJP*, 25 August 1957 (total population in 1949 and in 1956), 4 November 1958 (total population in 1952 and in 1957), and 27 December 1957 (agricultural population in 1956).

Fukien

Estimates are from figures in Ni and *An Economic Geography of South China*; and in *FJP*, 1 January 1958 (total population in 1952 and in 1957), 30 January 1957 (total population for 1955), 13 February 1957 (total population for 1956), 6 August 1955 (rural population for 1954, figure of the Ministry of Food), and 8 May 1957 (rural population for 1956).

Kwangsi

Very little evidence is available other than in Ni and in *An Economic Geography of South China*. Useful figures, however, are agricultural population in 1956 (*Mechanisation Bureau*) and total and agricultural populations in mid-1957 (*KWSINYTH* (no. 21), 1957).

Kwangtung

Some difficulties arise in making accurate estimates because of boundary changes during the period 1953 to 1957, and because some population figures include Hong Kong and Macau (for example, the 1953 Census figure). 1953 total population is estimated by deducting the populations of Hong Kong and Macau from the Census figure (cited by Ni). The resulting figure is confirmed by figures for grain output per head in *NFJP*, 23 July 1957 (which also provides total population in 1956). *TGY* gives total population for 1957, as does *An Economic Geography of South China*. The latter supplies evidence of the rural and urban populations in 1957, and *NFJP*, 13 April 1957 contains the same information for 1956.

Appendix 4 Sources of data for Table 5: Inequality of grain output per head of rural population at the Special District level in eleven provinces, 1952–57

Kansu

Rural populations for all Special Districts have been estimated from total populations given in *KAJP*, 27 February 1958. Rural population is assumed to be 94 per cent of total.

Yinch'uan. Grain output for **1952, 1955** and **1956**: *KAJP*, 26 October 1956.

Changyeh. Output per head for **1952, 1953** and **1957**: *KAJP*, 1 January 1958.

P'ingliang. Output for **1952**: *KAJP*, 17 August 1959. **1955** and **1956**: *ibid.*, 26 October 1956. **1957**: *ibid.*, 24 December 1958.

Tinghsi. **1957** output: *KAJP*, 7 December 1958.

Wutu. Output for **1955** and **1956**: *KAJP*, 19 November 1956. **1957**: *ibid.*, 3 January 1958.

Kan-nan. Output for **1952** and **1955**: *KAJP*, 9 October 1956. **1957**: *ibid.*, 16 November 1958.

Shensi

Hanchong. **1957**: Rural population *SESJP*, 22 November 1957. Output *ibid.*, 25 November 1959.

Yenan. **1952**: Output *SESJP*, 8 October 1959. Population estimated from 1957. **1957** output and population: *SESJP*, 15 October 1958.

Yülin. **1957**: Grain output *SESJP*, 2 February 1958. Population *ibid.*, 9 October 1958 and 28 June 1958. Earlier years: *Shen-hsi Nung-ts'un She-hu'e Chu-yi Chien-she (Shensi Rural Socialist Construction)* (Sian, 1956), vol. 1, p. 155.

Hopei

T'angshan. **1957**: Output *HOPJP*, 7 December 1957. Rural population from number of farm households (*HOPJP*, 5 April 1958) and estimated size of household (provincial average used). Same source and procedure used for Ch'engte, Tientsin, Changchiak'ou, Paoting, Hantan and Shihchiachuang.

Ch'engte. **1957**: Output *HOPJP*, 19 December 1957.

Ts'anghsien. **1957**: Output and population: *HOPJP*, 20 February 1958.

Tunghsien. **1955**: Output: *HOPJP*, 16 March 1956. Population estimated from number of households given in *ibid.*

Tientsin Special District. **1957**: Output, *HOPJP*, 8 January 1958.

Changchiak'ou. **1957**: Output from figures in *HOPJP*, 29 October 1958.

Paoting. **1957**: Output *HOPJP*, 25 October 1957.

Hantan. **1957**: Output *HOPJP*, 12 February 1958.

Shihchiachuang. **1957**: Output *HOPJP*, 11 January 1958.

Hsingt'ai. **1957**: Output: *HOPJP*, 21 November 1957. Rural population from figures in *ibid.*, 19 March 1956, projected to 1957.

Shansi

Ch'angchih. Output for **1956**: plan figure *SASJP*, 4 February 1956. Rural population for 1956 from figures in *ibid.*, 18 May 1958. Output for **1957** estimated from 1958 (*SASJP*, 21 October 1958), assumed to be double 1957 output. Rural population from figures in *ibid.*, 18 May 1958.

Chin-nan. **1952** estimate *SASJP*, 21 October 1958. **1955** and **1956:** From figures in *ibid.*, 21 November 1956.

Ying-pei. Average for **1953–57** from *SASJP*, 13 January 1958 and 18 May 1958.

Yütze. Output for **1955** and **1956** from figures in *SASJP*, 12 January 1958. Rural populations estimated from figures in *ibid.*, 18 May 1958.

Shantung

Grain production for each Special District is from *hsien* (county) data in *TCJP*, 21 January 1958, p. 3. Estimates of rural population are from the number of rural households in each *hsien* (from figures in *ibid.*, 26 January 1958 and 7 March 1958). The average size of rural households in Shantung is estimated from the provincial rural population and the number of rural households in the province.

Hunan

All estimates are from Hu Chiao-liang, *Hu-nan Sheng Ching-chi Ti-li* (*Economic Geography of Hunan Province*) (Changsha, 1956).

Anhwei

Wuhu. **1956**: Output *AJP*, 26 September 1957. Rural population *ibid.*, 20 August 1957.

Anking. **1956**: Estimate from Ministry of Food data in *AJP*, 4 May 1957.

Fouyang. Figures for four years, **1953–56**, given by the Ministry of Food in *AJP*, 7 October 1957.

Kiangsu

Soochow, Sunkiang, Yangchow and Nant'ung. Data in *Mechanisation Bureau*, pp. 207 and 234.

Yench'eng. Output *HHJP*, 22 January 1956 (communication from Dr R.F. Ash), and rural population, *HHJP*, 19 January 1958.

Hsüchow. Output for **1952** and **1955** given in *HCTC*, 1 October 1957 and 1 January 1958. Rural population for **1957** is in *ibid.*, 25 January 1958 and estimates for earlier years are derived from this.

Hwaiyin. The estimate for this very bad harvest year in Hwaiyin is based on figures for *k'ouliang* (grain rations) per head (*HHJP*, 17 August 1957) and grain imports of the Special District (*ibid.*, 5 October 1957). Rural population is estimated from the 1959 figure in *HHJP*, 19 January 1958. Grain 'requirements' for 1956 have been estimated (with an allowance for seed and feed added to rations). By deducting grain imports an indication of output is obtained. A check is provided by an estimate of grain output per head of rural population, 1956, in twenty poor *hsien* in Hwaiyin, Hsüchow and Yench'eng, of 207 kilograms. This is from figures in *CHCC* (no. 4), 1957, pp. 24–5, and in *Mechanisation Bureau*. A further indication of the poverty of Hwaiyin is the fact that grain output per head of rural population, 1957, in Hwaiyin and Hsüchow together was around 205 kilograms (*HHJP*, 19 December 1957 and 19 January 1958).

Szechuan

Wenchiang. Grain output for **1952, 1956** and **1957**: *SZJP*, 28 September 1958. Population estimates derived from figure for 1957 in *ibid.*, 17 March 1958.

Chiangchin. From data in *HHPYK*, vol. 107 (no. 9), 1957, pp. 92–3.

Neichiang. **1952**: Production estimated from data in *SZJP*, 27 January 1958. **1957**: Output *SZJP*, 30 September 1958. Rural population for 1957 estimated from total population for the District in *SZJP*, 27 March 1958. Population for 1952 derived from this.

Suining. Production for **1952** and **1957** in *SZJP*, 30 January 1958. Population for **1957**: *SZJP*, 30 January 1958 and *ibid.*, 27 March 1958. Population for **1952** estimated from 1957.

Yaan. Production for **1952** and **1955** and **1957** given in or estimated from *SZJP*, 1 October 1958. Population for **1957**: *SZJP*, 27 March 1958. Figures for earlier years are based on this.

Hsichang. **1957**: Output estimated from 1958 figure in *SZJP*, 17 November 1958. Figure for 1957 total population in the District (*SZJP*, 27 March 1958) provides the basis for estimate of 1957 rural population.

Nanch'ung. **1957**: Production estimated from grain ration data in *SZJP*, 1 October 1959. Population from figures in *SZJP*, 29 March 1958.

Fukien

Nanp'ing. **1957**: Production *FJP*, 31 December 1958. Rural population from total population (*FJP*, 22 November 1957).

Lungch'i. **1957**: Production in *FJP*, 2 February 1958. Rural population estimated from the number of rural households in the District: *FJP*, 2 July 1958.

Fuan. **1957**: Production, *FJP*, 27 December 1958. Rural population from total population (*FJP*, 1 July 1958).

Minhou. Production in **1954** and **1955**: *FJP*, 12 March 1956. Rural population estimated from rural household data in *ibid.*

Chinchiang. **1957**: Production, *FJP*, 18 November 1957. Rural population from figures in *ibid.*

Lungyen. **1957**: Production from *FJP*, 7 December 1958. Rural population estimated from total population: *FJP*, 1 July 1958.

Kwangtung

Fatshan. Grain output **1952–56** and an estimate for **1957**: *NFJP*, 13 August 1957. Rural populations derived from figure for **1956**: *NFJP*, 31 May 1958.

Swatow. **1957**: Production and rural population in *TLCS* (no. 9), 1958, pp. 422–4.

Hainan. Grain output **1952, 1954, 1955** and **1956**: *NFJP*, 12 August 1957. Rural populations derived from figure for 1957 in *An Economic Geography of Kwangtung*, pp. 53 and 93.

'*North Kwangtung*' *(including Chaokuan District)*. Grain production estimated from figures in *An Economic Geography of Kwangtung*, pp. 26 and 73. Rural population from total in *ibid*., p. 53.

Appendix 5 Grain procurement and sales, 1953–57

a. SOURCES OF DATA FOR CONSTRUCTION OF PROVINCIAL GRAIN BALANCES, 1953–57

Heilungkiang

Gross procurement. **1953–54** and **1954–55**: *HJP*, 9 December 1955. **1955–56**: *HJP*, 6 July 1956. **1956–57**: State Statistical Bureau (*HJP*, 7 August 1957) gives a reduction of 31 per cent in 1956–57; confirmed by data in *HJP*, 10 March 1957. **1957–58**: *HJP*, 13 October 1958.

Rural sales. **1953–54**: Total sales minus estimated urban sales. **1954–55**: From the amount of grain available in rural areas (*HJP*, 9 December 1955), from gross procurement and output. **1955–56**: From 'rural retention rate' in *HJP*, 24 September 1959, using gross procurement and output. **1956–57**: Total sales minus (estimated) urban sales. **1957–58**: Total sales minus urban sales.

Urban sales. **1953–54**: From 1954–55, said to be 13.62 per cent above 1953–54. (Fan Ching-yuan, *Liang Nien ti Liang-shih Chi-hua Shou-kou ho Chi-hua Kung-ying* (*Two Years of Grain Planned Purchases and Planned Supply*) Shanghai, 1955).) **1954–55** and **1955–56**: Total sales minus rural sales. **1956–57**: From figures for Harbin, applied to the urban population of the province. See *HAJP*, 15 November 1957. **1957–58**: An estimate (possibly an under-estimate) based on planned urban consumption (*HJP*, 16 October 1957).

Total sales. **1953–54** and **1954–55**: *HJP*, 9 December 1955. **1955–56**: *JMJP*, 24 August 1957. **1956–57**: Percentage rise given by State Statistical Bureau (*HJP*, 7 August 1957) and resulting figure confirmed in *JMJP*, 24 August 1957. **1957–58**: *HJP*, 31 December 1957.

Kirin

Gross procurement. **1953–54** and **1954–55**: *KJP*, 21 August 1957. **1955–56**: State Statistical Bureau percentage rise on 1954–55 (*KJP*, 20 April 1956). **1956–57**: Percentage decline given by State Statistical Bureau (*KJP*, 17 April 1957). **1957–58**: From five-year total gross procurement: *KJP*, 12 July 1958.

Rural sales. **1953–54, 1954–55, 1955–56** and **1956–57**: *KJP*, 21 August 1957. **1957–58**: From five-year total rural grain sales, *KJP*, 12 July 1958.

Urban sales. All by subtracting rural sales from total sales.

Total sales. **1953–54** and **1955–56**: *KJP*, 13 September 1957. **1954–55**: From four-year total (*KJP*, 21 August 1957). **1956–57**: *KJP*, 21 August 1957. **1957–58**: From five-year total (*KJP*, 12 July 1958).

Liaoning

Gross procurement. **1953–54**: From figures for 'rural grain availability' (*LJP*, 23 August 1957) and rural grain sales. **1954–55**: *LJP*, 22 October 1955. **1955–56**: *LJP*, 9 October 1956. **1956–57**: *LJP*, 23 August 1957; see also corroborating evidence in *LJP*, 2 July 1957. **1957–58**: *LJP*, 3 December 1958.

Rural sales. **1953–54**: Four-year total (*LJP*, 23 August 1957) minus the total of three years. **1954–55**: Total sales minus urban sales. Confirmed (approximately) in *LJP*, 22 October 1955. **1955–56**: From 'rural grain available' and rural population (see *LJP*, 29 September 1957). **1956–57**: Total sales minus urban sales, confirmed by figure for change in rural sales 1956–57, in *LJP*, 21 July 1957. **1957–58**: Planned figure implied by plan for total sales and for urban sales. See also *LJP*, 29 September 1957 for planned 'retained grain level' in rural areas; and *LSP* (no. 83), 1959, which records that rural sales, 1957–58, fell.

Urban sales. **1953–54**: *LJP*, 23 August 1957. **1954–55**: An estimate based on the rise in four Liaoning cities by 11.5 per cent given in *Two Years of Grain Planned Purchases and Planned Supply*. **1955–56** and **1956–57**: *LJP*, 13 September 1957. **1957–58**: Planned figure: *LJP*, 17 October 1957.

Total sales. **1953–54**: Rural sales plus urban sales. **1954–55**: *LJP*, 22 October 1955. **1955–56**: Rural sales plus urban sales. **1956–57**: *LJP*, 23 August 1957. **1957–58**: Plan: *LJP*, 14 December 1957.

Inner Mongolia

Gross procurement. **1953–54**: An estimate from index for central purchase for 1952–54 in *NMKJP*, 10 August 1955 and assumed tax (we have a guide from tax in 1958–59, *NMKJP*, 10 October 1959). **1954–55**: Given *NMKJP*, 28 April 1955. **1955–56**: Central purchase (figure supplied by Dr A.L. Erisman) and assumed tax. **1956–57** and **1957–58**: *NMKJP*, 16 December 1958.

Rural sales. **1953–54** and **1954–55**: *NMKJP*, 27 August 1955. **1955–56**: From gross procurement and 'retained level' in rural areas in *NMKJP*, 7 February 1958. **1956–57**: An estimate based on general indicators of the annual level of rural sales (which were very small). See *NMKJP*, 27 February 1957 and 29 September 1959. **1957–58**: 78.2 per cent of 1956–57, *NMKJP*, 1 May 1958.

Urban sales. **1953–54**: From percentage rise in 1954–55 compared with 1953–54, for the city of Paotou, *NMKJP*, 24 August 1955. **1954–55**: From ration data, *NMKJP*, 13 October 1955. **1955–56**: Estimated by assuming the national percentage decrease per head applied to the urban population of IMR. **1956–57**: Five year's urban sales (*NMKJP*, 29 September 1959) minus four years' total. **1957–58**: From ration data in *NMKJP*, 1 May 1958.

Total sales. **1953–57**: All by adding rural sales to urban sales.

Kansu

Gross procurement. **1953–54, 1954–55** and **1955–56**: All from gross procurement as a percentage of grain output, given in *KAJP*, 26 February 1958. **1956–57**: From *KAJP*, 8 March 1957 and 24 February 1958. **1957–58**: From figures in *KAJP*, 6 October 1959.

Rural sales. **1953–54** and **1954–55**: From grain per head of rural population, *KAJP*, 5 September 1957, given gross procurement. **1955–56**: Same method, relevent data in *JMJP*, 31 August 1957. **1956–57**: Same method. See *KAJP*, 5 September 1957.

Urban sales. All are estimated by subtracting rural sales from total sales.

Total sales. The starting point for our series is **1956–57** for which a figure is given in *TCKT* (no. 14), 1957, pp. 21 and 32. **1955–56**: Obtained from 1956–57, *KAJP*, 8 March

1957. **1954–55**: Estimated from 1955–56, *KAJP*, 12 March 1957. **1953–54**: Estimated roughly by assuming a small procurement–sales deficit (we know that Kansu imported grain in 1953–54).

Shensi

Gross procurement. **1953–54**: Four years' total, 1953–56 (*SESJP*, 4 September 1957) minus total for three years 1954–56. **1954–55, 1955–56** and **1956–57**: *SESJP*, 29 August 1957. **1957–58**: *SESJP*, 5 August 1958.

Rural sales. **1953–54, 1954–55, 1955–56** and **1956–57**: All from rural grain available (given procurement) in *SESJP*, 4 September 1957. **1957–58**: Estimated from consumption norm (*ibid.*) and from figures for rural population output and procurement.

Urban sales. **1953–54**: *SIAJP*, 3 November 1955. Rest: Total minus rural sales.

Total sales. **1953–54**: Urban plus rural sales. **1954–55**: *SESJP*, 4 September 1957. **1955–56**: *SESJP*, 10 May 1957. **1956–57**: From plan and degree of plan fulfilment (both *SESJP*, 10 May 1957). **1957–58**: A minimum estimate based on the plan for a rise of 2 per cent: *SESJP*, 1 October 1957. The result is almost identical to a figure obtained from five-year total in *SESJP*, 14 August 1958.

Sinkiang

Gross procurement. **1953–54**: Percentage of output given in *SINJP*, 3 October 1959. **1954–55**: A minimum, estimated with reference to gross procurement as a percentage of output in other years: said to be quite constant at 20 per cent: *LSP* (no. 81), 1959. **1955–56**: From figures in *SINJP*, 30 December 1955. **1956–57**: From 1957 and figures in *SINJP*, 4 December 1957. **1957–58**: *SINJP*, 1 September 1958 and 3 September 1958.

Rural sales. **1953–54**: Total sales minus (assumed) urban sales. **1955–56**: Assumed to be a slightly lower percentage of gross procurement than in 1956–57. **1956–57**: Rural sales a percentage of gross procurement given *SINJP*, 4 December 1957. **1957–58**: Assumed is a slight drop compared with 1956–57 in accordance with the good harvest and the anti-rightist campaign.

Urban sales. **1953–54, 1954–55** and **1955–56** all estimated for the very small urban population of Sinkiang (around 0.5 million) by assuming national average urban grain use per head was the same in this province. **1956–57**: Total sales minus rural sales. **1957–58**: Total sales minus (assumed) rural sales.

Total sales. **1953–54** and **1954–55** are estimates based on the knowledge that there were no procurement–sales surpluses either for exports or for stock accumulation (see *SNM*, 5 September 1956 for a clue relating to this point). We therefore assume that total sales were slightly below gross procurement. **1955–56**: (Estimated) urban sales plus (estimated) rural sales. **1956–57**: From figures in *SINJP*, 27 March 1957 and 16 July 1957. **1957–58**: Total sales 'required' or 'needed', *SINJP*, 4 December 1957.

Tsinghai

Gross procurement. **1953–54** and **1954–55**: *TSINJP*, 2 September 1955. **1955–56**: *TSINJP*, 6 September 1956. **1956–57**: State Statistical Bureau figure, *TSINJP*, 18 August 1957. **1957–58**: Planned figure, *TSINJP*, 13 September 1957.

Rural sales. Two main types of data are available: (1) Rural sales made in livestock areas (**1953–54**, **1954–55**, **1955–56** and **1956–57**), *TSLNJP*, 22 December 1957, and (2) figures of net procurement (*TSLNJP*, 13 September 1957) which can be used with gross procurement data to obtain rural sales. The resulting rural sales estimates are consistent with information on rural grain availability (*TSLNJP*, 21 November 1956). For 1956–57 rural sales are also given in *TSLNJP*, 13 August 1957. For **1957–58** we have a figure for planned total sales which we assume was fulfilled and this is divided between rural and urban sales by assuming that urban sales per head of the (very small) Tsinghai urban population fell by the same percentage as in China. An estimate of rural sales is thus obtained by subtraction. As a rough guide *TSLNJP*, 4 September 1957, comments on the high level of rural sales during summer 1957, above the monthly rate of 1956–57.

Urban sales. **1954–55, 1955–56** and **1956–57**: Total minus rural sales. **1953–54**: From 1956–57 and figure in *TSLNJP*, 13 September 1957. **1957–58**: See under rural sales.

Total sales. **1953–54** and **1954–55**: *TSLNJP*, 2 September 1955. **1955–56**: *TSLNJP*, 6 September 1956. **1956–57**: Total sales index in *TSLNJP*, 11 August 1957. **1957–58**: Plan in *TSLNJP*, 13 September 1957.

Honan

Gross procurement. **1953–54, 1954–55** and **1955–56**: *HONJP*, 24 August 1957. **1956–57**: *HONJP*, 27 August 1957. **1957–58**: *JMJP*, 1 December 1957.

Rural sales. **1953–54**: Four-year total 1953–56 (*HONJP*, 15 August 1957) minus total for 1954–56 (*HONJP*, 27 August 1957). **1954–55**: From figures in *HONJP*, 24 August 1957. **1955–56**: From figures in *HONJP*, 26 September 1957. **1956–57**: *HONJP*, 27 August 1957. **1957–58**: Estimate based on figures in *HONJP*, 15 August 1957.

Urban sales. All figures are obtained by subtracting rural sales from total sales.

Total sales. **1953–54, 1954–55** and **1956–57**: *HONJP*, 12 July 1957. **1955–56**: Four-year total (*HONJP*, 15 August 1957) minus three-year total (*HONJP*, 27 August 1957). **1957–58**: From figures in *HONJP*, 19 August 1958.

Hopei

Gross procurement. **1953–54, 1954–55, 1955–56**: *HOPJP*, 14 August 1957. **1956–57**: *HOPJP*, 7 August 1957.

Rural sales. All by subtracting urban from total sales.

Urban sales. **1953–54**: From 1954–55 and figures in *Nung-ts'un Liang-shih T'ung-kou T'ung-hsiao ho Shih-chen Liang-shih T'ing liang kung-ying* (*Rural Grain Central Purchase and Central Supply and Urban Grain Supplies*) (Peking, 1955). (Figures for Peking, Tientsin and Shanghai.) **1954–55**: Peking figure for urban sales per head (*HHYP* (no. 12), 1955) applied to Hopei province. **1955–56**: From 1956–57 and figure for Peking in *PKJP*, 25 August 1957. **1956–57**: Average of urban sales per head in Peking and Tientsin for 1956–57 applied to Hopei urban population. **1957–58**: From data for Tientsin; same percentage changes assumed to apply to Hopei urban population.

Total sales. **1953–54, 1954–55** and **1955–56**: *HOPJP*, 10 May 1957 and 14 August 1957. **1956–57**: *HOPJP*, 14 August 1957. **1957–58**: Five-year total for 1953–57 in *HOPJP*, 12 March 1958 (including an estimate for 1957–58) minus four-year total, 1953–56.

Peking

Urban sales. **1953–54:** From consumption data in *JMJP*, 3 November 1955, and from 1954–55 which is said to have risen by 14.8 per cent (*Rural Grain Central Purchase and Central Supply and Urban Grain Supplies*, p. 62). **1954–55:** *HHYP* (no. 8), 1955, pp. 112–13. **1955–56:** *PKJP*, 6 August 1957. **1956–57:** *PKJP*, 6 August 1957 and 25 August 1957. **1957–58:** *PKJP*, 1 November 1957 and guidance from the Tientsin data.

Shansi

Gross procurement. **1953–54:** *SASJP*, 8 December 1956. **1954–55:** 1953–54 and figures in *SASJP*, 12 September 1955. **1955–56:** By subtraction, using four-year total in *SASJP*, 24 August 1957. **1956–57:** *SASJP*, 12 April 1957 and 11 August 1957. **1957–58:** From planned figure in *SASJP*, 8 August 1957 (set at a time when a 20 per cent fall in grain output was predicted; in fact a 17.8 per cent drop occurred).

Rural sales. **1953–54:** By subtraction, using four-year total in *SASJP*, 24 August 1957. **1954–55:** Total minus urban sales. **1955–56:** Calculated from 'retained quantity', *SASJP*, 15 September 1957 and 11 August 1957. **1956–57:** *SASJP*, 11 August 1957. **1957–58:** Assumed to be slightly below the 1955–56 level (grain output was almost the same as 1955). This is consistent with the campaign to cut rural sales. The resulting estimated grain available in rural areas is in line with survey data in *Shansi Rural Economic Surveys*, vol. 1.

Urban sales. **1953–54:** Total minus rural sales. **1954–55:** From 1953–54 and figures in *SASJP*, 10 April 1956. **1955–56:** Total minus rural sales. **1956–57:** *SASJP*, 11 August 1957. **1957–58:** Estimated from ration data in *SASJP*, 20 November 1957. The implied reduction in monthly sales (compared with 1956–57) is assumed to have continued at that level throughout the grain year.

Total sales. **1953–54:** *SASJP*, 8 December 1956. **1954–55:** *SASJP*, 12 September 1955. **1955–56:** *SASJP*, 10 April 1956. **1956–57:** *SASJP*, 11 August 1957. **1957–58:** Estimate obtained by adding (estimated) rural and urban sales.

Shantung

Gross procurement. **1953–54:** *CTJP*, 11 May 1955. **1954–55** and **1955–56:** *TCJP*, 15 August 1957. **1956–57:** From 1955–56 and *LS* (no. 24), 1956. **1957–58:** *TCJP*, 8 April 1958.

Rural sales. **1953–54:** Estimated from 1954–55, with the help of figures in *TCJP*, 11 May 1955, 16 March 1955, and 16 August 1957. **1954–55:** Estimate derived from deducting (estimated) urban sales from total sales. **1955–56:** *LS* (no. 24), 1956, p. 4, and 1956–57 figure. **1956–57:** *TCJP*, 15 August 1957. **1957–58:** By subtracting (estimated) urban from total sales.

Urban sales. **1953–54:** Estimated from 1954–55 by assuming the national average change per head of urban population. **1954–55:** Again, an estimate, from 1955–56, based on the assumption that urban supplies per head moved in the same proportion as in the country as a whole. **1955–56** and **1956–57:** By subtracting rural from total sales. **1957–58:** Estimated by assuming a 5 per cent fall per head (national average decline).

Total sales: **1953–54:** Estimate, from (estimated) urban and rural sales. **1954–55:** Estimate, based on likely procurement-sales surplus, based on information on grain exports from Shantung. **1955–56:** *TCJP*, 4 September 1957. **1956–57:** *TCJP*, 10 August 1957 and 8 April 1958. **1957–58:** *Ibid.* (includes an estimate for April–June).

Tientsin

Urban sales. **1953–54**: From figures in *JMJP*, 3 November 1955 and grain output of Tientsin. **1954–55**: From percentage rise in *Rural Grain Central Purchase and Central Supply and Urban Grain Supplies*. **1955–56**: From ration data in *NCNA* (Tientsin), 6 December 1956 (*SCMP*, no. 1426), and *TJP*, 6 December 1956 and from output of grain. **1956–57**: From figures in *TKJJP*, 13 October 1957. **1957–58**: Consumption estimated from figures, *ibid.*, and urban sales from this and from grain output for 1957–58.

Hunan

Gross procurement. **1953–54**: Five-year total, 1953–57 (*HHNP*, 7 October 1959) minus sum of four years (1954–57). **1954–55**: *HHNP*, 7 October 1959. **1955–56**: *HHNP*, 2 March 1958. **1956–57**: From 1955–56 and figure in *HHNP*, 19 July 1957. **1957–58**: From data in *HHNP*, 2 March 1958 and 11 January 1958.

Rural sales. **1953–54, 1954–55** and **1955–56**: All from 'available grain' (given output and procurement), in *HHNP*, 19 July 1957. **1956–57**: Same method; figures in *HHNP*, 1 October 1957, corroborating data in *HHNP*, 19 July 1957 and 7 October 1957. **1957–58**: By subtraction, using five-year total in *HHNP*, 7 October 1959.

Urban sales. **1953–54**: From ration data in *HHNP*, 6 November 1957. **1954–55**: By subtraction: total sales minus rural sales. **1955–56** and **1956–57**: Both calculated from figures in *HHNP*, 31 August 1957 and 18 September 1957. **1957–58**: Calculated from ration data in *HHNP*, 7 October 1957.

Total sales. **1953–54**: By addition of rural and urban sales. **1954–55**: *HHNP*, 7 October 1959. **1955–56**, **1956–57** and **1957–58**: By adding rural and urban sales.

Hupei

Gross procurement. **1953–54, 1954–55** and **1955–56**: *LSWTCC*. **1956–57**: Index of gross procurement, applied to 1953–54, in *HUPJP*, 24 August 1957. **1957–58**: *LSP* (no. 85), 1959, p. 3.

Rural sales. **1953–54, 1954–55, 1955–56** and **1956–57**: *LSWTCC*, pp. 85–6. **1957–58**: From figures in *LSP* (no. 85), 1959, using figures for output and procurement.

Urban sales. **1953–54**: *LSP* (no. 85), 1959, p. 3. **1954–55, 1955–56** and **1956–57**: By subtraction of rural from total sales (checked against index of urban sales in *HUPJP*, 27 September 1957 and 31 December 1957). **1957–58**: *LSP* (no. 85), 1959, p. 3.

Total sales. **1953–54**: By adding rural and urban sales. **1954–55, 1955–56** and **1956–57**: *LSWTCC*, p. 78. **1957–58**: By addition of rural and urban sales.

Kiangsi

Gross procurement. **1953–54** and **1954–55**: *KSIJP*, 13 September 1955. **1955–56**: Tax plus purchase, *KSIJP*, 2 November 1956 and 1 July 1957. **1956–57**: *KSIJP*, 18 August 1957. **1957–58**: Plan figure, *KSIJP*, 12 December 1957.

Rural sales. **1953–54, 1954–55** and **1955–56**: From 'grain used' in *KSIJP*, 14 August 1957. **1956–57**: *KSIJP*, 18 August 1957. **1957–58**: Estimated from ration data in *KSIJP*, 8 January 1958.

Urban sales. **1953–54, 1954–55** and **1955–56**: Obtained by subtracting rural sales from total sales. **1956–57**: From ration data in *KSIJP*, 14 August 1957. **1957–58**: Same method, using data in *KSIJP*, 26 December 1957 and 9 August 1958.

Total sales. **1953–54** and **1954–55**: *KSIJP*, 31 August 1955. **1955–56** and **1956–57**: From gross procurement and procurement–sales gap (*LS* (no. 4), 1957, p. 18). (1956–57 is an estimate and must be regarded as a minimum figure.) **1957–58**: By adding rural and urban sales.

Anhwei

Gross procurement. **1953–54, 1954–55, 1955–56** and **1956–57**: Figures of the Grain Bureau in *AJP*, 6 October 1957. **1957–58**: *AJP*, 24 November 1959.

Rural sales. **1953–54, 1954–55** and **1955·56**: Calculated from Grain Bureau figures for 'grain used' in *AJP*, 6 October 1957. **1956–57**: Same method, using data in *NPC* (1957), pp. 343–7. **1957–58**: By deducting three-year total from four-year total given in *AJP*, 12 September 1957.

Urban sales. **1953–54, 1954–55, 1955–56** and **1956–57**: All by subtracting rural sales from total sales. **1957–58**: *AJP*, 9 October 1959.

Total sales. **1953–54, 1954–55, 1955–56** and **1956–57**: Figures of Grain Bureau in *AJP*, 6 October 1957. **1957–58**: By adding rural and urban sales.

Chekiang

Gross procurement. **1953–54**: Calculated from ration data in *JMJP*, 3 November 1955, given rural sales. **1954–55**: From 1955–56 and figures in *CHKJP*, 5 August 1956. **1955–56**: *CHKJP*, 10 May 1957. **1956–57**: *CHKJP*, 13 August 1957. **1957–58**: Planned figure, see *LSP* (no. 16), 1959.

Rural sales. **1953–54**: By subtracting estimate of urban sales from total sales. **1954–55** and **1955–56**: Calculated from 'used grain' figures in *CHKJP*, 23 December 1956 (given output and procurement). **1956–57**: Same method, using data in *CHKJP*, 11 July 1957. **1957–58**: From consumption data *CHKJP*, 29 September 1957, given gross procurement.

Urban sales. **1953–54**: By deducting three years' total from four-year total in *CHKJP*, 24 October 1957. **1954–55, 1955–56** and **1956–57**: By subtracting rural from total sales. **1957–58**: From ration data in *CHKJP*, 24 October 1957.

Total sales. **1953–54**: By subtracting three years' total sales from four-year total in *CHKJP*, 24 October 1957. **1954–55**: From gross procurement and procurement–sales surplus in *CHKJP*, 23 December 1956. **1955–56** and **1956–57**: *CHKJP*, 10 May 1957. **1957–58**: By adding rural sales to urban sales.

Kiangsu

Gross procurement. **1953–54, 1954–55** and **1956–57**: *HHJP*, 17 September 1957. **1955–56**: From 1954–55 and figures of State Statistical Bureau in *HHJP*, 28 April 1956, confirmed by *HHJP*, 25 August 1957. **1957–58**: Planned figure: *HHJP*, 5 January 1958.

Rural sales. **1953–54, 1954–55, 1955–56** and **1956–57**: *HHJP*, 17 September 1957. **1957–58**: Estimate based on plan for total sales and estimated urban sales.

Urban sales. **1953–54, 1954–55, 1955–56** and **1956–57**: By subtracting rural sales from total sales. **1957–58**: Estimate, using ration data for Shanghai (*JMJP*, 18 October 1957 and *Rural Grain Central Purchase and Central Supply and Urban Grain Supplies*, pp. 29 and 91).

Grain procurement and sales, 1953–57

Total sales. **1953–54**: By subtracting three years' total sales from given four-year total (*HHJP*, 12 September 1957). **1954–55**: State Statistical Bureau (*HHJP*, 28 April 1956) gives percentage reduction on 1953–54. **1955–56**: *HHJP*, 22 January 1957. **1956–57**: From figures in *HHJP*, 24 August 1957. **1957–58**: Plan, in *HHJP*, 1 September 1957.

Shanghai

Urban sales. **1953–54**: *SCMP*, no. 727. **1954–55**: Percentage increase given in *Rural Grain Central Purchase and Central Supply and Urban Grain Supplies*. **1955–56**: From consumption figures in *ibid.*, pp. 29 and 91; also *HWP*, 5 March 1957. **1956–57**: From consumption data in *CFJP*, 6 March 1957 and *HWP*, 5 March 1957. **1957–58**: From figures in *JMJP*, 18 October 1957.

Kweichow

Gross procurement. **1953–54**: *KCJP*, 6 December 1957. **1954–55, 1955–56** and **1956–57**: 1953–54 and percentage changes in *KCJP*, 12 July 1957; 1956–57 confirmed in *KCJP*, 12 July 1957. **1957–58**: Plan, *KCJP*, 6 December 1957.

Rural sales. **1953–54** and **1955–56**: From figure for grain used in rural areas, *KCJP*, 12 July 1957. **1954–55**: *KCJP*, 28 August 1957, given gross procurement. **1956–57**: By subtracting urban from total sales. **1957–58**: Six-year total (*LSP* (no. 81), 1959) minus five years (1958–59 estimated from total and urban sales, *KCJP*, 5 October 1959).

Urban sales. **1953–54, 1955–56** and **1957–58**: By subtraction of rural from total sales. **1955–56**: From 1956–57 and percentage given in *KCJP*, 28 August 1957. **1956–57**: From ration data in *ibid.*

Total sales. **1953–54**: *LSP* (no. 81), 1959. **1954–55**: Six-year total (*ibid.*) minus total for five years. **1955–56**: By adding rural and urban sales. **1956–57**: From 1955–56 and percentage in *KCJP*, 12 July 1957. **1957–58**: *LSP* (no. 81), 1959.

Szechuan

Gross procurement. **1953–54**: From 1954–55 and percentage in *NFJP*, 2 December 1954. **1954–55**: From percentage of output in *HHYP*, vol. 70 (no. 8), 1955, pp. 46–7. **1955–56**: By subtracting four years' total procurement from five years' total in *Economic Geography of SW China*, p. 25. **1956–57**: *SZJP*, 12 August 1957. **1957–58**: From plan (*ibid.*) and overfulfilment percentage in *SZJP*, 22 December 1957.

Rural sales. **1953–54**: *SZJP*, 12 August 1957 and *JMJP*, 31 August 1957. **1954–55**: *HHYP*, vol. 70 (no. 8), 1955, pp. 46–7. **1955–56**: *SZJP*, 23 August 1957 and *JMJP*, 26 March 1957. **1956–57** and **1957–58**: By subtracting urban sales from total sales.

Urban sales. **1953–54**: Estimated from figures for Chungking in *JMJP*, 3 November 1955. **1954–55**: *HHYP*, vol. 70 (no. 8), 1955, pp. 46–7. **1955–56, 1956–57** and **1957–58**: All estimated from ration data. See *CHCHJP*, 24 September 1957, *CHDJP*, 24 November 1957, and *SZJP*, 18 October 1957 and 6 January 1958.

Total sales. **1953–54** and **1955–56**: By adding rural to urban sales. **1954–55**: *HHYP*, vol. 70 (no. 8), 1955, pp. 46–7. **1956–57**: By subtracting four-year total from total for five years in *SZJP*, 30 September 1959. **1957–58**: Planned figure, *SZJP*, 12 August 1957.

Yunnan

Gross procurement. **1953–54, 1954–55, 1955–56** and **1956–57**: Gross procurement given as a percentage of output in *YJP*, 25 August 1957. **1957–58**: Is assumed as a minimum.

Rural sales. **1953–54, 1954–55, 1955–56** and **1956–57**: From 'retained grain' figures in *YJP*, 21 August 1957 (given output and procurement). **1957–58**: By deducting (estimated) urban sales from total sales.

Urban sales. **1953–54**: An estimate based on 1954–55 and national percentage change per head. **1954–55, 1955–56** and **1956–57**: By subtraction of rural sales from total sales. **1957–58**: Estimated by assuming national percentage fall per head.

Total sales. **1953–54**: By adding estimated urban sales to rural sales. **1954–55**: *HHYP*, vol. 70 (no. 8), 1955, pp. 193–4 (given procurement). **1955–56, 1956–57** and **1957–58**: From index in *LSP* (no. 78), 1959.

Fukien

Gross procurement. **1953–54**: From figures in *FJP*, 16 October 1955. **1954–55**: *FJP*, 6 August 1955, and 3 November 1955. **1955–56**: Drop in procurement recorded in *FJP*, 6 August 1957. **1956–57**: From figures in *FCY* (no. 2), 1958, pp. 20–2. **1957–58**: From figures in *FJP*, 15 January 1958 and 17 January 1957 (for tax and purchase).

Rural sales. **1953–54**: From consumption data in *JMJP*, 3 November 1955. **1954–55** and **1955–56**: *FJP*, 6 August 1957. **1956–57**: From grain used in rural areas (*ibid.*), given output and procurement. **1957–58**: An estimate by deducting estimated urban sales from total sales.

Urban sales. **1953–54, 1954–55, 1955–56** and **1956–57**: All by subtracting rural from total sales. **1957–58**: Calculated from ration data in *FJP*, 20 January 1958. The figures suggest a 6 per cent fall per head, compared with 1956–57.

Total sales. **1953–54**: By adding gross procurement to procurement–sales surplus estimated on a basis of known net exports from Fukien. **1954–55**: *FJP*, 6 August 1955. **1955–56**: From 1956–57 and percentage in *FJP*, 26 June 1957. **1956–57**: From procurement–sales deficit in *FJP*, 9 October 1957 (given procurement). **1957–58**: An estimate (which may be somewhat too low) based on figure for half year, in *LSP* (no. 6), 1959.

Kwangsi

Gross procurement. **1953–54, 1954–55, 1955–56** and **1956–57**: *KWSIJP*, 3 September 1957. **1957–58**: From figures in *LSP* (no. 81), 1959 and *LSP* (no. 90), 1959.

Rural sales. **1953–54, 1954–55, 1955–56** and **1956–57**: *KWSIJP*, 3 September 1957. **1957–58**: Assumed same as 1953–54 (output was the same).

Urban sales. **1953–54**: Obtained by subtracting rural from total sales. **1954–55**: *KWSIJP*, 1 September 1955. **1955–56**: From ration data in *KWSIJP*, 13 October 1955. **1956–57**: Assumes national percentage increase per head. **1957–58**: Assumes that urban sales per head were roughly equal to 1955–56, which is what was generally planned for throughout China at this time.

Total sales. **1953–54**: From procurement–sales surplus, *KWSIJP*, 9 October 1955. **1954–55**: By adding rural to urban sales. **1955–56**: By adding rural to urban sales.

1956–57: By adding our (assumed) urban sales to rural sales. **1957–58**: Little more than an assumption, by adding our estimated urban sales to (assumed) rural sales. We do know, however, that there was a procurement–sales deficit and that imports were needed (see *KWSIJP*, 31 December 1957).

Kwangtung

Gross procurement. **1953–54**: *NFJP*, 9 October 1957. (Gross procurement as a per cent of output.) **1954–55**: *NFJP*, 28 November 1957. **1955–56**: Central purchase given in *NFJP*, 20 July 1957 and tax in *NFJP*, 5 August 1956. Corroborating data are in *NFJP*, 28 November 1956 and 2 April 1957. **1956–57**: *NFJP*, 2 April 1957; also *NFJP*, 28 November 1957. **1957–58**: *NFJP*, 17 October 1959.

Rural sales. **1953–54** and **1954–55**: From rural sales as a percentage of grain procurement, *NFJP*, 28 November 1957. **1955–56**: From total and urban sales. **1956–57**: *KWCJP*, 20 July 1957. **1957–58**: From figure for rural grain available, *NFJP*, 17 October 1959.

Urban sales. **1953–54**: From Canton ration data, *JMJP*, 3 November 1955. **1954–55**: *KWCJP*, 20 July 1957. **1955–56** and **1956–57**: From figures in *NFJP*, 28 November 1957. **1957–58**: By deducting rural from total sales.

Total sales. **1953–54, 1954–55** and **1956–57**: By adding urban and rural sales. **1955–56**: *NFJP*, 28 November 1956. **1957–58**: *NFJP*, 17 October 1959.

Total grain sales, 1953–57 (thousand tons)

	1953	1954	1955	1956	1957
North East					
Heilungkiang	1853	1906	1749	2055	1583
Kirin	1160	1306	1136	1480	1535
Liaoning	3265	3498	3184	3477	3250[a]
North West					
IMR	390	472	436	730	522
Kansu	650	650	668	828	c.629
Shensi	831	934	895	945	964[b]
Sinkiang	c.275	c.300	c.217	c.375	360
Tsinghai	80	91	110	174	165
North					
Honan	2236	2397	2150	2657	2638
Hopei	2289	2959	2715	3650	2535
Shansi	910	985	965	1075	c.1085
Shantung	c.2617	c.2328	2496	2696	2800
Centre					
Hunan	1881	2600	1525	3175	1568
Hupei	1996	2982	2153	2295	2484
Kiangsi	1358	1650	1333	1293	776
East					
Anhwei	1967	3074	2161	3204	2600
Chekiang	c.1839	2117	1795	2050	c.1464
Kiangsu	3290	3726	3342	3953	3768[a]
South West					
Kweichow	500	730	510	621	750
Szechuan	3826	3400	3258	4280	3334
Yunnan	906	1131	1169	1347	1268
South					
Fukien	935	1225	1107	1239	900
Kwangsi	1052	1302	c.1301	c.1267	c.1009
Kwangtung	2966	3331	2786	2959	3355

Notes: a. Planned figure.　　b. Minimum figure.

Grain procurement and sales, 1953–57

b. NATIONAL GRAIN PROCUREMENT AND SALES, 1952–53 TO 1957–58
(MILLION TONS UNHUSKED GRAIN)

	Gross procurement	Total sales	Procurement sales ±	Rural sales	Urban sales	Net procurement
1952–53	32.25	35.70	−3.45	n.a.	n.a.	n.a.
1953–54	48.55	40.75	+7.80	20.05	20.70	28.50
1954–55	52.70	48.70	+4.00	25.90	22.80	26.80
1955–56	49.90	41.90	+8.00	21.10	20.80	28.80
1956–57	48.45	50.70	−2.25	26.70	24.00	21.75
1957–58	51.15	43.90	+7.25	17.75	26.15	33.40

SOURCES

Gross procurement. **1952–53**: Minister of Food, *JMJP*, 25 October 1959. **1953–54, 1954–55, 1955–56** and **1956–57**: *TCKT* (no. 19), 1957, pp. 31–2 and 28. **1957–58**: *JMJP*, 27 September 1958.

Rural sales. **1953–54, 1954–55, 1955–56** and **1956–57**: *TCKT* (no. 19), 1957, pp. 31–2 and 28. **1957–58**: Five-year total (Minister of Food, *JMJP*, 25 October 1959) minus four-year total.

Urban sales. **1953–54, 1954–55, 1955–56**: *TCKT* (no. 19), 1957, pp. 31–2 and 28. **1956–57** and **1957–58**: By subtracting rural from total sales.

Total sales. **1952–53**: From procurement–sales deficit in *LS* (no. 1), 1957, pp. 20–5. **1953–54, 1954–55, 1955–56**: *TCKT* (no. 19), 1957, pp. 31–2 and 28. **1956–57**: From total sales index in *CHCC* (no. 2), 1958, pp. 24–7. **1957–58**: From percentage rise in *Kuo-nei Shang-yeh Ching-chi* (*China's Internal Commercial Economy*), Trade and Economics Education Office of the Chinese People's University (Peking, 1960).

Appendix 6 Sources of grain tax data in twenty provinces, 1953–57

Heilungkiang

Tax in **1956–57** as a percentage of grain output is given in *HJP*, 25 September 1957. Said to be the same level as in former years, and described as 'not heavy'.

Liaoning

1954–55: *LJP*, 22 October 1955.

Inner Mongolia

Based on figure for **1958–59** in *NMKJP*, 10 October 1959.

Kansu

1953–56: Percentage of grain output given (*TCKT* (no. 14), 1957, pp. 21 and 32). **1957–58**: Plan in *KAJP*, 18 December 1957.

Shensi

1953–56: Tax as a percentage of output is given in *SESJP*, 18 July 1957. **1957–58**: *SESJP*, 5 August 1958.

Sinkiang

SNM, 5 September 1956, states that grain tax was 8 per cent of grain output, **1951–56**. A plan figure for **1955–56** (of 0.142 million tons, converted to raw grain) is found in *SINJP*, 23 September 1955. For **1957–58**: 8 per cent assumed.

Tsinghai

1955–56, 1956–57 and plan for **1957–58**: *TSINJP*, 13 September 1957.

Hopei

Tax as a percentage of output **1953–56** in *HOPJP*, 9 September 1957.

Shansi

1953–54: Percentage of output in *SASJP*, 6 October 1959, which states that the amount of tax was stable 1953–59.

Shantung

1956–57: Tax was 8 per cent of grain output, *CTJP*, 25 August 1957.

Hunan

1953–54, 1956–57 and **1957–58**: Percentage of output given in *HHNP*, 6 November

1959. **1955–56**: From 1956–57, which fell by 0.165 million tons (*HHNP*, 18 December 1956).

Hupei

1952–53 and **1956–57**: *LSWTCC*, p. 53.

Kiangsi

1955–56: *KSIJP*, 2 November 1956 and 1 April 1957. **1956–57**: From figures in *KSIJP*, 30 November 1956, 2 November 1956, and *LS* (no. 4), 1957. **1957–58**: *KSIJP*, 1 August 1958.

Anhwei

1953–56: All from percentages in *TC* (no. 9), 1957, confirmed by four-year average in *AJP*, 12 September 1957.

Kiangsu

HHJP, 16 April 1957, states that taxes were stable 1953–57 at the 1953 level. **1953–56**: From percentage of output: *TC* (no. 7), 1957, pp. 24–6.

Kweichow

KCJP, 15 August 1957 gives tax as a percentage of output, **1953–56**.

Szechuan

1956–57 and plan for **1957–58**: *SZJP*, 24 August 1957.

Yunnan

1955–56 and **1956–57**, as a percentage of output: *YJP*, 17 August 1957.

Fukien

1954–55, 1955–56 and **1956–57**: *FJP*, 6 August 1957. **1957–58**: *FJP*, 15 January 1958.

Kwangtung

1953–54: *NFJP*, 16 August 1954. **1954–55** and **1955–56**: *NFJP*, 5 August 1956. **1956–57**: By subtracting purchase from gross procurement. See *NFJP*, 20 July 1957 and 2 April 1957.

Appendix 7 Notes and sources on provincial grain exports and imports

1953–1957

Wherever possible all imports and exports refer to grain rather than calendar years and all figures have been expressed in unhusked grain equivalent.

Heilungkiang

1953 and **1954**: *HJP*, 9 December 1955. **1955**: From percentage of output exported in *TLCS* (no. 11), 1957, p. 497. **1956**: *HJP*, 3 August 1957, said to be the lowest ever and below the planned level. *SCMP*, no. 1662 refers to exports of coarse grains but imports of fine grains in 1956–57. Fine grain imports are given in *HJP*, 2 August 1957, and were from Inner Mongolia and Kiangsu. See also *HJP*, 21 June 1957, which indicates that rice was imported from Changsha. A further source is *HJP*, 15 December 1956. Some of these imports might belong to the 1957–58 grain year. Such imports are related to the failure of procurement in 1956–57. **1957**: This is a close approximation to what must have been the *maximum* export of grain in 1957–58. It has been estimated from figures in *LSP* (no. 10), 1959 for exports from Kirin, Heilungkiang and Inner Mongolia.

A further guide to Heilungkiang's grain exports is found in *HJP*, 29 October 1957 (four-year total), and *JMJP*, 14 December 1958 indicates that 23 per cent of the province's exports of grain were soya beans. Planned exports for 1958–59 are given in *HJP*, 17 November 1958, and *LSP* (no. 72), 1959 implies that this target was attained.

Kirin

1953: *KJP*, 12 July 1958. **1954**: Plan, assumed to have been fulfilled, *TKP*, 15 November 1954. Hong Kong *TKP*, 31 May 1955 (SCMP, no. 1064) states that Kirin exported one million tons plus per annum and that there were exports in 1953–54. **1955**: Arrived at from the procurement–sales deficit of 1953–54. **1956**: *KJP*, 5 September 1957. **1957**: *KJP*, 12 July 1958.

In general, *An Economic Geography of NE China* states that average grain exports were 0.6 million tons per year.

Liaoning

A four-year total of Liaoning's grain imports is given in *LJP*, 23 August 1957. Converted to raw grain this is almost identical to the four-year procurement–sales deficit. It is, therefore, safe to estimate annual imports around the annual deficits, but some allowance has been given to the increase in imports during 1956. Other evidence is found in *JMJP*, 26 May 1955 and *LJP*, 4 September 1957.

Inner Mongolia

1953 and **1954**: *NCNA*, 20 November 1954. **1955**: Average of two figures in *TLCS* (no. 7), 1957 and *NMKJP*, 29 November 1956. **1956**: *NMKJP*, 27 August 1957. **1957**: Five-year total grain exports (*NMKJP*, 5 February 1958) minus four-year total.

Further evidence is in *NMKJP*, 1 May 1959 (total exports of grain from 1947 to 1958), and *An Economic Geography of Inner Mongolia*, p. 28 states that grain exports averaged 20 per cent of output.

Kansu

No figures for individual years are available, but good qualitative evidence exists to form a basis for estimates, along with the annual procurement–sales deficits. We also have a four-year total for grain exports (calendar years) in *KAJP*, 1 January 1958.

1953: *KAJP*, 16 August 1958 refers to exports in 1953–54. **1954**: The same article also reveals that in the early post-liberation years the Central Government imposed a light export burden on Kansu but increased this in 1954 in view of increases in production and consumption which had occurred: 'This met with a protest.' *KAJP*, 23 November 1956 states that Kansu exported grain in 1954–55. **1955**: *KAJP*, 16 August 1958 refers to 'first exports' of grain from Kansu in that year. **1956**: Exports were planned in 1956–57 for disaster areas such as Hopei; see *JMJP*, 12 September 1956. **1957**: From procurement–sales deficit (as for 1953–56) and from the four-year total in *KAJP*, 1 January 1958.

Shensi

Very little evidence exists other than the annual procurement–sales gap, but *SESJP*, 4 September 1959, gives a five-year total for grain exports, 1953–57, and these have been apportioned to individual years on a basis of the procurement–sales surpluses or deficits.

Sinkiang

NPC (1957), pp. 399–405 states that as the cotton area grew during the Second Five Year Plan period (1958–62) grain and oil self-sufficiency was to be attained. *SNY*, p. 4, pointed to the fact that Sinkiang would 'in future' be able to serve as a granary for the North East of China. However, *JMJP*, 4 October 1957, reveals that Sinkiang, formerly in deficit, was now a surplus area.

From the small annual procurement–sales surpluses, it is clear that there was no significant 'external' grain trade. Possibly there might have been a small export surplus in 1957–58.

Tsinghai

The main indicator of Tsinghai's status relating to grain self-sufficiency is the minute annual procurement–sales surpluses and deficits. *TSINJP*, 17 August 1957, records that stocks were used to finance such a deficit in 1956–57, while *TSINJP*, 6 September 1956, states that the province was self-sufficient in 1954–55.

Honan

Exports of **1953, 1954** and **1955**: *HONJP*, 12 July 1957. Exports in 1956 are obtained by subtraction of 1953–55 total from 1953–56 total given in *Ch'üan mien Yüeh-chin chung ti liang-shih Kung-tso (Grain Work During the Great Leap Forward)* (Chengchow, 1958), 3 volumes, vol. 3, p. 6.

1954 and **1956** grain imports: The total for the two years (given *HONJP*, 24 August 1957) has been apportioned equally. The situation in 1957–58 is confused. 1957 was a bad harvest year, with wheat output down by 0.524 million tons. (This would affect Honan's export capability.) On the other hand, a procurement–sales surplus of 0.285 million tons was achieved. We know that Honan's position *vis-à-vis* the grain trade was the subject of intense political struggle, in which provincial leaders demanded imports of over one million tons. Since it was stated that this view was defeated during the anti-rightist struggle it is safe to assume that there were no such imports and it is probable that no grain was exported in 1957–58.

Hopei

1953 and **1954**: *HOPJP*, 10 May 1957. **1955**: *HOPJP*, 17 March 1956 (used in conjunction with 1954 figure), and *HOPJP*, 26 October 1956. **1957**: *HOPJP*, 12 March 1958. These annual figures are consistent with a four-year total for grain imports in *HOPJP*, 3 September 1957.

It is interesting to note that *An Economic Geography of N. China*, p. 59, relates the large amount of *fine* grain imports to the low fine grain output per head in Hopei.

Peking, Tientsin and Shanghai

All estimates are based on the gap between output and consumption (for all users) plus an allowance (an arbitrary 5 per cent) for stocks. Sources of data for output have been given in Appendix 2, and those for 'consumption' or grain sales are listed in Appendix 5.

Shansi

1953–56: Exports for 1953 and 1954 and imports for 1955 and 1956 all given in *SASJP*, 11 August 1957; see also *SASJP*, 10 April 1956. **1957**: An estimate based on the procurement–sales deficit of 0.110 million tons.

Shantung

1953: *CTJP*, 30 May 1955 and *TCJP*, 22 September 1957. **1954**: *CTJP*, 30 August 1955. Note that *TKP*, 17 November 1954 reported that Shantung exported *wheat* to Peking and Tientsin. **1955**: An assumption based on the statement in *An Economic Geography of N. China* that in a good year 10–15 per cent of wheat output was exported. 1955 was an average year, therefore, 10 per cent of output is assumed to have been exported. **1956**: An assumption. There was bumper wheat harvest in 1956, but a fairly big procurement–sales deficit. It is reasonable therefore to assume no exports or imports. **1957**: *TCJP*, 18 October 1957.

Hunan

In relation to its importance as a grain exporter, annual figures are surprisingly lacking. *An Economic Geography of Central China* cites an average figure per year, and states that the province's rice exports were 'second only to Szechuan'. *LSP* (no. 8), 1959, records the gross grain exports 1949–59 (0.613 million tons per annum). A further guide comes from the statement in *HHNP*, 24 November 1958, that 'stocks are low', which tends to confirm that most of the annual procurement–sales surpluses were exported. For 1953 we have no guidance. **1954**: Rice was *imported* from Szechuan (*HHNP*, 20 October 1957). Further details are available from *LSP* (no. 82), 1959, which lead to our estimate of 0.3 million tons. **1955**: *HHNP*, 25 August 1955 states that Hunan hoped to increase its rice exports. **1956**: Exports for August are given in *HHNP*, 7 September 1956, while *HHNP*, 18 December 1956 reports that there had been a big reduction in export tasks for 1956–57. **1957**: Given in *LSP* (no. 80), 1959.

Hupei

1953, 1955 and **1956**: Exports in *HUPJP*, 17 July 1957. **1954**: Imports in Hupei Daily Propaganda Compendium, *Strive to Carry out Completely the First Five-Year Plan* (Wuhan, 1955), p. 71. **1957**: Assumed on a basis of the procurement–sales surplus; with assistance from figures for average exports 1953–58 in *LSP* (no. 85), 1959.

Kiangsi

1953 and **1954**: *KSIJP*, 23 September 1955. **1955**: Obtained by assuming exports were 96 per cent of the procurement–sales surplus (based on earlier years). **1956**: By subtracting three-year total from four-year total (*KSIJP*, 10 August 1957). **1957**: By deducting total exports over seven years (*KSIJP*, 9 November 1957) from eight-year total (*HHPYK*, vol. 128 (no. 6), 1958, pp. 27–30).

Note that the highest exports were in 1952 (*KSIJP*, 23 September 1955) but, with output stagnating during the First Five-Year Plan period, such a level could not be sustained.

Anhwei

Imports for **1954**: *AJP*, 9 October 1959. Imports for **1956**: From figures in *AJP*, 6 October 1957, and from procurement–sales deficit.

No figures are available for exports in individual years, but some guidance as to their probable level is available. *AJP*, 6 October 1957, states that Anhwei exported grain in good harvest years and imported in bad years. A six-year total for grain exports (1953–58) is given in *AJP*, 9 October 1959. If 1953, 1955, 1957 and 1958 are all exporting years, each year's exports must have been high to be consistent with the six-year total, and the annual procurement–sales surpluses can be used with confidence to estimate the likely amounts. Finally, we have a further general indication of the 'average annual surplus' in *AJP*, 23 September 1957.

Chekiang

Only one 'semi' hard figure is available: plan for 1956 in *CHKJP*, 10 May 1957 (assumed to have been fulfilled). However, a four-year total for grain exports (1954–57) is in *CHKJP*, 11 January 1958 and this implies large annual exports in relation to the procurement–sales surpluses. *CHKJP*, 23 July 1957 states that Chekiang was one of China's top eight grain-exporting provinces, which puts annual exports, therefore, at 0.3–0.5 million tons per year. *HHPYK*, vol. 128 (no. 6), 1958, pp. 107–9, reports that Chekiang's grain exports 'can be' around 0.315 million tons per year.

Kiangsu

Very few annual figures available but there are several important pointers. One report (*FBIS*, 1 August 1978) indicates that Kiangsu was either self-sufficient or it exported grain in six out of the ten years of the 1950s. *An Economic Geography of East China*, p. 16, is cautious about Kiangsu's grain exports, stating that only a 'little' rice and flour was exported in view of the high internal, urban demand. Two items of evidence suggest that there was very fine tuning indeed relating to grain imports and exports as output (and as procurement, compared with sales) varied: (1) Kiangsu exported grain in the first half of 1954–55 and imported during the second half (*Rational Transport*); (2) grain imports for 1956 match very closely the fall in output and the procurement–sales deficit; see *HHJP*, 12 September 1957. Procurement–sales surpluses for 1953, 1954, 1955 and 1957 have therefore been used as the main indicator of annual exports.

Kweichow

1953: Some contradictory statements exist. *NCNA*, no. 1121 states that no grain was exported, but *KSIJP*, 12 November 1957 reports that as a result of high output in 1953, Kweichow sent out its first exports. *An Economic Geography of SW China*, p. 110, states that in 'recent years', 6, 7 or 10 per cent of rice output had been exported: 6 per cent of 1953 output = 0.226 million tons. The procurement–sales surplus was 0.560 million tons. **1954**: *JMJP*, 3 November 1955. **1955**: By subtracting three years' exports from a four-year total in *KSIJP*, 28 August 1957. **1956**: *JMJP*, 13 November 1957. **1957**: From figures for July–October 1957 (*ibid.*, and *KSIJP*, 12 November 1957) and the procurement–sales surplus.

Szechuan

1953–56: *HH* (no. 16), 1957, pp. 121–3. **1957**: *CHCHJP*, 30 December 1957. **1958**: Six-year total (*LSP* (no. 73), 1959) minus five-year total.

Calendar year figures have been converted to grain year estimates by taking two-year averages (1953–58).

Yunnan

Very little evidence is available, but there are some statements which indicate when grain was exported. First exports were in 1955 (*SCMP*, no. 1152). *HHYP*, vol. 70 (no. 8), 1955, pp. 193–4, states that, although output had risen, no exports had been required from Yunnan, and our assumed exports for 1955 may be regarded as a minimum in the light of the procurement–sales surpluses accumulated 1953–55. **1956**: Calculated from figures in *HHPYK*, vol. 124 (no. 2), 1958, pp. 36–9, for grain exports from the South West Region. Yunnan exports have been obtained by subtraction. **1957**: Assumed, based on the procurement–sales surplus and the statement that Yunnan had a 'small surplus' (*YJP*, 16 August 1957). We know from *KWSIJP*, 31 December 1957, that Yunnan exported grain to Kwangsi in 1957.

Fukien

1953: Exports: *CNS*, 27 July 1954 ('first year of grain exports'). Imports: *FJP*, 4 January 1955. *FJP*, 30 September 1959 records that Fukien became self-sufficient in 1957–58 and exported some grain in 1958–59. However, *An Economic Geography of South China* claims that the province had been self-sufficient since 1952 and this is what we accept.

Kwangsi

1953: From 1954–55 and *TKP*, 17 November 1954. **1954**: *KWSIJP*, 28 August 1955. **1955**: Assumed on a basis of the procurement–sales gap. **1956**: Assumed no imports or exports. **1957**: 'Imports are needed' according to *KWSIJP*, 31 December 1957, and, bearing in mind the procurement deficits of 1956 and 1957, the level must have been fairly high. *LSP* (no. 3), 1959, states that Kwangsi became a surplus province in 1958.

Kwangtung

1953 and **1954**: *NFJP*, 12 January 1955. **1955** and **1956**: *NFJP*, 30 August 1956. **1957**: No evidence of either imports or exports, and in view of T'ao Chu's cancellation of exports in 1956, it is safe to assume that there were none.

PRE-COMMUNIST CHINA

Two books in English have been valuable sources for all these data: T.H. Shen, *Agriculture Resources of China*, and D.H. Perkins, *Agricultural Development in China 1368–1968* (Chicago, 1969). For Manchuria the best source was Wang Ch'eng-ching, *Tung-pei chih Ching-chi Tzu-yuan (Economic Resources of the North East)* (Shanghai, 1947). For the central and eastern provinces, in addition to data in Shen and Perkins, detailed Japanese figures are available in *Shina Keizai Nampo (China Economic Yearbook)* (South Manchuria Railway Department, Tokyo, 1939) (kindly provided and translated by Professor C.B. Howe). Pre-communist grain imports of Chekiang are also given in *CHKJP*, 29 September 1959, and *HHPYK*, vol. 128 (no. 6), 1958, pp. 107–9. For the status of the South West Region see data in Chiang Chün-chang, *Hsi-nan Ching-chi Ti-li (An Economic Geography of the South West)* (Shanghai, 1945). Pre-war grain imports of Fukien are given in *FJP*, 29 September 1959. Good data on Kwangtung's pre-war grain trade are in *NFJP*, 23 July 1957; also Government of Kwangtung, *Kuang-tung Liang-shih T'ung-chi (Grain Statistics of Kwangtung)* (Canton, 1933).

Appendix 8 Estimated grain consumption per head of total and of rural population in Chinese provinces, 1953–57, in kilograms unhusked grain

Estimated grain consumption per head of total population 1953–57 (kilograms unhusked)

	1953	1954	1955	1956	1957	Average 1953–57
North East						
Heilungkiang	364	337	375	443	339	372
Kirin	333	322	314	336	359	333
Liaoning	294	309	303	351	293	310
North West						
IMR	280	270	192	327	205	255
Kansu	164	185	205	299	241	219
Shensi	241	231	206	260	202	228
Sinkiang	227	227	244	232	219	230
Tsinghai	164	230	260	295	272	244
North						
Honan	194	199	212	230	203	208
Hopei	183	186	210	214	205	200
Shansi	234	211	207	235	186	215
Shantung	192	211	217	245	211	215
Centre						
Hunan	245	248	258	287	253	258
Hupei	275	244	286	316	323	289
Kiangsi	263	274	281	298	273	278
East						
Anhwei	232	229	272	305	291	266
Chekiang	270	262	265	280	253	266
Kiangsu	230	226	245	244	234	236
South West						
Kweichow	185	205	194	240	257	216
Szechuan	221	220	239	262	250	238
Yunnan	215	235	245	289	288	254
South						
Fukien	245	240	242	283	247	251
Kwangsi	245	275	263	n.a.	n.a.	261
Kwangtung	247	263	253	289	288	268
Peking[a]	246	270	222	234	229	240
Tientsin[a]	243	265	231	253	222	243
Shanghai[a]	282	296	236	270	233	263
Average for China	233	237	246	273	250	248

Note: a. Overwhelmingly urban population; no differentiation between rural and urban made.

Estimated grain consumption per head of population

Estimated grain consumption per head of rural population 1953–57 (kilograms unhusked)

	1953	1954	1955	1956	1957	Average 1953–57
North East						
Heilungkiang	397	348	440	532	404	424
Kirin	344	324	336	365	404	355
Liaoning	259	279	291	362	295	297
North West						
IMR	280	271	185	313	198	249
Kansu	152	183	205	304	min.240	217
Shensi	242	229	206	261	206	229
Sinkiang	c.224	c.222	c.245	c.228	c.216	c.227
Tsinghai	155	221	252	281	258	233
North						
Honan	185	194	213	228	199	204
Hopei	178	179	208	210	201	195
Shansi	216	188	188	222	167	196
Shantung	186	206	215	239	203	210
Centre						
Hunan	244	244	258	289	256	258
Hupei	281	242	297	328	336	297
Kiangsi	260	273	284	294	280	278
East						
Anhwei	228	223	270	310	281	262
Chekiang	275	264	270	287	258	271
Kiangsu	222	212	243	241	233	230
South West						
Kweichow	177	192	194	242	259	213
Szechuan	220	218	241	265	254	240
Yunnan	209	227	235	281	284	247
South						
Fukien	241	244	252	300	259	259
Kwangsi	238	272	263	245	n.a.	255
Kwangtung	254	270	263	300	294	276
Average for China	227	228	245	274	251	245

Appendix 9 Estimated grain seed requirements in Chinese provinces per year, 1953–57 (thousand tons)

	1953	1954	1955	1956	1957	Seed requirement as % of grain output, 1953–57
North East						
Heilungkiang	312	317	304	297	323	4.07
Kirin	162	167	168	176	174	3.09
Liaoning	149	145	160	179	173	2.52
North West						
IMR	209	216	217	235	231	6.09
Kansu	227	236	251	262	235	5.64
Shensi	282	284	286	295	271	5.78
Sinkiang	75	90	74	81	86	4.30
Tsinghai	22	22	22	25	32	4.55
North						
Honan	931	954	929	950	914	7.66
Hopei	448	486	469	522	517	5.60
Shansi	240	244	237	250	232	6.00
Shantung	732	765	740	754	730	5.69
Centre						
Hunan	337	361	398	423	425	3.70
Hupei	388	388	406	416	415	4.23
Kiangsi	222	237	246	256	292	3.99
East						
Anhwei	602	653	660	675	663	6.30
Chekiang	222	227	231	255	227	3.10
Kiangsu	650	650	650	700	665	5.49
South West						
Kweichow	127	132	138	155	162	3.20
Szechuan	732	760	798	851	848	3.85
Yunnan	162	168	173	195	206	3.14
South						
Fukien	160	163	171	173	176	4.13
Kwangsi	274	273	294	299	278	5.08
Kwangtung	537	547	581	592	594	5.05
China (million tons)	8.202	8.485	8.603	9.016	8.869	4.77

Appendix 10 Livestock and estimated livestock grain feed in Chinese provinces, 1953–57

a. PROVINCIAL AND NATIONAL PIG POPULATIONS 1952–57 (MILLIONS)

	1952	1953	1954	1955	1956	1957	Average 1952–57
North East							
Heilungkiang	1.913	n.a.	2.887	2.350	2.667	3.060	2.575
Kirin	2.390	n.a.	2.260	1.926	1.630	2.067	2.055
Liaoning	4.920	n.a.	n.a.	3.765	2.580	4.580	3.961
North West							
IMR	1.542	n.a.	n.a.	n.a.	0.959	1.680	1.394
Kansu	1.114	1.180	<1.953*	1.190	1.412	2.307	1.441
Shensi	1.784	n.a.	1.950	1.751	1.900	2.742	2.025
Sinkiang	0.213	n.a.	n.a.	n.a.	n.a.	0.160	0.187
Tsinghai	0.104	0.109	0.118	0.160	0.206	0.216	0.152
North							
Honan	n.a.	4.176	4.175	2.942	3.590	7.460	4.469
Hopei	5.294	c.5.100	c.5.000	3.845	5.100	8.560	5.483
Shansi	0.660	n.a.	0.845	0.690	0.996	1.910	1.020
Shantung	5.410	6.643	n.a.	3.098	5.239	8.030	5.684
Centre							
Hunan	6.830	7.023	n.a.	5.790	6.079	10.910	7.326
Hupei	4.500	5.182	5.101	3.400	4.994	8.447	5.271
Kiangsi	2.837	3.180	3.120	2.980	2.840	4.260	3.203
East							
Anhwei	3.380	3.780	n.a.	2.650	3.410	7.020	4.048
Chekiang	2.780	3.373	3.730	2.648	2.920	5.680	3.522
Kiangsu	5.984	n.a.	n.a.	5.140	7.000	9.500	6.906
South West							
Kweichow	3.599	n.a.	>4.300*	4.300	3.680	6.150	4.432
Szechuan	13.770	17.130	20.140	19.100	20.000	25.000	19.190
Yunnan	3.710	3.880	5.549	6.046	4.732	6.520	5.073
South							
Fukien	2.410	3.560	2.700	2.468	2.600	4.010	2.958
Kwangsi	3.807	n.a.	4.560	4.130	3.760	5.560	4.363
Kwantgung	6.550	7.004	8.625	7.040	6.060	7.790	7.178
China (official)	89.765	96.131	101.718	87.920	97.800	144.670	103.001

Note: * These figures are not used in the calculation of the 1952–57 average.

SOURCES

All are for end of year unless stated otherwise.

Heilungkiang

1952 and **1957**: *An Economic Geography of NE China*. **1953**: n.a. **1954**: (High point according to *HJP*, 3 January 1957), *CKNP* (no. 16), 1957. **1955**: *Ibid*. **1956**: *Ibid*.

Kirin

1952: *KJP*, 1 March 1957. **1953**: n.a. **1954**: *Economic Geography of NE China*. **1955**: *KJP*, 1 March 1957. **1956**: *Ibid*. **1957**: *Economic Geography of NE China*.
  June 1954: 2.26 (*KJP*, 7 December 1956). **June 1955**: 1.937 (*ibid*.). **June 1956**: 1.64 (*ibid*.).

Liaoning

1952: SSB in *JMJP*, 10 May 1957. **1953–54**: n.a. **1955**: From figures in *LJP*, 5 January 1957 and number of rural households. **1956**: SSB in *JMJP*, 10 May 1957. **1957**: *NTKTTH* (no. 7), 1958, p. 40.

Inner Mongolia

1952 and **1957**: *NMKTC*. **1953–55**: n.a. **1956**: *NMKJP*, 5 February 1957.

Kansu

1952: From 1957 and percentage in *KAJP*, 12 June 1958. **1953**: *KAJP*, 11 March 1957. **1954**: Less than 1953 (*KAJP*, 11 March 1957). **1955**: *KAJP*, 11 March 1957. **1956** and **1957**: *KAJP*, 29 October 1958.

Shensi

1952: *SESJP*, 14 August 1958. **1953**: n.a. **1954**: (High point) *SESJP*, 6 November 1957. **1955** and **1956**: *SESJP*, 4 May 1957. **1957**: *SESJP*, 5 August 1958.

Sinkiang

1952: *SINJP*, 23 September 1955. **1953–56**: n.a. **1957**: *NTKTTH* (no. 7), 1958, p. 40.

Tsinghai

1952: *TSINJP*, 17 August 1955. **1953, 1954** and **1955**: From 1952 and index in *TSINJP*, 1 September 1957. **1956**: From 1955 and percentage in *TSINJP*, 6 March 1957. **1957**: *TSINJP*, 17 February 1958.

Honan

1952: n.a. **1953**: *HONJP*, 27 November 1956. **1954** and **1955**: *HONJP*, 12 December 1956. **1956** and **1957**: *JMJP*, 13 February 1958. June figure: *HONJP*, 12 December 1956.

Hopei

1952: *HOPJP*, 22 September 1955. Was highest 1952–December 1957 (*HOPJP*, 10 December 1957). **1953**: Above 1954 (and below 1952), *HOPJP*, 7 February 1955. **1954**: From 1955 and *HOPJP*, 22 September 1955. **1955**: *KWCJP*, 3 March 1957. **1956**: *HOPJP*, 10 December 1957. June figure, *HOPJP*, 23 August 1957. **1957**: *NTKTTH* (no. 7), 1958, p. 40.

Shansi

1952 and **1954**: *SASJP*, 24 February 1955. **1953**: n.a. **1955** and **1956**: *SASJP*, 31 January 1957. June 1956 figure, *SASJP*, 5 September 1957. **1957**: *NTKTTH* (no. 7), 1958, p. 40.

Shantung

1952: *CTJP*, 16 August 1957. **1953**: From figures in *An Economic Geography of N. China*, and arable area for 1953. **1954**: n.a. **1955** and **1956**: *TCJP*, 16 August 1957. June 1956 figure *TCJP*, 9 August 1957. **1957**: *NTKTTH* (no. 7), 1958, p. 40.

Hunan

1952: *HHNP*, 7 December 1957. **1953**: *HHNP*, 26 August 1954. **1954**: n.a. **1955** and **1956**: SSB, in *HHNP*, 15 February 1957. **1957**: *Economic Geography of Central China*.

Hupei

1952: *HUPJP*, 1 October 1957. **1953** and **1954**: *LSWTCC*, p. 88 (June figures). **1955** and **1956**: *HUPJP*, 4 November 1957. Spring **1956**: *HUPJP*, 22 November 1956. **1957**: *TLCS* (no. 1), 1959.

The pig population of Hupei fell from 5.182 million at the end of June 1953 to 2.5 million in spring 1956 (*TKP*, 22 November 1956), a fall of 52 per cent.

Kiangsi

1952: *KSIJP*, 30 September 1955. **1953–56**: *KSIJP*, 23 January 1957. End May 1956, *ibid.* **1957**: *KSIJP*, 1 January 1958.

Anhwei

1952: *AJP*, 1 January 1958. **1953**: *TTKP*, 12 July 1956 (end of June figure). **1954**: n.a. **1955** and **1956**: *AJP*, 23 September 1957. **1957**: *NTKTTH* (no. 7), 1958, p. 40.

Chekiang

1952 and **1957**: *HHPYK*, vol. 128 (no. 6), 1958, pp. 107–9. **1953**: From 1954 and percentage in *CHKJP*, 9 February 1955. **1954** and **1955**: SSB in *CHKJP*, 5 August 1956. **1956**: *CHKJP*, 26 April 1957. June **1956**: *CHKJP*, 28 October 1957.

Kiangsu

1952 and **1957**: *HHJP*, 10 January 1958. **1953** and **1954**: n.a. **1955**: *HHJP*, 1 October 1957. **1956**: *HHJP*, 3 August 1957.

Kweichow

1952 and **1957**: *KCJP*, 29 September 1959. **1953** and **1954**: n.a. *KCJP*, 12 January 1957 states that pigs declined in 1955 and 1956, therefore the peak must have been in 1954. **1955**: *KCJP*, 20 December 1957. **1956**: *KCJP*, 30 August 1957.

Szechuan

1952–56: *HH* (no. 17), 1957, pp. 25–8. **1957**: *An Economic Geography of SW China.*

Yunnan

1952 and **1957**: *An Economic Geography of SW China.* **1953**: From 1952 and index in *YJP*, 10 May 1957. **1954, 1955** and **1956**: *YJP*, 23 December 1957.

Fukien

1952: *SCMP*, no. 1624. **1953**: *CKNP* (no. 21), 1955, p. 32. **1954**: *FJP*, 26 June 1957. **1955** and **1956**: SSB in *FJP*, 26 June 1957. June **1956**: *FJP* 30 January 1957. **1957**: *An Economic Geography of South China.*

Kwangsi

1952: *KWSIJP*, 5 October 1955. **1953**: n.a., but about 4 million: see 1954. **1954**: Said to be the high point of the First Five Year Plan period, *KWSIJP*, 21 February 1958. **1955**: *KWSIJP*, 27 September 1956. **1956** and **1957**: *KWSIJP*, 21 February 1958. June **1956**: *NTKTTH* (no. 2), 1957.

Kwangtung

1952: *NFJP*, 8 December 1957. **1953**: Hsü Chün-ming (ed.), *Liang-Kuang Ti-li* (*A Geography of the Two 'Kwangs', Kwangsi and Kwangtung*) (Shanghai, 1956), p. 84. **1954**: *NFJP*, 5 August 1956. **1955** and **1956**: SSB in *NFJP*, 18 August 1957. **August 1956**: *NFJP*, 30 August 1956. **1957**: *NTKTTH* (no. 7), 1958, p. 40.

China

1952 and **1957** (end year): *JMJP*, 6 April 1958. **1953–55** (mid-year): *NYHTH*. **1956** (end year): *HHPYK*, vol. 112 (no. 14), 1957, pp. 28–9. Note that the mid-year figure was 84.026 million (*NYHTH*).

Livestock and estimated livestock grain feed

b. DRAUGHT ANIMALS IN CHINESE PROVINCES, 1952–57 (MILLIONS)

	1952	1953	1954	1955	1956	1957	Average 1952–57
North East							
Heilungkiang	2.515	2.715	n.a.	2.395	2.470	2.057	2.430
Kirin	c.2.000	2.220	2.315	2.192	1.984	1.705	2.069
Liaoning	4.090	n.a.	n.a.	2.630	2.370	2.410	2.875
North West							
IMR	4.448	4.985	5.494	n.a.	5.835	5.465	5.245
Kansu	3.078	n.a.	4.218	n.a.	4.848	3.720	3.966
Shensi	2.042	2.369	c.2.800	2.829	2.629	2.530	2.533
Sinkiang	3.569	n.a.	n.a.	n.a.	c.4.705	c.5.026	4.433
Tsinghai	1.924	n.a.	n.a.	0.626	n.a.	1.700	1.417
North							
Honan	6.870	7.334	7.880	7.549	6.710	6.763	7.184
Hopei	3.816	4.018	4.479	4.219	c.3.300	3.223	3.843
Shensi	1.910	2.015	2.140	2.157	2.158	2.037	2.070
Shantung	c.5.000	4.856	n.a.	5.210	4.760	4.992	4.964
Centre							
Hunan	2.694	2.814	n.a.	2.730	2.910	3.057	2.841
Hupei	n.a.	n.a.	n.a.	2.718	2.919	2.740	2.792
Kiangsi	1.843	1.958	1.981	1.964	1.996	2.160	1.984
East							
Anhwei	2.640	n.a.	n.a.	2.720	2.840	2.770	2.743
Chekiang	1.091	n.a.	n.a.	1.057	1.063	1.009	1.005
Kiangsu	1.799	n.a.	n.a.	c.1.933	c.2.043	1.882	1.914
South West							
Kweichow	2.700	2.450	n.a.	3.250	3.550	3.730	3.136
Szechuan	c.7.419	c.7.266	n.a.	c.7.643	c.8.103	c.8.065	7.699
Yunnan	c.3.807	n.a.	4.579	5.110	5.290	5.310	4.819
South							
Fukien	0.851	n.a.	n.a.	0.973	1.035	0.948	0.961
Kwangsi	3.830	n.a.	n.a.	4.800	4.143	4.293	4.267
Kwangtung	3.870	n.a.	4.200	4.588	4.597	4.340	4.319

SOURCES

Heilungkiang

1952 and **1957**: *An Economic Geography of NE China.* **1953**: From 1952 and increase recorded in *NCNA*, 23 March 1954. **1954**: n.a. **1955** and **1956**: SSB figures in *HJP*, 7 August 1957.

Kirin

1952: Assumed from the fact that the number exceeded that of 1957. (*CKNP* (no. 5), 1958, pp. 22–4.) **1953**: *KJP*, 24 January 1958. **1954** and **1957**: *An Economic Geography of NE China.* **1955** and **1956**: *KJP*, 7 December 1956.

Liaoning

1952: *LJP*, 1 October 1959. **1953** and **1954**: n.a. **1955**: From 1956 and figures in *LJP*, 28 December 1956. **1956**: From 1957 and figures in *LJP*, 2 December 1957. **1957**: *LJP*, 28 January 1958.

Inner Mongolia

1952 and **1957**: *NMKTC.* **1953** and **1954**: From 1952 and index in *NMKJP*, 10 August 1955. **1955**: n.a. **1956**: *NMKJP*, 5 February 1957.

Kansu

1952: From 1957 and figures in *KAJP*, 23 May 1958 and 12 June 1958. **1953**: n.a. **1954**: *KAJP*, 6 March 1955. **1955**: n.a. **1956**: From 1952 and figures in *KAJP*, 26 September 1957. **1957**: *KAJP*, 23 May 1958.

Shensi

1952 and **1957**: *SESJP*, 14 August 1958. **1953**: From 1952 and percentage in *SESJP*, 18 December 1953. **1954**: Estimated from figures in Ch'iu Huai, *Yang Niu Hsüeh (Cattle Rearing)*, vol. 1 (Nanking, 1957), pp. 6–7. **1955** and **1956**: *SESJP*, 4 May 1957.

Sinkiang

1952: *SINJP*, 23 September 1955. **1953–55**: n.a. **1956** and **1957**: Figures for horses and cattle are in *SINJP*, 22 February 1957 and an estimate for camels has been added, using percentages in Wang Wei-p'ing and Hu Ying-mei, *Hsin-chiang Wei-Wu-Erh Tzu-chih ch'ü (Sinkiang-Uighur Autonomous Region)* (Peking, 1959).

Tsinghai

A major difficulty is how to differentiate between data relating to (1) all large animals; (2) all large animals in agricultural areas (i.e., excluding the province's extensive pasture lands), and (3) 'plough animals'. The three figures available relate to (2).

1952: From figures in *TSINJP*, 17 August 1955. **1955**: *TSINJP*, 13 December 1955. **1957**: *TSINJP*, 15 December 1957.

Honan

1952: *HONJP*, 29 September 1956. **1953**: *An Economic Geography of N. China*. **1954**: *HONJP*, 17 January 1958. **1955** and **1956**: Figures of SSB in *HONJP*, 18 September 1957. **1957**: 1956 figure and information in *HONJP*, 17 January 1958.

Hopei

1952: *HOPJP*, 22 September 1955. **1953**: From figures in *An Economic Geography of N. China*. **1954**: From 1955 and information *HOPJP*, 22 September 1955. **1955**: *HOPJP*, 13 March 1956. **1956**: An estimate from figure for 'working animals' (Spring 1957) in *Mechanisation Bureau*, and evidence relating to the ratio of working to total draught-type animals. **1957**: From figures in *HHPYK*, vol. 124 (no. 2), 1958, pp. 101–3; approximately confirmed by the statement in *CKNP* (no. 5), 1958, pp. 22–4.

Shansi

1952: *SASJP*, 24 February 1955. **1953** and **1954**: *SASJP*, 23 February 1955. **1955** and **1956**: *SASJP*, 31 January 1957. **1957**: *SASJP*, 12 May 1958.

Shantung

1952: A rough estimate from 1957 and the fact that 1952 was above 1957 (*CKNP* (no. 5), 1958, pp. 22–4). **1953**: From figures in *An Economic Geography of N. China*. **1954**: n.a. **1955**: From 1956 and information in *TCJP*, 25 December 1956. **1956**: *TCJP*, 17 August 1957. **1957**: From figures in *Mechanisation Bureau*.

Hunan

1952 and **1957**: *HNNY*, p. 88. **1953**: From 1952 and information in *HHNP*, 27 January 1954. **1954**: n.a. **1955** and **1956**: Figures of SSB in *HHNP*, 15 February 1957.

Hupei

1955 and **1956**: *JMJP*, 2 June 1957. **1957**: *TLCS* (no. 1), 1959.

Kiangsi

1952–56: *KSIJP*, 23 February 1957. **1957**: *An Economic Geography of Central China*.

Anhwei

1952: *AJP*, 18 March 1958. **1953** and **1954**: n.a. **1955** and **1956**: *AJP*, 23 September 1957. **1957**: *An Economic Geography of East China*.

Chekiang

1952: From 1956 and percentage in *Mechanisation Bureau*. **1953** and **1954**: n.a. **1955**: SSB figure in *CHKJP*, 5 August 1956. **1956**: *CHKJP*, 23 December 1956. **1957**: *CHKJP*, 15 January 1958. *CKNP* (no. 5), 1958, pp. 22–4, confirms that 1957 was below 1952.

Kiangsu

1952: *HHJP*, 28 December 1955. **1953** and **1954**: n.a. **1955**: Estimated from 1956 with the aid of figures in *HHJP*, 28 January 1957 (SSB report). **1956**: From 1957 and figures in *HHJP*, 25 December 1957. **1957**: *HHJP*, 25 December 1957.

Kweichow

1952 and **1957**: *An Economic Geography of SW China*. **1953**: *KCJP*, 21 December 1957. **1954**: n.a. **1955**: *KCJP*, 30 December 1957. **1956**: *KCJP*, 1 January 1957.

Szechuan

There are some figures for total cattle, some for 'plough' cattle and one figure for horses. We require an estimate of total cattle plus horses: i.e., the stock out of which working animals are drawn. Horses (*c.* 0.5 million) are around 7 per cent of this total and working cattle are approximately 70 per cent of total cattle. These ratios have been used in making estimates.

1952: From total cattle (*An Economic Geography of SW China*). **1953**: From total cattle calculated from figures in *SZJP*, 5 October 1954, and in *An Economic Geography of SW China*. **1954**: n.a. **1955**: From working cattle (*SZJP*, 5 December 1957) and horses (*ibid.*). **1956**: From total cattle calculated from 1949 (*An Economic Geography of SW China*) and percentage in *SZJP*, 29 August 1957. **1957**: From total cattle in *An Economic Geography of SW China*.

Yunnan

1952: From total cattle (around 83 per cent of all large animals), *An Economic Geography of SW China*. **1953**: n.a. **1954** and **1955**: SSB data in *YJP*, 11 June 1956. **1956**: *YJP*, 1 May 1957. **1957**: *YJP*, 14 December 1957

Fukien

1952: From 1957 and percentage in *FJP*, 1 January 1958. **1953** and **1954**: n.a. **1955** and **1956**: SSB report in *FJP*, 26 February 1957. **1957**: *An Economic Geography of S. China*.

Kwangsi

1952 and **1955**: *A Geography of the two 'Kwangs'*, p. 84. **1953** and **1954**: n.a. **1956**: *KWSINYTH* (no. 1), 1957. **1957**: *KWSIJP*, 25 February 1958.

Kwangtung

1952: *NFJP*, 22 December 1957. **1953**: n.a. **1954**: From 1957 and change in number recorded in *NFJP*, 11 April 1958. **1955**: *NFJP*, 24 March 1056. **1956**: *NCNA*, 6 August 1957. **1957**: *An Economic Geography of S. China*, p. 31.

C. NUMBER OF WORKING DRAUGHT ANIMALS DURING 1953–57 IN CHINESE
PROVINCES, AND IN CHINA

	Working draught animals (million)	Working animals as percentage of total draught-type animals (%)	Years for which data available
North East			
Heilungkiang	1.541	68	1956 & 1957
Kirin	1.179	58	1954, 1955, 1956 & 1957
Liaoning	1.244	52	1956 & 1957
North West			
IMR	4.196	80[a]	1952–54 & 1956–57
Kansu	2.083	56	1957
Shensi	1.910	75	1957
Sinkiang	3.623	77	1956
Tsinghai	0.315	50	1955
North			
Honan	5.602	77	1953–57
Hopei	2.962	77	1952, 1954 & 1957
Shansi	1.594	77[a]	1952–57
Shantung	4.218	84	1956
Centre			
Hunan	2.227	75	1956 & 1957
Hupei	2.094	75[a]	1952–57
Kiangsi	1.714	83	1955 & 1957
East			
Anhwei	1.702	62	1957
Chekiang	0.801	76	1952, 1956 & 1957
Kiangsu	1.457	74	1956 & 1957
South West			
Kweichow	2.241	70	1952 & 1957
Szechuan	4.795	62	1953, 1954, 1956 & 1957
Yunnan	3.790	72	1956
South			
Fukien	0.716	73	1957
Kwangsi	2.906	69	1956 & 1957
Kwangtung	3.373	74	1955
China	52.637	64	1952, 1956 & 1957

Note: a. Assumed figure.

SOURCES

Heilungkiang

1956: *HJP*, 12 January 1957. **1957**: *CKNPTK* (no. 5), 1958, p. 14.

Kirin

1954: From 1957 and information given by Teng Tzu-hui in *HHPYK*, vol. 124 (no. 2), 1958, pp. 101–3. **1955 and 1956**: From figures in *KJP*, 25 April 1957 and 7 December 1956. **1957**: *An Economic Geography of NE China*, p. 118.

Liaoning

1956 and 1957: From figures in *LJP*, 24 March 1957.

Inner Mongolia

80 per cent of total assumed. Although Inner Mongolia was an important livestock rearing province, a shortage of draught animals is recorded in *NMKJP*, 5 February 1958.

Kansu

1957: *KAJP*, 23 May 1958.

Shensi

1957: *SESJP*, 4 February 1958.

Sinkiang

1956: *SINJP*, 22 February 1957.

Tsinghai

1955: *TSINJP*, 13 December 1955.

Honan

1953: *An Economic Geography of N. China*, p. 162. **1954–56**: *HHPYK*, vol. 99 (no. 1), 1957, pp. 88–90. **1957**: Average of two figures, *Mechanisation Bureau*, p. 169 and *CKNP* (no. 14), 1958, pp. 26–7 (the latter is considerably lower than the former).

Hopei

1952: *HHPYK*, vol. 124 (no. 2), 1958, pp. 101–3. **1954 and 1957**: *Mechanisation Bureau*, p. 44.

Shansi

Assumed percentage of total draught-type animals in work. We have considerable qualitative evidence of draught animal shortage: see for example, *SASJP*, 30 March 1958, which refers to a deficit of 0.6–0.7 million. *An Economic Geography of N. China*, p. 105, reports that the burden of farm land per animal was greater than in other northern provinces (1953–54). Our estimated sown area per working animal exceeds that of Kansu, Shensi and Honan, but is slightly less than the burden in Hopei and Shantung.

Shantung

1956: *Mechanisation Bureau*, p. 196.

Hunan

1956: *HHNP*, 26 February 1957. **1957:** *HHNP*, 5 March 1958.

Hupei

Assumed with reference to Hunan. *An Economic Geography of Central China*, p. 29, states that the burden of land per head in the plains of Hupei was high, at around 3.3 hectares per animal, and in some Special Districts it exceeded 5.3 hectares per beast.

Kiangsi

1955: *KSIJP*, 8 January 1956. **1957**: *An Economic Geography of Central China*, p. 130.

Anhwei

1957: *AJP*, 28 September 1959; also *An Economic Geography of East China*, p. 83, which states, in addition, that the burden of land per working animal exceeded 50 *mou*. We assume that it was 55 *mou* and have expressed this in terms of working animals from 1952–56 from the arable area data.

Chekiang

1952 and **1956**: *Mechanisation Bureau*, p. 282. **1957**: From figures in *CHKJP*, 24 February 1957.

Kiangsu

1956: *NTKTTH* (no. 8), 1957. **1957**: *HHYP*, 25 December 1957.

Kweichow

1952 and **1957**: *KCJP*, 29 September 1959. Note that the figure for the burden per beast (in *mou*) for 1957 recorded in *An Economic Geography of SW China*, p. 109, implies a much smaller number of working animals, and a 12.5 per cent decline, 1952–57, but this must be rejected in the face of all other evidence, including the figures for total draught-type animals, and the fact that Kweichow exported draught animals.

Szechuan

1953: *SZJP*, 5 October 1954. **1954**: *SZJP*, 6 January 1955. **1956**: From 1949 figure (*SZJP*, 5 October 1954) and percentage in 29 August 1957. **1957**: *SZJP*, 29 August 1957.

Yunnan

1956: *NTKTTH* (no. 8), 1957, pp. 22–3.

Fukien

1957: *An Economic Geography of S. China*, p. 126.

Kwangsi

1956: *KWSINYTH* (no. 7), 1957, p. 196. **1957**: *An Economic Geography of S. China*, p. 82.

Kwangtung

1955: *An Economic Geography of Kwangtung*, p. 34.

China

1952 and **1956**: *CHCC* (no. 9), 1957, pp. 5–8. **1957**: Teng Tzu-hui in *HHPYK*, vol. 124 (no. 2), 1958, pp. 101–3.

d. ESTIMATED GRAIN FEED ALLOCATIONS IN CHINESE PROVINCES AND IN
CHINA, 1953–57, USED IN MAKING GRAIN CONSUMPTION ESTIMATES FOR THE
CHINESE POPULATION (THOUSAND TONS)

	1953	1954	1955	1956	1957	% Output 1953–57
North East						
Heilungkiang	592	663	623	616	549	7.98
Kirin	504	515	486	442	401	8.56
Liaoning	761	665	561	497	546	9.46
North West						
IMR	304	316	335	355	350	9.12
Kansu	593	686	736	806	764	16.70
Shensi	398	466	466	439	441	9.05
Sinkiang	446	490	533	565	608	28.02
Tsinghai	44	48	38	40	34	7.55
North						
Honan	881	940	875	801	900	7.20
Hopei	988	973	903	746	951	10.46
Shansi	343	364	361	368	367	8.99
Shantung	611	603	598	607	620	4.65
Centre						
Hunan	324	308	282	298	246	2.78
Hupei	307	300	257	303	379	3.25
Kiangsi	129	128	124	121	167	2.13
East						
Anhwei	319	308	303	329	394	3.20
Chekiang	123	131	112	119	186	1.79
Kiangsu	213	216	222	246	323	2.02
South West						
Kweichow	213	251	258	258	327	5.85
Szechuan	796	842	765	831	957	4.05
Yunnan	533	566	622	624	491	10.54
South						
Fukien	166	133	124	131	186	7.10
Kwangsi	204	225	216	218	254	4.00
Kwangtung	278	305	294	270	305	2.57
China	10.070	10.442	10.094	10.030	10.746	5.67

Appendix 11 Arable and total sown areas of Chinese provinces, 1952–57

a. PROVINCIAL ARABLE AREAS, 1952–57 (MILLION HECTARES)

	1952	1953	1954	1955	1956	1957
North East						
Heilungkiang	6.472	6.941	6.605	6.700	7.200	7.289
Kirin	4.662	4.585	4.627	4.636	4.795	4.720
Liaoning	4.790	4.749	4.749	4.701	4.827	4.750
North West						
IMR	5.020	5.199	5.248	5.248	5.584	5.543
Kansu	4.469	4.566	4.592	4.734	5.111	4.960
Shensi	4.537	4.550	4.552	4.521	4.553	4.520
Sinkiang	1.593	1.557	1.645	1.701	1.858	2.021
Tsinghai	0.455	0.455	0.461	0.473	0.492	0.500
North						
Honan	9.052	9.093	9.106	9.081	9.039	9.067
Hopei	8.780	8.780	8.776	8.776	9.000	9.000
Peking	0.087	0.087	0.083	0.081	n.a.	n.a.
Shansi	4.623	4.679	4.688	4.649	4.550	4.541
Shantung	9.219	9.293	9.289	9.301	9.296	9.267
Tientsin	0.088	0.088	0.088	0.087	0.092	0.095
Centre						
Hunan	3.679	3.680	3.729	3.750	3.853	3.863
Hupei	4.064	4.097	4.107	4.276	4.200	4.366
Kiangsi	2.747	2.756	2.756	2.760	2.756	2.813
East						
Anhwei	5.895	5.914	6.014	6.003	6.001	5.920
Chekiang	2.223	2.226	2.247	2.274	2.238	2.277
Kiangsu	6.178	6.263	6.325	6.330	6.263	6.272
Shanghai	0.036	0.035	0.037	0.037	0.037	0.020
South West						
Kweichow	1.913	1.926	1.958	2.001	2.227	2.091
Szechuan	7.468	7.470	7.477	7.611	7.607	7.666
Yunnan	2.407	2.448	2.599	2.665	2.780	2.787
South						
Fukien	1.468	1.471	1.474	1.475	1.489	1.479
Kwangsi	2.316	2.385	2.267	2.468	2.432	2.531
Kwangtung	3.678	3.759	3.761	3.786	3.786	3.860

Arable and total sown areas, 1952–57

SOURCES

Heilungkiang

1952, 1953 and **1956**: State Statistical Bureau in *HJP*, 10 October 1957. **1954**: *NYHTH*. **1955**: *JMJP*, 16 December 1955. **1957**: *An Economic Geography of NE China*.

Kirin

1952–55: *NYHTH*. **1956**: *KJP*, 9 July 1957. **1957**: *An Economic Geography of NE China*.

Liaoning

1952: *LJP*, 28 September 1957. **1953–55**: *NYHTH*. **1956**: 1955 figure and *JMJP*, 18 January 1957. **1957**: *JMJP*, 3 May 1958.

Inner Mongolia

1952 and **1957**: *NMKTC*. **1953–55**: *NYHTH*. **1956**: *NMKJP*, 5 February 1957.

Kansu

1952–55: *NYHTH*. **1956**: 1952 figure and *KAJP*, 23 November 1956. **1957**: *KAJP*, 19 July 1957.

Shensi

1952–56: *NYHTH*. **1957**: *JMJP*, 3 May 1958.

Sinkiang

1952–56: *NYHTH*. **1957**: *SNY*.

Tsinghai

1952–55: *NYHTH*. **1956**: *TSINJP*, 18 August 1957. **1957**: *JMJP*, 3 May 1958.

Honan

1952–55: *NYHTH*. **1956**: State Statistical Bureau, *HONJP*, 18 September 1957. **1957**: *KWSIJP*, 6 February 1958.

Hopei

1952–55: *NYHTH*. **1956**: *Mechanisation Bureau*. **1957**: *JMJP*, 3 May 1958.

Peking

1952–55: *NYHTH*.

Appendix 11

Shansi

1952–55: *NYHTH.* **1956:** *SASJP,* 31 January 1957. **1957:** *TLCS* (no. 1), 1959.

Shantung

1952–55: *NYHTH.* **1956:** State Statistical Bureau in *TCJP,* 9 August 1957. **1957:** *TCJP,* 9 March 1957.

Tientsin

1952–55: *NYHTH.* **1956:** *TJP,* 2 July 1956. **1957:** *TJP,* 30 April 1959 (SSB figure).

Hunan

1952–57: *HNNY.*

Hupei

1952–55: *NYHTH.* **1956:** *Shui-t'ien Nung-ch'ü kung-tso ts'an-k'ao tzu-liao* (Reference Materials on Farm Implements used in Paddy Fields) (Peking, 1957), p. 83. **1957:** *An Economic Geography of Central China.*

Kiangsi

1952–55: *NYHTH.* **1956:** *Mechanisation Bureau.* **1957:** *An Economic Geography of Central China.*

Anhwei

1952–55: *NYHTH.* **1956:** *Mechanisation Bureau.* **1957:** *AJP,* 6 December 1957.

Chekiang

1952–55: *NYHTH.* **1956:** *Mechanisation Bureau.* **1957:** From total sown area and multiple cropping index, both given by State Statistical Bureau in *CHKJP,* 30 September 1957, and 23 January 1958, respectively.

Kiangsu

1952–55: *NYHTH.* **1956:** *Mechanisation Bureau.* **1957:** *HHJP,* 7 February 1958.

Shanghai

1952–55: *NYHTH.* **1956:** *CFJP,* 12 August 1956. **1957:** From figures in *CFJP,* 19 May 1958.

Kweichow

1952–55: *NYHTH.* **1956:** *KCJP,* 8 August 1957. **1957:** *An Economic Geography of SW China.*

Szechuan

1952–55: *NYHTH.* **1956**: *SZJP*, 13 April 1957, and China's arable area. **1957**: *An Economic Geography of SW China.*

Yunnan

1952–55: *NYHTH.* **1956**: *YJP*, 4 September 1957. **1957**: *YJP*, 27 December 1957.

Fukien

1952–55: *NYHTH.* **1956**: State Statistical Bureau in *FJP*, 26 June 1957. **1957**: *An Economic Geography of S. China.*

Kwangsi

1952–55: *NYHTH.* **1956**: *Mechanisation Bureau.* **1957**: *KWSINYTH* (no. 7), 1957.

Kwangtung

1952 and **1953**: *NYHTH.* **1954** and **1955**: State Statistical Bureau figures in *NFJP*, 7 April 1956. **1956**: *Mechanisation Bureau.* **1957**: *An Economic Geography of S. China.*

b. TOTAL SOWN AREAS IN CHINESE PROVINCES, 1952–57 (MILLION HECTARES)

	1952	1953	1954	1955	1956	1957
North East						
Heilungkiang	6.445	—	—	6.640	7.160	7.140
Kirin	4.611	—	4.553	4.566	4.779	4.609
Liaoning	4.943	—	—	—	—	4.945
North West						
IMR	4.806	c.4.650	—	4.730	5.150	5.117
Kansu	—	—	—	—	—	4.689
Shensi	5.216	—	—	—	—	5.514
Sinkiang	1.402	1.381	1.398	1.489	1.645	1.715
Tsinghai	—	—	—	0.397	0.436	0.433
North						
Honan	13.940	14.421	14.642	14.566	14.680	14.616
Hopei	10.330	10.185	10.630	—	11.088	10.567
Peking	—	—	—	—	—	—
Shansi	4.935	4.866	5.002	5.016	5.014	4.891
Shantung	13.257	13.410	13.738	13.561	13.563	13.668
Tientsin	—	—	—	—	—	—
Centre						
Hunan	5.202	5.472	5.780	6.236	6.816	6.841
Hupei	—	—	—	6.414	7.140	7.248
Kiangsi	—	—	4.823	4.824	5.212	5.300
East						
Anhwei	8.112	8.759	—	10.463	10.784	9.957
Chekiang	3.917	—	4.067	4.159	4.538	4.406
Kiangsu	—	—	—	—	—	10.412
Shanghai	—	—	—	—	—	0.040
South West						
Kweichow	2.202	—	—	—	3.078	3.137
Szechuan	10.754	—	11.066	11.797	12.293	13.032
Yunnan	2.908	—	3.211	3.358	3.613	3.818
South						
Fukien	2.099	—	2.152	2.207	2.408	2.381
Kwangsi	3.140	—	3.971	4.288	4.368	4.257
Kwangtung	6.555	7.132	—	7.425	7.617	7.642

SOURCES

Heilungkiang

1952: SSB figure in *HJP*, 1 October 1957. **1955** and **1956**: SSB report, *HJP*, 7 August 1957. **1957**: Figures in *An Economic Geography of NE China*.

Kirin

1952 and **1957**: *An Economic Geography of NE China*. **1955** and **1956**: SSB report, *KJP*, 17 April 1957. **1954**: From arable area and *KJP*, 20 April 1956.

Liaoning

1952 and **1957**: *An Economic Geography of NE China*.

Inner Mongolia

1952 and **1957**: *NMKTC*. **1953**: From figures in *An Economic Geography of Inner Mongolia*, p. 30, and grain sown area. **1955** and **1956**: *NMKJP*, 25 April 1957.

Kansu

1957: From figures in *KAJP*, 10 July 1957 and 3 January 1958.

Shensi

1952: From 1957 figure and information in *SESJP*, 14 August 1958. **1957**: *SESJP*, 5 August 1958.

Sinkiang

1952, 1953 and **1957**: *SNY*. **1954**: *SINJP*, 22 September 1955. **1955** and **1956**: *SINJP*, 18 January 1957.

Tsinghai

1955: From 1956 and figures in *TSINJP*, 13 December 1955. **1956**: *TSINJP*, 13 August 1957. **1957**: *TSINJP*, 18 August 1957.

Honan

1952–55: From arable area and multiple cropping indexes 1952–54 (*CKNP* (no. 15), 1957), and for 1955 (*HONJP*, 15 March 1956). **1956**: SSB report, *HONJP*, 18 September 1957. **1957**: From arable area and multiple cropping index (*CKNP* (no. 12), 1957).

Hopei

1952 and **1957**: Calculated from figures in *CHYTC* (no. 9), 1959, and net grain sown area. **1953**: From arable area and multiple cropping index (*An Economic Geography of N.*

China). **1954:** From wheat sown area and figures in *An Economic Geography of N. China.*
1956: From arable area and multiple cropping index (*CKNP* (no. 12), 1957, pp. 16–19).

Shansi

1952: From 1954 and percentage in *SASJP*, 5 September 1955. **1953:** From arable area
and multiple cropping index in *Economic Geography of N. China.* **1954** and **1955:** From
arable area and multiple cropping index (*SASJP*, 10 April 1956). **1956:** From arable
area and multiple cropping index (*JMJP*, 9 February 1958). **1957:** From arable area
and multiple cropping index (*SASJP*, 21 December 1957).

Shantung

1951–55: All from arable area and multiple cropping indexes (*CKNP* (no. 15), 1957).
1956: From arable area and multiple cropping index in *ibid.* **1957:** *TCJP*, 6 January
1958.

Hunan

1952–57: *HNNY.*

Hupei

1952: An estimate from known arable area and 1955 multiple cropping index (*HUPJP*,
8 January 1960). **1955:** From arable and cropping index, *ibid.* **1956:** From arable area
and multiple cropping index, *ibid.* **1957:** From arable area (*An Economic Geography of
Central China*) and multiple cropping index (*CHCJP*, 14 January 1958).

Kiangsi

1952: From arable area and multiple cropping index (*KSIJP*, 27 April 1957 and 21
April 1957, both excluding green fertiliser crop sown area, but converted to include such
crops from figures in *KSIJP*, 31 March 1956, and *KSIJP*, 27 August 1955). **1954:** From
arable area and multiple cropping index (*FJP*, 10 April 1955). **1955:** From arable area
and multiple cropping index (*KSIJP*, 31 March 1956). **1956:** From arable area and
multiple cropping index (*KSIJP*, 21 April 1957). **1957:** From arable area and multiple
cropping index (*KSIJP*, 4 October 1957).

Anhwei

1952: From arable area and multiple cropping index (*KSIJP*, 21 April 1957). **1953:**
From arable area and multiple cropping index (*JMJP*, 12 April 1956). **1955:** From
arable area and multiple cropping index (*AJP*, 19 January 1957). **1956:** From arable
area and multiple cropping index, *ibid.* **1957:** From arable area and multiple cropping
index (*AJP*, 12 December 1957).

Chekiang

1952 and **1957:** Figures of SSB in *CHKJP*, 30 September 1957. **1954** and **1955:** Figures in
SSB in *CHKJP*, 5 August 1956. **1956:** Figures in SSB in *CHKJP*, 29 May 1957.

Kiangsu

1952: Estimated from arable area and multiple cropping index (including Shanghai) in *An Economic Geography of East China*. An adjustment made to the index is based on figures in *HSCP*, 21 January 1958. **1957**: From arable area and multiple cropping index, *ibid*.

Shanghai

1957: From arable area and multiple cropping index (*TLCS* (no. 1), 1959, pp. 28–31).

Kweichow

1952: From arable area and multiple cropping index (*CIAAA*). **1956**: From arable area and multiple cropping index (*KCJP*, 8 August 1957 and index for 1952). **1957**: From arable area and multiple cropping index (*An Economic Geography of SW China*).

Szechuan

1952: From arable area and multiple cropping index (*An Economic Geography of SW China*). **1954**: From arable area and multiple cropping index (Wang Ch'eng-ching, *Chung-kuo Liang-shih Tseng-ch'an Wen-t'i* (*Problems of Raising Grain Production in China*) (Peking, 1958), p. 69. **1955**: From arable area and multiple cropping index in *SZJP*, 13 February 1957. **1956**: From arable area and multiple cropping index (*Problems of Raising Grain Production*, p. 69). **1957**: From arable area and multiple cropping index (*SZJP*, 16 November 1957).

Yunnan

1952: From arable area and multiple cropping index (*YJP*, 30 September 1957). **1954**: From 1955 (SSB figures, *YJP*, 11 June 1956). **1955**: From arable area and multiple cropping index in *YJP*, 14 January 1957. **1956**: From 1955 and SSB figures in *YJP*, 1 May 1957. **1957**: From arable area and multiple cropping index in *An Economic Geography of SW China*.

Fukien

1952: From arable area and multiple cropping index (*FJP*, 12 October 1957). **1954**: From arable area and multiple cropping index (SSB report in *FJP*, 1 April 1956). **1955** and **1956**: SSB figures in *FJP*, 26 June 1957. **1957**: From arable area and multiple cropping index in *FJP*, 12 October 1957.

Kwangsi

1952: From arable area and multiple cropping index in *KSIJP*, 21 April 1957. **1954** and **1955**: *CIAAA*. **1956**: From arable area and multiple cropping index in *KSIJP*, 21 April 1957. **1957**: From arable area and multiple cropping index (*An Economic Geography of S. China*).

Kwangtung

1952 and **1957**: *An Economic Geography of S. China*. **1953**: *CIAAA*. **1955**: *HHPYK*, vol. 95 (no. 21), 1956, pp. 68–70. **1956**: From arable area and multiple cropping index in *KSIJP*, 21 April 1957.

Appendix 12 Provincial grain sown areas in 1958 and 1959: sources of data

Heilungkiang

1958. Total grain: *CIAAA*. Wheat: *CIAAA*. Rice: *HJP*, 11 November 1958. Soya: *CIAAA*. Potatoes and coarse: by subtraction.

1959. Total grain: *CIAAA*.

Kirin

1958. Total grain: *KJP*, 7 October 1958. Wheat: *CIAAA*. Rice: *CIAAA*. Soya: *KJP*, 7 October 1958. Coarse: *CIAAA*. Potatoes: By subtraction.

1959. Total grain: *CIAAA*.

Liaoning

1958. All data: *An Economic Geography of NE China*.

1959. Not available.

Inner Mongolia

1958. Total grain: *NMKJP*, 11 November 1958. Wheat, rice, soya: *NMKTC*. Potatoes: *NMKJP*, 11 November 1958. Coarse: By subtraction.

1959. Total grain: *NMKTC*.

Kansu and Ningsia

1958. Total grain: *KAJP*, 18 September 1959 (old boundaries) plus Ningsia (*CIAAA*). Wheat and rice: *CIAAA*. Soya is assumed to be the same as 1957. Potatoes and coarse: *CIAAA*.

1959. Total grain: *CIAAA*, including an estimate for Ningsia.

Shensi

1958. Total grain: *CIAAA*. Wheat: *ibid*. Other: Assumed.

1959. Estimated from contraction reported in *SESJP*, 25 November 1959.

Sinkiang

1958. Total grain: *SNY*. Wheat, rice and soya: *ibid*. Other: By subtraction.

1959. Total grain: *CIAAA*.

Tsinghai

1958. Total grain: *SCMP*, no. 1912. Wheat: Assumed equal to 1956. Rice: Nil. Soya: Negligible. Potatoes: *CIAAA*. Other: By subtraction.

1959. Not available.

Provincial grain sown areas, 1958 and 1959

Honan

1958. Total grain: Net grain sown area (*Honan Tsai-p'ei Hsüeh* (*A Study of Wheat Cultivation in Honan*), Honan Agricultural Science Academy (Peking, 1960)) plus assumed soya area (six-year average for 1952–57). Rice, wheat and potatoes: *TLCS* (no. 1), 1959. Coarse: By subtraction.

1959. Total grain: *CIAAA*.

Hopei

1958. Total grain: By addition of individual crop sown areas. Wheat and coarse: *CIAAA*. Rice: From 1957 and increase in *HOPJP*, 11 March 1958. Soya: Assumed, using four-year average. Potatoes: *JMJP*, 17 October 1958.

1959. Not available.

Shansi

1958. Total grain: *SASJP*, 9 September 1959. Wheat and soya: *CIAAA*. Rice: By subtraction (total for rice, potatoes and maize given in *SASJP*, 9 September 1959). Potatoes: *SASJP*, 18 August 1958. Maize: *CIAAA*. Coarse: By subtraction.

1959. Total grain: *CIAAA*.

Shantung

1958. Total grain: By addition. Wheat: *TCJP*, 18 November 1958. Rice: *CKNP* (no. 4), 1959, and 1957 figure. Soya: *CIAAA*. Potatoes: *CKNP* (no. 18), 1958. Coarse: By subtraction.

1959. Total grain: Average of two estimates: (1) based on decline of wheat sown area in 1959 (*JMJP*, 18 September 1959) and of potato sown area (*CIAAA*), and (2) *CIAAA* gives sown area of rice, wheat, potatoes and soya. An estimate for coarse grains is added, by assuming that they maintained the six-year average of 1952–57.

Hunan

1958. Total grain: *HHPYK*, vol. 167 (no. 21), 1959, pp. 77–80. Wheat, soya and rice: *HNNY*. Potatoes: *HHNP*, 29 September 1958. Coarse: By subtraction.

1959. Total grain: *CIAAA*.

Hupei

1958. Total grain: Estimated from the grain arable area (*TLCS* (no. 1), 1959) and an assumed grain multiple cropping index, using data for earlier years. Wheat: *CIAAA*. Rice: *HUPJP*, 8 January 1960. Soya and potatoes: Assumed from figures relating to 1952–57. Coarse: By subtraction.

1959. Total grain: Estimated from decline in rice sown area (area for 1959 is in *TJP*, 24 November 1959) and in wheat sown area (1959 is in *CIAAA*.)

Kiangsi

1958. All data: *CIAAA*.

1959. Total grain: *ibid.*

Anhwei

1958. Total grain: *AJP*, 28 September 1959. Rice: *NTKTTH* (no. 18), 1958. Wheat, soya and potatoes: *CIAAA*. Coarse: By subtraction.

1959. Estimate based on decline in Summer 1959 grain sown area (*AJP*, 24 November 1959).

Chekiang

1958. Total grain: From *net* sown area (*CIAAA*) and assumed soya area (which in Chekiang was very small). Rice: From rice arable and double-cropped area (*CHKJP*, 29 September 1959). Wheat and soya: Assumed. Potatoes: *CIAAA*. Coarse: By subtraction. (Maize is given in *CIAAA*.)

1959. Not available.

Kiangsu

1958. Total grain: *TLCS* (no. 6), 1959. Rice, wheat and soya: *ibid*. Potatoes: *HHJP*, 6 October 1959. Coarse: By subtraction.

1959. Total grain: Estimated from known output and average yield for 1952–57.

Kweichow

1958. Total grain: From 1949 (*CIAAA*) and percentage in *KCJP*, 30 September 1959, plus soya (*CIAAA*). Rice: *KCJP*, 25 September 1958. Wheat: *CIAAA*. Potatoes: *KCJP*, 25 September 1958. Coarse: By subtraction.

1959. Not available.

Szechuan

1958. Total grain: *SZJP*, 26 September 1959. Rice: A compromise between the large area recorded in *SNMJP*, 16 May 1958 and lower figures in *An Economic Geography of SW China*, p. 29 (for double-cropped area) and in *CIAAA*. Wheat: *CIAAA*. Soya: Assumed equal to average for 1952 and 1957. Potatoes: *SZJP*, 25 November 1958. Coarse: By subtraction.

1959. Total grain: Based on the contraction of rice sown area (1959 is in *CIAAA*) and of spring wheat (see *SZJP*, 24 March 1959).

Yunnan

1958. Total grain: *CIAAA*. Rice: *YJP*, 19 August 1959. Wheat: *YJP*, 21 May 1958. Soya: Assumed equal to the average in earlier years. Potatoes: From 1957 and figures in *YJP*, 12 August 1958. Coarse: By subtraction.

1959. Not available.

Fukien

1958. Total grain: Net grain sown area (*FJP*, 28 September 1959) plus soya (*FJP*, 4 June 1958). Rice: *CIAAA*. Wheat: *FJP*, 10 December 1959. Potatoes: From figures in *CKNP* (no. 7), 1958, p. 26. Coarse: By subtraction.

1959. Total grain: *CIAAA*.

Kwangsi

1958. No figure for total grain sown area but *planned* figure is consistent with all evidence. See *KWSINYTH* (no. 21), 1957. Rice: From figures in *JMJP*, 19 June 1958 and *CNS*, 26 November 1958. Wheat: Assumed average for 1954–57. Soya and potatoes: *CIAAA*. Coarse: By subtraction.

1959. Not available.

Kwangtung

1958. Total grain: From net area (*TLCS* (no. 5), 1959) plus an estimate for soya. Rice: *TLCS*, *ibid*. Wheat and potatoes: *CIAAA*. Coarse: By subtraction.

1959. Total grain: Estimated from data relating to the decline in the rice sown area in 1959 (see *CNS*, 30 March 1960 and *NFJP*, 3 October 1959); in potatoes (*CIAAA*); in the later coarse sown area (*NFJP*, 3 October 1959); and in the winter sown area for 1958–59 (*NCNA*, 15 April 1960).

Appendix 13 Provincial total populations, 1974–80

Total population figures used in estimated grain output per head during the period 1974–80 (millions)

	1974	1975	1976	1977	1978	1979	1980
North East							
Heilungkiang	29.729	30.175	30.597	30.995	31.372	31.690	31.963
Kirin	20.183	20.546	20.895	21.229	21.547	21.846	22.057
Liaoning	32.209	32.724	33.215	33.647	34.051	34.426	34.726
North West							
IMR	—	—	—	—	18.272	18.510	18.765
Kansu	—	—	18.277	18.515	18.737	18.940	19.109
Ningsia	3.313	—	3.379	3.440	3.500	3.640	3.737
Shensi	26.313	26.734	27.108	27.460	27.789	28.070	28.272
Sinkiang	11.553	11.773	11.985	12.189	12.384	12.560	12.711
Tsinghai	3.355	3.432	3.508	3.582	3.654	3.719	3.720
North							
Honan	66.479	67.676	68.826	69.927	70.976	71.890	72.575
Hopei	47.915	48.634	49.315	49.956	50.555	51.046	51.680
Peking	8.191	8.289	8.372	8.429	8.496	8.706	c.8.767
Shansi	23.074	23.397	23.701	23.985	24.249	24.472	24.765
Shantung	67.063	68.136	69.158	70.126	71.038	72.310	72.818
Tientsin	—	—	—	—	7.319	7.390	7.789
Centre							
Hunan	48.665	49.395	50.087	50.738	51.347	52.230	52.810
Hupei	43.020	43.751	44.451	45.118	45.759	46.320	46.840
Kiangsi	—	—	30.597	31.240	31.853	32.290	32.584
East							
Anhwei	44.377	45.176	45.944	46.679	47.379	48.030	48.920
Chekiang	34.943	35.712	36.462	37.140	37.549	37.920	38.242
Kiangsu	55.964	56.692	57.372	58.003	58.417	58.930	59.380
Shanghai	—	—	11.120	11.198	11.255	11.321	11.463
South West							
Kweichow	—	—	—	—	26.918	27.310	27.770
Szechuan	93.799	94.925	95.655	96.484	97.070	97.740	98.175
Yunnan	—	—	—	30.337	30.920	31.350	31.671
South							
Fukien	—	—	23.575	24.046	24.477	24.800	25.031
Kwangsi	31.306	32.026	32.731	33.418	34.086	34.700	35.380
Kwangtung	52.968	53.761	54.438	55.120	55.930	56.810	57.800
China (official)	905.39	919.70	935.36	946.68	958.09	970.92	982.55

SOURCES

Heilungkiang

1980: From 1979 and natural increase in *JMJP*, 25 March 1981. **1979**: *Encyclopaedia* (1980). **1978**: Official figure cited by Jowett in *CQ* (no. 81), March 1980, pp. 105–10. **1977**: From 1978 and natural increase in *NYCCWT* (no. 1), 1980, pp. 37–9. **1976, 1975** and **1974**: From 1977 and assumed natural increases.

Kirin

1980: From 1979 and natural increase in *SWB*, 25 March 1981. **1979**: *Encyclopaedia* (1980). **1978**: From 1979 and natural increase in *SWB*, 25 March 1981. **1977, 1976, 1975** and **1974**: From 1978 and assumed natural increases.

Liaoning

1980: From 1979 and natural increase in *SWB*, 15 April 1981. **1979**: *Encyclopaedia* (1980). **1978, 1977, 1976, 1975** and **1974**: From 1979 and assumed natural increases.

Inner Mongolia

1980: From 1979 and planned natural increase in *SWB*, 9 January 1981. **1979**: *Encyclopaedia* (1980). **1978**: From 1979 and natural increase in *SWB*, 9 January 1981.

Kansu

1981: From 1980 and assumed natural increase. **1980**: From natural increase in *JMJP*, 25 March 1981 and 1979 figure. **1979**: *Encyclopaedia* (1980). **1978**: From 1979 and natural increase in *JMJP*, 25 March 1981. **1977** and **1976**: From 1978 and assumed natural increases.

Ningsia

1981: Assumed same natural increase as Kansu. **1980**: From 1979 and assumed natural increase. **1979**: *Encyclopaedia* (1980). **1978**: *PR* (no. 52), 1978, p. 25. **1977, 1976, 1975** and **1974**: From 1978 and assumed natural increases.

Shensi

1981: From 1980 and assumed natural increase. **1980**: From 1979 and natural increase in *JMJP*, 10 March 1981. **1979**: *Encyclopaedia* (1980). **1978**: From 1979 and natural increase in *ibid*. **1977, 1976, 1975** and **1974**: From 1978 and assumed natural increases.

Sinkiang

1980: From 1979 and natural increase in *SWB*, 25 March 1981. **1979**: *Encyclopaedia* (1980). **1978**: From 1979 and natural increase in *ibid*. **1977, 1976, 1975** and **1974**: From 1978 and assumed natural increases.

Tsinghai

1980: *SWB*, 15 April 1981. **1979**: *SWB*, 10 December 1980. **1978**: From 1979 and natural increase in *Encyclopaedia* (1980). **1977, 1976, 1975** and **1974**: From 1978 and assumed natural increases.

Honan

1980: From 1979 and natural increase in *JMJP*, 10 March 1981. **1979**: *Encyclopaedia* (1980). **1978**: From 1979 and natural increase in *SWB*, 25 March 1981. **1977, 1976, 1975** and **1974**: From 1978 and assumed natural increases.

Hopei

1980: From 1979 and assumed natural increase. **1979**: *Encyclopaedia* (1980). **1978**: From 1979 and natural increase in *ibid*. **1977, 1976, 1975** and **1974**: From 1978 and assumed natural increases.

Peking

1980: From 1979 and assumed natural increase. **1979**: *Encyclopaedia* (1980). **1978**: *JKYC* (no. 1), 1980, pp. 39–45. **1977**: From 1978 and assumed natural increase. **1976**: From 1977 and natural increase in *PR* (no. 32), 1979, p. 9. **1975** and **1974**: From 1976 and assumed natural increases.

Shansi

1980 and **1979**: SSB report in *SASJP*, 16 August 1981. **1978**: From 1979 and natural increase in *Encyclopaedia* (1980). **1977, 1976, 1975** and **1974**: From 1978 and assumed natural increases.

Shantung

1980: From 1979 and natural increase in *SWB*, 25 March 1981. **1979**: *Encyclopaedia* (1980). **1978**: From 1979 and natural increase, *ibid*. **1977, 1976, 1975** and **1974**: From 1978 and assumed natural increases.

Tientsin

1980: *SWB*, 18 February 1981. **1979**: *Encyclopaedia* (1980). **1978**: From 1979 and natural increase, *ibid*.

Hunan

1980: From 1979 and assumed natural increase. **1979**: *Encyclopaedia* (1980). **1978**: From 1979 and natural increase, *ibid*. **1977, 1976, 1975** and **1974**: From 1978 and assumed natural increases.

Hupei

1980: From 1979 and assumed natural increase. **1979**: *Encyclopaedia* (1980). **1978**: From 1979 and natural increase, *ibid*. **1977, 1976, 1975** and **1974**: From 1978 and assumed natural increases.

Kiangsi

1980: From 1979 and natural increase in *JMJP*, 3 March 1981. **1979**: *Encyclopaedia* (1980). **1978**: From 1979 and natural increase, *ibid.* **1977**: From 1978 and natural increase in *SWB*, 10 December 1980. **1976**: From 1977 and assumed natural increase.

Anhwei

1980: From 1979 and assumed natural increase. **1979**: *Encyclopaedia* (1980). **1978**: From 1979 and natural increase, *ibid.* **1977, 1976, 1975** and **1974**: From 1978 and assumed natural increases.

Chekiang

1980: From 1979 and natural increase in *SWB*, 25 March 1981. **1979**: *Encyclopaedia* (1980). **1978**: From 1979 and natural increase, *ibid.* **1977**: From 1978 and assumed natural increase. **1976**: From 1977 and natural increase in *SWB*, 25 March 1981. **1975** and **1974**: From 1976 and assumed natural increases.

Kiangsu

1980: From 1979 and assumed natural increase. **1979**: *Encyclopaedia* (1980). **1978**: From figures in *ibid.* and *CFJP*, 1 December 1980. **1977**: From figures relating to grain output and output per head, given to author by Agriculture Office, Nanking. **1976, 1975** and **1974**: From 1977 and assumed natural increases.

Shanghai

1980 and **1979**: SSB report in *SWB*, 15 July 1981. **1978**: From 1979 and natural increase in *SWB*, 4 March 1981. **1977**: From 1978 and natural increase in *PR* (no. 22), 1979. **1976**: From 1977 and assumed natural increase.

Kweichow

1980: From 1979 and assumed natural increase. **1979**: *Encyclopaedia* (1980). **1978**: From 1979 and natural increase, *ibid.*

Szechuan

1980: From 1979 and natural increase in *SWB*, 25 March 1981. **1979**: *Encyclopaedia* (1980). **1978**: From 1979 and natural increase in *SWB*, 25 March 1981. **1977**: From 1978 and natural increase, *ibid.* **1976**: From 1977 and natural increase in *JMJP*, 11 August 1979. **1975**: From grain output and output per head (*Szechuan Ta-hsüeh Hsüeh-pao* (*Szechuan University Journal*) (no. 1), 1981, pp. 30–4). **1974**: From 1975 and assumed natural increase.

Yunnan

1981: From 1980 and assumed natural increase. **1980**: From 1979 and natural increase in *SWB*, 25 March 1981. **1979**: *Encyclopaedia* (1980). **1978**: From 1979 and natural increase, *ibid.* **1979**: From 1978 and natural increase in *ibid.*

Appendix 13

Fukien

1980: From 1979 and natural increase in *SWB*, 25 March 1981. **1979**: *Encyclopaedia* (1980). **1978**: From 1979 and natural increase, *ibid*. **1977**: From 1978 and natural increase in *JMJP*, 19 April 1980. **1976**: From 1977 and assumed natural increase.

Kwangsi

1980: From 1979 and assumed natural increase. **1979**: *Encyclopaedia* (1980). **1978**: From 1979 and natural increase, *ibid*. **1977, 1976, 1975** and **1974**: From 1978 and assumed natural increases.

Kwangtung

1980: From 1979 and assumed natural increase. **1979**: *Encyclopaedia* (1980). **1978**: From 1979 and natural increase in *NFJP*, 4 July 1979. **1977**: From 1978 and natural increase, *ibid*. **1976, 1975** and **1974**: From 1977 and natural increases; figures given to author in Canton.

China

1980: SSB report *JMJP*, 30 April 1981. **1979** and **1975**: *Economic Yearbook* (1981). **1978**: SSB report *PR* (no. 20), 1980, p. 24. **1977**: From 1978 and natural increase in *CCKH* (no. 3), 1980, pp. 54–8. **1976**: From 1977 and natural increase in *ibid*. **1974**: From 1975 and natural increase in *Economic Yearbook* (1981).

Appendix 14 Provincial total grain output, 1974–80

Grain output 1974–80 (million tons)

	1974	1975	1976	1977	1978	1979	1980
North East							
Heilungkiang	13.833	14.723	11.803	c.12.983	14.690	14.625	14.625
Kirin	8.550	9.056	7.566	8.307	9.100	9.035	8.585
Liaoning	9.806	10.418	9.553	10.350	10.720	11.940	12.215
North West							
IMR	—	—	—	—	4.970	5.100	3.970
Kansu	—	—	4.138	4.670	4.717	4.620	4.930
Ningsia	1.182	—	c.0.798	c.0.990	c.1.164	1.061	1.204
Shensi	7.560	7.500	7.700	5.765	8.000	9.099	7.570
Sinkiang	2.735	3.145	3.560	3.410	3.700	3.940	3.890
Tsinghai	0.888	0.977	c.0.750	0.818	0.857	0.820	0.960
North							
Honan	c.18.784	19.904	21.726	21.000	20.000	21.340	21.480
Hopei	14.990	14.990	15.000	14.595[a]	16.850	17.795	15.220
Peking	—	1.835	—	1.512	1.860	1.724	1.860
Shansi	6.903	7.593	—	—	6.744	8.008	6.855
Shantung	17.250	20.000	22.500	22.010	22.864	24.715	23.840
Tientsin	—	—	—	—	1.264	1.390	1.378
Centre							
Hunan	16.907	18.006	18.552	19.623	20.800	22.180	21.240
Hupei	15.025	16.250	17.250	16.203	17.253	18.496	15.360
Kiangsi	9.931	—	9.929	10.922	11.250	12.970	12.400
East							
Anhwei	15.552	15.750	17.325	14.515	14.825	16.090	14.540
Chekiang	12.040	13.760	9.040	12.450	14.200	16.120	14.350
Kiangsu	19.674	20.251	21.871	18.300	22.735	25.140	23.570
Shanghai	2.334	2.201	2.459	2.034	2.509	2.590	1.869
South West							
Kweichow	—	—	—	—	6.460	6.230	6.480
Szechuan	25.279	25.250	24.850	27.500	29.500	32.010	32.640
Yunnan	—	—	—	7.578	8.640	7.930	8.656
South							
Fukien	—	—	6.034	6.517	7.260	7.620	8.020
Kwangsi	9.520	9.996	10.121	10.432	10.861	11.730	11.910
Kwangtung	16.610	16.100	15.810	17.435	16.235	17.380	18.080
China (official)	275.15	284.50	286.21	283.12	304.75	332.12	318.22

a. Assumed figure.

Appendix 14

SOURCES

Heilungkiang

1974 and **1975**: From graph in *Chung-kuo Nung-yeh Ti-li Tsung-luen (General Agricultural Geography of China)*, Geography Research Institute, Chinese Academy of Social Sciences (Peking, 1980), p. 343. **1976:** From 1975 and figure in *ibid.*, p. 342. **1977:** From 1976 and percentage in *FBIS*, cited in Tuan (1981). **1978:** Figure supplied by Dr A.L. Erisman. **1979** and **1980:** *FBIS*, 23 June 1981.

Kirin

1974: *SWB*, 10 December 1980. **1975:** From 1978 and percentage in *JMJP*, 21 February 1979. **1976:** From 1975 and figure in *General Agricultural Geography*, p. 342. **1977:** *JMJP*, 25 April 1979. **1978:** *CNS*, 27 September 1979. **1979:** *Encyclopaedia* (1980), p. 75. **1980:** *SWB*, 27 May 1981.

Liaoning

1974: From 1949, 1965 and percentage in Tuan (1981). **1975:** From 1974 and percentage in *ibid.* **1976:** From 1975 and decline recorded in *General Agricultural Geography*, p. 342. **1977:** *FBIS*, 18 August 1981. **1978:** *HNY* (no. 20), 1979. **1979** and **1980:** *SWB*, 17 June 1981 (SSB figures).

Inner Mongolia

1978: *SC* (no. 6), 1979, p. 44, gives output per head. Output is calculated from this and population. **1979** and **1980:** *Encyclopaedia* (1981), p. 277.

Kansu

1976 and **1977:** From 1978 and percentage given to author by Dr A.L. Erisman. **1978:** *NYCCWT* (no. 1), 1980, pp. 26–8 and p. 52. **1979** and **1980:** *Encyclopaedia* (1981), p. 277. **1981:** From 1980 and percentage decline given in *SWB*, 23 December 1981.

Ningsia

1974, 1979 and **1980:** *JPRS*, no. 78238. **1975:** n.a. **1976:** From 1977 and percentage given by Tuan (1981). **1977:** From 1949 output and information in *PR* (no. 52), 1978, p. 25. (1949 is from 1974 and *Shen-chou Chu-pien (China's Great Changes)* (Hong Kong, 1976).) **1978:** From 1977 and percentage cited by Tuan (1981). **1981:** Expected output given in *SWB*, 9 December 1981.

Shensi

1974: From 1949 (*SESJP*, 30 September 1957 and output of 1956) and *Great Changes*, p. 233. **1975, 1976** and **1977:** Communication to the author in Sian, 1982, by Provincial Agriculture Office. **1978:** *SWB*, 25 April 1979. **1979** and **1980:** SSB in *SESJP*, 20 June 1981. **1981:** *SWB*, 15 January 1982 (7.5 million tons).

Sinkiang

1974: From 1975 and percentage in *SWB* cited by Tuan (1981). **1975**: *NYCCWT* (no. 3), 1980, pp. 34–6 and p. 4. **1976**: From 1977 and *JMJP*, 4 November 1978. **1977**: From 1978 and *JMJP*, 13 May 1979. **1978**: *PR* (no. 38), 1979, p. 5. **1979** and **1980**: *Encyclopaedia* (1981), p. 277.

Tsinghai

1974: From 1949 (*LS* (no. 22), 1956, p. 11) and percentage in Tuan (1981). **1975**: From 1974 and *JMJP*, 26 December 1975. **1976**: Estimate based on 1971; *KMJP*, 12 April 1978 states that 1976 was below 1971. 1971 = 0.751 million tons (from 1970; 1970 is from 1975 and *FBIS* cited by Tuan (1981). **1977**: From 1978 and percentage given by Tuan (1981). **1978**: *JMJP*, 14 April 1979. **1979** and **1980**: *Encyclopaedia* (1981), p. 277.

Honan

1974: Estimate from 1965 and information in *Great Changes* (1965 given by Tuan 1981). **1975**: From 1965 and figures in Tuan (1981). **1976** and **1977**: From 1949 and information in Tuan (1981). (1949: from output for 1955 and 1953 and percentages in *An Economic Geography of N. China*.) **1978**: From 1970 and percentage in *JMJP*, 30 December 1979. **1979** and **1980**: *Encyclopaedia* (1981), p. 277.

Hopei

1974: From 1965 and *PR* (no. 26), 1976, p. 24 (1965 given by Tuan (1981)). **1975**: Said to equal 1974: *PR* (no. 26), 1976, p. 24. **1976** and **1979**: *Encyclopaedia* (1980), p. 69. **1977**: n.a. **1978**: *CCKL* (no. 3), 1981, pp. 3–5; also *JMJP*, 8 January 1980. **1980**: *Encyclopaedia* (1981), p. 277.

Peking

1974: n.a. **1975** and **1978**: *JKYC* (no. 1), 1980, p. 40. **1976**: n.a. **1977**: From 1978 and percentage in Tuan (1981). **1979**: *SWB*, 1 April 1981. **1980**: *Encyclopaedia* (1981), p. 277.

Shansi

1974: From 1949 and percentage in *Great Changes*, p. 37. (1949 is in *SASJP*, 10 October 1959.) **1975**: From 1974 and percentage in *JMJP*, 26 December 1975. **1976** and **1977**: n.a. **1978**: *Encyclopaedia* (1980), p. 69. **1979** and **1980**: SSB figures in *SASJP*, 16 August 1981.

Shantung

1974: From 1975 and Ch'en Yung-kuei's figures in *KMJP*, 24 December 1976. **1975**: *HC* (no. 9), 1978, p. 35. **1976**: *Chia-su Shih-hsien Nung-yeh Chi-hsieh-hua (Speed Up the Realisation of Agricultural Mechanisation)* (Peking, 1978), p. 12. **1977**: From 1974 and data given by Yu Ch'iu-li in *Ch'uan Tang Dong Yuan Chue-chou san nien wei chi-pen shang shih-hsien Nung-yeh Chi-hsieh-hua er Fen-tou (The Whole Party Mobilises Cadres in a Decisive Fight to Struggle for Three Years Basically to Achieve Agricultural Mechanisation)* (Peking, 1978), p. 19. **1978** and **1979**: *Encyclopaedia* (1980), pp. 86 and 87. **1980**: *Encyclopaedia* (1981), p. 277.

Tientsin

1978: From 1979 and percentage in Tuan (1981). **1979:** *Encyclopaedia* (1981), p. 277. **1980:** *TJP*, 27 June 1981.

Hunan

1974: From 1949 (*TCKT* (no. 1), 1958, p. 13) and *Great Changes*, p. 173. **1975:** From 1974 and percentage in *JMJP*, 30 December 1975 (1975 said to be 65 per cent above 1965, which is cited by Tuan (1981)). **1976:** From 1965 and percentage in Tuan (1981). **1977:** From 1978 and percentage in *SWB*, 20 June 1979. **1978:** Tuan (1981). **1979** and **1980:** *Encyclopaedia* (1981), p. 277.

Hupei

1974: From Dr A.L. Erisman. **1975:** From 1976 and percentage given by Tuan (1981). **1976:** *JMJP*, 9 December 1976. **1977:** From 1978 and percentage given by Tuan (1981). **1978** and **1979:** *Encyclopaedia* (1980), p. 102. **1980:** *Encyclopaedia* (1981), p. 277.

Kiangsi

1974: From 1949 (*KSIJP*, 1 January 1958) and *Great Changes*, pp. 148–9. **1975:** n.a. **1976** and **1977:** From 1977 and 1978 respectively, and percentage in *JMJP*, 16 May 1979. **1978:** *Encyclopaedia* (1980), p. 94. **1979** and **1980:** *Encyclopaedia* (1981), p. 277.

Anhwei

1974: From 1949 (*SWB*, 10 December 1980) and *Great Changes*, p. 129. **1975:** Tuan (1981). **1976:** From 1975 and *JMJP*, 6 December 1976. **1977:** *NYCCWT* (no. 6), 1980, pp. 51–3, and output for 1976 and 1978. **1978:** *Encyclopaedia* (1980), p. 92. **1979** and **1980:** *Encyclopaedia* (1981), p. 277.

Chekiang

1974 and **1975:** From 1949 (*JMJP*, 21 February 1979) and percentages in Tuan (1981). **1976:** From 1974 and *JMJP*, 18 December 1978. **1977:** From 1978 and *ibid.* **1978:** Tuan (1981). **1979** and **1980:** *Encyclopaedia* (1981), p. 277.

Kiangsu

1974: From 1963 (given to the author in Nanking) and growth rate in *Great Changes*, p. 119. **1975:** From 1976 and percentage in *JMJP*, 4 December 1976. **1976:** From 1970 (figure obtained in Nanking) and growth rate in *HC* (no. 10), 1980, pp. 15–21. **1977:** From figures in *ibid.* **1978:** *Encyclopaedia* (1980), p. 89. **1979** and **1980:** *Encyclopaedia* (1981), p. 277.

Shanghai

1974 and **1975:** Figures given to the author in Shanghai, 1982. **1976:** From 1978 and increase 1976–79 in Tuan (1981). **1977:** From 1978 and increase 1977–78 in Tuan (1981). **1978:** Materials published at the Shanghai Agricultural Exhibition, 1979, visited by the author. **1979:** *Encyclopaedia* (1981), p. 277. **1980:** SSB in *SWB*, 15 July 1981.

Kweichow

1978: From output per head in *JMJP*, 27 December 1979 and total population (*Encyclopaedia* 1980, p. 111). **1979** and **1980**: *Encyclopaedia* (1981), p. 277.

Szechuan

1974: From output per head (*Szechuan Ta-hsüeh Hsüeh-pao* (*Szechuan University Journal*) (no. 1), 1981, pp. 30–4), and estimated total population. **1975**: From 1977 and figures in *JMJP*, 23 November 1978. **1976**: From 1977 and *JMJP*, 29 November 1978. **1977**: From 1976 and *JMJP*, 23 November 1978. **1978**: *JMJP*, 22 March 1979. **1979** and **1980**: *Encyclopaedia* (1981), p. 277.

Yunnan

1977, 1978, 1979: Figures in *Ching-chi Wen-t'i T'an-tso* (*Discussions of Economic Problems*) (no. 1), 1980, pp. 31–6. **1980**: *SWB*, 3 June 1981. **1981**: *SWB*, 24 February 1982.

Fukien

1976: From 1977 and *JMJP*, 25 December 1977. **1977**: From 1978 and *SWB*, 28 March 1979. **1978**: *Encyclopaedia* (1980), pp. 95 and 96. **1979** and **1980**: *Encyclopaedia* (1981), p. 277.

Kwangsi

1974: From 1950 (*FBIS*, 29 June 1978) and Tuan (1981). **1975**: From 1974 and *JMJP*, 26 December 1975. **1976**: From 1965 (from 1975 and *JMJP*, 26 December 1975) and figures in Tuan (1981). **1977**: From 1957 and *JMJP*, 12 December 1978. **1978**: From 1979 and *Encyclopaedia* (1980), p. 107. **1979** and **1980**: *Encyclopaedia* (1981), p. 277.

Kwangtung

1974–78: Supplied to the author in Canton. **1979** and **1980**: *Encyclopaedia* (1981), p. 277.

China

1974: From 1975 and growth, 1974–75 in Yang Chien-pai, *Luen Kung-yeh ho Nung-yeh ti kuan-hsi* (*On the Relations between Industry and Agriculture*) (Peking, 1981), p. 124. **1975**: *Economic Yearbook* (1981). **1976**: From 1975 and figures in *On the Relations between Industry and Agriculture*, p. 126. **1977, 1978** and **1979**: *JMJP*, 12 September 1980. **1980**: SSB figure in *JMJP*, 30 April 1981.

INDEX OF NAMES

GENERAL INDEX

Reference to the appendices are not included.

General index

as an inferior food: 65, 74, 75, 141, 195
importance in grain self-sufficiency: 132n
as a high-yielding crop: 132, 132n, 195
Malnutrition, 29, 154, 156
Meat, consumption
in China: 193, 194, 195, 197, 198
in Taiwan: 195
Millet
importance in north China: 21, 74, 195
declining output: 132, 197
Nanking, 135n
Natural disasters, 3, 31, 34, 48, 59, 60, 63, 64, 77, 81, 86, 134, 138, 146, 158, 167
Ningsia, 135, 173, 176
Oedema, 156n, 157
Peanuts, in Shantung, 14
Peking, 6, 29, 59, 76, 77, 81, 86, 90, 127, 128, 134, 161, 165, 186, 192
People's communes, 139, 141, 142
Pigs, 106, 111–14, 177, 178, 186
Population
rural, broad categories of grain self-sufficiency in 1950s: 3–4; provincial distribution in 1950s: 5; migration of: 122, 124, 157, 161
total, vital rates in Great Leap Forward: 156
urban, size in 1950s: 21; control of: 86, 122, 161; in Great Leap Forward: 139–40, 161; preference for fine grain: 21–3, 68, 74–5, 122; low average age in Canton: 117; high average age in Shansi: 117; wages and demand for grain: 68, 117
Pork
consumption in China: 112–13, 192, 197
in Taiwan: 113, 194, 197
Potatoes
as an inferior food: 22, 22n, 65, 67, 67n, 74, 122, 141, 195
importance in grain self-sufficiency: 66–7, 122n
role in Great Leap Forward: 132, 135, 138, 141, 148, 157, 158

as high-yielding crop: 67, 67n, 195
reweighting of: 167
Potential provincial grain surpluses and deficits, 6, 23–7, 135, 138, 149, 176–81
Private plots, 190–1
Provincial grain exports, 42, 77–8, 79, 80–1, 86–91, 92–5, 124–8, 145, 149, 155, 158, 159–60, 165, 184, 185–9
Provincial grain imports, 67n, 77, 78, 79, 80, 81, 86–90, 92–5, 124–8, 149, 157, 158, 165, 184, 185–9
Redistribution of grain, effect on consumption, see Central purchase and supply of grain
Refugees, from China to Hong Kong, 158
Rice
as a fine grain: 21, 75, 91, 195
double-cropping in 1956: 110
extension in north China: 132, 132n, 134, 135
sown area in Great Leap Forward: 146–7
in Szechuan: 158, 185
output growth: 197
consumption in Taiwan: 194
Seed grain, 1, 3, 21, 43, 61, 62, 97, 97n, 141, 143, 153, 176, 177, 178, 179, 185, 192
Shanghai, 6, 27, 59, 67n, 68, 76, 77, 81, 86, 90, 128, 134, 161, 165, 178, 186, 190, 192, 193n
Shansi, 22, 29, 35, 59, 75, 77, 78, 79, 80, 86, 98, 102, 104, 111, 112, 117, 123, 124, 135, 138, 147n, 149, 153, 173
Shantung, 6, 10–14, 22n, 27, 29, 34, 35, 45, 49, 58, 64n, 65n, 66n, 72, 75, 76, 77, 78, 80, 94, 102, 124, 134, 134n, 135, 138, 138n, 141, 147n, 149, 153, 157, 170, 173, 176
Shensi, 10, 22, 35, 45, 59, 65n, 72, 77, 78, 79, 81n, 90, 102, 104, 116, 122, 127, 135, 141n, 147n, 149, 153, 173, 176, 186
Shenyang, 68
Sinkiang, 40, 72, 111, 172
Soya beans
rationing in Canton: 70

328

C